Death Sentences
Literature and State Killing

LEGENDA

LEGENDA is the Modern Humanities Research Association's book imprint for new research in the Humanities. Founded in 1995 by Malcolm Bowie and others within the University of Oxford, Legenda has always been a collaborative publishing enterprise, directly governed by scholars. The Modern Humanities Research Association (MHRA) joined this collaboration in 1998, became half-owner in 2004, in partnership with Maney Publishing and then Routledge, and has since 2016 been sole owner. Titles range from medieval texts to contemporary cinema and form a widely comparative view of the modern humanities, including works on Arabic, Catalan, English, French, German, Greek, Italian, Portuguese, Russian, Spanish, and Yiddish literature. Editorial boards and committees of more than 60 leading academic specialists work in collaboration with bodies such as the Society for French Studies, the British Comparative Literature Association and the Association of Hispanists of Great Britain & Ireland.

The MHRA encourages and promotes advanced study and research in the field of the modern humanities, especially modern European languages and literature, including English, and also cinema. It aims to break down the barriers between scholars working in different disciplines and to maintain the unity of humanistic scholarship. The Association fulfils this purpose through the publication of journals, bibliographies, monographs, critical editions, and the MHRA Style Guide, and by making grants in support of research. Membership is open to all who work in the Humanities, whether independent or in a University post, and the participation of younger colleagues entering the field is especially welcomed.

ALSO PUBLISHED BY THE ASSOCIATION

Critical Texts
Tudor and Stuart Translations • *New Translations* • *European Translations*
MHRA Library of Medieval Welsh Literature

MHRA Bibliographies
Publications of the Modern Humanities Research Association

The Annual Bibliography of English Language & Literature
Austrian Studies
Modern Language Review
Portuguese Studies
The Slavonic and East European Review
Working Papers in the Humanities
The Yearbook of English Studies

www.mhra.org.uk
www.legendabooks.com

STUDIES IN COMPARATIVE LITERATURE

Studies in Comparative Literature are produced in close collaboration with the British Comparative Literature Association, and range widely across comparative and theoretical topics in literary and translation studies, accommodating research at the interface between different artistic media and between the humanities and the sciences.

ALSO PUBLISHED IN THIS SERIES

Death Sentences

Literature and State Killing

EDITED BY
BIRTE CHRIST AND ÈVE MORISI

LEGENDA
Studies in Comparative Literature 49
Modern Humanities Research Association
2019

Published by Legenda
an imprint of the Modern Humanities Research Association
Salisbury House, Station Road, Cambridge CB1 2LA

ISBN 978-1-78188-557-4

First published 2019

Copy-Editor: Charlotte Brown

CONTENTS

❖

ACKNOWLEDGEMENTS

The editors would like to thank the Humanities Division of the University of Oxford for an award from the REF Strategic Research Assistance Fund that enabled the completion of this volume. They are also grateful to all the contributors and to Graham Nelson at Legenda for their benevolence and patience since the inception of this project. Thanks are due to Leonie Schmidt for her editorial help with two of the chapters that follow and to Madeline Kienzle for the preparation of the index. The editors are also much indebted to Jim House for his careful proofreading of two sections in the collection, to Jacqueline Uren for her meticulous editorial assistance throughout the preparation of the manuscript, to the Institut d'Études Avancées in Paris and in particular to Élodie Saubatte for her generous help with the cover illustration, and to Robert Priseman for permission to include his oil painting *No Human Way to Kill: Electric Chair* (2007–08) on the cover.

INTRODUCTION

Capital Literature

Ève Morisi

Capital punishment incarnates sovereign power's ultimate right, the right of death.[1] Irreversible and paradoxical, it institutionalizes killing in societies which otherwise largely define this act as criminal. It interrogates the limits of humanity in several respects — the limits we impose on certain human lives and those through which we define humaneness. The death penalty also has other far-reaching political, ethical, and symbolic ramifications: it puts to the test realities and principles such as individual and state responsibility, the conditions of legitimacy of extreme violence, the moral foundations of punishment and the law, and democracy, to name but a few. *Death Sentences* attends to the specifics and possibilities of literature as they illuminate these singular characteristics of state killing, understood here as execution following due judicial process.

The Death Penalty and Recent Western History

One may have the impression that, by and large, the exceptional institution of capital punishment has long been obsolete in the Western world. Yet modern and contemporary history demonstrates otherwise. Numerous nations did not abolish the death penalty for all crimes — times of war included — until the 1960s, 70s and 80s, even if the last executions or abolition in time of peace generally occurred earlier. Austria, East Germany, Finland, Luxemburg, the Netherlands, Norway, Portugal, Romania, Slovenia, and Sweden were among these states in Europe. Similarly, New Zealand and Australia's last state to abolish capital punishment did so in the 1980s. Such countries as Albania, Armenia, Belgium, Bulgaria, Croatia, Cyprus, the Czech Republic, Denmark, Georgia, Greece, Hungary, Ireland, Italy, Lithuania, Malta, Poland, Serbia, Slovakia, Spain, Switzerland, Turkey, Ukraine, and the United Kingdom officially did away with the death penalty for all offences later, in the 1990s and 2000s. In North America, the same can be said of Canada.[2] Latvia was the last member state of the European Union to abolish capital punishment in war time, in 2012.

Protocol No. 6 to the European Convention for the Protection of Human Rights (ECHR) from 1983 abolishing the death penalty in times of peace has now been ratified by all but one member state of the Council of Europe.[3] In 1998, the Rome

Statute — the treaty that founded the International Criminal Court — excluded capital punishment from the penalties applicable to the most serious crimes affecting the international community.[4] In 2002, Protocol No. 13 to the ECHR banned the death penalty in all circumstances, including for crimes committed in times of war and imminent threat of war.[5] Since then, most member states have ratified it.

A worldwide trend towards abolition, markedly perceptible in Europe, was thus established and then bolstered by international statutes in the last third of the twentieth century. This has resulted in 142 countries being abolitionist either in law or in practice today. Nevertheless, fifty-six countries currently retain the death penalty, according to Amnesty International's global report published in 2018.[6] Despite an overall decline, at least 1032 legal executions were carried out in twenty-three countries — that is about one in eight countries worldwide — in 2016 and 3117 death sentences were recorded in fifty-five countries, so that at least 18,848 people were known to be under sentence of death worldwide at the end of that year.[7] In 2017, excluding the thousands of executions carried out in China, at least 993 individuals were put to death in twenty-three countries, at least 2591 death sentences were pronounced in fifty-three countries, and 21,919 people were known to be on death row worldwide.[8]

Although the advancement of Europe and the Western world on the abolitionist front is significant, they are not altogether done with lethal justice. Belarus is yet to abolish capital punishment; Russia currently retains the death penalty, although its application has been forbidden since 2009 following a decision of the Constitutional Court; Recep Tayyip Erdoğan expressed the wish to re-instate the death penalty after the 2016 *coup d'état* attempt against Turkey's state institutions, notwithstanding Ankara having abolished it in 2004; and the United States of America was consistently among the biggest executioner countries worldwide from 2006 to 2015, alongside such nations as China, Iran, Iraq, Pakistan, and Saudi Arabia.

As the largest Western democracy still practising state killing, including that of people with mental illness, the US evidently stands out in the contemporary penal landscape. At present, there are thirty-one retentionist states in that country, and, at the end of 2016, a decreased but non-negligible number of individuals — 2832 — were on death row.* By 2017, a total of 1465 people had been executed since the US Supreme Court's approval of new capital laws in 1976, following a hiatus in executions that had lasted for almost ten years.[9] In spite of the inconsistent application of the death penalty in the US, the role played by racial discrimination in its enforcement, the frequent revelation of miscarriages of justice, and the legal doubt over whether it constitutes 'cruel and unusual punishment' prohibited by the Eighth Amendment, several dozen new death sentences are still being pronounced annually. Since a limited number of executions are carried out each year, an ageing population finds itself on death row and inmates sometimes die while awaiting their killing.

---

* On 13 March 2019, just as the present volume was being indexed, Governor Gavin Newsom reprieved all 737 condemned inmates of California, a state in which executions had been stayed since 2006. Yet two voter initiatives aiming to end the death penalty each failed by a narrow margin over the past eight years, and a proposition to speed up executions by shortening appeals was adopted in 2016.

Indeed, execution protocols have been increasingly questioned, and reports of botched lethal injection have regularly surfaced in retentionist American states. The Old World was instrumental in this predominant method of execution until recently. In 2011, the European Union imposed an export ban on sodium thiopental — the same year the last US manufacturer of this drug stopped producing it. Previously, a number of European pharmaceutical companies had supplied the United States with this anaesthetic drug, typically used during the first phase of lethal injection before additional substances paralyze the prisoner and then stop their heart. The EU now advocates universal abolition of the death penalty, and between 2009 and 2016 the European Instrument for Democracy and Human Rights allocated several million euros to US-based campaigns and non-profit organizations supporting the fight against capital punishment.[10]

These latest practical, diplomatic, and financial interventions by the European Union in the US have not led to the desired outcome. Over the past few years, the US has experimented with alternative sedatives in lethal injections with sometimes catastrophic results.[11] Several states have also passed laws that prevent courts and the media from identifying the private compounding pharmacies that supply lethal injection drugs and from accessing execution records. This arrangement prevents the investigation of the lawfulness and constitutionality of execution procedures.

Situating Literature Within Capital Punishment

What does literature have to do with this complex Western history and, in some cases, ongoing implementation of lethal justice? It intersects with them in significant and related ways. Literary works have informed and deepened the philosophical and political debates about the death penalty throughout the modern and contemporary periods. They have ceaselessly generated scenarios, characters, and discourses that shed light on the conception and practice of capital punishment. They have also participated in the spectacularity or controlled figuration on which the death penalty relies in order to be operative (the above-mentioned secrecy laws recently adopted by some American states are but one of many instances of this reliance). In other words, literature has critically thought through capital punishment and given shape to an imaginary that itself feeds into state killing.

Influential reflections on the legitimacy and illegitimacy of the death penalty emerged in the writings of European Enlightenment thinkers and their American peers. Montesquieu's *De l'esprit des lois* [The Spirit of the Laws] (1748) argued that the severity of punishments is fitter for despotic governments.[12] Jean-Jacques Rousseau supported capital punishment in *Du contrat social* [The Social Contract] (1762) on account of society's supposed right to take the life of any individual threatening the conservation of the State.[13] Shortly thereafter, Voltaire's *Traité sur la tolérance* [Treatise on Tolerance] (1763) exposed the iniquitous process through which the Protestant merchant Jean Calas, an innocent father, was unjustly sentenced to death and ended up being broken on the wheel in a France still marked by the Revocation of the Edict of Nantes. A year later, the Italian jurist Cesare Beccaria, who was well acquainted with the works of Montesquieu, Voltaire, and the French encyclopaedists, published the ground-breaking treatise *Dei delitti e delle pene* [On Crimes and Punishments] anonymously. It founded a secular and liberal definition of penalty, provocatively stating in its twenty-eighth chapter:

> Non è dunque la pena di morte un *diritto* [...] ma è una guerra della nazione con un cittadino, perché giudica necessaria o utile la distruzione del suo essere. Ma se dimostrerò non essere la morte né utile né necessaria, avrò vinto la causa dell'umanità.
>
> [The death penalty is not a matter of *right* [...] but is an act of war on the part of society against the citizen that comes about when it is deemed necessary or useful to destroy his existence. But if I can go on to prove that such a death is neither necessary nor useful, I shall have won the cause of humanity.][14]

Abbé Morellet translated Beccaria's essay into French at the end of 1765 and such major figures as D'Alembert and Voltaire warmly welcomed it. In 1766, Voltaire also circulated a *Commentaire* on the treatise and addressed the Italian thinker in his account of the condemnation and execution of the chevalier de La Barre for profanation — La Barre was tortured, decapitated, and burnt at the stake with Voltaire's *Dictionnaire philosophique* [Philosophical Dictionary] nailed to his chest that same year. At the end of the century, former Attorney General of Pennsylvania William Bradford published *An Enquiry: How Far the Punishment of Death is Necessary in Pennsylvania* (1793), which included an epigraph by Montesquieu. Bradford supported capital punishment but considered its usefulness and the juries' resort to it in the most pragmatic terms, ultimately leading his state to reduce drastically the number of crimes punishable by death. In England, Jeremy Bentham partly echoed Beccaria's conception of punishment in his *Rationale of Punishment* (1775/1830) and 'On Death Punishment' (1831), which criticized the death penalty on utilitarian grounds. In Germany, Immanuel Kant, who had also read Beccaria, preferred to advocate for a retributive approach to punishment and made room for the death penalty in the *lex talionis* defended in *Die Metaphysik der Sitten* [The Metaphysics of Morals] (1795).

The chapters in this volume attest that, either through anticipation or through rehearsal, Western literature has infiltrated both the abolitionist and the retentionist arguments articulated by these thinkers and others. It has probed their considerations, be they strategic, utilitarian, retributivist, religious, deterrence-centred, or dictated by moral imperatives. Literary writing has also contributed to understanding the death penalty by giving shape, and flesh, to the reflections of philosophers, jurists, and political theorists. In doing so, it has sometimes counterbalanced their inclination towards abstraction and political pragmatism.

Narratives short and long, poetry, and the theatre are well-equipped to reflect on state killing in ways that other discourses and arts sometimes cannot rival. They may create new idioms to ask what constitutes a capital crime. They have the ability to invent forms that dissect the circumstances, the experiences, and the gestures that can characterize such crimes, for both the offender and the victim. Their plots explore the subtlest mechanisms susceptible to inform and inflect lethal justice.

Their staging reveals the partly rational, partly irrational processes of judging and sentencing. Their multiple characterization and focalization can elucidate the thinking and behaviour of the guilty and the innocent, of the lay citizen and the man of law, of the individual and the community. Their dramatization highlights the rituals and the affects of all those who participate in state killing, directly and indirectly. Their descriptions portray the clinical specificities of various modes of execution. The works at hand also deploy an array of registers — tragic, realistic, comical, ironic, didactic, pathetic, or satirical — liable to highlight the miscarriages of justice, the possibility of clemency, pardon, or commutation, or the aftermath of punishment. And their self-referentiality may unveil the processes of representation that mediatize and transfigure the death penalty, from the cliché to the myth, and influence its reception.

At bottom, the poetic and imagistic capacities of literary works enable us to penetrate the world of capital justice, the condemned man, and the executioner, worlds that would otherwise remain radically foreign to us, or known only vaguely. In immersing readers in these mental and physical spaces, literary writing makes them better grasp the troubled nature of this penalty, which appears to draw, and cross, a fine line between crime and punishment. Literature therefore is capital not only because it takes the death penalty as its subject matter, but also because its art sharpens our critical understanding of this institution.[15]

Presentation of the Volume and Chapters

This volume sets out to analyze a wide range of major literary representations of state killing from the pivotal Enlightenment period to the twenty-first century in both Europe and the United States. It aims to shed light on the craft of poetics all the while being mindful of the historical specificity of the works at hand. *Death Sentences* therefore combines fine-grained readings of key texts with the careful identification of the political, legal, and judicial contexts in which they appeared. In doing so, the collection attempts to complement examinations of other cultural representations of capital punishment.[16] It also strives to prolong studies of its literary figuration that have focused on a single genre, moment, or national tradition.[17] While our volume lays no claim to exhaustiveness, the mosaic of literatures and moments under investigation can hopefully invite transversal readings that tease out parallels and contrasts between major novels, poems, and plays, conjuring up possible transnational and transhistorical dialogues among them.

Part i, entitled 'Fact and Fiction', interrogates the respective roles played by, and the interactions between, these two poles in writings that weave together actual personal experience and external realities into their narrative fabric. In Chapter 1, William Mill Todd III explores the strategies of indirection and displacement that Dostoevsky, who was himself once subject to a mock execution, sets in place in *Записки из мертвого дома* [Notes from the House of the Dead] (1860–62), *Идиот* [The Idiot] (1868–69), and *Братья Карамазовы* [The Brothers Karamazov] (1879–80). Todd notably demonstrates how all three works scrutinize the death penalty from a multiplicity of perspectives, not least from that of the condemned man whose inner life the novelist exposes in extraordinary detail. Norman Mailer's *The Executioner's Song* (1979) transposes the question of the interface between real life and storytelling into the twentieth century, as Brian Jarvis shows in Chapter 2. Mailer chronicles the crime, trial, and execution of murderer Gary Gilmore, who waived his right to appeal and was ultimately presented to a shooting squad in Utah in 1977 — Gilmore's execution thereby ended the de facto moratorium on the death penalty that had been in place in the US for about ten years. In unpacking Mailer's exploration and hybridization of styles, genres, and registers, Jarvis brings to light the ethical and political impact of poetics.

Following this opening reflection on 'capital works' of narrative fiction that incorporate elements of non-fiction, Part II, 'Punishment and Performance', turns to the role played by representation and performativity in state killing. Chapter 3 focuses on pamphlet plays featuring the death penalty in late eighteenth- and early nineteenth-century France. Jessica Goodman examines how they establish a critique of state execution at this crucial historical juncture that made the guillotine both famous and infamous. Revolutionary pamphlet theatre, she reveals, puts revolutionary justice as well as its political tenets on trial, notably by restaging a central actor, the people. Chapter 4 draws on Jacques Derrida's seminars on the death penalty and on psychoanalysis to analyze Oscar Wilde's poem 'The Ballad of Reading Gaol' (1897), written after the author involuntarily witnessed a hanging while in prison. E. S. Burt reviews the Millian reformist take on the nineteenth-century British penal system before arguing that Wilde's ballad shows both to misfire. Unnecessary state cruelty is presented as displacing suffering from the condemned man to his fellow convicts, whose imagination and language run amok as the execution draws near. The performative language of and model behind the death sentence, Burt demonstrates, fall prey to various dysfunctions. Although Wilde does not appear to prescribe a particular corrective to this forbidding diagnosis, his use of testimony, oral language, and allegory condemn state killing. Chapter 5 confirms that the critical potential of performance — or counter-performance — in lethal punishment may reach beyond the stage. In a cross-examination of Franz Kafka's posthumous novel *Der Proceß* [The Trial] (1925) and Bertold Brecht's play *Die Maßnahme* [The Measures Taken] (1930), David Pan argues that capital punishment is inseparable from a process of representation whereby a particular account of the state is constructed and enacted. He shows how both works trace their protagonists' gradual acceptance of this particular narrative — a sacrificial one — and how it contributes to the construction of meaning for the individual and to shaping a conception of both sovereign authority and justice.

Part III, 'Lyric and Law', considers Romantic poetry and the ways in which it may confront lethal justice. Paying particular attention to William Wordsworth's 'The Thorn', in Chapter 6, Mark Canuel reflects on the Romantic ballad as it echoes the sensationalism and didacticism of a long-standing tradition all the while morphing into a critical space. This renewed space, Canuel explains, distances itself from penal harshness and favours rehabilitation over brutal retribution. Chapter 7 offers an in-depth examination of another poem, José de Espronceda's 'El reo de muerte' [The Convict Condemned to Death] (1837). Michael Iarocci investigates how the text modulates a main intertext, Victor Hugo's *Le Dernier Jour d'un condamné* (1829), to better reach its Spanish Catholic audience, and how it interacts with its immediate literary, political, and penal contexts. Using Adorno, Iarocci identifies the ways in which poetic form, with its aesthetic and rhythmic inflections, establishes a distance from reality that paradoxically captures the convict's suffering more efficiently, thereby sharpening the critique of state killing in constitutionally liberal Spain. Concomitantly, the poem points to the pleasure of song and thus to a possible move beyond the world of execution.

Part IV, 'Poetics and Politics', examines particular manipulations of language and form insofar as they intersect with the political foundations and the practice of state killing. Chapter 8 returns to the French novel with which Espronceda — and Dostoevsky — engaged: Hugo's *Le Dernier Jour d'un condamné*. It proposes that this novel denounces the modern death penalty through a kind of poetic activism that centres on the condemned man's mental torture. A disorderly representation indicative of his terror, the staging of an impossible communication with the world around him, and the emergence of a new expressive regime that mirrors his distorted conscience shatter the claim that death by guillotine is humane and painless, as the proponents of the machine and modern French penal law argued. John Cyril Barton in turn sheds light on the formal anti-gallows strategies developed by highly popular antebellum American author E. D. E. N. Southworth in *The Lost Heiress* (1854) and *The Gipsy's Prophecy* (1859). Chapter 9 scrutinizes the two novels' ability to mobilize empathy and sensation and to question lethal justice pointedly. Plot, characterization, incident, core tropes such as condemned innocence and the revelation of fallible evidence, as well as narrative structures stressing the responsibility and potential shortcomings of sovereign power all coincide to strip capital punishment of its legitimacy.

In Chapter 10, Birte Christ considers Stephen King's *The Green Mile* (1996) as a fiction that also seeks to elicit sympathy at every turn. Serialization, parallel narratives, and a sophisticated paratextual and intertextual arrangement radically subvert deterrence, a central component of retentionist argumentation. They respectively force us to feel the pain of waiting on death row; emphasize alienation by institutions that control and persecute, and open up meta-reflections not only on the passing of time, but also on the persistence of memory, including a certain literary memory, part of which signals fiction's potential to improve both law and society.

Muted language has often been used to write about the death penalty, as Albert Camus argued.[18] These ten chapters show that, in contrast, literature has cultivated voices that imaginatively speak up about state killing, thus constituting a vibrant forum of debate.

Notes to the Introduction

1. For a history of this right and its inflection into bio-power, see Michel Foucault, *Histoire de la sexualité 1. La Volonté de savoir* (Paris: Gallimard, 1976); *'Il faut défendre la société': Cours au Collège de France 1975–1976* (Paris: Gallimard-Seuil, 1997); *Surveiller et punir: naissance de la prison* (Paris: Gallimard, 1975). See also Giorgio Agamben, *Homo sacer: il potere sovrano e la nuda vita* (Turin: Einaudi, 1995).
2. Roger Hood and Carolyn Hoyle, *The Death Penalty: A Worldwide Perspective*, 5th edn (Oxford: Oxford University Press, 2015), pp. 504–05.
3. Council of Europe, 'Protocol No. 6 to the Convention for the Protection of Human Rights and Fundamental Freedoms Concerning the Abolition of the Death Penalty', <https://www.echr.coe.int/Documents/Library_Collection_P6_ETS114E_ENG.pdf> [accessed 24 February 2018].
4. International Criminal Court, Rome Statute, 'Part 7: Penalties', <http://legal.un.org/icc/statute/romefra.htm> [accessed 24 February 2018].
5. Council of Europe, 'Protocol No. 13 to the Convention for the Protection of Human Rights and Fundamental Freedoms, Concerning the Abolition of the Death Penalty in All Circumstances', <https://www.echr.coe.int/Documents/Library_Collection_P13_ETS187E_ENG.pdf> [accessed 24 February 2018].
6. Amnesty International, 'Annex II: Abolitionist and Retentionist Countries as of 31 December 2017', *Global Report on Death Sentences and Executions 2017* (April 2018), pp. 40–41 (p. 40), <https://www.amnesty.org/download/Documents/ACT5079552018ENGLISH.PDF> [accessed 3 August 2018].
7. Amnesty International, 'The Use of the Death Penalty in 2016', *Global Report on Death Sentences and Executions, 2016* (April 2017), pp. 3–10 (pp. 4–6), <https://www.amnesty.org/download/Documents/ACT5057402017ENGLISH.PDF> [accessed 24 February 2018]. Some countries such as China classify information about capital punishment as a state secret. Amnesty International stopped publishing estimated figures for this country in 2009.
8. Amnesty International, 'The Use of the Death Penalty in 2017', *Global Report on Death Sentences and Executions 2017* (April 2018), pp. 5–11 (pp. 6–8), <https://www.amnesty.org/download/Documents/ACT5079552018ENGLISH.PDF> [accessed 3 August 2018].
9. Amnesty International, 'United States of America', *Amnesty International Report 2017/18. The State of the World's Human Rights*, pp. 384–89 (p. 388), <https://www.amnesty.org/download/Documents/POL1067002018ENGLISH.PDF> [accessed 24 February 2018].
10. European Commission, International Cooperation and Development, 'Fight Against the Death Penalty', <https://ec.europa.eu/europeaid/sectors/human-rights-and-governance/democracy-and-human-rights/fight-against-death-penalty_en> [accessed 24 February 2018].
11. In 2014, the botched executions of Dennis McGuire in Ohio and Clayton Lockett in Oklahoma exemplified the failure of new drug protocols. A mix of midazolam and hydromorphone was administered to McGuire. According to Father Lawrence Hummer, who witnessed the execution, it took twenty-six minutes before McGuire, who gasped and seized after the injection, was pronounced dead. Lawrence Hummer, 'I Witnessed the Execution of Dennis McGuire. What I Saw was Inhumane', *Guardian*, 22 January 2014, <https://www.theguardian.com/commentisfree/2014/jan/22/ohio-mcguire-execution-untested-lethal-injection-inhumane> [accessed 15 August 2018]. It reportedly took one hour and forty-four minutes for Lockett to die following the failure of the intravenous line that had to be put into his groin (a suitable vein could not be found on his other limbs). He was declared unconscious by the authorities although he attempted to speak and he succumbed after the execution was eventually officially called off. Robert Patton, the director of the Oklahoma Department of Corrections, published a timeline of the botched procedure on 1 May 2014: <https://www.theguardian.com/world/interactive/2014/may/01/oklahoma-execution-clayton-lockett-timeline-document> [accessed 24 February 2018]. For an examination of executions gone wrong in the United States, see Austin Sarat's *Gruesome Spectacles: Botched Executions and America's Death Penalty* (Stanford, CA: Stanford University Press, 2014).

12. Montesquieu, 'De la sévérité des peines dans les divers gouvernements', *De l'esprit des lois*, in *Œuvres complètes*, ed. by Roger Caillois, 2 vols (Paris: Gallimard, 1951), II, 227–995 (pp. 318–19).

13. Jean-Jacques Rousseau, 'Du droit de vie ou de mort', *Du contrat social ou principes du droit politique*, in *Œuvres complètes*, ed. by Bernard Gagnebin and Marcel Raymond, 4 vols (Paris: Gallimard, 1959–69), III, 376–77.

14. Cesare Beccaria, *Dei delitti e delle pene*, ed. by Franco Venturi (Turin: Einaudi, 1994), p. 62; *On Crimes and Punishments, and Other Writings*, ed. by Richard Bellamy, trans. by Richard Davies with Virginia Cox and Richard Bellamy (Cambridge & New York: Cambridge University Press, 1995), p. 66.

15. As such artists and thinkers as Iris Murdoch, Martha Nussbaum, and Hayden White have argued, literary language is an essential prism through which we process and critique historical, socio-political, and cultural realities. See, for example, Iris Murdoch, 'Vision and Choice in Morality', *Proceedings of the Aristotelian Society*, supplementary vol. 30, (1956), 32–58; Martha Nussbaum, *The Fragility of Goodness: Luck and Ethics in Greek Tragedy and Philosophy* (Cambridge: Cambridge University Press, 1986), and *Love's Knowledge: Essays on Philosophy and Literature* (Cambridge: Cambridge University Press, 1992); *Renegotiating Ethics in Literature, Philosophy, and Theory*, ed. by Jane Adamson and others (Cambridge: Cambridge University Press, 1998); and Hayden White, *The Practical Past* (Evanston, IL: Northwestern University Press, 2014).

16. Since the publication of Wendy Lesser's *Pictures at an Execution: An Inquiry into the Subject of Murder* (Cambridge, MA: Harvard University Press, 1993) and Austin Sarat's important books on capital punishment (*The Killing State: Capital Punishment in Law, Politics, and Culture* (New York: Oxford University Press, 1999); *When the State Kills: Capital Punishment and the American Condition* (Princeton, NJ: Princeton University Press, 2001); and, edited with Christian Boulanger, *The Cultural Lives of Capital Punishment; Comparative Perspectives* (Stanford, CA: Stanford University Press, 2005)), much scholarship on the death penalty within the field of cultural studies has tended to set aside the specificities of literature. Mary Welek Atwell's *Evolving Standards of Decency: Popular Culture and Capital Punishment* (New York: Peter Lang, 2004) and *Wretched Sisters: Examining Gender and Capital Punishment* (New York: Peter Lang 2007), as well as Kerstin-Susanne Kurdzel's *The Machinery of Death on Screen: Die Darstellung der Todesstrafe im US-amerikanischen Spielfilm* (Saarbrücken: Dr. Müller, 2008) reflect on the death penalty in film, culture, and other non-literary discourses. A number of studies on the cultural representations of capital punishment have emphasized news reporting, theoretical and philosophical writings, congressional hearings, political speeches, and visual and digital media: Claire Grant's *Crime and Punishment in Contemporary Culture* (London: Routledge, 2004), Philip Smith's *Punishment and Culture* (Chicago, IL: University of Chicago Press, 2008), Michelle Brown's *The Culture of Punishment: Prison, Society, and Spectacle* (New York: New York University Press, 2009), Anne-Marie Cusack's *Cruel and Unusual: The Culture of Punishment in America* (New Haven, CT: Yale University Press, 2009), and Daniel LaChance's *Executing Freedom: The Cultural Life of Capital Punishment in the United States* (Chicago, IL: University of Chicago Press, 2016). Literature is not considered in some recent analyses of punishment in contemporary popular culture, such as *Punishment and Popular Culture*, ed. by Charles J. Ogletree and Austin Sarat (New York: New York University Press, 2015).

17. On American literature and state killing, see for instance Ann M. Algeo, *The Courtroom as Forum: Homicide Trials by Dreiser, Wright, Capote, and Mailer* (New York: Peter Lang, 1996); David Guest, *Sentenced to Death: The American Novel and Capital Punishment* (Jackson: University Press of Mississippi, 1997); Kristin Boudreau, *The Spectacle Death: Populist Literary Responses to American Capital Cases* (Amherst, MA: Prometheus Books, 2006); Paul Christian Jones, *Against the Gallows: Antebellum American Writers and the Movement to Abolish Capital Punishment* (Iowa City: University of Iowa Press, 2011); Jeannine Marie DeLombard, *In the Shadow of the Gallows: Race, Crime, and American Civic Identity* (Philadelphia: University of Pennsylvania Press, 2012); John Cyril Barton, *Literary Executions: Capital Punishment and American Culture, 1820–1925* (Baltimore, MD: Johns Hopkins University Press, 2014). On British literature and state killing, see Mark Canuel, *The Shadow of Death: Literature, Romanticism, and the Subject of Punishment* (Princeton, NJ: Princeton University Press, 2007). On French literature and state killing, see Paul Savey-Casard,

Le Crime et la peine dans l'œuvre de Victor Hugo (Paris: Presses universitaires de France, 1956); Patrick Wald Lasowski, *Les Échafauds du romanesque* (Lille: Presses universitaires de Lille, 1991); Christine Marcandier-Colard, *Crimes de sang et scènes capitales: essai sur l'esthétique romantique de la violence* (Paris: Presses universitaires de France, 1998); Laura Jean Poulosky, *Severed Heads and Martyred Souls: Crime and Capital Punishment in French Romantic Literature* (New York: Peter Lang, 2003); Regina Janes, *Losing Our Heads: Beheadings in Literature and Culture* (New York: New York University Press, 2005); Patrick Wald Lasowski, *Guillotinez-moi! Précis de décapitation* (Paris: Le Promeneur, 2007); Loïc Guyon, *Les Martyrs de la veuve: romantisme et peine de mort* (Oxford: Peter Lang, 2010); Ève Morisi, *Albert Camus contre la peine de mort* (Paris: Gallimard, 2011).
18. Albert Camus, 'Réflexions sur la guillotine', in *Œuvres complètes*, ed. by Raymond Gay-Crosier and others, 4 vols (Paris: Gallimard, 2006–08), IV, 125–67 (p. 128).

PART I

Fact and Fiction

CHAPTER 1

Fedor Dostoevsky's Death Sentences: Strategies of Indirection

William Mills Todd III

On 22 December 1849, sixteen young utopian socialists, members of the Petrashevsky Circle, were driven to Semenovsky Square in St. Petersburg, sentenced to death, allowed to kiss the cross, and dressed in long white shirts. Sabres were broken over their heads, signifying forfeit of noble rank. The first three were led to the stakes to be shot. Three quarters of an hour after the prisoners learned their intended fate, retreat was sounded, the three were led away from the stakes, and a decree was read in which His Imperial Majesty, Nicholas I, sentenced the prisoners to exile and penal servitude. Had this reprieve, carefully choreographed by the emperor himself, not been carried out, it would have been Russia's first public execution since the beheading and quartering of the Cossack rebel Pugachev and his lieutenants in 1775. Even considering the wave of revolutions sweeping Europe in 1849, revolutions that deeply disturbed Nicholas and his government, the execution of these few young idealists would have been disproportionate to their activities and aspirations and to their degree of influence in public life. As historian Igor Volgin notes, their conspiracy left fewer traces in the Russian historical consciousness than other nineteenth-century intellectual movements, before and after.[1]

Among the prisoners waiting in the second set of three was Fedor Mikhailovich Dostoevsky, a promising young journalist and fiction writer. That same evening, he was able to send off a brief description of these events to his brother before being transported to what would become four years in prison on the eastern limits of the Russian empire, then four more years of army service, also in the far east.[2] His description of the execution scene is as terse as my summary of it, perhaps to spare his brother's feelings. He focuses, instead, on his hope for survival, concerned mainly about whether he would be able to continue writing. Through extraordinary effort and determination, this talented young dreamer had, within a half century, made himself a fixture of world literature, his works translated into many languages. The bare facts of his biography — the death sentence, prison, exile, epilepsy, indebtedness, a gambling addiction — became nearly as famous as his works, enhanced by the theories and imagination of such readers as Freud and Nietzsche, as well as by the use he put them to in his imaginative writing. The death sentence and surrounding events proved a turning point in his career, and I will discuss them in this paper, focusing in particular on three major works, *Записки из мертвого дома* [Notes from the House of the Dead] (1860–62), *Идиот* [The Idiot] (1868–69), and *Братья Карамазовы* [The Brothers Karamazov] (1879–80). I will examine the conditions which did not allow him openly to discuss execution in Russia and explore how he expanded his understanding of 'death sentences' from state-performed execution to include vicious corporal punishment. Dostoevsky would become arguably Russia's most insightful and incisive court reporter during the 1870s, but I will argue that death penalties were not just a matter of the legal system to Dostoevsky, but that he incorporated, quite literally, into them a set of moral, psychological, and spiritual issues. Neither he nor his readers, contemporary and subsequent, would forget that he had experienced a death sentence himself. But unlike the vast majority of Russian and Soviet writers condemned to death, he lived to reflect upon it. As his post-exile career advanced, the spectre of capital punishment came increasingly to haunt his work. My core argument is that the experience of a death sentence, which he could not directly address for reasons of censorship, found expression in his writing through a consistent set of strategies of indirection and displacement that he employed throughout his mature work. While providing the necessary historical and biographical background, I will focus on the passages from his novels in which he marshals these strategies. I will further show how he exploits narrative possibilities, especially multiple narration and point of view, in treating capital punishment, but that his treatment is remarkable for the weight it gives to the experience of the human being under sentence of death.

The Theatricality of Capital Punishment in the Russian Empire

Reading through the legal terminology of Dostoevsky's death sentence, we see that freedom of speech and of association were not civil liberties enjoyed by the subjects, even noble ones, of the Russian empire:

> The Military Court finds the defendant Dostoevsky guilty of, upon receiving in March of this year from Moscow, from the nobleman Pleshcheev (a defendant), a copy of a criminal letter by Belinsky, having read this letter at meetings: first, at the home of the defendant Durov and then at the home of the defendant Petrashevsky, eventually giving it to the defendant Mombelli to be copied. Dostoevsky was at the home of the defendant Speshnev when the subversive work by the lieutenant Grigoriev entitled 'A Soldier's Conversation' was read. Hence the Military Court has sentenced him, the retired engineer-lieutenant Dostoevsky, for the failure to report the dissemination of the littérateur Belinsky's letter that constitutes a criminal offense against church and government and of the pernicious work of the lieutenant Grigoriev — to be deprived, on the basis of the Code of Military Degrees [...] of ranks, of all rights concomitant to his social estate and to be subjected to the death penalty by shooting.[3]

The sentence lists nine separate articles in support of the sentence, all involving crimes against the state as opposed to civil crimes, such as murder.

The Russian Empire and its successor states, the Soviet Union and the Russian Federation, have, not unlike other European nations, a long, complicated history of capital punishment, both in terms of legal status and concrete implementation. What has generally distinguished this history from those of other nations is the relatively weak rule of law in this succession of authoritarian or totalitarian states, which have rarely featured an independent judicial system that could not be circumvented by repressive state apparatuses (police, military, or prison authorities) or by the directives of those in power, primarily the autocrat.

Russia's first emperor, Peter the Great, inherited from medieval Muscovy a significant list of capital crimes and increased it to 123, preserving such gruesome means as impaling and burning at the stake; execution was primarily used to punish mutiny, murder, and treason. His daughter, Elizabeth II, curtailed the number of offences and the brutality of the executions. She assumed the power to review all death sentences and in 1754 declared a moratorium on capital punishment, replacing it with disfigurement, branding, and lashing with the knout, followed by exile and forced labour. Siberian exile served pragmatic imperial purposes: populating Russia's expanding eastern regions, sparsely peopled with non-Slavic, non-Orthodox native groups, building fortifications and towns, and exploiting rich natural resources.

Elizabeth's successor, Catherine the Great, wrote a famous 'Instruction' to her Legislative Commission, inspired, among other Enlightenment writings, by Montesquieu (*De l'esprit des lois* [The Spirit of Laws], 1748) and Beccaria (*Dei delitte e delle pene* [On Crimes and Punishments], 1764), in which she argued for the presumption of innocence, against torture, and against capital punishment in times of peace and stability.[4] The stipulation of 'peace' justified the execution of participants in the devastating Pugachev rebellion (1773–74), but it was a sign of the amelioration of punishments that he was beheaded before being quartered. The stipulation of 'stability' covers the death penalty for the writer Aleksandr Radishchev, whose polemical *Путешествие из Петербурга в Москву* [Journey from St. Petersburg to Moscow] (1790) had infuriated Catherine, leading her to compare him to Pugachev and accusing him of propagating the ideas which had led to the French Revolution. For this he was sentenced in a criminal court to death by beheading, a sentence commuted to loss of noble rank and exile in Siberia when it turned out that he was acting alone, not as a member of a conspiracy.[5]

Radishchev was a little-known writer, and all but a few copies of his book were quickly destroyed. Like the Petrashevsky Circle, to which Dostoevsky belonged, he did not make an immediate impact on Russian public life. Far more important for Russian awareness of capital punishment was the Decembrist uprising of 14 December 1825. Although it was quickly repressed, the arrest of nearly 600 young men astounded St. Petersburg. Few members of educated westernized society did not have a son, husband, relative, or friend among the conspirators. Of the thirty-one death sentences, only five were carried out and were done so in secret, but the details of the botched hanging became known and deeply imprinted on successive generations of the incipient Russian intelligentsia. Those spared capital punishment received ruthless sentences to exile, hard labour, and dangerous military missions.

Their grace and courage under harsh conditions earned them widespread respect, not only in the capital cities, Petersburg and Moscow, but in the far reaches of the empire. This, in turn, could support the Enlightenment ideas that execution proves no deterrent to the spread of revolutionary ideas and actions. Subsequent Russian writers, including Dostoevsky and Tolstoy, did not share the ideas of the Decembrists, but they inevitably mentioned them with respect. Dostoevsky would always remember the Decembrist's widow who gave him a Bible and some money as he was being conducted to his own Siberian exile.[6]

Like Radishchev, like his fellow members of the Petrashevsky Circle, and like the majority of the condemned Decembrists, then, Dostoevsky was threatened with capital punishment, but ultimately spared. But his forty-five minutes of anticipation made real what had previously been a literary experience, his reading of and admiration for Victor Hugo's searing *Le Dernier Jour d'un condamné* [The Last Day of a Condemned Man] (1829), in which the narrative is presented through the voice and vision of the man condemned to public execution by guillotine. As Joseph Frank has noted, Dostoevsky cites a phrase from this novel in the letter he wrote to his brother immediately after the mock execution.[7] Perhaps that phrase conveyed to his brother the horror of the experience, in ways that Dostoevsky's brief summary did not.

If, before his sentence, crime in his fiction would be for the most part petty transgressions occasioned by poverty, it would now become stark violence, beating and murder, harshly answered by state-sponsored punishment. Dostoevsky's four years in prison would provide a lifetime of material for his novels and essays on crime, punishment, and regeneration. In his pre-exile fiction he had mastered such literary techniques as parody, the fantastic, the Doppelgänger, and interior monologue, and he had learned to translate Utopian Socialist insights and romantic psychology, respectively, into his first novels, *Бедные люди* [Poor Folk] (1846) and *Двойник* [The Double] (1846), doing so in imaginative, non-doctrinaire fashion and beginning to develop his ability to depict perverse psychological motivations. Now his writing would focus on the horror of violence as it was seen and experienced by perpetrators and victims.

Notes from the House of the Dead: Strategies of Indirection

Dostoevsky's *Notes from the House of the Dead* was eagerly awaited and positively received by the Russian reading public as it was serialized, first in an obscure newspaper, then in a journal, *Time*, published by Dostoevsky's brother. The years 1860 to 1862 were ripe for such a public airing of the failures and brutality of the Russian penal system, as this was the era of the Great Reforms, the emancipation of the serfs, and the restructuring of the legal system along Western models. But it was also a time for writers and publishers to be cautious, because suspicious fires and the distribution of inflammatory pamphlets in Petersburg were leading to the arrest of intellectuals and the suppression of periodicals. Nobody was more aware of this than Dostoevsky, who had recently returned from Siberian exile and would remain under official surveillance until 1875.[8] Indeed, he would encounter censorship problems throughout the serialization process, including a complaint from the censor that he might mislead the public by depicting prison life with insufficient harshness.[9]

Many readers took this book to be a thinly fictionalized digest of Dostoevsky's prison experience. While that approach certainly lent the novel an undeniable aura of authenticity and its author an aura of martyrdom (in the etymological sense of 'witness'), it does little justice to the structure, rhetoric, and range of the narrative. For this novel, Dostoevsky first adapted strategies of indirection which he would also use with variations in his later work. The first and most important of these strategies involved framing the protagonist-prisoner's unfolding narrative with another, a narrative by a civilized, lightly ironical, generally optimistic gentleman who observes the narrator after his release from prison and eventually publishes a selection of the principal narrator's papers. By making his hero-narrator, Gorianchikov, a murderer, a crime which was typically punished not by execution but by a long term of penal servitude, Dostoevsky ostensibly took capital punishment, and his own sentence, off the table, as he would take it off the table for the convicted murderers in his future novels, *Преступление и наказание* [Crime and Punishment] (1866) (Raskolnikov), *The Idiot* (Rogozhin), and *The Brothers Karamazov* (Dmitri). It is doubtful that a discussion of capital punishment, reserved principally for political criminals and members of the military, would have passed the censorship at this tense time in Russian civic life. This did not prevent Dostoevsky's contemporary or subsequent readers from seeing Gorianchikov's narration as being shaped by Dostoevsky's experience of a death sentence.

Dostoevsky manages, within this constraint, to give a profound psychological account of the de facto capital punishment that these long sentences occasioned through harsh conditions, violence among the prisoners, and savage corporal punishment.[10] He does this through the narration of two unfolding and intertwining processes of realization. The first involves a critique of the penal system's dehumanization of the inmates; the second involves a growing awareness of certain irrational, spiritual aspects of the human personality, ones ill-served by the system of penal servitude. The frame narrative, which opens *Notes from the House of the Dead*, activates both processes of realization in its presentation of Gorianchikov, released from prison and living out his life in a small Siberian town, angry, isolated, crushed by his experience, unable to associate with anyone except a young girl he tutors, mysteriously having requiems sung for someone (his murdered wife?) on St. Catherine's day. Robert Louis Jackson has aptly characterized him as a victim of traumatic shock.[11] This despair contrasts sharply with the joy and optimism Gorianchikov had expressed as he was released from prison at the end of his ten-year term: 'Да, с Богом! Свобода, новая жизнь, воскресенье из мертвых... Экая славная минута!' (IV, 232) ['Yes, God go with you! Freedom, a new life, resurrection from the dead... What a glorious moment!'].[12] The elevated lexicon here (God, new life, resurrection) contrasts sharply with the harsh conditions the prisoner is leaving behind and with the vision of his subsequent life the reader has encountered in the frame narrative. This contrast begs an explanation, and the prisoner provides it through the stories of the inmates, through reflections on his own experience, and implicitly, by relying on the reader to draw conclusions from the novel's juxtaposition of its many scenes and capsule biographies.

Gorianchikov suggests that penal servitude is a death sentence from the very title he gives his notes, 'Сцены из Мертвого дома' (IV, 8) ('Scenes from The Dead House') (p. 26). His account, which begins with his first impressions, insists on the 'dead house' as an antithesis to the world outside the stockade: 'Тут был свой особый мир, ни на что более не похожий, тут были свои особые законы, свои костюмы, свои нравы и обычаи, и заживо Мертвый дом, жизнь — как нигде, и люди особенные' (IV, 9) ('Here was our own world, unlike anything else; here were our own laws, our own dress, our own manners and customs, here was the house of the living dead, a life like none other upon earth, and people who were special, set apart') (p. 27). These laws, manners, and customs served to negate not only the possibility of normal human interaction and returning to civil society, but also the possibility of finding spiritual healing through the remorseful acknowledgment of transgression. At the centre of this realization is the narrator's growing understanding about the complexity of the human personality and about the nature of crime, which arises in this novel from every aspect of the human psyche (passion, reason, will) and which cannot be explained by simple recourse to environmental determinism (IV, 142; p. 224). Noting the absence of inner anguish among the inmates (and manifesting none of it himself until released from prison), Gorianchikov reflects on the moral and mental impact of the 'dead house':

> В преступнике же острог и самая усиленная каторжная работа развивают только ненависть, жажду запрещенных наслаждений и страшное легкомыслие. Но я твердо уверен, что знаменитая келейная система достигает только ложной, обманчивой, наружной цели. Она насасывает жизненный сок из человека, энервирует его душу, ослабляет ее, пугает ее и потом нравственно иссохшую мумию, полусумасшедшего представляет как образец исправления и раскаяния. Конечно, преступник, восставший на общество, ненавидит его и почти всегда считает себя правым, а его виноватым. К тому же он уже потерпел от него наказание, а чрез это почти считает себя очищенным, сквитавшимся. (IV, 15)

> [In the criminal, prison and the most intense penal labour serve only to develop hatred, a thirst for forbidden pleasures and a terrible flippancy. But I am firmly convinced that the famous system of solitary confinement achieves only a spurious, deceptive, external goal. It sucks the vital sap from a man, enervates his soul, weakens it, intimidates it, and then presents the withered mummy, the semi-lunatic as a model of reform and repentance. Of course, the criminal, who has rebelled against society, hates it and nearly always considers himself to be in the right and it to be in the wrong. What is more, he has already suffered its punishment, and he nearly always considers that this has cleansed him and settled his account.] (p. 36)

In Gorianchikov's view, neither the barracks system he experienced, nor the European panopticon system that Nicholas I considered in 1845, solves the problem of restoring the criminal to life. Gorianchikov himself, as we see in the novel's framing introduction, has become just such a mummy and semi-lunatic.

While the prison regime contributes to the moral, spiritual, and psychological death of the inmates, it does not neglect bodily harm, at times fatal. Gorianchikov discovers that all but some inmates imbued with religious faith (be it Christian, Jewish, or Islamic) attempt to express their will in acts of hopeless defiance: gambling, fighting, swearing, binge drinking, and attempting escape. This, in turn, subjects them to a second de facto form of capital punishment, savage beating with switches and rods. Noblemen were, by this time, exempt from corporal punishment, but, because prisoners of noble origin had lost that status upon conviction, they, too, could be beaten. Dostoevsky found himself in this position while in prison, narrowly escaping a flogging for malingering.[13] During his four years of military service after imprisonment, however, Dostoevsky was forced to take part in the disciplinary beating of fellow soldiers. The penalty for not doing so or for doing so with insufficient force, carefully monitored by an attending officer, was to oneself undergo this punishment.[14]

Gorianchikov captures the brutality of this punishment, and its futility as a deterrent or corrective early on, in his brief tale of a gentle Bible-reading prisoner who threw a brick at the major in charge of the inmates: 'Его схватили, судили и наказали. Все произошло очень скоро. Через три дня он умер в больнице. Умирая, он говорил, что не имел ни на кого зла, а хотел только пострадать' (IV, 29) ['The man had been seized, tried and flogged. All this had happened very swiftly. Three days later he had died in hospital. As he had lain dying, he had said that he intended no harm to anyone, but simply wanted to suffer'] (p. 55). Disproportionate official violence, a de facto death sentence, senselessly answers inexplicable, irrational violence, directed by the inmate more towards himself than towards the major. The extreme brutality that the inmate knowingly courts and the blunt simplicity of his explanation ('wanted to suffer') make this a primitive form, if not a travesty, of Christian repentance.

When Gorianchikov enters the prison hospital, he details the full horror of these beatings as he witnesses the treatment of those who had been punished, hears their stories, and learns of the pervasiveness of this brutal regime. His dispassionate analysis of it focuses, in turn, upon the failure of the beatings to deter defiance of authority and upon the prisoner's lack of guilty feelings:

> Арестант, хоть и всегда наклонен чувствовать себя правым в преступлениях против начальства, так что в самый вопрос об этом для него немыслим, но все-таки он практически сознавал, что начальство смотрит на его преступление совсем иным взглядом, а стало быть, он и должен быть наказан, и квиты. Тут борьба обоюдная. Преступник знает притом и не сомневается, что он оправдан судом своей родной среды, своего же простонародья, которое никогда, он опять-таки знает это, его окончательно не осудит, а большею частию и совсем оправдает, лишь бы грех его был не против своих, против братьев, против своего же родного простонародья. Совесть его спокойна, а совестью он и силен и не смущается нравственно, а это главное. (IV, 147)

[Although a convict is always inclined to consider himself in the right with regard to crimes against figures of authority, so that no question ever arises in his mind, he is none the less perfectly aware that the authorities look upon his crime from quite a different standpoint, and that therefore he must be punished, so that they may be quits. Here there is a two-sided struggle. Besides, the criminal knows for a certainty that he will be acquitted by the judgment of his own people, who will never finally condemn him and who will for the most part fully acquit him, as long as his crime is not against one of his own kind, his brothers, his common kith and kin. His conscience is untroubled; and this freedom from moral embarrassment gives him strength, and that is the main thing.] (p. 231)

The convict needs this strength, because the punishments are so excessive that the prison authorities administered them in instalments:

Это разделение наказания на две половины случается всегда по приговору лекаря, присутствующего при наказания. Если назначенное по преступлению число ударов большое, так что арестанту всего разом не вынести, то делят ему это число на две, даже на три части, судя по тому, что скажет доктор во время уже самого наказания, то есть может ли наказуемый продолжать идти сквозь строй дальше, или это будет сопряжено с опасностью для его жизни. Обыкновенно пятьсот, тысяча и даже полторы тысячи выходятся разом; но если приговор в две, в три тысячи, то исполнение делится на две половины и даже на три. (IV, 153)

[This division of the punishment into two parts always occurred on the ordering of the doctor who is present when the man is flogged. If the crime entailed a large number of strokes, so many that the victim could not take them all at once, the flogging was divided into two or even three parts, depending on the doctor's opinion, once the flogging had got under way, as to whether the man would be able to go on walking up and down the line, or whether this would put his life at risk. Sentences of five hundred, a thousand or even fifteen hundred strokes were normally taken in one go; but if the sentence called for two or three thousand, its execution would be divided into two or even three parts.] (p. 239)

It would seem that this concern by the medical staff argues against these beatings as de facto death sentences, but at least one of the convicts, the cold-blooded murderer Orlov, knew better:

Он еще перед первой половиной наказания думал, что его не выпустят из-под палок и что он должен умереть. До него доходили уже разные слухи о мерах начальства, еще когда он содержался под судом; он уже и тогда готовился к смерти. Но, выходив первую половину, он ободрился. Он явился в госпиталь избитый до полусмерти; я еще не видал таких язв; но он пришел с радостью в сердце, с надеждой, что останется жив, что слухи были ложные, что его вот выпустили же теперь из-под палок, так что теперь, после долгого содержания под судом, ему уже начинали мечтаться дорога, побег, свобода, поля и леса... Через два дня после выписки из госпиталя он умер в том же госпитале, на прежне же койке, не выдержав второй половины. (IV, 153)

[Before the first part of his punishment he had thought he was not going to survive the beating and that it was intended he should die. Various rumours about how the authorities proposed to treat him had reached him while he had been detained awaiting sentence; it was at that time that he had begun to prepare himself for death. But when he survived the first part of the beating, his spirits revived. He had been brought to the hospital half beaten to death; I have still to this day never seen wounds such as those had had then; but he arrived among us with joy in his heart, in the hope that he would survive, that the rumours had been untrue; here he was, after all, after his long period of confinement as he had awaited trial and sentence, he was beginning to dream of the road, of escape, of freedom, the fields and woods... Two days after his discharge from the hospital he died in the same hospital, in the same bed, having failed to survive the second half of his sentence.] (p. 240)

This mixture of hope and resignation, reinforced rhetorically by pounding repetitions, marks Dostoevsky's later treatment of those doomed to death. The harsh corporal punishments in *Notes from the House of the Dead* give him an opportunity to develop this psychological pattern and rhetorical technique.

Gorianchikov's treatment of these punishments is remarkable for its attention to the psyche of those involved, the punishers and the punished, even as he does not display his own sentiments or reactions. He focuses on the psychological impact of these sentences on the prisoners as the punishment approaches: 'Тут вообще находит на осужденного какой-то острый, но чисто физический страх, невольный и неотразимый, подабляющий все нравственное существо человека' (IV, 152) ['A keen but purely physical terror usually descends on the condemned man. It is a terror that is involuntary and inexorable, and it overwhelms a man's entire moral being'] (p. 239). The first-person account does not afford a privileged inner view inside the prisoner's mind, but Gorianchikov's generalization has the authority of Dostoevsky's experience, which for his readers lay behind it.

Corporal punishment not only fails to reform the prisoners, either spiritually or socially, it also psychologically corrupts those who perform it. And 'perform' is the appropriate term, for the officers and executioners responsible are shown to take sadistic delight in choreographing the beatings. Lest we miss his point, Gorianchikov uses the phrases 'theatrical pomp' and 'art' of flogging, the latter five times in eight pages (IV, 148–57; pp. 232–44). This section on 'executioners' is the longest in his critique of corporal and, by extension, capital punishment. He begins with a specific example, Lieutenant Zherebyatnikov:

Это был человек лет под тридцать, росту высокого, толстый, жирный, с румяными, заплывшими жиром щеками, с белыми зубами и с ноздревским раскатовским смехом. По лицу его было видно, что это самый незадумывающийся человек в мире. Он до страсти любил сечь и наказывать; палками, когда, бывало, назначали его эксекутором... Поручик же был чем-то броде утонченнейшего гастронома в исполнительном деле. Он любил, он страстно любил исполнительное искусство, а любил единственно для искусства. Он наслаждался им и, как истаскавшийся в наслаждениях, полинявший патриций времени Римской империи, изобретал себе разные утонченности, разные противуестественности, чтоб сколько-нибудь расшевелить и приятно пощекотать свою заплывшую жиром душу. (IV, 147–48)

[He was a tall, fat, oily man of about thirty, with red, pudgy cheeks, white teeth and a booming laugh. From his face it was obvious that he was an extremely unreflective individual. He was very fond of administering floggings and beatings whenever it was his turn to do so. The lieutenant was a sort of ultra-refined gourmet in this sphere. He loved, he passionately loved the art of administering corporal punishment, and he loved it for its own sake. He took real pleasure in it, and like some patrician from the time of the Roman Empire, worn out in delights and amusements, he devised various refinements, various unnatural practices, in order to arouse and agreeably titillate his greasy sensibilities.] (p. 232)

But even his supposed antithesis, Lieutenant Smelakov, a 'simple man', resorted to a favourite 'joke', telling the prisoner to recite verses which, when one came up that rhymed with the order to commence beating, would start the process. Gorianchikov speculates that he always repeated the joke because he had composed it: 'Может быть именно потому, что он ее сам сочинил, из литературного самолюбия' (IV, 151) ['Maybe [...] because he had made it up himself, out of literary vanity'] (p. 237). Gorianchikov's vocabulary in these passages, which engages both the native Russian word for 'executioner' (палач) as well as the direct foreign borrowing (экзекутор), reminds us that he considers these corporal punishments a kind of death sentence.[15]

Ultimately, he addresses not just the aestheticization of punishment, but the sensuality of it, in a passage which entwines together the terms of his psychological, spiritual, and civil condemnation of the practice, one which destroys the humanity of its practitioners as much as it tortures their victims:

Я не знаю, как теперь, но в недавнюю старину были джентльмены, которым возможность высечь жертву доставляла нечто, напоминающее маркиз де Сада и Брнвилье. Я думаю, что в этом ощущении есть нечто такое, отчего у этих джентльменов замирает сердце, сладко и больно вместе. Есть люди как тигры, жаждущие лизнуть крови. Кто испытал раз эту власть, это безграничное господство над телом, кровью и духом такого же, как сам, человека, так же созданного, брата по закону Христову; кто испытал власть и полную возможность унизить самым высочайшим унижением другое существо, носящее на себе образ божий, тот уже поневоле как-то делается не властен в своих ощущениях. Тиранство есть привычка; оно одарено развитием, оно развивается, наконец, в болезнь. Я стою на том, что самый лучший человек может огрубеть и отупеть от привычки до степени зверя. Кровь и власть пьянят: развиваются загрубелость, разврат; уму и чувству становятся доступны и, наконец, сладки самые ненормальные явления. Человек и гражданин гибнут б тиране навсегда, а возврат и человеческому достоинству, к раскаянию, к возрождению становится для него уже почти невозможен. К тому же пример, возможность такого своеволия действуют и на все общество заразительно: такая власть соблазнительна. Общество, равнодушно смотрящее на такое явление, уже само заражено в своем основании. Одним словом, право телесного наказания, данное одному над другим, есть одна из язв общества, есть одно из самых сильных средств для уничтожения в нем всякого зародыша, всякой попытки гражданственности и полное основание к непременному и неотразимому его разложению. (IV, 154–55)

[I don't know how it is nowadays,[16] but in the not so distant past there were certain gentlemen who obtained from the freedom to flog their victims something that was reminiscent of the Marquis de Sade and the Marquise de Brinvilliers. There was, I believe, something about this sensation that made the hearts of these gentlemen stop beating, something at once sweet and painful. There are people like tigers, who thirst for blood to lick. Whoever has experienced this power, this unlimited mastery over the body, blood and spirit of another human being, his brother according to the law of Christ; whoever has experienced this control and this complete freedom to degrade, in the most humiliating fashion, another creature made in God's image, will quite unconsciously lose control of his own feelings. Tyranny is a habit; it is able to, and does, develop finally into a disease. I submit that habit may coarsen and stupefy the very best of men to the level of brutes. Blood and power make a man drunk; callous coarseness and depravity develop in him; the most abnormal phenomena become accessible, and in the end pleasurable to the mind and the senses. The human being and the citizen perish forever in the tyrant, and a return to human dignity, to repentance, to regeneration becomes practically impossible for him. What is more, the example, the possibility of such intransigence have a contagious effect upon the whole of society; such power is a temptation. A society which can look upon such a phenomenon with indifference is already contaminated to its foundations. Put briefly, the right given to one man to administer corporal punishment to another is one of society's running sores, one of the most effective means of destroying in it every attempt, every embryo of civic consciousness, and a basic factor in its certain and inexorable dissolution.] (pp. 241–42)

The cascade of metaphors (wild beasts, drunkenness, running sores) and discourses (psycho-sexual, medical, Christian, political) in this passage, unusual in Gorianchikov's normally controlled and analytic narration, lends depth and power to his argument, as does its comprehensiveness, which ranges from the individual psyche to the health of society as a whole. His relentlessly orchestrated syntactic repetitions reinforce his condemnation. The narrator concludes the passage by generalizing still further, seeing the executioner in anyone who exercises despotic power over another. His examples are manufacturers and employers, and he refers to awareness of this expressed in books. But the most convincing example of the crushing power of the system of state punishment is the novel's vision of Gorianchikov himself, physically, psychologically, socially, and spiritually destroyed by his experience of prison, able to interact only with the young girl he tutors. The image of him in the publisher's introduction is a classic example of novelistic 'showing'; as a reader encounters Gorianchikov's analytic, hopeful account of his stay in prison, he or she can never forget the final chapter of that account, presented at the outset of the novel.

Notes from the House of the Dead was the book that secured Dostoevsky's reputation as a major writer, and for a number of his readers, including Tolstoy and Turgenev, it was their favourite of his writings. Its strategy of indirection in dealing with death sentences, i.e. its focus on often fatal corporal punishment and on the destructive aspects of prison life, allowed Dostoevsky to evade censorship and, more importantly, to convey a sense of what it was to be condemned to a living death. As searing as the prison experience was for Dostoevsky, it was far from his only treatment of the death penalty. As Russia's radical movements developed and resorted to political terror and assassination, he had new opportunities to confront capital punishment, if not to write about it directly.

Beyond the Novelistic Pseudo-Memoir to the Mature Novels: Death Sentences from Multiple Perspectives

On 4 April 1866, Dmitry Karakozov attempted to murder Emperor Alexander II, an event which deeply shocked the increasingly patriotic and nationalistic Dostoevsky, who was in the process of composing and serializing *Crime and Punishment* at the time. But, as historian Claudia Verhoeven convincingly argues, the extraordinary parallels between Dostoevsky's fictional Raskolnikov and Karakozov (their age, their status as former law students, their nebulous ideas, their unclear motivation) cannot be seen as a matter of influence, at least in this novel, from which the political is virtually absent.[17] A harsh crackdown on periodicals and writers in the wake of the assassination attempt did not invite Dostoevsky to incorporate political conspiracy, mock execution (one of Karakozov's alleged confederates), or execution by firing squad (Karakozov himself) into the remaining instalments of the novel. Raskolnikov twice feels like a man condemned to death, once before and once after he commits murder, but this comes in instalments published before Karakozov's trial and is a matter of pangs of conscience, not physical state-sponsored execution (VI, 52, 146). Neither passage develops the theme of a death sentence. Punishment in the last novels of Dostoevsky is internalized and, lacking the finality of physical execution, can become a prolonged event in his famously excruciating, never-quite-completed plots of crime, suffering, repentance, and redemption. As was the case with the prisoners in *Notes from the House of the Dead*, the criminals will be moved by conscience, not by the power of the state, to feel guilt, repent, and seek redemption.

The Idiot, Dostoevsky's next and arguably darkest novel, reads like an extended meditation on anticipating, witnessing, and experiencing death sentences in a broad sense, be they medical (Ippolit's immanent death from consumption; Prince Myshkin's excruciating attacks of epilepsy), psychological (Nastasia Filippovna's suicidal attachment to the murderously jealous Rogozhin), or state-inflicted (the prince's memory of a French execution; Holbein's painting *The Body of the Dead Christ in the Tomb*, Figure 1.1).

FIG. 1.1. Hans Holbein der Jüngere, *Der Tote Christus im Grab*, 1521–22

The apocalyptic phrase 'time shall be no more' (Revelation 10:6) echoes through the novel, capturing this sense of life on the edge of extinction. But it is legal execution that sets the pattern, and the novel's protagonist, just returned to Russia from four years of treatment in Switzerland for mental issues, raises it at the very beginning of the novel. Unsocialized in the conventions of polite conversation, Prince Myshkin appears at the home of distant relatives and immediately issues Dostoevsky's strongest pronouncement on capital punishment, first in a conversation with a servant, later with his host's young daughters. The author's strategy is, again, one of indirection, locating the execution in France and focalizing it through his profoundly empathetic hero. Russia's political executions, such as Karakozov's, could still not be discussed in print, especially by Dostoevsky, a former political prisoner, and Russia's civilian courts did not issue death sentences.

The Prince introduces the topic abruptly, apropos of the great legal reforms of the 1860s, noting that Russia does not have capital punishment, then turns to France:

> — Да. Я во Франции видел, в Лионе. Меня туда Шнейдер с собою брал.
> — Вешают?
> — Нет, во Франции все головы рубят.
> — Что же, кричит?
> — Куды! В одно мгновение. Человека кладут, и падает этакий широкий нож, по машине, гильотиной называется, тяжело, сильно... Голова отскочит так, что и глазом не успеешь мигнуть. Приготовления тяжелы. Вот когда объявляют приговор, снаряжают, вяжут, на эшафот взводят, Вот тут ужасно! Народ сбегается, даже женщины, хоть там и не любят, чтобы женщины глядели. (VIII, 19–20)

> > ['Yes, I saw it in France, at Lyons. Schneider took me with him to see it.'
> > 'Do they hang them?' [asks the footman]
> > 'No, in France they cut off their heads.'
> > 'Does the fellow yell, then?'
> > 'Oh no! It takes only a single instant. the man is put in place and a sort of broad knife falls on him, it's part of a machine called a guillotine, it's a heavy thing, powerful... The head flies off so quickly you don't have time to blink. The preparations are hideous. It's when they read out the sentence, set up the machine, bind the man, lead him out to the scaffold, that's the dreadful part! People gather round, even women, though they don't like women to watch.][18]

This is a fictional character speaking, of course, but, replacing the firing squad with the guillotine, it resembles the scene of Dostoevsky's own near execution. The prince then speaks of the criminal, saying nothing about his crime, but viewing, as Victor Hugo had taught Dostoevsky to do, the execution from the point of view of the condemned man, expanding upon his initial 'dreadful':

> Этакую муку!... Преступник был человек умный, бесстрашный, сильный, в летах. Легро по фамилии. Ну вот, я вам говорю, верьте не верьте, на эшафот всходил — плакал, белый как бумага. Разве это возможно? Разве не ужас? Ну кто же по страху плачет? Я и не думал, чтоб от страху можно было заплакать не ребенку, человеку, который никогда не плакал,

человеку в сорок пять лет. Что же с душой в эту минуту делается, до каких судорог ее доводят? Надругательство над душой, больше ничего! Сказано: 'Не убий', так за то, что он убил, и его убивать? Нет, это нельзя. Вот я уж месяц назад это видел, а до сих пор у меня как пред глазами. Раз пять снилось. (VIII, 19–20)

[Such torment!... The criminal was an intelligent man, fearless, strong, getting on in years, Legros by name. Well, I'll tell you, believe it or not, when he mounted the scaffold he wept, with a face as white as a ghost. Is it possible? Isn't it horrible? Whoever weeps from fear? I'd never imagined that a man could weep from fear — not a child, after all, but a man who'd never wept in his life, a man of forty-five. What must be happening in his soul at that moment for a man to be brought to such convulsions? An outrage on the soul, nothing less! It is said: 'Thou shalt not kill' — so does that mean because he had killed he, too, must be killed? No, it's wrong. I saw it a month ago, and I can still see it even now. I've dreamed about it repeatedly.] (p. 26)

The prince's empathy infects his interlocutor:

Камердинер с сочувствующим интересом следил за ним, так что оторваться, не хотелось; может быть, тоже был человек с воображением и попыткой на мысль.
— Хорошо еще вот, что муки немного, — заметил он, — когда голова отлетает. (VIII, 20)
[The valet followed his words with sympathetic interest, reluctant, it appeared, to tear himself away; he was also, perhaps, a man with imagination who made some attempt to think for himself.
'It's a good thing at least that the suffering is short,' he observed, 'when the head falls off.'] (p. 26)

But the prince will not let him off so easily, and the novelist raises the issue of anticipation, which he himself had experiences, and which the flogged prisoners in *Notes from the House of the Dead* certainly had experienced:

— Вот вы это заметили, и это все точно так же замечают, как вы, и машина для того выдумана, гильотина. А мне тогда же пришла в голову одна мысль: а что, если это даже и хуже? Вам это смешно, вам это дико кажется, а при некотором воображении даже и такая мысль в голову вскочит. Подумайте: если, например, пытка; при этом страдания и раны, мука телесная, и, стало быть, все это от душевного страдания отвлекает, так что одними только ранами и мучаешься, вплоть пока умрешь. А ведь главная, самая сильная боль, может, не в ранах, а вот что вот знаешь наверно, что вот через час, потом через десять минут, потом через полуминуты, потом теперь, во сейчас — душа из тела вылетит, и что человеком уж больше не будешь, и что это уж наверно; главное то, что *наверно*. Вот как голову кладешь под самый нож и слышишь, как он склизнет над головой, вот эти-то четверть секунды всего и страшнее. Знаете ли, что это не моя фантазия, а что так многие говорили? Я до того этому верю, что прямо вам скажу мое мнение. Убивать за убийство несоразмерно большее наказание, чем самое преступление. Убийство по приговору несоразмерно ужаснее, чем убийство разбойничье. Тот, кого убивают разбойники, режут ночью, в лесу, или как-нибудь, непременно еще надеется, что спасется, до самого последнего мгновения. Примеры бывали, что уж горло перерезано, а он еще надеется, или бежит, или просит. А тут всю эту последнюю надежду, с которою умирать в десять раз легче, отнимают *наверно*; тут пригбор, и в том, что наверно не избегнешь, вся ужасная-то мука и сидит, и сильнее этой муки нет на свете. Приведите и поставьте солдата против самой пушки на сражении и стреляйте в него, он еще будет надеяться, но прочтите этому самому солдату приговор *наверно*, и он с ума сойдет или заплачет. Кто сказал, что человеческая природа в состоянии вынести это без сумасшествия? Зачем такое ругательство, безобразное, ненужное, напрасное? Может быть, и есть такой человек, которому прочли приговор, дали помучиться, а потом сказали: 'Ступай, тебя прощают'. Вот этакой человек, может быть, мог бы рассказать. Об этой муке и об этом ужасе и Хростос говорил. Нет, с человеком так нельзя поступать! (VIII, 19–21)

[You've made that observation, it's exactly the same observation that everyone makes, and that's why this machine, the guillotine, was invented. But then a thought came into my head: what if it's even worse? You may find this ridiculous, it may seem outrageous to you, but if you've any imagination, an idea like this will leap into your head. Just think: if there was torture, for example, it would involve suffering and injuries, physical torment and all that would probably distract you from the mental suffering, so that your injuries would be all that you'd suffer, right up to the time you died. For, after all, perhaps the worst, most violent pain lies not in injuries, but in the fact that you know for certain that within the space of an hour, then ten minutes, then half a minute, then now, right at this moment — your soul will fly out of your body, and you'll no longer be a human being, and that this is certain; the main thing is that it's *certain*. When you put your head right under the guillotine and hear it sliding above your head, it's that quarter of a second that's most terrible of all. This isn't my imagination, you know, many people have said the same thing. I believe this so strongly that I'll tell you my opinion straight out. To kill for murder is an immeasurably greater evil than the crime itself. Murder by judicial sentence is immeasurably more horrible than murder committed by a bandit. The person who's murdered by a bandit has his throat cut at night, in a forest, or somewhere like that, and he certainly hopes to be rescued, right up to the very last moment. There have been examples of people whose throats have been cut still hoping, or running away, or begging for their lives. But here, all this final hope, with which it's ten times easier to die, is taken away *for certain*; the terrible torment remains, and there's nothing in the world more powerful than that torment. Take a soldier and put him right in front of a cannon in a battle and fire it at him, and he'll go on hoping, but read out a *certain* death sentence to that same soldier, and he'll go mad, or start to weep. Who can say that human nature is able to endure such a thing without going mad? Why such mockery — ugly, superfluous, futile? Perhaps the man exists to whom his sentence has been read out, has been allowed to suffer, and then been told: 'Off you go, you've been pardoned'. A man like that could tell us, perhaps. Such suffering and terror were what Christ spoke of. No, a human being should not be treated like that!] (pp. 25–28)

This is the longest argument against capital punishment that we find in Dostoevsky's works, and it joins empathetic imagination, humane argument, psychological insight, and Christian narrative (Christ in the Garden of Gethsemane) to sway the prince's listener and, by extension, the reader. Dostoevsky merges his own experience with his profound sense of Christ's suffering to make the passage particularly vivid. The Prince's engaged, empathetic narration, sensitized (as we will subsequently learn) by his experience of epilepsy, contrasts with Gorianchikov's more distant, analytical narration in *Notes from the House of the Dead*.

The prince reduces the servant-interlocutor to pensive silence, but he is far from finished with his discourse on capital punishment. Soon, in the midst of a comic scene with the wife of the Epanchin family and their three young daughters, the eldest daughter's request that the prince suggest to her the topic for a painting leads him to suggest she paint an execution scene. This sets the prince off on another extended passage on about execution, all the more striking because it is so inappropriate for polite social discourse. Here the prince focuses less on arguments against capital punishment and more on the condemned man's dreadful process of anticipation through his last hours to the last seconds — physical sensations, psychic horror — which the prince imagines in an act of simultaneous remembering and empathetic anticipatory ecphrasis, addressing his audience, the Epanchin women, and beyond them, the novel's readers, and involving them in the prisoner's experience:

В низу лесенки он был очень бледен, а как поднялся и стал на эшафот, стал вдруг белый как бумага, совершенно как белая писчая бумага. Наверно, у него нога слабела и деревенели, и тошнота была, — как будто что его давит в горле, и от этого точно щекотно, — чувствовали вы это когда-нибудь в испуге или в очень страшные минуты, когда и весь рассудок останется, но никакой уже власти не имеет? Мне кажется, если, например, неминуемая гибель, дом на вас валится, то тут вдруг ужасно захочется сесть и закрыть глаза и ждать — будь что будет!... Вот тут-то, когда начиналась эта слабость, священник поскорей, скорым таким жестом и молча, ему крест к самым губам вдруг подставлял, маленький такой крест, серебряный, четырехконечный, — часто подставлял, поминутно. И как только крест касался губ, он глаза открывал, и опять на несколько секунд как бы оживлялся, и   ноги шли. Крест он с жалостью целовал, спешил целовать, точно спешил не забыть захватить что-то про запас, на всякий случай, но вряд ли в эту минуту что-нибудь религиозное сознавал. И так было до самой доски... Странно, что редко в эти самые последние секунды в обморок падают! Напротив, голова ужасно живет и работает, должно быть, сильно, сильно, сильно, как машина в ходу; я воображаю, так и стучат разные мысли, все неконченные, и может быть, и смешные, посторонние такие мысли: 'вот этот глядит — у него бородавка на лбу, бот у палача одна нижняя пуговица заржавел'... а между тем все знаешь и все помнишь; одна такая точка есть, которой никак нельзя забыть, и в обморок упасть нельзя, и все около нее, около этой точки, ходит и вертится. И подумать, что это так до самой последней четверти секунды, когда уже голова на плахе лежит, и ждет, и *знает*, и вдруг услышит над собой, как железо склизнуло! Это непременно услышишь! Я бы, если бы лежал, я бы нарочно слушал и услышал! Тут, может быть, только одна десятая доля мгновения, но непременно услышишь! И представьте же, до сих пор еще с секунду, может быть, знает, что она отлетела, — каково понятие! А что если пять секунд!... Нарисуйте эшафот так, чтобы видна была ясно и близко одна только последняя ступень; преступник ступил на нее: голова, лицо бледное как бумага, священник протягивает крест, тот с жадностью протягивает свои синие губы, и глядит, и — *все знает.* Крест и голова — вот картина, лицо священника, палача, его двух служителей и несколько голов и глаз снизу, — все это можно нарисовать как бы на третьем плане, в тумане, для аксессуара... Вот какая картина. (VIII, 55–56)

[At the foot of the steps he was very pale, but when he had climbed them and stood on the scaffold he suddenly turned as white as paper, just like white writing paper. His legs had probably gone weak and numb, and then he felt nausea — as though his throat were being constricted, making it tickle — have you ever felt that, when you were frightened or at moments of great terror, when all of your reason remains but has no power anymore? I think that if, for example, doom is inevitable, and the house is collapsing on top of one, one will have a sudden urge to get down and close one's eyes and wait for what may come next!... it was at this point that the priest rather more quickly, with a swift gesture, suddenly began to put the cross right to the man's lips without a word, a small cross, silver, four-pointed — doing so frequently, every minute. And as soon as the cross touched his lips, he would open his eyes, and again for a few seconds come to life again, as it were, and his legs moved forward. He kissed the cross avidly, hurried to kiss it, as though he were hurrying lest he forget to take something with him in reserve, just in case, but he would hardly have been aware of anything religious at that moment. And so it continued right up to the plank itself... It's strange that men seldom faint at those very last seconds! On the contrary, the brain is horribly alive and must work fiercely, fiercely, fiercely, like an engine in motion; I imagine various thoughts chattering, all unfinished, and perhaps ridiculous ones, too, irrelevant ones: 'Look at that man staring — he has a wart on his forehead, look at the executioner, one of his lower buttons is rusty'... and all the while you keep remembering; there is one point like that, which you cannot forget, and you must not faint, and everything moves and whirls around it, around that point. And to think that this goes on until the very last quarter of a second, when your head lies on the block, waits, and *knows*, and suddenly it hears above it the sliding of the iron! That you would certainly hear! If I were lying there I would make a special point of listening for it and hearing it! At that point there would perhaps only be one-tenth of a moment left, but you would certainly hear it! And imagine, to this day there are those who argue that when the head flies off it may possibly for a second know that it has flown off — what a conception! And what if it were five seconds?... Paint the scaffold so that only the last stair can be seen clearly and closely; the condemned man has stepped on to it; his head, white as paper, the priest holding out the cross, the man extending his blue lips and staring — and *knowing everything.* The cross and the head — that is the painting, the face of the priest, of the executioner, of his two assistants and a few heads and eyes from below — all of that may be painted on a tertiary level, as it were, in a mist, as a background... that's what the painting should be like.] (pp. 76–78)

As he does in his conversation with the servant, the prince focuses not on what the criminal has done, but on what society is doing to the condemned man and how the condemned man experiences it as torture. While some of the details about the prisoner's sense of time echo those Dostoevsky wrote to his brother after his own near-execution, as Joseph Frank has noted, the detail and the sense of horror are much amplified in this scene, in which the prince takes no pains to spare the feelings of his audience.[19] The prince's combination of narrative and imagined painting effectively capture the intensity of the moment, the prisoner's senses at work, and the prisoner's desperation.

How Not to Imagine and Represent Execution: Further Practices of Indirection

It is in light of this feeling for the condemned that we may understand Dostoevsky's harsh reaction to Ivan Turgenev's article, 'The Execution of Tropmann'. As Robert Jackson and Joseph Frank have noted, Dostoevsky took issue with the focus of Turgenev's article, not with Turgenev's opposition to capital punishment, which Dostoevsky, after all, shared.[20] Writing about a public execution he had attended in Paris in 1870, Turgenev narrates primarily his own feelings, self-indulgently, in what Dostoevsky found a 'pompous and fussy' manner. Even worse, he does so in a way that Dostoevsky found cowardly and immoral because Turgenev averts his eyes at the moment of execution itself, ashamed to have joined the huge crowd of vulgar curiosity seekers.[21] While Dostoevsky, as we have seen, had analyzed the brutalizing impact of such spectacles on their audience in *Notes From the House of the Dead*, he had, even in that earlier work, but increasingly in his later ones, taken the condemned man's perspective in treating capital punishment, and it was that empathy he found lacking in Turgenev's account.

A salient example of egocentric inattention to the condemned person occurs in Dostoevsky's final novel, *The Brothers Karamazov*, but with a different twist, not sentimental (as in Turgenev's case), but angry, satirical. Ivan's rebellion against 'God's world' and his simultaneous attack on the faith of his younger brother Alesha includes another execution scene, once again set in Switzerland, once again featuring the guillotine, once again referring to Russia's lack of capital punishment, a partial fiction understood by most of Dostoevsky's contemporary readers, who would have known that the government could and did use military tribunals to condemn political terrorists. The case Ivan depicts was a real one, as are all of Ivan's examples in his brief against divine justice, and the execution of Richard did take place in Geneva in 1850. Ivan sarcastically summarizes the religious brochure devoted to it, translated from French to Russian in 1877.[22] The condemned man, Richard, was an illegitimate child, illiterate and mistreated throughout his childhood:

Дикарь стал добывать деньги поденною работой в Женеве, добытое пропивал, жил как изверг и кончил тем, что убил какого-то старика и ограбил. Его схватили, судили и присудили к смерти. Там ведь не сентиментальничают. И вот в тюрьме его немедленно окружают пасторы и члены разных Христовых братств, благотворительные дамы и проч. Научили они его в тюрьме читать и писать, стали толковать ему Евангелие, усовещивали, убеждали, напирали, пилили, давили, и вот он сам торжественно сознается наконец в своем преступлении. Он обратился, он написал сам суду, что он изверг и что наконец-таки он удостоился того, что и его озарил Господь и послал ему благодать. Все взволновалось в Женеве. Все, что было высшего и благовоспитанно, ринулось к нему в тюрьму; Ришара целуют, обнимают: 'Ты брат наш, на тебя сошла благодать'! А сам Ришар только плачет в умилении: 'Да, на меня сошла благодать! Прежде я все детство и юность мою рад был корму свиней, а теперь сошла и на меня благодать, умираю во Господе'! — 'Да, да, Ришар, умри во Господе, ты пропил кровь и должен умереть во Господе. Пусть ты невиновен, что не знал совсем Господа, когда завидовал корму свиней и когда тебя вили за то, что ты крал у них корм (что ты делал очень нехорошо, ибо красть не позволено), — но ты пролил кровь и должен умереть'. И вот наступает последний день. Расслабленный Ришар плачет и только и делает, что повторяет ежеминутно: 'Это лучший из дней моих, я иду к Господу'! — 'Да, — кричат пасторы, судьи и благотворительные дамы, — это счастливейший день твой, ибо ты идешь' к Господу'! Все это двигается к эшафоту вслед за позорною колесницей, в которой везут Ришара, в экипажах, пешком. Вот достигли эшафота: 'Умри, брат наш, — кричат Ришару, — умри во Господе, ибо и на тебя сошла благодать'! И вот покрытого поцелуями братьев брата Ришара втащили на эшафот, положи на гильотину и оттяпали-таки ему по-братски голову за то, что и на него сошла благодать. (XIV, 218–19)

[The savage began to earn his living as a day labourer in Geneva, he drank what he earned, he lived like a monster and finished by killing and robbing an old man. He was caught, tried, and condemned to death. They do not sentimentalize there. And in prison he was immediately surrounded by pastors, members of Christian brotherhoods, philanthropic ladies, and the like. They taught him to read and write in prison, and expounded the Gospel to him. They exhorted him, worked upon him, drummed at him incessantly, till at last he solemnly confessed his crime. He was converted, he wrote to the court himself that he was a monster, but that in the end God had sent him light and shown grace. All Geneva was in excitement about him, all philanthropic and religious Geneva. All aristocratic and well-bred society of the town rushed to the prison; they kiss Richard and embrace him: 'you are our brother, you have found grace... Though it's not your fault that you knew not the Lord, when you coveted the pigs' food and were beaten for stealing it (which was very wrong of you, for stealing is forbidden); but you've shed blood and you must die'. And so the last day comes. Limp Richard cries and does nothing but repeat every minute: 'This is my best day. I am going to the Lord!' 'Yes,' cry the pastors, judges and philanthropic ladies, 'this is your happiest day, for you are going to the Lord!' Everything [sic] moves, in carriages and on foot, toward the scaffold behind the cart of shame bearing Richard. They reach the scaffold: 'Die, brother,' they cry to Richard, 'die in the Lord, for grace has come upon you!' And so, covered with his brothers' kisses, Richard is dragged on to the scaffold, and led to the guillotine. And they chopped off his head in brotherly fashion, because he had found grace.][23]

Ivan's carefully crafted repetitions and short angry sentences ruthlessly hammer everything they touch: organized religion, the legal system, human indifference, the third hypostasis of the Trinity, the Holy Spirit, grace descending (Ivan will also attack God the Father and, in 'The Grand Inquisitor', God the Son). Lost in the cornucopia of absurdity is Richard himself, who becomes a limp puppet, manipulated by church, state, society, and Ivan's rhetoric. Ivan's anger, like Turgenev's civilized squeamishness, but unlike Prince Myshkin's empathy, gives little insight into the feelings of the condemned prisoner and gives little sense of the torture that capital punishment entails. In place of Prince Myshkin's or Gorianchikov's attention to the executed man's suffering, Ivan offers merely the terse 'dragged'. His exemplary role in Ivan's brief against God concluded, Richard disappears from the novel, leaving the reader with a powerful sense of the absurdity of first condemning the barely human Richard and only then seeking to awaken his mind and conscience. Dostoevsky, in this 'little picture', as Ivan calls it, proves a master of novelistic perspectivalism, as we see the events from several points of view: Ivan's satiric and rebellious rhetoric, his brother's crushed silence, the self-satisfied hypocrisy of the Genevans, the eager embrace of the travestied Christian beliefs by Richard. The reader is left to infer the brutality of execution from the verbs 'dragged' and 'chopped off'. As the novel moves forward, the implied author is careful to counter these perversions of 'grace' with more positive and empathetic narrations of repentance, forgiveness, and quests for reconciliation. Capital punishment by the state and Ivan's ruthless travesty of redemption figure as two unsatisfactory solutions to problems of human transgression.

Conclusions: Dostoevsky, the Death Penalty, and Novelistic Representation

The rapidly increasing terrorist incidents in Russia of the 1870s and 1880s brought Dostoevsky the inhabitant of Petersburg into close proximity with the capital punishment reserved for violent political activists. On 22 February 1880 he witnessed the public hanging of Ippolit Mlodetsky, who had attempted to assassinate Count Loris-Melikov, the official given dictatorial powers to quell the disturbances. It took place on the same square where Dostoevsky had himself awaited execution three decades before. But this time there was no last-minute reprieve. Exceedingly upset, Dostoevsky talked about the execution in several social gatherings during the days that followed, including one hosted by a member of the imperial family, Grand Duke Konstantin Konstantinovich.[24] He did not incorporate the execution into *The Brothers Karamazov*, which was still being serialized, as he had not incorporated the execution of Karakozov into *Crime and Punishment*. But he did raise the possibility of a sequel to *The Brothers Karamazov*, one in which the saintly youngest brother, Alesha, would become a political radical and be executed. Had he done so, and this is only one of the possibilities he explored, he would have for the first time abandoned the strategy of indirection we have seen in his earlier works and confronted directly the remaining recourse to capital punishment in the Russian empire.[25] It would have been a bold move, but no less bold than Ivan's attack on God's world, which Dostoevsky was able to get past the censorship, a cautious editor, and the Chief Procurator of the Holy Synod. But it would have also run counter to Dostoevsky's novelistic treatment of controversial issues, showing them from a variety of conflicting perspectives and inviting the reader to see beyond the individual viewpoints of characters and narrators.

Dostoevsky died shortly after sharing his plans for the sequel. He did not live to see it into print or even into a draft. He spoke little of his own mock execution, mentioning it only three times to his wife during a quarter century of marriage.[26] In his best-known fictions, severe punishment is something that transgressors impose upon themselves more harshly than the state imposes it on them. Dostoevsky never wrote a tract against capital punishment, although, as we have seen, his characters and narrators do confront it. He does not deal with Russian executions directly in his writing, fictional or non-fictional. And yet his strategy of indirection enabled him to address it from a variety of viewpoints: the executioner's, the witnesses', and, most vividly, that of the condemned prisoner. His brief, yet powerful, depictions, always integrated into the plot and characterization patterns of his fictions, capture the prisoner's anguish, hopes, dread, and sense of time. From this last perspective, the prisoner's, capital punishment was nothing less than prolonged torture, a violation of Christian forgiveness, and, even more, a repetition of the violence done to Christ, Dostoevsky's indelible image of perfect beauty, goodness, and truth.

Notes to Chapter 1

1. Igor Volgin, *Propavshii zagovor: Dostoevsky i politicheskii protsess 1849 g.* (Moscow: Izdatel'stvo Libereia, 2000), p. 652.

2. Fedor Dostoevsky, *Polnoe sobranie sochinenii v tridtsati tomakh*, 30 vols (Leningrad: Nauka, 1972–90), XXVIII: i, 161–62. Letter of 22 December 1849 to M. M. Dostoevsky. All subsequent quotations from the works of Dostoevsky in this paper are taken from this edition, with references in the main text (with the number of the volume preceding the page reference).

3. Quoted in *Dostoevsky as Reformer: The Petrashevsky Case*, ed. and trans. by Liza Knapp (Ann Arbor, MI: Ardis, 1987), p. 91.

4. Isabel de Madariaga, *Russia in the Age of Catherine the Great* (New Haven, CT: Yale University Press, 1981), p. 155.

5. John T. Alexander, *Catherine the Great: Life and Legend* (Oxford: Oxford University Press, 1989), pp. 283–85.

6. A vast Soviet literature on the Decembrists served both the official goal of developing a history of radical thought in Russia and the unofficial, dissident goal of preserving ideals of intellectual independence and individual dignity under conditions of oppression. Useful studies in English include Anatole G. Mazour, *The First Russian Revolution, 1825*, 2nd printing (Stanford, CA: Stanford University Press, 1961); and *The Decembrist Movement*, ed. by Marc Raeff (Englewood Cliffs, NJ: Prentice-Hall, 1966). On the behavior and cultural models for the Decembrists, see Iurii M. Lotman, 'The Decembrist in Daily Life (Everyday Behavior as a Historical-Psychological Category)', in *The Semiotics of Russian Cultural History*, ed. by Alexander D. Nakhimovsky and Alice Stone Nakhimovsky (Ithaca, NY: Cornell University Press, 1985), pp. 95–149.

7. Joseph Frank, *Dostoevsky: The Seeds of Revolt, 1821–1849* (Princeton, NJ: Princeton University Press, 1976), p. 109.

8. I. L. Volgin, *Poslednii god Dostoevskogo: Istoricheskie zapiski* (Moscow: Sovetskii pisatel, 1986), p. 131.

9. Edward Wasiolek, *Dostoevsky: The Major Fiction* (Cambridge, MA: M.I.T. Press, 1964), p. 201.

10. Abby M. Schrader, *Languages of the Lash: Corporal Punishment and Identity in Imperial Russia* (DeKalb: Northern Illinois University Press, 2002), gives a thorough and sophisticated overview of Russian disciplinary measures. Anna Schur, *Wages of Evil: Dostoevsky and Punishment*

(Evanston, IL: Northwestern University Press, 2012), gives a thorough analysis of Dostoevsky's fictional and journalistic treatment of punishment in general. A concise version of her argument appears in Anna Schur, 'Punishment and Crime', in *Dostoevsky in Context*, ed. by Deborah A. Martinsen and Olga Maiorova (Cambridge: Cambridge University Press, 2015), pp. 30–38.

11. Robert Louis Jackson, 'The Narrator in Dostoevsky's *Notes from the House of the Dead*', in *Studies in Russian and Polish Literature in Honor of Waclaw Lednicki*, ed. by Zbigniew Folejewski and others (The Hague: Mouton, 1962), pp. 192–216 (p. 197). For an extended, highly sophisticated analysis of the novel, especially of its narrator's 'conversion experience,' see Nancy Ruttenburg, *Dostoevsky's Democracy* (Princeton, NJ: Princeton University Press, 2008).

12. Fedor Dostoevsky, *The House of the Dead*, trans. by David McDuff (London: Penguin, 1985), p. 357. Subsequent references to this edition will appear in the main text.

13. Joseph Frank, *Dostoevsky: The Years of Ordeal, 1850–1859* (Princeton, NJ: Princeton University Press, 1983), pp. 78–80. Frank judiciously weighs and rejects the legend that Dostoevsky was subjected to corporal punishment and that this was a source of his epilepsy.

14. Ibid., p. 178.

15. On the range of meanings of 'palach' see Schrader, *Languages of the Lash*, p. 191, n. 1.

16. In a footnote, Gorianchikov notes that reforms had ameliorated this harsh regime in the years after he left prison (IV, 152; p. 238). He is alluding to the phasing out of the harshest corporal punishments during the period of the Great Reforms (1855–67) and their concomitant limitation, in ameliorated form, to exiles and male peasants. Schrader, *Languages of the Lash*, pp. 144–90.

17. Claudia Verhoeven, *The Odd Man Karakozov: Imperial Russia, Modernity, and the Birth of Terrorism* (Ithaca, NY: Cornell University Press, 2009), pp. 85–103. Without mentioning Verhoeven's study, a well-argued new study of the novel's treatment of Petersburg argues that Raskolnikov's route to the murder of the stockbroker and her sister is not random, but takes him to places associated with political prisoners and regicide. The itinerary in question, however, is established in the first installments of the novel, published before Karakozov's attempt. Ulrich Schmid, 'Dostoevsky and Regicide: The Hidden Topographical Meaning of *Crime and Punishment*', *Dostoevsky Studies*, n.s., 19 (2015), 51–62.

18. Fedor Dostoevsky, *The Idiot*, trans. by David McDuff (London: Penguin, 2004), pp. 25–26. Subsequent references to this edition will appear in the main text.

19. Joseph Frank, *Dostoevsky: The Miraculous Years, 1865–1871* (Princeton, NJ: Princeton University Press, 1995), p. 312.

20. Frank, *Dostoevsky: The Miraculous Years*, p. 423; Robert Louis Jackson, 'The Ethics of Vision I: Turgenev's "Execution of Tropmann" and Dostoevsky's View of the Matter', in *Dialogues with Dostoevsky: The Overwhelming Questions* (Stanford, CA: Stanford University Press, 1993), pp. 29–54. Jackson's sophisticated and persuasive reading defends Turgenev's strategy by differentiating between Turgenev the author-narrator of the piece and Turgenev the character.

21. Dostoevsky, *Polnoe sobranie sochinenii*, XXIX, i, 128–29. Letter to N. N. Strakhov of 11 June 1870.

22. *Obrashchenie i smert' l.f. Richara, kazennogo v Zhjeneve 11-go iunia 1850 goda*, per. s frantsuzskogo (St. Petersburg: Tip. A. Iakobsona, 1877). Dostoevsky had a copy of this anonymous tract in his personal library. For a discussion of the pamphlet and his use of it see N. F. Budanova, 'Istoriia "Obrashcheniia I smerti" Richara, rasskazannaia Ivanom Karamazovym', *Dostoevskii: Materialy I issledovaniia*, 13 (1996), 106–19.

23. Fedor Dostoevsky, *The Brothers Karamazov*, ed. and trans. by Susan McReynolds Oddo (New York: W. W. Norton & Company, 2011), pp. 207–08.

24. The episode is analyzed in similar terms by Volgin, *Poslednii god Dostoevskogo*, pp. 134–63, and Joseph Frank, *Dostoevsky: The Mantle of the Prophet, 1871–1881* (Princeton, NJ: Princeton University Press, 2002), pp. 484–87.

25. For an analysis of Dostoevsky's very preliminary thoughts about the sequel, see James L. Rice, 'Dostoevsky's Endgame: The Projected Sequel to *The Brothers Karamazov*', *Russian History*, 33.1 (2006), 45–62.

26. Volgin, *Poslednii god Dostoevskogo*, p. 150.

CHAPTER 2

Matters of Grave Importance:
Style in Norman Mailer's
The Executioner's Song

Brian Jarvis

To write about myself is to send my style through a circus of variations and
postures, a fireworks of virtuosity designed to achieve... I do not even know
what. Leave it that I become an actor, a quick-change artist, as if I believe I
can trap the Prince of Truth in the act of switching a style.

NORMAN MAILER, *Advertisements for Myself*

At 8:07 a.m. on 17 January 1977, Gary Mark Gilmore was executed just outside
the grounds of Utah State Prison. Six months earlier, on the morning of 21 July
1976, Gilmore had been arrested on the outskirts of Provo in Utah on suspicion
of armed robbery and double homicide. Gilmore's victims were Max Jensen, a gas
station attendant in Orem, and Ben Bushnell, a motel manager in Provo. In both
incidents, Gilmore instructed his compliant victim to lie face down on the floor
before shooting him in the head. The subsequent trial commenced on 5 October
and was concluded in two days. Gilmore was convicted and sentenced to death.
Given the opportunity to choose the mode of his execution, the condemned
man elected to be shot by a firing squad. The date of the execution was set for 15
November 1976, but, when Gilmore waived his right to appeal, both the American
Civil Liberties Union and the National Association for the Advancement of
Colored People attempted to intervene. There had been a de facto moratorium on
the death penalty in the United States for around a decade and opponents of capital
punishment were deeply concerned that this might be overturned by the precedent
of the Gilmore case. A number of judicial stays were issued right up to the eve of
the execution, when the legitimacy of Gilmore's punishment was authoritatively
determined by a Supreme Court ruling based on a majority of five to four. Five
local police officers were recruited as executioners. With no recent experience
of carrying out capital punishment, prison officials converted a space in a nearby
disused cannery into a bespoke execution facility. The marksmen were positioned
behind a makeshift curtain with small holes cut out through which to shoot. Their

target was hooded and strapped to an office chair positioned in front of a dirty mattress and some sandbags. Asked for any last words, Gilmore responded bluntly: 'Let's do it'. Allegedly, this infamous phrase inspired the Nike slogan: 'Just do it'. This may be the most conspicuous legacy of the Gilmore execution, but it is not the most momentous. As opponents of the death penalty feared, by insisting on his inalienable right to die, Gilmore re-opened the door to the death chamber in the US. Inadvertently, 'let's do it' issued an imperative to the killing state which since 1977 has carried out almost 1,500 legal homicides.

The story of Gary Gilmore's crime, trial, and execution captivated America in the mid-seventies. Intense media interest turned Gilmore into a national celebrity although the condemned man's time in the limelight was short-lived. Whilst the media circus swiftly moved on, this crucial chapter in the history of punishment in the US was memorialized by Norman Mailer in *The Executioner's Song* (1979). Although it covers a relatively brief span of just nine months, from shortly before the murders until just after the execution, this is a hefty slab of a text that stretches over 1000 pages. *The Executioner's Song* took fifteen months to write and required a mammoth research effort. Mailer made field trips to Utah and Oregon and conducted over 100 face-to-face and telephone interviews with family, friends, lawyers, lobbyists, and journalists. In addition, he consulted transcripts of interviews at which he was not present, legal testimony, newspaper and police reports, psychological profiles, and Gilmore's voluminous correspondence with his girlfriend, Nicole Baker. In an afterword, over several pages, Mailer acknowledges his debt to a vast gallery of participants and assistants in compiling a prodigious archive.

The Executioner's Song represented a significant departure for Mailer in terms of his customary mode of composition and it also involved a major transformation in his signature style. Mailer's fiction and essays from the 50s and 60s often engaged and at times indulged in surrealist experimentation, pugilistic polemic, and purple prose. The central figure, typically, was 'Norman Mailer'. In a *New York Times* review of *The Executioner's Song* entitled 'The Ballad of Gary G.', fellow author Tim O'Brien responded favourably to the new style:

> No gimmicks, no tricks, no *Advertisements for Myself*. The prose is spare and dry and clean. Most important, Mailer does not inject his own personality or judgement into the narrative, doesn't sermonize or philosophize, and doesn't attempt to force his material into any preconceived moulds.[1]

Intriguingly, for a text of such epic scope and detail, O'Brien's review focuses almost exclusively on what is absent. My own analysis of *The Executioner's Song* below will similarly attempt to adumbrate its critical lacunae, but will challenge other aspects of O'Brien's assessment. The apparent simplicity and neutrality of *The Executioner's Song* is deceptive. This begins at the beginning with the title. The title may not be a trick, but it is not as 'spare and dry and clean' as, say, *The Execution of Gary Gilmore*, or perhaps *Gilmore's Tale*. Readers waiting for a scene in which an executioner literally sings will be disappointed and so we know that Mailer intends us to read metaphorically. However, once the trope is recognized we are confronted and possibly confounded by a supplementary puzzle: who, exactly, is the intoning

'Executioner'? The firing squad can be dismissed as they are plural and hardly seen behind the curtain and so perhaps the 'Executioner' is a synecdoche for the killing state as it chants its death song. An alternative possibility is that the eponymous executioner and the condemned man are one and the same. Gary Gilmore murders his victims 'execution style'. He persuades his partner to commit suicide. Gilmore's vehement insistence on his own execution spectacularly accelerates the reintroduction of capital punishment in the US. Unwittingly, Gilmore thus becomes the 'executioner' of other Death Row inmates right up to the present day. Alongside this speculation, we should note more decisively, that Mailer had already used 'The Executioner's Song' as the title of a poem in *Cannibals and Christians* (1966) and as a chapter heading in *The Fight* (1975). Lyricism, suggestive ambiguity, and auto-plagiarism follow the reader as we move from title to epigraph:

> Deep in my dungeon
> I welcome you here
> Deep in my dungeon
> I worship your fear
> Deep in my dungeon
> I dwell.
> I do not know
> If I wish you well.[2]

This *'old prison rhyme'* reappears with a second stanza at the end of the text. However, in the 'Afterword' which follows, Mailer makes the following confession: 'the *old prison rhyme* at the beginning and the end of this book is not, alas, an ancient ditty but a new one, and was written by this author ten years ago for his movie *Maidstone*' (p. 1052). This is not quite as perplexing as Tim O'Brien's *The Things They Carried* (1990) (a novel about the Vietnam War which starts with a disclaimer stating that all the characters in the book are imaginary, but then follows with a dedication to the characters which makes them seem real), but the title and epigraph to *The Executioner's Song* should alert the attentive reader to messy complicating factors beneath the apparently 'spare and dry and clean' surface of the text.

It may have been noticed that, so far, *The Executioner's Song* has exclusively been referred to as a 'text'. This, in part, is a defensive gesture resorted to because other genre labels are problematic. In 1979, Mailer's text won the Pulitzer Prize for Fiction and in 1980 it was nominated for the National Book Critics Circle Award for 'nonfiction'.[3] Mailer's own classifications fail to resolve the issue. In the 'Afterword', he informs us that this book 'does its best to be a factual account', but also admits to certain editorial omissions and revisions. He suggests 'there would not have been a way to do this factual account — this, dare I say it, *true life story*, with its real names and real lives — as if it were a novel' (p. 1053). At the same time, Mailer actively encouraged his publishers to market the book with the vaguely oxymoronic epithet of 'true-life novel'. In 'The True Story of an American Writer', Jean Radford proposes that across his career Mailer 'developed into a stylistic chameleon (realist, allegorist, journalist), crossing generic border-lines [...] raiding a number of ideological positions (Marxist, existentialist, left conservative, Zen)'.[4] In the reading below, deploying a cultural materialist methodology, I aim to demonstrate that an eclectic and at times unstable compound of styles, genres, and ideological formations are evident not only across the Mailer *oeuvre*, but specifically within *The Executioner's Song*. The core of the text is broadly realist, but in a reflexive fashion that incorporates metafictional and meta-nonfictional impulses which challenge a naively empirical model of 'reality'. Grafted onto the realist spine there are strands of romance, gothic, western, and prison narrative genres. *The Executioner's Song* looks back to the Puritan execution sermon and early American crime writing, resonates with the emergent dirty realist aesthetic and looks forward to the tone and thematics of blank fiction from the 80s and 90s. Alongside the variations in genre, Mailer ventriloquizes vernacular diction (East Coast, western, and prison argot) and incorporates as well as critiques the stylistics of different institutions: the state, the judiciary, the media, and the church. Radford goes so far as to propose that Mailer's novel addresses the 'state of the nation's language'.[5] Gary Gilmore was executed in the bicentennial year of 1976. At a distinct historical juncture between the end of the Vietnam era and the rise of the New Right, *The Executioner's Song* interrogates the impact that execution has on individuals, institutions, and society at large. In this task, the intricate imbrication of ethical and political modalities with aesthetic practices is underscored. Like Oscar Wilde, the ex-inmate of Reading Gaol, Mailer understands the grave importance of style.[6]

Breaking the Law of Genre

> Genres are not to be mixed. [...]
>
> 'Do', 'Do not' says 'genre', the word 'genre', the figure, the voice, or the law of genre. [...]
>
> The clause or floodgate of genre declasses what it allows to be classed. It tolls the knell of genealogy or genericity, which it however also brings forth to the light of day. Putting to death the very thing that it engenders, it cuts a strange figure;
>
> JACQUES DERRIDA, 'The Law of Genre'[7]

For Derrida, genre is bound up with law in an unstable dialectic. Each attempt to define, demarcate, and lay down the rules governing a particular genre is shadowed by that which it seeks to exclude. This process resonates beyond the realm of critical theory. The state and various institutions aim to label subjects and place limits, but the law which intends to police a boundary produces and thus contains its Other. It is not a matter of a law being broken, but of an edict which establishes the conditions in which it is always already transgressed. We might feel it is safe to assume that *The Executioner's Song* belongs to the genre of the law: this is, after all, a narrative of crime and punishment, death row, and courtroom drama. However, Mailer's 'act of switching style' foregrounds the instability of the genre of genre itself. In the early stages of *The Executioner's Song*, style is relatively stable, but once the murders take place the genre code begins to multiply and mix and cuts an increasingly 'strange figure'.

The breaking of the law seems to release disruptive energies within the text: an explosive proliferation of supergenres, sub-genres, and hybrids emerge at both the general and local level. There are over ninety extracts from personal correspondence (letters and telegrams), more than sixty citations from official documentation (including transcripts from interviews with Gilmore, his family and friends, agents and lawyers, and police and prison staff, alongside a number of legal texts and psychiatric records) and an excess of fifty quotations from newspaper reports and articles.[8] Inevitably, the overall tone of the text gravitates towards tragedy, but this mode is interspersed with numerous instances of comedy. Gallows humour seeps in with allusions to newspaper comic strips and cartoons about Gilmore's execution. At one point the self-condemned man participates in the comedy by offering his cell mate, Gibbs, a fake invitation card:

> Mrs. Bessie Gilmore of Milwaukie, Ore cordially invites you to the execution
> of her son: Gary Mark Gilmore, 36
> Place: Utah State Prison, Draper, Utah
> Time: Sunrise
> EARPLUGS AND BULLETS WILL BE FURNISHED. (p. 663)

Many of the genre labels which might be affixed to *The Executioner's Song* require supplementation. Given the extent of the citations from correspondence, Mailer's text can be addressed as an epistolary narrative whilst specific letters display additional generic affiliations. On Death Row, Gilmore's voluminous correspondence effectively becomes an extended auto-obituary. *Dead Man Writing*. His most intimate correspondence with Nicole interweaves strands of poetry, humour, romance, pornography, self-mythologizing fantasy, surrealism, and gothic colourings:[9]

> *I've told you that I haven't slept lately — the ghosts descended and set upon me with a force I didn't believe they possessed. I smack 'em down and they sneak back and climb in my ear [...] foul demon motherfuckers with dirty furry bodies whispering vile things in the nite [...] Dirty inhuman beasts jackals hyena rumor monger plague ridden unhappy lost ghostly foul ungodly things unacceptable creeping crawling red eyed bat eared soulless beasts [...]*
>
> The demon ghosts
> trick tease tantalize
> bite and claw scratch and screech
> weave a web of oldness. (p. 362)

Gothic shading in *The Executioner's Song* is not restricted to the couple's death row correspondence. Family legends surrounding Gary are steeped in the supernatural. Bessie Gilmore believes that her son is possessed: 'the haunted house on Salt Lake [...] whatever it was that lived in that house [...] must in those years have begun to live in Gary' (p. 1049). This superstition is oddly echoed by psychiatric reports which refer to the 'ghost ridden' psychotic (p. 397), hinting at the generic contamination of a professional discourse. After Gilmore's execution, Nicole's sister, April, is haunted by nightmares of a spectral Gary returning from the grave. Gary is also asked if he is the devil and is described as 'the demon that got into Linda Blair in *The Exorcist*' (p. 613). After an angry meeting with his client, the attorney Ron Stanger says 'it was like a horror film. I could almost see his teeth getting longer' (p. 746). The autopsy procedure which follows Gary's execution dramatizes the sadism of state slaughter by shifting from a mode of gothic suggestion to a scene of spectacular body horror (a generic requirement which appeared to become practically compulsory in police procedurals and serial killer narratives during the 80s and 90s):

> Then they removed the pituitary, put it aside, and sliced the brain like meat loaf [...] and they took all the organs they did not need for dissection and put them back into the body and head cavities, and drew his face up, pulled it right back taut over the bones and muscles, like putting on the mask again, fit the sawed-off bone-cap back on the skull, and sewed the scalp, and body cavity. When they were all finished, it looked like Gary Gilmore again. (p. 1001)

In their death row letters, Gary and Nicole repeatedly assure each other that death is not the end. The lovers subscribe to a New Age mystical faith in reincarnation and the doctrine of karmic debts. Gary, in fact, believes that he has already been executed in England in the eighteenth century and still has to atone for some crime from the past.

> *I owe a debt, from a long time ago [...]. There have been years when I haven't even thought much of it at all and then something (a picture of a guillotine, a headmans block, or a broad ax, or even a rope) will bring it all back and for days it will seem I'm on the verge of knowing something very personal, something about myself.* (p. 305)

Elsewhere in their correspondence, Gary and Nicole secretly plan suicide and promise to meet each other in 'the darkness'. The film-maker Larry Schiller recognizes that 'these letters still offered the love story. He not only had the man's reason for dying but Romeo and Juliet, and life after death' (p. 709).

Romance is one of the most significant narrative strains within *The Executioner's Song*. Mailer appears keen to uncover a partially redemptive quality in the intensity of Gary and Nicole's relationship. There are different 'chapters' to the love story. At times, their relationship seems like the sort of tempestuous affair narrated in a country-and-western ballad: a thirty-five-year old ex-con meets a nineteen-year old widowed divorcee and mother of two and they spin into a whirlwind cycle of alcohol, abuse, break-up, and reunion. In their letters, Gilmore appears sensitive and solicitous and his fear of death is dwarfed by the fear of losing Nicole. Some of their correspondence is highly explicit: '*fucked your belly button pushed my tongue in your mouth in your cunt in your ass*' (p. 404). The couple's erotic intimacy is undergirded by a vivid and self-mythologizing fantasy life. Gilmore reinvents Nicole as his '*little elf sweet*' (p. 545) and offers to transport her to '*places i loved as a child, a dark little glen in the forest of pines [...] Listen to my enchanted forest talking softly in its thousand tongues*' (p. 808). Nicole pleads with her lover to '*Touch my soul with your truth*' (p. 699).

Writing to Nicole from his cell, Gary declares with equal fervour: '*I love you more than God*' (p. 486). Religion typically plays a pivotal role in American narratives of punishment and is evident throughout *The Executioner's Song*. In the beginning, one of Gilmore's cousins, Brenda, shares her 'earliest recollection of Gary' (p. 5) in which Christian imagery is prominent. At the age of six, Brenda had fallen from an apple tree she was not supposed to climb and Gary caught her: a Fall, forbidden fruit, and a Saviour. The opening chapter is entitled 'The First Day' and is followed by others with more explicitly religious signposting. Chapter 32, for example, announces 'The Angels and the Demons Meet the Devils and the Saints'. If the possibility of Gary as a saviour is muted in the opening anecdote, it becomes louder as his Day of Judgement approaches. One of his lawyers, Dennis Boas, confesses that he 'feel[s] like Judas helping get you executed' (p. 527). At the execution, Gary's final words to Father Meersman are '*Dominus vobiscum*' (p. 984). After he is shot, Gary's hand is seen 'rising and falling' (p. 1005) perhaps in *signum crucis*. In a continuation of this motif, the post-autopsy donation of parts of Gary's body might be read as a surgical sacrament. Whilst the messianic imagery around Gilmore could be ironic, the insistence on execution for his sins appears sincere and linked to doctrine in the Church of Jesus Christ of the Latter-day Saints. Both of Gilmore's victims were Mormons and his own father had been raised within the LDS. In this context, Gary's determination to die might be seen as a confirmation of the efficacy of the Mormon credo of 'blood atonement [...] "Those who shed blood must pay in blood"' (p. 776). The principle of punishment as retribution increased in currency during the late 1970s. The post-Vietnam period between Gilmore's execution and the publication of Mailer's novel saw a sea-change from the progressive impulses of the 60s which utilized psychological and sociological models to understand social deviance and promoted a rehabilitative ideal to the rise of the New Right with a fundamentalist insistence on theological approaches to crime as 'sin' — an expression of 'evil' — and a concomitant emphasis on a retributive model of criminal justice.

The genealogy of the Mormon tenet of blood atonement can be traced back to a Puritan penology based on Old Testament teachings. Daniel A. Cohen has argued persuasively that the Puritan execution sermon can be read as 'the first dominant American crime genre'.[10] From the mid-seventeenth to the early eighteenth century the gallows sermon was an integral part of the dramatized spectacle of public execution. The homily issued dire warnings on the social and spiritual perils of wrongdoing and underlined the extent to which the acts of one rogue backslider could jeopardize the salvation of the entire community. The condemned subject played a crucial role in this performance as a willing scapegoat. A full confession and repentance were compulsory for redemption. In this manner, the act of execution was not an expulsion, but an ecstatic embrace of the outcast back into the moral folds of the community. At a time when the authority of Puritan theocracy was largely sacrosanct, lengthy execution sermons were delivered to crowds in their thousands and underscored a religious master narrative on the meaning of punishment. Over the course of the eighteenth and nineteenth centuries, as the authority of the Puritan Church waned, the meaning of execution became increasingly plural and contested as new genres of crime and punishment writing began to emerge. As legal authority took over from clerical, extensive trial reports sought to record meticulously the details of crimes as well as statements made by criminals, witnesses, lawyers, judges, and jurors. Another challenge to the theological narrative came from a burgeoning newspaper industry.

With the development of the penny press from the 1830s, print media sought to increase their circulation with broadsides and lurid accounts of crimes and trials and punishments. Cohen demonstrates how both lawyers and journalists routinely resorted to literary conventions in their presentations. In certain cases, for example crimes of passion, tropes were routinely deployed from the gothic and romance genres, and from melodrama and sensation fiction, which represented a radical departure from the pious restraint of the Puritan sermon. This was supplemented by a number of popular literary contributions which gave a voice to the criminal: the criminal biography and autobiography, the crime ballad, and the 'last words' of the condemned which sometimes appeared in verse form. Over the course of the nineteenth century, as it became more commercially successful, the literature of crime and punishment increased in scope with the addition of supplementary texts. This literature was characterized by contrary impulses towards materialism and the mythological. On the one hand, there was an increasing willingness to consider the cogency of medical and environmental factors, but, on the other, this supergenre began to exercise a literary license that blurred the distinctions between fact and fiction and either demonized the criminal in gothic mode or romanticized them as a free-spirited outlaw. The cultural history here is worth sketching briefly since key aspects of the tradition in the representation of capital punishment are evident in *The Executioner's Song*. The Puritan idea of peril for the community as well as the condemned is echoed since the execution of the one is implicitly offered by Mailer as symptomatic of a profound social and spiritual crisis for the many. As in the colonial era, the condemned man embraces his execution which is then publicized widely to an eager audience. The details of the crime, trial, and punishment are meticulously documented by legal, medical, and journalistic bodies. At times these sources also sensationalize and deploy literary tropes as part of a messy miscegenation of genres which blurs the lines between fact and fiction.[11] Cohen illustrates how the 'certain, unitary, and rigidly patterned' truth of the Puritan sermon gave way to 'complex, elusive and fragmented' meanings in eighteenth- and nineteenth-century representations of execution.[12] Mailer replaces the theocratic monologue and clear moral imperative with a chorus of voices and conflicting perspectives which seek to explain, or romanticize, or demonize Gary Gilmore.

According to Cohen's account, discursive constructions of capital punishment were wrested from ecclesiastical authority and taken into the marketplace. The commodification of execution comes to the fore in the second half of *The Executioner's Song*. Mailer's book, and, by implication, the nation itself, is divided in two. 'Western Voices' (pp. 3–503) and 'Eastern Voices' (pp. 507–1050) are polarized in key respects. In Book Two, the reader witnesses power plays by representatives of the state, the judiciary, and commercial agents within the media industry. Most of the key figures in this respect are male and middle class. In contrast, the focal point in Book One is blue-collar lives, and women such as Nicole Baker and Bessie Gilmore play significant roles. The 'Western Voices' are often female, poor, and rendered in a colloquial drawl. By contrast, the 'Eastern Voices' which drown out their western counterparts in Book Two are typically faster and more formal. An implicit move from slow country cadences to snappy urban professional discourse is accompanied by a geographical migration: an emphasis on the outdoors in 'Western Voices' is replaced by claustrophobic confinement in prison cells and motel rooms. From the opening scene in the apple orchard, 'Western Voices' declares its generic identity as a western: 'Right outside was a lot of open space. Beyond the backyards were orchards and fields and then the mountains. A dirt road went past the house and up the slope of the valley into the canyon' (p. 5). Even when the action moves into cities such as Provo, 'the desert [is] at the end of every street, except to the east' (p. 28) and 'overhead [is] the immense blue of the strong sky of the American West. That had not changed' (p. 19). The trailer-bound Bessie forms a bond with 'the beautiful peak she [calls] Y Mountain because the first settlers had put down flat white stones on its flank to make a great big white "Y" [...] That mountain belongs to me' (p. 319). The focus on landscape and sky, guns, violent crime, and criminal justice are all markers of the classic western. Gary sounds 'like a cowboy' (p. 1047) and when asked which actor he would cast as himself in a movie he chooses an iconic figure from classic westerns: 'Gary Cooper [...] I was named after him' (p. 659). Although Gary's story ends in familiar fashion with the cowboy achieving a stoic dignity as he is gunned down, *The Executioner's Song* is less a classic western than a contribution to the post-Western revisionism of the 60s and 70s.[13] The absence of a clear moral schema (an omission we will address below) means that, to invoke and partly revoke Richard Slotkin's seminal phrase, there is no regeneration through violence.[14]

The Real Story of the Real Story

> Schiller said to himself, there is a story and it's real. Since it's real, it has, in this case, to be fantastic.
>
> NORMAN MAILER, *The Executioner's Song* (p. 598)

Our whistle-stop tour of genre and style in *The Executioner's Song* has covered a lot of ground — from the seventeenth-century Puritan execution sermon to the contemporary post-western — but there has been a significant omission. The aesthetic background to all of Mailer's stylistic switching is realism: the style which aspires to be without style. Very few death row stories venture beyond realism, as though the seriousness of the subject demanded this aesthetic choice. 'Real' and 'reality' are keywords in *The Executioner's Song* which appear around 200 times and are often connected to Gary, the murders, and the execution. In terms of its genre and genealogy, *The Executioner's Song* is routinely linked to Truman Capote's *In Cold Blood* (1966) with its account of the murder of the Clutter family and the subsequent hanging of Dick Hickock and Perry Smith. Mailer, however, insisted that the style of *In Cold Blood* was incongruous with its subject: 'Edith Wharton [has] reappeared as Truman Capote, even more of a jewel'.[15] The obvious implication here is that, stylistically at least, *In Cold Blood* is rather genteel, ornamental, and aesthetically feminine. Mailer's alternative literary role model for realism in *The Executioner's Song* is 'Papa' Hemingway. In general terms, Mailer's prose style aims for simplicity and an economy of expression. Sentences are typically short, uncluttered by florid embellishment or complex grammar and syntax, and focus instead on functional nouns and verbs rendered in everyday cadences: 'The morning went like that. It was a good morning' (p. 36). As in Hemingway's fiction, a lot of the story is carried by conversation. Much of 'Eastern Voices' and 'Western Voices' is devoted to dialogue where verisimilitude is attained by the careful rendition of regional dialect, vernacular contractions, 70s slang, and assorted professional vocabularies. Mailer works hard to make these voices sound like motel managers from Provo, New York journalists, and Los Angeles film-makers. He reproduces grammatical errors in speech, and typos are also common in the correspondence, alongside underlining, capitalization, and changes in font size. Since the reader knows that the letters are historical documents and can see how accurately extracts are being reproduced, the aura of authenticity extends to adjacent material.

It would be a mistake, however, to assume that *The Executioner's Song* subscribes to a guileless model of realism. Borrowing from Henry James, we might say that the 'air of reality' in Mailer's work is polluted by the presence of other genre codes and by the marked transition from 'the story of one's hero [...] [to] the story of one's story'.[16] In 'Western Voices', the imprisonment and execution of Gilmore threatens to become secondary to questions of the construction and ownership of the Gilmore narrative. On Death Row, Gilmore becomes the eye at the dead centre of a textual hurricane of legal documents, media reports, interviews, letters, and contracts. According to Phyllis Frus, 'the process of production of *The Executioner's Song* is revealed in the narrative, since the second half (book 2) is "about" how the information in book 1 was gathered'.[17] This process ends precisely at the point when all of the materials which have been meticulously collated in the book are about to be handed over to the writer Norman Mailer. Self-reflexivity, which as Christine Brooke-Rose reminds us, 'is a form of stylization', problematizes and at times threatens to negate the classical realist code.[18] Metafictional discourses which foreground questions of reading, writing, and authorship challenge naive positivist assumptions with a version of 'reality' as a social and, in this instance, a specifically literary construction.

A key figure in this regard, one who vies with Gilmore for the limelight in Book Two, is Larry Schiller. A former journalist who went on to become a writer, photographer, and producer, Schiller established a relationship with Gilmore and purchased the media rights to his story. Schiller conducted extensive interviews with Gilmore, Nicole Baker, and others. He became the curator of Gilmore's correspondence, collated trial testimony, and commissioned others to write pieces. Ultimately, having laid the groundwork, Schiller handed over the project of writing to Mailer and the two also collaborated on the film adaptation of *The Executioner's Song*.[19] Schiller expresses a determination to bear witness and record with absolute fidelity:

> He realized that if he was going to take accurate notes at the execution, he might not have a second to remove his glance from the scene and so he would have to learn to separate his hand from his eye, and do it without ever referring to the pad, and to himself he said, 'For the first time, Schiller, you can't fictionalize, you can't make it up, you can't *embroider*. (p. 859)

As a surrogate author within the text, Schiller implicitly subscribes to a realist aesthetic which opposes the camera eye which merely records empirical detail to exercises in fictional 'embroidery' (a trope with similar gender connotations to the 'jewellery' of Capote's style). At the same time, however, Schiller openly entertains different ways of telling the tale:

> A scenario could be worked up of a guy who comes out of prison and struggles with his old con habits, but finally kills a man, a real study of the pains of getting out of jail. That way they could do capital punishment and whether a man had a right to die, and never touch upon a love story. (p. 595)

The 'real study' still has to be 'worked up' and genre codes (prison drama, romance) must come into play. Schiller's commitment to objectivity is at odds with a recognition of the impossibility of the hand erasing itself as it writes: 'Actually,' said Schiller to himself, 'I have become part of it. All around me, I'm becoming part of the story' (p. 714). The same recognition is achieved by freelance writer Dennis Boaz: 'I'm a character in this thing I'm writing [...] so I don't plan out everything I do. I'm being acted upon by the real author of these events. Whoever or whatever that is' (p. 627). The ethical and political consequences of the writer's involvement in their subject is grasped even more keenly by Barry Farrell when he is hired by Schiller to interview Gilmore for *Playboy*: '[of] course, one Barry Farrell had become an integral part of this machine that was making it impossible for Gilmore to take an appeal' (p. 832).

Especially in the second half of *The Executioner's Song*, the story talks to itself at a volume which interrupts the possibility of the reader simply listening to a straightforward account of historical events. The implicit stylistic allusions to Hemingway are gestured towards by a telegram that Schiller sends to Gary and that borrows from Schiller's report on Hemingway's suicide (p. 763). In an earlier telegram, Schiller reassures Gilmore and perhaps threatens to unsettle the reader with the following: 'WE WISH TO PRESENT YOUR STORY AS TRUTH NOT FICTION STOP' (p. 598). At High School, Grace McGinnis taught Gary in a Creative Class and remembers an insightful conversation with his brother, Mikal, about Capote's *In Cold Blood* (p. 456). In their childhood the Gilmore brothers had studied the dictionary avidly. Gary encourages Nicole to do the same, but she misreads a word: '*anyhow it's TAUTOLOGIC not TANTALOGIC. Look again*' (p. 478). Irony is evident in the lexical choice here (the tautological repetitions of metafictional self-reflexivity) and in the steady stream of meta-commentaries by characters on the state of the story we are reading. The producer David Susskind is initially excited: 'I think this story's got several layers of importance and interest and could make very exciting, dramatic material' (p. 603). However, following Nicole's suicide attempt, Susskind revises his original assessment:

> The story was getting to be, in Susskind's view, a very sensational, malodorous, exploitative mess [...] It's no longer a story about the breakdown of the criminal justice system, it's a farce [...] 'I think anybody who does the story now is jumping on a dead and putrefying body. It's bizarre and sick'. (p. 629)

Philip Roth famously complained that:

The American writer in the middle of the 20th century has his hands full in trying to understand, describe and then make credible much of American reality. It stupefies, it sickens, it infuriates and finally it is even a kind of embarrassment to one's own meager imagination. The actuality is continually outdoing our talents, and the culture tosses up figures almost daily that are the envy of any novelist.[20]

Mailer had anticipated Roth's grievance in 'The Man Who Studied Yoga', an early short story where a frustrated writer, Sam Slovoda, gives up on his novel because 'he cannot find a form [...] He does not want to write a realistic novel because reality is no longer realistic'.[21] Much of the surface of *The Executioner's Song* appears to suggest an unruffled realism guided by the principles of transparency, comprehensiveness, and coherence, but there are undercurrents which take the story into troubled waters. The 'real story' becomes increasingly elusive and torn between conflicting aesthetic, commercial, legal, and political frames. Nicole confesses that 'some of it was real, some was made-up' (p. 728) and even when the 'real' is present at crucial points, its meaning is far from immanent: 'the news lived in the air of the courtroom. [...] a man was going to be executed. It was real but it was not comprehensible. The man was standing there' (p. 447). The air of reality threatens to become toxic.

In his cell at one point, Gary engages in what might be read as a metafictional allegory of the naïvely realist author:

Then he fell in love with the Magic Marker. [...] on all the walls, he wrote 'WALL', wrote 'CEILING' on the ceiling, 'TABLE' on the table, 'BENCH' on the bench, 'CHOWER' in the shower. [...] Finally, he printed on Gibbs's face and his own: 'FOREHEAD', 'NOSE', 'CHEEK', 'CHIN'. (p. 388)

On occasion, this process appears to be taken to parodic excess by Mailer himself. After he has murdered Bennie Bushnell, Gary hides out in a room at the Holiday Inn. Chapter 14, 'The Motel Room', offers a remarkable density of descriptive detail for what one might assume to be a rather bland interior: the curtains, the chairs, the desk, the beds, the laminated swimming pool regulations. The reader's eye is taken from the television to the television stand, from the chromium ball feet of the television stand to their rubber casters, and on to the impression they leave on the 'blue shaggy synthetic-fabric rug' (p. 233). To return to Henry James, there is no 'figure in the carpet' here, but only a manic accumulation of empirical details which seems compensatory for a lack of answers to the mystery posed by the murders. The forensic scrutiny of the motel room finishes in the bathroom with a close-up on the softness and absorbency of toilet paper which 'would stick to the anus' (p. 234). Drawing attention to the messy materialism beneath the plastic surfaces of consumer society is a signature move by Mailer, but it leaves the reader no closer to understanding why Gilmore has committed murder. If the pages of *The Executioner's Song* are to absorb the reality of the Gilmore story something more than realism is required.

A similar recognition was at the heart of an emergent school of fiction in the late 1970s; Raymond Carver was the head teacher and notable pupils included

Richard Ford and Jayne Anne Phillips. Both individually and collectively, these writers were tagged with a variety of labels: 'dirty realism' was the most popular but others included 'new social realism' and 'K-Mart realism', 'hick chic', 'Diet-Pepsi minimalism', and even 'post-Vietnam, post-literary, postmodernist blue-collar neo-early-Hemingwayism'.[22] *The Executioner's Song* shares key socio-political and aesthetic affinities with dirty realism. Mailer offers a sympathetic but unsentimental portrayal of the working class and the unemployed: people who live in trailer homes, work in gas stations and motels, and shop, as Gary is seen to do, at K-Mart. The main stylistic signature of dirty realism was minimalism. Carver's short stories avoided figurative language in favour of everyday speech and precise physical description. Much of Book One is written in precisely this style and, whilst this is a very long novel, it is composed from a series of short sections punctuated by innumerable breaks which might have appeared as self-contained stories in an anthology of dirty realist prose. Central to the minimalism of dirty realist writing and of Mailer's work is the act of leaving a lot unsaid. The empty spaces between sections in Mailer's work become increasingly conspicuous as visual markers of absence, mystery, and a profound sense of the ultimate impenetrability of actions and events.

There is a hole in the heart of *The Executioner's Song* and its formal emblem is the line break. The thousands of blank white spaces between sections evoke the absolute extinction of being involved in execution, but even before he is shot in the heart Gilmore is repeatedly associated with a troubling absence. The decisive act in Book One, the murder of Max Jensen, is condensed into a series of short single clause sentences delivered in an uncannily anaesthetized aesthetic which mirrors the automaton behaviour of the killer. This anti-epiphany is rendered in the same numbed naturalism evident subsequently in the Holiday Inn:[23]

> It was a bathroom with green tiles that came to the height of your chest, and tan-painted walls. The floor, six feet by eight feet, was laid in dull gray tiles. A rack for paper towels on the wall had Towel Saver printed on it. The toilet had a split seat. An overhead light was in the wall.
>
> Gilmore brought the Automatic to Jensen's head. 'This one is for me,' he said, and fired.
>
> 'This one is for Nicole,' he said, and fired again. The body reacted each time.
>
> He stood up. There was a lot of blood. It spread across the floor at a surprising rate. Some of it got onto the bottom of his pants.
>
> He walked out of the rest room with the bills in his pocket, and the coin changer in his hand, walked by the big Coke machine and the phone on the wall, walked out of this real clean gas station. (p. 224)

Immediately after the murders Gary's face is 'blank' (p. 245). His account of the night is oddly atonal (p. 799) and riddled with blind spots: 'some of it is totally blank' (p. 440). Gary claims that when his sentence was delivered he 'probably felt less than anyone in the courtroom' (p. 693) and during interviews he frequently disappears inside himself: 'blank space was there to look back at Schiller' (p. 693). These affective aporia and the flat prose style move beyond the emotional reticence of Hemingway and towards the formal and thematic signatures of blank fiction: with their numb recitation of the surfaces of consumerist non-places and spree killings by charismatic but oddly detached killers, a line might be drawn from *The Executioner's Song* to Bret Easton Ellis's *American Psycho* (1991).[24] Gilmore, like Patrick Bateman, occupies the 'psychopathic flats' (p. 799). Passages in *The Executioner's Song* read like proto-blank fiction with their insensate commentary on incidents of extreme violence: 'Martin took his new wife in the woods and stabbed her twenty times, cut her throat, cut the unborn baby out of her body, stabbed at the baby, went home' (p. 413).

In his seminal work on postmodernism, Fredric Jameson identified a 'new kind of flatness' as the 'supreme formal feature' of contemporary cultural production.[25] Jameson paired this depthlessness with a 'waning of affect' and sought to map both phenomena onto developments in global capitalist economic and social relations.[26] Connections between formal and affective flattening and consumerism in *The Executioner's Song* might confirm Jameson's pronouncement. Whilst Gilmore claims that one of the bullets is for him and one for Nicole, the presence of a third party at the crime scene might be detected. In the build-up to the murders, much of Gilmore's frustration is tied to his inability to keep up payments on his prize possession: a six-cylinder '66 Mustang. In a letter to Nicole he seems to confess that he has destroyed their lives 'because I was so spoiled and couldn't immediately have a white pickup truck I wanted' (p. 306). It might be noted that the commodity Gary covets is branded after a breed of horse iconically associated with the American West and that his violent disappointment is directed at people in the workplaces which service a car culture (a gas station and a motel).

Whilst Gary's anger is fuelled by pecuniary debt, he comes to terms with his fate in relation to the mystical notion of 'Karmic debt'. We might, at this point, consider the extent to which punishment itself is underpinned by the economic principle of restitution. As Derrida observes in his work on the death penalty, 'the origin of the legal subject, and notably of penal law, is commercial law; it is the law of commerce, debt, the market, the exchange between things, bodies and monetary signs'.[27] Although Gilmore conceptualizes his punishment as the price to be paid for injuries he has inflicted in this and previous lives, part of Mailer's focus is on commodity envy as a cause of crime and how the media (including best-selling novels) capitalize on capital punishment. This process, of course, includes the condemned man himself as he sells his story to the highest bidder. Gilmore recognizes the irony of his situation when he proposes using his execution as a means of advertising Timex watches (p. 831). His status as commercial opportunity and brand is ironically underscored at a public talk by his agent, Larry Schiller, who is challenged by a Mormon student for wearing 'a Gary Gilmore belt' (p. 876) when in fact the interlocking G's on the buckle are the Gucci logo. Whilst Gilmore's defiant last words were the inspiration for a global marketing brand, the fate of his body underscores Mailer's contempt for (and, as a successful novelist and media personality, inevitable complicity with) a style-less and soul-less corporate

America: 'Gary's ashes had been put into a plastic bag of the sort you sell bread in, a cellophane bag with the printing from the bread company clearly on it. That freaked Schiller out [...] coloured printing all over it, not festive, but cheap, a 59 cents loaf of bread' (p. 1022).

The Ideology of the Form

> The secret that Truth is entirely and absolutely a matter of style.
> — Oscar Wilde, 'The Decay of Lying'[28]

Whilst 'Western Voices' combines the western genre with a dirty realist and proto-blank fiction aesthetic, meta-fictional and meta-nonfictional discourses come to the fore in 'Eastern Voices'. As noted in our introduction, the generic indeterminacy of *The Executioner's Song* is evidenced by the fact that it garnered awards as both 'fiction' and 'nonfiction'. This hybridity is a signature of the new journalism to which Mailer's work made a powerful contribution alongside that of Tom Wolfe and Truman Capote.[29] New journalism emerged in the 60s and 70s in part as a response to developments in media ecology. At the same time that novelists such as Philip Roth were expressing exasperation at their inability to compete with 'reality' as it was reported by a burgeoning media industry, challenges were being issued to the ability of conventional journalism to report the full story of events such as the Vietnam War. Both genres, accordingly, pushed at their boundaries and converged on a middle ground. In the context of accelerating hypermediation — of which the Gilmore execution is a prime-time example — Mailer seeks to forge new modes of self-reflexive literary journalism in his 'true-life novel'.

Meta-journalism takes different forms in *The Executioner's Song*. Firstly, and most visibly, there is the inclusion of numerous quotations from newspapers and television reports. Secondly, there is extensive commentary on and critique of aspects of the media coverage and in particular the lurid and ghoulish entertainment served up by 'yellow journalism' (p. 807). Thirdly, as discussed above, Mailer employs a journalistic style which — following in the footsteps of the *Toronto Star*'s most famous reporter, Ernest Hemingway — prioritizes the crisp and succinct reporting of factual detail. Fourthly, *The Executioner's Song* both employs and reports on journalistic methodology — the legwork of interviewing and ascertaining facts. At the same time, however, Mailer's approach does not subscribe to a naive model of journalistic objectivity, but instead poses challenging questions of point of view and veracity. In the 'Afterword', Mailer begins with the following confession:

> This book does its best to be a factual account of the activities of Gary Gilmore and the men and women associated with him in the period from April 9, 1976, when he was released from the United States Penitentiary at Marion, Illinois, until his execution a little more than nine months later in Utah State Prison [...] This does not mean that it has come a great deal closer to the truth than the recollections of the witnesses. (p. 1051)

The epistemological borders between 'fact', 'fiction', and 'truth' are clouded by the simultaneous insistence on accuracy and artistic license: Mailer admits that some of the interviews, letters, newspaper quotations, and dialogue have been altered. In addition, and inevitably, the materials require editing, arranging, condensing, and crafting. Journalism is not a passive and innocent relaying of an a priori narrative, but the active construction of a story.

This is a recognition which Schiller offers his audience of Mormon students after explaining the sign of the double 'G' on his belt: 'You are a journalist, because you have turned one thing into another, and that is journalism' (p. 876). Schiller seems to distinguish between the creative role of the journalist and the historian whose job it is to remain 'accurate to the facts [...] You recorded history right' (p. 600). Conversely, Mailer's approach to writing the past anticipates the principles of new historicism. In 'The Historical Text as Literary Artefact', Hayden White reminds us that all stories which claim to be based on fact are still 'verbal fictions, the contents of which are as much *invented* as *found*'.[30] The sub-title of Mailer's *Armies of the Night* — 'History as a Novel: The Novel as History' — underscores the contention that history must be plotted and that fictions are inevitably historical.[31] The meta-nonfictional discourses in *The Executioner's Song* precisely encourage the reader to challenge historical and journalistic accounts of the Gilmore execution including the one which is encouraging this challenge. A hermeneutic of suspicion is cultivated by the intentionally indeterminate borders Mailer traces between history, journalism, and fiction. The 'Prince of Truth' is not confined to any one territory. As Gary suggests in one of his letters to Nicole: 'I was looking for a truth that was very rigid, unbending, a single straight line that excluded everything but itself. A simple Truth, unadorned. I was never quite satisfied — I found many truths though' (p. 345).

The search for a single truth which splinters apart is repeated throughout the text and is especially evident during and after the execution scene. Larry Schiller aims to capture the event with absolute fidelity by painstakingly recording every sensory detail of the condemned man's final moments and in particular the colours Gary sees before they place the hood over his head. Banishing all 'journalistic assumptions' and relying instead on his 'photographer's eye' (p. 981), Schiller observes 'the yellow line and the black hood and the black T-shirt Gary was wearing and the white pants, and the shots' (p. 990). The myopic concentration on material facts again seems compensatory for the impenetrable mystery of time and death, and Schiller's empirical fetishism is subsequently shown to be suspect:

> They drove over together to the execution site. When they got inside the cannery, Schiller couldn't believe what he now saw. His description of the events had been accurate in every way but one. He had gotten the colours wrong. The black cloth of the blind was not black but blue, the line on the floor was not yellow but white, and the chair was not black but dark green. He realized that during the execution something had altered in his perception of colour. (p. 992)

The execution scene is the moment at which for 'the first time [...] it became real a man was about to be killed' (p. 977), but it is at precisely the existential epiphany of the final seconds of a man's life that the realist aesthetic breaks down. Concerns about phenomenological stability and thus reliable narration are aggravated by the sheer number of focalizers in the text. In his seminal study of narrative, Gérard Genette reminds us to pose the critical questions 'who speaks?' and 'who sees?'[32] The answer to these questions in *The Executioner's Song* is almost everybody. Although the execution itself lasts only ten pages, it is seen from seven separate points of view. Alongside Schiller there are two lawyers, a sheriff, Gary's uncle, a counsellor, and a priest, and each hones in on different details: from the warmth of the condemned man's final handshake, to the surreal theatricality of proceedings and the deafening blast of the rifles. Following the execution, the emotional recoil of over twenty different characters is relayed in short fragments again over the space of ten pages. Across the 1000-page text the reader encounters over 100 distinct focalizers. Whilst many of Mailer's sentences are indebted to Hemingway's style, the structure of *The Executioner's Song* (with its epic scale, prodigious cast including historical figures, multiple genre codes, and inclusion of newspaper clippings) is modelled on Dos Passos's epic trilogy *U.S.A.* (1937). This is not an arbitrary aesthetic choice. The form of the novel reflects the suturing of punishment practices within the intricate fabric of social relations. Gilmore's crime and punishment are woven together with the lives of lovers, family and friends, working class communities in Utah, national and local legal systems and media grids, religious institutions and subcultures (the Mormon and Catholic Churches and New Age mysticism), and political factions (including the NAACP and the Utah Coalition against the Death Penalty). Writing in a different context about repressive cold war cultural pathologies in the US and the potential antidote of a liberating 'hip' perspective, Mailer insisted that subjects need to be 'seen more as a vector in a network of forces than as a static character in a crystallized field'.[33] By positioning Gilmore within a network of forces, Mailer undermines the dominant punitive ideology which seeks to erase structural determinants and isolate individuals as responsible agents.

The heteroglossia of *The Executioner's Song* is dialectically inclusive, but the Prince of Truth is lost in the crowd. Notable absences from the chorus of voices are Mailer and Gilmore: the normally vocal author imposes a strict silence on himself and the reader rarely gets unmediated access to Gilmore's interiority. The condemned man is a dead centre without being central and ultimately eludes a panoptic web of speculative gazes. Near the beginning, when Gary takes a job at an insulation plant, he eats lunch on his own: 'just sat on a piece of machinery off to the side and ate the food in all the presence of his own thoughts. Nobody knew what he was thinking' (p. 55). As the moment of death moves closer, the reader is taken further away from Gilmore's thoughts and our reliance on third parties means that 'Gary Gilmore' is shattered in a prism of perspectives. Mailer's literary cubism wilfully cultivates contradiction. On the one hand, Gilmore might be valorized as a class hero. In his introduction to Jack Abbott's prison autobiography, *In the Belly of the Beast*, Mailer proclaimed that 'not only the worst of the young are sent to prison, but the best — that is, the proudest, the bravest, the most daring, the most enterprising, and the most undefeated of the poor'.[34] On the other hand, whilst posing a subversive challenge to the authority of the judiciary, Gilmore might also be vilified as a class traitor who sold out his peers on Death Row for blood money and a short stint in the media spotlight.

While there is compelling evidence to suggest that Gilmore is simply a narcissistic and manipulative murderer, certain of his features also match Mailer's photo-fit for the 'philosophical psychopath'.[35] Alternately classified in Mailerean mythology as the 'hipster' or 'white negro', this is an existentialist rebel who discovers their being on the brink of nothingness. Gilmore chooses to embrace death rather than resign himself to the living death of a life sentence in prison. Within the context of a bland, sterile, and repressed Mormon culture, Gilmore embodies the spontaneous nonconformity of the subject who embraces sex, violence, and creativity and attempts to find their own unique style rather than simply following a social script. Art is central to this process of self-creation and Gilmore is repeatedly associated with writing and the visual arts. He composes letters and poetry and reads widely including the work of counter-cultural icons such as Ginsberg, Kerouac, and Kesey. He sketches and paints and alludes to the work of Michelangelo, Bernini, and Van Gogh. Mailer's portrait of the artist as a condemned man concludes with Gilmore's final gesture just after he has been shot: he lifts the hand with which he committed his crimes with, according to Schiller, a movement 'as delicate as the fingers of a pianist raising his hand before he puts it down on the keys' (p. 986). Previously, watching Gilmore perform for the cameras in the courtroom, Schiller was struck by his star persona: 'Everybody in that crowded, steaming, incandescent room fixed on him. He drew all eyes, all lenses. Schiller was now twice impressed with Gilmore as an actor [...] the kind of acting that makes you forget you are in the theatre' (p. 675). Adding the performing arts to Gilmore's aesthetic repertoire raises the uncomfortable possibility that what appears to be authentic existentialist rebellion is actually Sartrean bad faith. Gilmore might be impersonating himself for posterity: a condemned man pretending to be a condemned man.

Mailer provides no final verdict on Gilmore. The reader is left hanging between precariously poised possibilities: class hero and traitor, poet and psychopath, victim and villain. Evidence exists to support each case, and the hermeneutic and ethical burden of judgement falls to the reader-as-juror. Mailer's refusal to take the stand might be misread as a failure of commitment.

In terms of its content, *The Executioner's Song* is not a strident critique of capital punishment, but the literary execution tells another story. The formal and stylistic complexity of the text engages the reader's participation in aesthetic processes which in themselves foster empathy and critical consciousness. As Susan Sontag reminds us in her seminal essay 'On Style', the content of the form is crucial:

> Art is not only about something; it is something. A work of art is a thing in the world, not just a text or commentary on the world [...] the qualities which are intrinsic to the aesthetic experience (disinterestedness, contemplativeness, attentiveness, the awakening of the feelings) and to the aesthetic object (grace, intelligence, expressiveness, energy, sensuousness) are also fundamental constituents of a moral response to life [...]. All great art induces contemplation, a dynamic contemplation [...]. It is an experience of the qualities or forms of human consciousness.[36]

Circuitous stylistic strategies in *The Executioner's Song* compel the reader's awareness of their active participation in and responsibility for the production of meaning within the literary text and beyond. As Phyllis Frus suggests, Mailer's metafictional experimentation counters 'the consequences of reification with a reflexive conception of art'.[37] The social practice of reifying 'criminals' by abstracting them from social and historical processes can be mitigated by aesthetic forms. Ultimately, style is of grave importance in *The Executioner's Song* because it compels us to confront the meanings and mystery of violence and murder in America, thus ensuring that the death sentence of the killing state is not the last word.

Notes to Chapter 2

1. Tim O'Brien, 'The Ballad of Gary G.', *New York Times*, 15 October 1979, p. 67.
2. Norman Mailer, *The Executioner's Song* (London: Vintage, 1991). All subsequent references are to this edition and are in the main text.
3. On the back cover of the 1991 Vintage classics edition, the text is classified as 'TRUE CRIME/ BIOGRAPHY'.
4. Jean Radford, 'Norman Mailer: The True Story of an American Writer', in *American Fiction: New Readings*, ed. by Richard Gray (London: Vision Press, 1983), pp. 222–37 (p. 222).
5. Ibid., p. 224.
6. 'In matters of grave importance, style, not sincerity is the vital thing'. Oscar Wilde, *The Importance of Being Earnest* (Oxford: Heinemann, 1994), p. 56.
7. Jacques Derrida, 'The Law of Genre', *Critical Inquiry*, 7.1 (Autumn 1980), 55–81 (pp. 55, 56, 65).
8. Mailer refers to his various sources in an afterword.
9. Mailer claims that he has not tampered with the original correspondence but does confess to occasional minor revisions.
10. Daniel A. Cohen, 'Blood Will Out: Sensationalism, Horror, and the Roots of American Crime Literature', in *Mortal Remains: Death in Early America*, ed. by Andrew Burstein and Nancy Isenberg (Philadelphia: University of Pennsylvania Press, 2003), pp. 31–55 (p. 51).
11. Taking my cue from the Derrida quotation at the start of this section, I apply a loose definition of genre as 'type' here. It includes the multiple discourses (including non-literary) surrounding the practice of capital punishment.
12. Daniel A. Cohen, *Pillars of Salt, Monuments of Grace: New England Crime Literature and the Origins of American Popular Culture, 1647–1860* (Liverpool: Liverpool University Press, 1993), pp. 248, 251.
13. For example, we might see Gilmore's tale as a re-run of *Badlands* (1973) which follows the love affair between an older outlaw figure and his teenage girlfriend as they commit a series of apparently motiveless murders. Malik's film was inspired by the spree killings of Charles Starkweather and his fourteen-year-old girlfriend Caril Ann Fugate. Starkweather's first murder was of a gas station attendant who refused to sell him a toy dog on credit. He was executed in 1957.
14. Richard Slotkin, *Regeneration Through Violence: The Mythology of the American Frontier, 1600–1860* (Norman: University of Oklahoma Press, 1973).
15. Cited in Chris Anderson, *Style as Argument: Contemporary American Nonfiction* (Carbondale & Edwardsville: Southern Illinois University Press, 1987), p. 117.
16. The phrase 'air of reality' comes from James's 'The Art of Fiction', in *Partial Portraits* (London: Macmillan, 1888), p. 390. The subsequent quotation comes from the preface to *The Ambassadors* collected in Henry James's *The Art of the Novel: Critical Prefaces* (Chicago, IL: University of Chicago Press, 2011), p. 313.
17. Phyllis Frus, *The Politics and Poetics of Journalistic Narrative: The Timely and the Timeless* (Cambridge: Cambridge University Press, 1994), p. 189.
18. Christine Brooke-Rose, *A Rhetoric of the Unreal: Studies in Narrative and Structure, Especially of the Fantastic* (Cambridge: Cambridge University Press, 1981), p. 371.
19. *The Executioner's Song* (1982) was directed by Schiller whilst Mailer wrote the screenplay.

20. Philip Roth, 'Writing American Fiction', *Commentary* (March 1961), 223–33 (p. 225).
21. Norman Mailer, 'The Man Who Studied Yoga', in *Advertisements for Myself* (Cambridge, MA: Harvard University Press, 1992), p. 175.
22. John Barth, 'A Few Words About Minimalism', *New York Times*, 28 December 1986, section 7, p. 1.
23. Mailer was intimately familiar with the legacy of an American literary naturalism — specifically, the understated depiction of violence and the focus on painterly depictions of low-rent interiors — in Dreiser, Crane and Norris.
24. For more on this subgenre of millennial US fiction see James Annesley's *Blank Fictions: Consumerism, Culture and the Contemporary American Novel* (London: Pluto, 1998).
25. Fredric Jameson, *Postmodernism: Or, the Cultural Logic of Late Capitalism* (London: Verso, 1992), p. 9.
26. Ibid., p. 10.
27. Jacques Derrida, *The Death Penalty*, trans. by Peggy Kamuf (vol. 1) and Elizabeth Rottenberg (vol. 2), 2 vols (Chicago, IL: University of Chicago Press, 2013–17), I, 152.
28. Oscar Wilde, 'The Decay of Lying', in *The Decay of Lying and Other Essays* (London: Penguin, 2010), p. 20.
29. Specifically in the context of execution, one could note George Orwell's 'A Hanging' (1931) as an early precedent for the new journalism (in *Why I Write* (London: Penguin, 2004), pp. 95–101).
30. Hayden White, 'The Historical Text as Literary Artefact', in *Tropics of Discourse: Essays in Cultural Criticism* (Baltimore, MD: Johns Hopkins University Press, 1985), p. 82.
31. Norman Mailer, *Armies of the Night* (New York: Plume, 1968).
32. Gérard Genette, *Narrative Discourse: An Essay in Method* (New York: Cornell University Press, 1983).
33. Norman Mailer, 'The White Negro: Superficial Reflections on the Hipster', in *Advertisements for Myself*, p. 348.
34. Norman Mailer, 'Introduction', in Jack Henry Abbott, *In the Belly of the Beast* (New York: Vintage, 1991), p. xi.
35. Mailer, 'The White Negro', p. 344.
36. Susan Sontag, 'On Style', in *Against Interpretation and Other Essays* (London: Penguin, 2009), p. 23.
37. Frus, *The Politics and Poetics of Journalistic Narrative*, p. 179.

PART II

Punishment and Performance

CHAPTER 3

'Le peuple veut du sang': The Guillotine and the General Will in Revolutionary Pamphlet Theatre

Jessica Goodman

In 1790s France, the always porous boundary between theatre and politics was particularly blurred. From dramatic speeches in the National Assembly, to public executions and funerals, to festivals that used theatrical techniques to create a sense of national community, the spectacles of the Revolution were everywhere.[1] Public execution held a complex and troubled position in this theatrical political arena. The guillotine — employed for the first time in 1792 — was conceived as a humane, equalizing manner of dispatch.[2] Its mechanical nature allowed it to be viewed as an instrument of justice divorced from individual human intervention: the incarnation of the general will, removing at a stroke those elements of society who posed a threat to the health of the whole. Yet the very same speed and efficiency that had made it so attractive also risked diminishing the efficacy of execution as an exemplary deterrent to those very people whose will it purported to enact. Death by guillotine, whilst spectacular for the mechanics of the machine itself, lasted mere seconds and thus each individual death offered none of the visual representation of agonizing punishment provided by its predecessors, hanging and the wheel.[3] Thus, in this period of highly theatrical politics, state execution was — like many reimagined instruments of authority — problematic and unstable, and its specific instability rested precisely on the tensions it exposed in the position of the public with respect to the state authorities that claimed to carry out its desires.

Where politics is theatrical, theatre naturally interests itself in the political; and indeed, the political theatre of the period played on the insistent presence of a public in the theatrical *salle* to comment on and enact the central role the people now ostensibly held in contemporary political discourse. Newly free to represent recent historical events, authors and troupes did so with great enthusiasm, in particular drawing on the emotional appeal of the *drame* theorized by Diderot and Beaumarchais to stage trial plays in which the audience became witness, judge, and jury. This facet of revolutionary culture has received significant attention in recent years in useful work by Yann Robert and Thomas Wynn, among others.[4] The guillotine itself, however, did not appear on stage, un-representable in both literal and perhaps moral terms.[5]

In order to find onstage discussion of the guillotine we must turn instead to texts produced by anti-revolutionaries. Without an officially sanctioned theatrical outlet, such authors produced pamphlet plays: printed play texts whose dissemination contributed to the vast, largely ephemeral print output of the period.[6] Though these texts may not be theatre in the strict sense of assuming performance before an audience, their conception within dramatic conventions plays on the same sense of a relationship with a collective public employed by the 'true' courtroom plays mentioned above. Indeed, in a handful of pamphlet plays printed around the turn of the nineteenth century, the role of the public in the revolutionary theatre–politics of the period is explicitly both parodied and exploited, in particular with respect to their role in state execution.[7] Through their representation of the public and the political authorities 'on stage', the authors of these pamphlets demonstrate how — in their view — the revolutionaries both manipulated and misrepresented the opinions of the public, using the guise of the 'general will' to justify carrying out personal vendettas through the medium of the guillotine.

This chapter focuses on three such play texts in order to examine different articulations of this theatrical critique of state execution at three distinct moments around the turn of the century: *La Journée des dupes* [The Day of the Dupes] (1790), *Le Martyre de Marie-Antoinette* [The Martyrdom of Marie-Antoinette] (1794), and *Le Cri de l'innocence, ou le tribunal coupable* [The Cry of Innocence, or the Guilty Tribunal] (1816?).[8] It explores questions of responsibility and the status of truth in the texts, evaluates how the victims of public execution are configured with respect to their executioners, and sets out how the content of the plays draws on techniques of representation and non-representation to figure the manipulation of the concept of democracy. Furthermore, it considers how the presentation of these critiques as theatre can both serve to implicate their readers as part of this public-employed-as-personal-weapon, and encourage them to become, in turn, judges of the revolutionary leaders who are implicitly put on trial before the theatre public, thus inciting their allegiance to the anti-revolutionary cause.

Theatre, Revolution, Judgement

The spectacular nature of revolutionary politics and culture has been well documented by Susan Maslan, Mona Ozouf, and Marie-Hélène Huet, among others, and this is not the place for a detailed rehearsal of their useful and comprehensive investigations.[9] Suffice it to say that the role of the public was key to all revolutionary performances, for not only did they bear witness to the acts represented before them, but their very presence sanctioned their political leaders as their (political and literal) representatives, enacting the law that had been officially defined as 'l'expression de la volonté générale' [the expression of the general will].[10] Robespierre frequently referred to the exercise of power as a quasi-religious act which incarnated the collective in the individual: the pronouncement of a legal sentence was, he stated, a 'devoir sacré que le vœu de la nation [...] impose' [sacred duty imposed by the will of the nation].[11]

It was inevitable in this context that the theatre itself should come to play an important role. The eighteenth century had seen a vast increase in the number of performance spaces across the country: in Paris alone, the number of theatres tripled between 1716 and 1789.[12] The Le Chapelier Law, passed in 1791, permitted the performance of plays by any private individual, removing at a stroke the laws of cultural *privilège* that had governed the theatrical output of the previous 150 years. Whilst Napoleon would reinstate direct state control of theatre when he came to power, the 1790s was a period of theatrical freedom unlike any that had gone before, not least because the associated removal of theatrical censorship meant contemporary events could be represented in the theatres for the first time.[13] This did not, however, mean that those in power took no interest in what appeared on the public stage. Instead, the widespread hunger for public spectacle was directly harnessed by the revolutionary authorities. A long debate about the function of theatre in the new regime culminated in a series of decrees ratified by the Convention on 2 August 1793 which required theatres to produce plays exemplifying civic virtues and portraying the glorious events of recent revolutionary history in order to encourage patriotism among their spectators.[14]

The representation of the history of the nation played its role in the creation of a new national identity crucial to the establishment of a new, free France.[15] This was a process wrought through collective experience: Philippe Bourdin describes how the recreation of a militant act on stage was able to 'le rendre immédiatement signifiant dans son partage collectif' [make it immediately meaningful by being shared].[16] Those who had not been present could feel as if they had been and thereby take their own place in the story of their developing nation. The symbiotic affective link between stage and audience had its roots in the *drame*, theorized from the 1750s onwards by Diderot, Beaumarchais, and later Mercier. Diderot's *Fils naturel* stages the annual re-enactment of a family history in which an onstage spectator feels so drawn in that he nearly becomes part of the action (a step he eventually takes in the accompanying *Entretiens*).[17] Robert tracks how in later re-enactments of recent political events the same sort of emotional engagement was turned to political ends, with the moral values represented on stage generalized and made accessible to the audience, now configured as a single affective community with a common political goal.[18]

As Robert shows, the blurring of lines between theatrical and political publics was especially evident in the courtroom plays that experienced particular popularity in the early years of the decade.[19] Five different representations of the iconic trial of Jean Calas (1762) were performed in the period from 1790 to 1791. The defendant was a Protestant, tortured and condemned to death for the alleged murder of his Catholic son — later revealed to be a suicide. Though he had posthumously been recognized as innocent, in part thanks to the efforts of Voltaire, no public exoneration had yet taken place: the theatre provided a forum that paralleled the courtroom, and allowed this *Ancien Régime* injustice to be redressed by a new jury of the 'peuple'. If the Calas plays set out to overturn the judgements of the past, plays representing more recent trials sought the affirmation of the general will by inciting public support for the sentences passed by the revolutionary courts.[20] Yet the emotional potential of theatrical performance could also have its drawbacks: Robespierre worried that a representation of Louis XVI's trial ran the risk of humanizing the defendant and thus drawing his guilt into question.[21] This is a feature of the theatrical trial that would be exploited by the anti-revolutionaries in the plays to be examined here.

A celebrated example of theatrical judgement is Sylvain Maréchal's *Le Jugement dernier des rois* [The Last Judgement of the Kings] (1877) in which all of Europe's monarchs are taken to an almost deserted island and destroyed by a volcano.[22] Sanja Perovic situates this text precisely within the framework of an attempt to reconfigure the public response to political events. She argues that the execution of Louis XVI, met as it was with an uncomfortable silence from the spectators, had not been accepted as generated by the general will and suggests that the authorities therefore set out to ensure that the killing of Marie-Antoinette did take on this status. Though the trial and execution of the queen on 16 October 1793 was also greeted by public silence, Maréchal's play — performed at the Théâtre de la République just two days later — used comedy and an incitement to audience participation through shouting and catcalling to break this silence, and recast the destruction of monarchy as 'a collective action performed by the sovereign body as a whole'.[23] Nowhere is this clearer than in the statement made by the *sans-culotte* who accompanies the exiled monarchs: 'Le peuple Français s'est levé. Il a dit: je ne veux plus de roi; et le trône a disparu. Il a dit encore: je veux la république, et nous voilà tous républicains' [The French people has risen. It said: I no longer want a king; and the throne vanished. It then said: I want a republic; and here we are, all of us republicans].[24] This evocation of the 'peuple' as motivation for destructive acts is another feature that anti-revolutionaries pick up and invert in their own theatrical trial texts.

The Spectacle of Public Death

If the law is the expression of the general will, then the guillotine is, in the words of the staunch abolitionist Victor Hugo, 'la concrétion' of this law: the machine that enacts the collective desire to purge the nation of its rotten elements.[25] In Daniel Arasse's detailed account of the conception and evolution of the instrument it not only symbolized, but actually helped to construct the concept of the general will, and of a unified demos, turning the 'peuple' into the 'Peuple'.[26] Like Maréchal's impersonal volcano, whose status as natural underlined its claim to rightful destruction of the European monarchs, the guillotine — situated from May 1793 to June 1794 directly in front of the National Assembly and operated with only the most minimal human intervention — was presented as an almost autonomous instrument, driven only by the will of the multitude and thus by natural right.[27]

An embodiment *of* the people, the guillotine also performed *before* the people, and yet its operations — whilst spectacular in their precision and novelty — were

FIG. 3.1. Jean-François Janinet, *Machine proposée à l'Assemblée nationale pour le supplice des criminelles [sic] par M. Guillotin: les exécutions se feront hors de la ville...*, 1791, in: Bibliothèque nationale de France.

largely invisible.[28] Though the stagey trappings of public killings still existed, the moment of death happened in the blink of an eye; life separated from afterlife by the single swish and thump of the blade. The celebrated doctor Cabanis noted the contrast this created with the drawn-out spectacle of earlier methods of execution: 'Les spectateurs ne voient rien; il n'y a pas de tragédie pour eux; ils n'ont pas le temps d'être émus' [The spectators see nothing; there is no tragedy for them; they do not have the time to be moved].[29] An engraving, produced in 1791, represents this paradox of invisible spectacle, showing a guillotine whose operation is obscured from public view by soldiers and a ministering priest, and where the executioner himself averts his eyes as he lifts his blade to strike the fatal blow (Figure 3.1).

With the moment of punishment itself so difficult to see — let alone capture in any lasting representation — the focus quickly moved to what came before and after. Verbal accounts tended to linger on the emotions generated by anticipation and post-hoc contemplation rather than the act itself, whilst images increasingly focused on the procession to the guillotine: the only point at which the public could look directly into the face of the accused.[30] Of course, public reaction to executions varied: the famously silent receptions of the deaths of Louis XVI and Marie-Antoinette not only contrasted with the shouting and confusion at other executions, but also suggested that 'the public' as an entity was not always at ease with its role as de facto jury.[31] It is just such unease that the anti-revolutionary pamphleteers would exploit in their theatrical texts, to which we can now turn.

In the remainder of this chapter it will be my contention that the pamphlet plays examined here — all set in a revolutionary period in which public interactions were dominated by suspicion, paranoia, and the fear of an unpredictable form of justice — bring together the notions of state punishment as the expression of the general will and of the theatre as courtroom, both to call for a retrial of their executed protagonist-victims and to put the revolutionary authorities themselves on trial, accused of appropriating the voice of the public to their own ends.[32] Moreover, they do this in a manner that allows their readers-figured-as-theatre-audience a choice: to become implicated as part of the public used to justify these killings, now recast as unlawful, or to step outside themselves and take their place on the very jury that now condemns their leaders. The three plays examined, all published anonymously, present different models for how the public was configured with respect to state killing and thus different ways in which their authors appealed to an imagined theatre public. This public did, as far as we know, remain imaginary: as we shall show, the plays were almost certainly not performed. But this absence of a viewing audience should not prevent us from considering them as theatre and commenting on their theatrical effects, for their authors' decision to produce them within the conventions of theatre necessitates a consideration of their relationship to an (imagined) collective audience.[33]

La Journée des dupes

Printed anonymously in 1789, this *'pièce tragi-politi-comique'* pre-dates the guillotine by several years. Its frontispiece claims it was performed at the Théâtre de la Nation, but no record exists of any such performance. Contemporary critics attributed it to Nicolas Bergasse, the lawyer and politician now best remembered for the attacks made on him by Beaumarchais as the thinly disguised Bégearss in his 1792 *La Mère coupable*.[34] Just such an obvious anagram disguises the main target of this text, Mirabeau, who — as Bimeaura — appears alongside an equally transparent Laibil (Bailli), Yetafet (La Fayette), and others. The play follows the group as, motivated by pure self-interest, they whip up the public to carry out the march on Versailles. The title links the events portrayed to the day in November 1630 on which the enemies of Cardinal Richelieu mistakenly believed that they had succeeded in persuading Louis XIII, then king, to dismiss Richelieu from power, following an ultimatum from Marie de Médicis. The evocation of this moment, known as the 'journée des dupes', suggests that the author of this play is interested in the location of power during attempts at revolt or revolution. Although the guillotine had not been used in France at the point at which this play was written, the piece nonetheless presents the manipulation of the public will in a manner that will have consequences for our understanding of later representations of state execution. In particular, we find a series of calls for public lynching which resemble those that the revolutionary authorities in the later *Le Martyre de Marie-Antoinette* will claim are made with respect to Marie-Antoinette's execution. In this regard, the movement between the two texts seems to enact what Wilda Anderson describes as the 'fusion of the lynch mob into the virtuous general will',[35] a movement that is also embodied in the 1793 institutionalization of insurrection as a 'sacred right'.[36]

'Le Peuple' is a character in its own right, sometimes appearing under that name and at other moments given the more class-specific title 'Les Poissardes': the market traders of Les Halles, traditionally characterized as vulgar in both habits and language. In virtually all of its appearances this 'peuple' speaks with one voice despite its plurality, even in the most long and complex sentences, reflecting the then-nascent concept of unified public opinion. This slippage between singular and collective is compounded by the use of a *poissard*-type dialect which conflates first person singular and first person plural pronouns and verb endings: a comic tic — '[La justice], ç'a va bien mieux da! depuis que je nous en melons' [Justice is going much better, right, since I are getting us involved in it] (p. 37) — that also eerily pre-empts Robespierre's later adoption of the rhetorical 'nous' to convey his status as representative of the general will.[37]

The first time 'le peuple' appears, it 's'attroupe' [gathers round or flocks] (p. 13), and the animalistic undertones are surely not accidental, for the sheep-like qualities of these impressionable individuals-made-one are continually emphasized. It repeats the same phrases over and over, often in response to specific trigger words. Thus, at the mention of a 'gentilhomme' or a 'comte' it automatically calls for a public lynching, whilst in response to any opposition it throws itself on the offender. The latter prefigures a later play, *La Journée du dix août 1792*, [The Day of August 10,

1792] in which a traitor is attacked and killed by a raging crowd of indistinguishable individuals. Pierre Frantz suggests that the appeal with which a Jacobin character follows this act — 'courage citoyens' [courage, citizens] — speaks not to the onstage mob but to the theatre audience, who are thus implicated alongside the true perpetrators of the act.[38]

In *La Journée des dupes*, the violence of the people is not valorized; nor, though, are the people merely dismissed as stupid despite the comedy of unthinking repetition. Rather, their behaviour is presented as the result of their manipulation by a cruel and self-interested political power. The dissimulation this entails is rather crudely spelled out. In a monologue, Mirabeau refers to 'la crédulité de cette tourbe ignorante' [the credulity of this ignorant rabble] whom he is easily able to persuade (p. 11). Lines later he performs just such manipulative persuasion, assuring them: 'mes enfans, je veille toujours pour votre bonheur' [my children, I always watch out for your happiness] (p. 15). He explains the meaning of the royal veto in terms he believes they will understand — related to the theft of food — and thus instils in them the idea that all aristocrats are their enemies, resulting in the calls for lynching mentioned above. And persuasion can happen via the printed word too: elsewhere, we learn the people have been convinced to call for the death of a guard because 'je l'avons lu dans un petit imprimé' [I are read it in a little pamphlet] (p. 42).

The key point here is that this suggestible, manipulated public, whose conditioning we witness again and again, is continually cited as the sovereign 'nation' on the basis of which all decisions are made. Thus, when a guard warns the royalist La Peyrouse: 'Vous voyez que [vos réponses] ne plaisent pas à la nation; elle finir[a] par vous pendre' [You see that the nation does not like your responses; it [will] end up hanging you] (p. 26), the mob has already become an official institution of the French state. Moreover, the public has clearly been fed a corrupted version of the language of enlightenment and revolution, for it rejects the legal interrogation of La Peyrouse on the basis that 'c'est inutile, la nation l'a condamné. Qu'eu ce que c'est que la liberté, si je ne pouvons faire tout ce que je voulons?' [it's useless, the nation has condemned him. What do freedom mean, if I are not allowed to do what I want?] (p. 36). The reader is already well aware of just how far — 'séduit et ignorant' [seduced and ignorant] as they are (p. 31) — this 'peuple' is not doing 'ce que je voulons', but the message is driven decisively home at the moment at which one of their number wonders who, in the end, is benefitting from the changes to which they are witness:

— On dit que c'est l'homme.
— Mais quel homme?
— Ma foi, ce n'est pas nous toujours. (p. 52)

['They say it's [the] man.'
'But which man?'
'By my faith, it's never us.']

The 'peuple' are not the only 'dupes' exposed here: politicians are revealed as blind to each other's manipulation and the concluding theme is that everyone is a 'dupe' of politics. But it is less the trickery, and more the services in which that trickery is employed, that are of interest. Each politician claims to be acting according to the wishes of the people and by exposing 'le langage du démagogue [qui] doit l'attribuer tout au peuple qu'il conduit' [the language of the demagogue, [who] must attribute it all to the people he leads] (p. 82), this play acts — as Eleanor F. Jourdain argues — as a 'political orator, who is forcing attention from the mob in the effort to make the people rationally conscious of their actions', and, we might add, of the manipulation of those actions.[39]

Le Martyre de Marie-Antoinette

In a second anonymous text, published five years later, the process of manipulation is no longer so straightforwardly exposed. Nor, indeed, is the 'peuple' itself even present on stage. Rather, an invisible public is continually cited as justification for the actions of the political authorities; its insistent presence in the wings recalls the pressure exerted on Titus by the Roman people in Racine's classical tragedy Bérénice (1670). Whether or not it has expressed — or been made to express — the opinions attributed to it is apparently irrelevant: the mere reference to it, and its untouchable status as the sovereign populace, is enough. Moreover, the actions at stake here are imbued with far more political weight than the marches and calls for lynching of the previous text: now, the 'peuple' provides justification for the state execution of Marie-Antoinette herself.[40]

   This construction of the 'peuple' as a weapon is insistent and overt. Its status as an uncontrollable force is hinted at in Marie-Antoinette's memories of her husband's death 'au nom de ses sujets' [in the name of his subjects] (p. 12), an experience that has left her terrified of 'ce peuple effréné' [this wild people]. Yet it quickly becomes apparent that this force — or rather the idea of it — has been harnessed by the revolutionary authorities to support their own plans. The clearest demonstration of this is the various interventions of the Mayor of Paris, for whom 'le peuple' becomes a verbal tic with which he prefaces every demand. 'Le peuple vous demande' [the people asks for you], he tells the imprisoned queen, followed closely by 'le peuple vous commande' [the people commands you], repeated twice within a handful of lines (p. 17). Most significant though, is the moment just a few lines further on where this same 'peuple' becomes 'les bourreaux' [the executioners], against whom Marie-Antoinette is enjoined to defend herself (p. 18). Not content with casting the people as jury, political authority, and executioner, in a later scene Barère elevates them to divine status: 'Nous obéissons au peuple souverain; [...] Le peuple est tout-puissant' [We obey the sovereign people; [...] The people is all-powerful] — the latter in comparison to the 'grand être' [great being] who is now 'néant' [nothing] (p. 32).

   Yet whilst this construction allows ultimate blame for the planned death of Marie-Antoinette to fall squarely in the lap of the populace — after all, 'le peuple veut du sang' [the people wants blood] (p. 21) — the question of responsibility here is far more complex in that it is continually deferred. What the play in fact exposes is the construction of a plot by a self-interested triumvirate (Robespierre, Barère, Danton), acting to exert pressure within a broader committee, including a

President who, according to Barère, is 'un instrument [...] à mon plan nécessaire' [an instrument [...] necessary to my plan] (p. 29), which in turn manipulates the Senate into ordering what is explicitly termed 'un nouvel attentat' [a new attack] (p. 11) by the medium of the supposedly institutionalized guillotine. At every stage, the 'peuple' is invoked as the guarantor that what is requested is right. But in this complex series it is clear that every reference to 'nos lois' [our laws] must be treated with caution, for the 'nous' that generates this law — and thus sanctions the 'state' killing — is in fact continually shifting.

The illegality of supposedly legal, state-sanctioned operations is made explicit by the anonymous author, not least in the repeated reference to fabricated charges. The particular invented charge in question here, that of incest, was indeed applied to Marie-Antoinette.[41] The revelation of its status as false is accompanied by the more general admission that:

> Tout homme est criminel: il suffit qu'on l'accuse:
> Le peuple malheureux exige qu'on l'amuse. (p. 26)
>
> [Every man is criminal: let him only be accused:
> The unfortunate people demand to be amused.]

The supposed public appetite for blood as entertainment, which, as we shall see, contrasts sharply with discussion of public humanity elsewhere in the play, thus becomes its own, secondary form of motivation located in the 'peuple', to parallel the official line on public justice:

> L'honnête homme mourant, à ce peuple inhumain,
> Fournit, depuis quatre ans, un brillant jour de fête. (p. 59)
>
> [For four years the [spectacle of] an honest man dying
> Has provided a wonderful feast day for this inhuman people.]

The revolutionary powers are fully aware of the criminal nature of their actions: both Danton and Robespierre refer to their 'crimes' and call the supposedly legal executions 'assassinations'. The moment at which the illegal nature of the killing is clearest is when the queen's executioner, acting according to Robespierre's wishes, determines that if a legal death is not provided for, 'je la poignarderai' [I will stab her] (p. 44): the individual charged with carrying out the will of the people as commanded by their representatives in power is revealed to be no more than a personally directed instrument of murder. Significantly, however, without the public witnessing the execution it will lose its official status. Thus it is that earlier in the play, when Marie-Antoinette pre-emptively presents her breast to be struck, Robespierre hurriedly calls upon the rhetoric of exemplarity and public punishment to justify the need to wait:

> Non, non, dans les tourments,
> Pour le salut du peuple, il est bon qu'elle expire. (p. 22)
>
> [No, no, for the salvation of the people
> It is as well that she should die in torment.]

It is only once the execution is underway that the possibility of a less official death becomes acceptable. The crowd is then said to be whipped up to such an extent that:

> Si cette tigresse échappe à l'échafaud,
> Un zélé citoyen deviendra son bourreau. (p. 57)

> [If this tigress escapes the scaffold,
> A zealous citizen will become her executioner.]

A murder, as opposed to an execution, at this later stage would not undermine the constructed justification by public will, for it would be seen to stem from the zeal of the righteous crowd and from outrage at the idea of this general will being overturned. To each of these illegal actions, then, the officializing stamp of the 'peuple' is applied: though in reality this justification is no more true or legal than the acts it justifies, nonetheless:

> Quand le peuple consent, nos lois en vérité
> Pour condamner à la mort, changent l'absurdité. (p. 31)

> [When the people consents, our laws change absurdity
> Into truth, in order to pronounce a death sentence.]

The absurd — or, implicitly, the illegal — can become legal truth simply by being expressed as the will of the multitude.

In this play, then, whilst the now invisible 'peuple' continues to serve as official justification for the self-interested actions of the few, in its invisibility it is also absolved of true responsibility. The direct manipulation that was such a key part of *La Journée des dupes* is still to some extent present: we see the members of the Comité planning to spread false rumours that will turn a tale of defeat into one of victory, and to announce a grain shortage in order to stir up unrest (p. 3). However, the people themselves are accorded more intelligence and independence, and the authorities seem to have less control than their counterparts in the earlier play, with Robespierre warning:

> Citoyen, prenez garde
> Que le peuple inquiet en tous lieux nous regarde. (p. 7)

> [Citizen, be careful:
> The troubled people watches us all around.]

The 'peuple' is, moreover, endowed with a potential for humanity that recalls the concerns surrounding the potential dangers of representing the royal trials on stage in later years: 'le peuple nous résiste, en voyant leurs vertus' [the people resist us, seeing their virtues] (p. 4), whilst:

> Des hommes inconnus, à Louis, à sa mère
> Proposent de leurs bras le secours salutaire. (p. 9)

> [Unknown men offer the salutary aid of their arms
> To Louis and his mother.]

Barère — one of the key drivers of the plan to guillotine Marie-Antoinette — remains largely sanguine about where the loyalties of 'cette race imbécile' [this imbecile race] lie (p. 10), terming them 'le servile instrument [...] de notre cruauté' [the servile tool of our cruelty] (p. 7). Marie-Antoinette, he determines, in a definitive future tense 'périra sous l'effort de ma rage discrète' [will perish thanks to my hidden rage] (p. 8), for in the end, of course, what the people do or do not say is outweighed by what he can claim that they have said. Their invisibility renders them a far more convenient weapon than the 'peuple' of the earlier play, whose pronouncements had to be made to match the required outcome.

Yet if this ability of the people to empathize with the imprisoned queen does not prevent their use as a weapon to those plotting against her, it nonetheless presents a more hopeful vision than that painted by the previous play. For here, there is the prospect that the people might be redeemed. Marie-Antoinette herself notes that 'le peuple est entraîné par un Sénat féroce' [the people is dragged along by a ferocious Senate], and recognizes that even if they do at times express the anti-royalist sentiments which are attributed to them they are 'des hommes malheureux' [unfortunate men], whom she could not countenance killing even to save her own son (p. 19). Her hope lies in a justice beyond the corrupt, earthly system to which she is subject. 'Mon juge est Dieu' [my judge is God] (p. 55), she states, a sentiment that is echoed in her final, heroic speech which condemns the unnatural actions of the revolutionaries (pp. 60–61). All of this underlines the anonymous author's rejection of the manipulated will of the people as a basis for right. It also extends beyond the queen's own interests when she appeals:

> Dieu de miséricorde, oubliant ta justice,
> Sur le peuple François, jette un regard propice. (p. 14)

> [God of mercy, forgetting your justice,
> Cast a benevolent eye over the French people.]

This plea demonstrates her selflessness in her concern for a 'peuple' that otherwise, she fears, 'va s'égorger lui-même' [is going to destroy itself (literally, 'cut its own throat')] (p. 34). At the same time, it offers the reader or spectator a way out precisely via the empathy incited by a human presentation, just as the revolutionaries had feared. Robespierre articulates this fear in the play when he states: 'elle parle, et déjà ses crimes ne sont plus' [she speaks, and already her crimes are no more] (p. 54). Her presence is clearly presented as moving, as it is elsewhere in contemporary textual and visual productions: Marie-Antoinette's jailer himself is deeply touched by the sight of his poor charge and as a result defines his own actions in harming her as 'méprisable' [contemptible] (p. 52).[42] The 'peuple', when asked to give an official view on the imminent execution, fails to respond, pre-empting the silence that will surround her death (p. 58). The reader, though, can potentially go a step further. Benefitting, perhaps, from the 'regard propice' of a benevolent God, he can be part of a regenerated 'peuple' whose humanity is not stamped out or twisted by the corrupt authorities that represent him. Before proceeding with this line of thought, however, it is as well to examine the third and final play in this corpus.

Le Cri de l'innocence, ou le tribunal coupable

This text, listed in the Soleinne catalogue as printed in 1816, represents a further evolution in the presentation of the relationship between the public voice and state killing.[43] It recounts a true but little-known episode, the 'Affaire des Galettes', which took place in Montpellier in 1794. During a period of famine, a shortage of flour led to a proclamation that individuals were forbidden from making bread or cakes. However, certain bakers were discovered to be producing small batches of *galettes* in secret, and the authorities accused them of plotting to supply the enemy Spanish army (when in fact the *galettes* were intended to feed non-juror priests).[44] The *arrêt* pronounced against them immediately couched their crime in terms of an affront to the collective:

> Ces êtres sont d'autant plus criminels qu'ils poignardent le peuple en lui enlevant les moyens d'existence, et d'autant plus méprisables qu'ils peuvent, en l'inquiétant sur les subsistances, lui faire oublier ses devoirs les plus chers et ses serments les plus sacrés: *La liberté ou la mort!*[45]

> [These beings are even more criminal in that they injure [literally: stab] the people by taking from them their very means of existence, and even more despicable because, by causing the people to worry about food, they may cause them to forget their most dear duties, and their most sacred oath: *Liberty or death!*]

In the resulting trial a majority verdict found the defendants guilty: eight were ultimately released, but four were executed in the city's first use of the guillotine.

The play is attributed to 'M. J. C.'. One library catalogue reads this as referring to Pierre-Joseph Cambon, a politician who had some involvement in the Revolution.[46] Originally from Montpellier, he was in hiding from 1795 as an opponent of Robespierre, then returned to be a part of Napoleon's 100-day legislature in 1815, before being exiled in 1816. The preface to the text describes Napoleon as 'notre auguste chef' [our august leader], and Cambon is known to have had an interest in the enactment of fair trials by jury, so the attribution is plausible: little more can be ascertained on this count.[47] Though no known source testifies to its performance, theatre is at the very heart of this text.[48] The trial itself took place on the stage of the Montpellier theatre, which had been used as a meeting place since a fire destroyed the interior in 1789, and the *avant-propos* self-consciously sets up the event as spectacle, describing 'l'art de la cruauté' [the art of cruelty], 'la scène la plus tragique' [the most tragic scene], and the 'spectacle déchirant' [harrowing spectacle] (pp. 3–4). That this already spectacular event, steeped in the revolutionary sense of justice-as-theatre, should then be turned into a play, whose author even imagines it being performed on the very stage where the original trial took place, could not be a clearer demonstration of how theatre can act as retrial and theatre audience as judge and jury.[49]

The title of the play spells out this idea of a retrial — or at least a new trial with defendant and accuser in opposing roles — with the image of 'le tribunal coupable'.[50] As in *Le Martyre de Marie-Antoinette*, responsibility and the locus of legal authority are blurred: evidence is lacking or falsified, witnesses are primed, and 'un général infâme et complice' [an odious and conniving general] works in partnership with the judges (p. 3). The 'good' characters are highly aware of how truth is being manipulated: Constance, whose husband is on trial, refers to the tribunal as 'assassins' (p. 19), whilst Fabius, son of one of the defendants, reminds the jury that the accused are 'des mères, des époux, que des êtres pervers ont traduit [*sic*] devant vous' [mothers, husbands, that [these] perverse beings have brought before you] (p. 29). But the treacherous president of the committee adopts the language of enlightenment and reason to support his stance: he claims he is acting 'par humanité' [out of humanity] and refers to 'la clarté du procès, les témoins entendus' [the transparency of the trial, the witnesses heard] (p. 31). As in the previous play, the corruption depicted here is not a new accusation: contemporary documents report that the president of the jury had been chosen illicitly by the president of tribunal, and was in fact the author of the letter that had originally condemned the defendants.[51] The play rather acts to dramatize and publicize this fact.

That the corruption goes to the heart of the jury itself is clearly troubling given the emphasis on the voice of the people. Here, this specific set of individuals is called upon to take responsibility on behalf of the rest of the 'peuple' for condemning those that threaten the wellbeing of the collectivity. The public prosecutor unsurprisingly calls for a guilty verdict:

> Jurés républicains, sachez avec courage,
> Venger les droits sacrés d'un peuple qu'on outrage.
> C'est en vous acquitant de ce pénible emploi
> Que vous satisferez aux désirs de la loi. (p. 27)

> [Republican jurors, know how
> To avenge with courage the sacred rights of a people that has been affronted.
> It is by taking on this difficult task
> That you will satisfy the desires of the law.]

But the juror Casca not only pushes for the use of the guillotine as superior to the 'fade logique' [dull logic] of the law: he describes the pressure that the people — invisible in their full masses, yet visible in the audience of the theatrical trial — place on him and his fellow representatives, in a fantastically contradictory image of simultaneous freedom and coercion:

> Le peuple impatient autour de vous s'empresse;
> Emettez librement un vœu qui l'intéresse. (p. 33)

> [The impatient people presses about you;
> Speak freely a judgement that concerns it.]

Once again, the 'peuple' acts as a justification, but here its expression, funneled through the jurors, takes on actual — and not merely symbolic — legal weight in the imposition of a death sentence.

As in *Le Martyre de Marie-Antoinette*, those on the side of 'right' in *Le Cri de l'innocence* look beyond earthly justice for their final judgement. But again we see more than just blind faith in an external correction to the corrupt human system. Whilst certain characters might appeal to the heavens, hope also remains located in the prospect of a better earthly future. Constance suggests that the death of her innocent husband will 'exciter [...] les bras d'un peuple impatient de venger son trépas' [stir up [...] the arms of a people impatient to avenge his demise] (p. 20): the 'peuple', then, can also potentially be convoked as a positive force; its energy 'un feu qui ne pourra s'éteindre' [a fire that cannot be put out] (p. 20).[52] Though revolution was a natural force in Maréchal's play, here, as in *Le Martyre de Marie-Antoinette*, nature is recuperated as a force for good by the anti-revolutionaries; a force that, though perhaps still an articulation of divine power, nonetheless encourages its followers to put heavenly justice to work in their own lives. In Constance, 'la nature a parlé' [nature has spoken], whilst the defence lawyer maintains 'je défends l'innocence et je sers la nature' [I defend innocence and I serve nature] (p. 29). These individuals act as models for the 'peuple' who is presented as waking up to 'le cri de la nature' [the cry of nature] (p. 9) and refusing to sanction, or be employed to justify, any more crimes. Thus, though the killings do in fact take place, the implication is that the population has learned from its mistakes. The condemned Lorand tells the children he leaves behind to 'respecter les lois jusqu'au dernier soupir' [respect the laws until [your] last breath] (p. 34); a desire that can only be possible if he believes in the law as an essentially good and hopeful force which is only temporarily misused.

This later play — written after the Terror when a new order has been restored — can allow itself hope for redress precisely because its author has seen the chaos and disorder come to an end. Indeed, in July 1795 a trial of the 'tribunal coupable', including its president, really did take place in the same Montpellier court, where it was decreed that 'le meurtre commis sous le glaive de la loi doit être poursuivi comme celui commis avec le poignard de l'assassin' [murder committed with the sword of the law must be prosecuted in the same way as that committed with the assassin's dagger]. The image of legal killing as assassination had made it into the official rhetoric of the court. Justice was not entirely served, however, for just months after that ruling, a law was passed stating that former members of revolutionary committees could not be condemned for carrying out the laws of the time at which they acted. Thus these 'assassins juridiques' [legal assassins] escaped judgement.[53] What this play does, then, is precisely what the Calas plays had done in 1790–91: provide the (imagined) public exoneration of the innocent, and, here, condemnation of the guilty, that the court itself had never quite allowed. In doing so, the play includes the reader/audience in the 'peuple' in whom hope is invested; the new jury that can also go on to enact the civilizing process that will not just correct this single case, but better society as a whole.

★   ★   ★   ★   ★

All three of these plays explicitly set out how responsibility for a personally motivated act is deferred and placed in the hands of a public which is manipulated or misrepresented, its voice appropriated to sanction 'official' actions, in particular killings that are in reality no more than assassinations. The removal of responsibility recalls the very rationale for the guillotine itself, which took the requirement to bring down an axe away from an individual executioner, mechanizing and depersonalizing the process of killing until it became merely the enactment of an equally impersonal legal decree.[54] But this depersonalization of such an essentially human moment left spectators unable to react in an appropriate manner, and made the act itself un-representable. Only by considering the before and after could emotion — so essential for both a negative and a positive reaction to the death penalty — be restored to the process.[55] These plays thus engage with both the problem of depersonalization, and that of emotion, arguing, alongside the marquise de la Tour du Pin in her *Journal d'une femme de cinquante ans*, that it is the executioner who is in fact human, whilst the revolutionaries who order the use of the guillotine are the true 'bourreaux' [executioners].[56]

The theatrical presentation of these arguments is key to their effect. These anti-revolutionaries did not have an actual public stage on which to hold their retrials, as the revolutionary authorities themselves did. But the notion that these texts are theatre — the implied audience, the demonstration rather than account of the claimed injustice, the continual nods to an off-stage 'peuple' — plays on precisely the same questions of spectacle that were being used in official events. In his discussion of revolutionary trial plays, Robert argues that re-enacting the past can serve either to master it, redressing the injustice perpetrated against Calas, or to create disunity: what would happen if a theatre audience, drawn in by a humanizing representation of Louis XVI's final days, were to contest the validity of his execution?[57] In either case the creation of a public reaction that either accords with or differs from the 'official' view is the key outcome, even if the official view itself was also already predicated upon public consensus. These pamphlet plays employ exactly the same tactic, encouraging the 'audience', whether or not it is actually present, to judge. But in their insistent focus on the reactions and status of the onstage public, the hope seems to be that for the real public this judgement will take place in a more self-aware manner; that the readers of these texts will choose to extricate themselves from the sheep-like populace, whose members risk being condemned as collaborators, and instead side with the independent, natural, moral incarnation of the 'peuple' in whom hope is invested, and who not only refuses to be used as an excuse for crime, but turns on the criminals, and condemns them in turn.

Insofar as the united 'peuple' straddles a difficult line between force for good and justification for evil, the fact that these theatrical texts remain unperformed may in fact work in their favour. Whilst they incite the sense of public unity and collective reasoning implied by theatre, they are nonetheless read by individuals in reality isolated from the peaks of emotions created by experience in a crowd, and thereby potentially endowed with clearer sight. This is not entirely a vision of a 'true' general will, generated by the people rather than imposed upon them, for the plays very strongly suggest the line that is to be taken. But the 'peuple' clearly still has a place in the revised systems of 'loi' in which these authors place their faith. It might be, then, that in order to regain the natural, just perspective that is believed to be theirs, it is necessary for them to become individuals again for a moment; to evaluate their own reactions before coming together once more as an imagined theatrical public, and thus to avoid being swept up in the 'torrent' that is the creation — both internally and externally motivated — of the general will. In a period that promoted both the importance of being guided by a personal, emotional 'inner conviction', and the idea of collective, unmediated, insurrectional justice, the tension between individual and group judgement as a basis for legal right was constant: the unperformed play perhaps provides one way out of that bind.

In addressing the contemporary debate regarding the source of true justice, these pamphlet plays fit into a paradigm set out by Scott S. Bryson: that in the late eighteenth century, theatrical and legal reform had a common goal in constructing a self-contained, autonomous system, which nonetheless had to draw and fascinate the outside gaze, specifically by engaging the spectator through his shared humanity with those within.[58] Sharing humanity, with a theatrical character or an individual on trial, involves that same negotiation of the individual and the collective we have identified in these plays: finding points that are already held in common, but also being able to imagine the specific, individual experiences of the other. But in both cases, it is vital that this moment of contact and crossover be recognized, for it is always there: the system is never entirely divorced from human intervention, a purely mechanical guillotine, operating of its own accord. Rather, the public, whether theatrical or legal, necessarily has a continued interaction with the system, both as individual and collective. This vital, specifically human interaction, when employed correctly, sanctions and justifies the functions of both theatre and the law; even the anti-revolutionary writers here seem to put forward a version of this view. But it also condemns both theatre and the law to uncertainty, to subjectivity, and to a sceptical response that royal justice, founded on divine right, had never had to face.

That gap between the ideal theatrical or political public and the reality of lost control is perhaps responsible for one final irony regarding the (probable) unperformed status of these texts. It is a commonplace that the theatrical author dreads handing his work over to the actors, liable as it is to be pulled out of shape before being subjected to judgement by an audience beyond his control. The inclusion of a character on stage who performs an act of interpretation — the role many have argued is occupied by Molière's *raisonneurs* — can serve to direct the audience response; one tool to stamp authority on a slippery text.[59] These unperformed pamphlet plays go a step further: not only do they stage the public, but this fictional 'peuple', constructed and controlled by the author, is in fact the only collective judgement to which the events of the play will be exposed. For all their apparent aims to the contrary, these authors may in the end be seen as performing the very same act of appropriation and manipulation that they so roundly condemn. They create their ideal 'peuple', and claim to represent its will, all the while excising the unpredictable, emotional, and human reaction of a real crowd of individuals, who threaten the unity of the vision their masters wish to present. In the imagined theatre-courtroom, the anti-revolutionary can console himself with a hopeful version of reality, in which he really does have a public stage from which to call his supporters to action and enlist them on the side of 'right'. But in fact, he remains confined to the sidelines, part of the anonymous masses who are told they control the operation of the guillotine, even as the true puppeteers show themselves to be pulling the strings.

Notes to Chapter 3

Many thanks to Yann Robert, Alexey Evstratov, and the editors of this volume for their useful comments on this essay prior to submission. Thanks also to the participants in the British Society for Eighteenth-Century Studies panel (January 2017), at which I first presented this research, and to Claire Siviter for her assistance regarding the Montpellier text. Translations from French are my own.

1. Susan Maslan, *Revolutionary Acts: Theater, Democracy and the French Revolution* (Baltimore, MD: Johns Hopkins University Press, 2005), Mona Ozouf, *Festivals and the French Revolution*, trans. by Alain Sheridan (Cambridge, MA: Harvard University Press, 1988), and Marie-Hélène Huet, *Rehearsing the Revolution: The Staging of Marat's Death, 1793–1797* (Berkeley: University of California Press, 1982).
2. Raymonde Monnier, 'La Question de la peine de mort sous la Révolution française', in *Révolution et justice pénale en Europe: modèles français et traditions nationales (1780–1830)*, ed. by Xavier Rousseaux, Marie-Sylvie Dupont-Bouchat, and Claude Vael (Paris: L'Harmattan, 1999), pp. 225–42.
3. Daniel Arasse, *La Guillotine et l'imaginaire de la Terreur* (Paris: Flammarion, 1987), pp. 27–29.
4. For example Yann Robert, *Dramatic Justice: Trial by Theater in the Age of the French Revolution* (Philadelphia: University of Pennsylvania Press, 2019), and *Representing Violence in France, 1760–1820*, ed. by Thomas Wynn (Oxford: SVEC, 2013).
5. Conversely, in the early 1790s, complaints were made about the depiction of early forms of more spectacular capital punishment onstage on the grounds that it risked offending female audience members (Robert, *Dramatic Justice*, p. 289).
6. Between the declaration of the freedom of the press in the *Déclaration des droits de l'homme et du citoyen* (August 1789) and the start of the Terror, ephemeral pamphlet publications proliferated in France, produced by authors of all political persuasions and circulating quickly and relatively widely in the streets, coffee houses, and taverns; see Antoine de Baecque, 'Pamphlets: Libel and Political Mythology', in *Revolution in Print: The Press in France 1775–1800*, ed. by Robert Darnton and Daniel Roche (Berkeley: University of California Press, 1989), pp. 165–76, and Carla Hesse, *Publishing and Cultural Politics in Revolutionary Paris, 1789–1810* (Berkeley: University of California Press, 1991). Thousands of these pamphlets survive in library collections across the world, many of them still to be fully catalogued. Theatre, and dialogue more broadly, are popular forms in such collections: Michel Biard, in a recent study of the 'dialogues of the dead' genre, examines ninety-six dialogue pamphlets in the period from 1789 to 1795, though points out that this is by no means exhaustive; see *La Révolution hantée* (Paris: Vendémiaire, 2012).The index of the French Revolutionary Collection in the British Library, which contains over 48,500 items, lists over 200 items relating to theatre — without including all the dialogue or theatrical pamphlets that may exist classified under different headings; see G. K. Fortescue, *French Revolutionary Collections in the British Library* (London: The British Library, 1979). To my knowledge, no specific study has yet been undertaken on this genre — though on comparable pamphlet plays in the American Revolution, see Ginger Strand, 'The Many Deaths of Montgomery: Audiences and Pamphlet Plays of the Revolution', *American Literary History*, 9.1 (1997), 1–20.
7. The three plays explored here are selected for the manner in which — albeit in three quite different ways — their theatrical structure seems intrinsic to their specifically critical argument regarding the role of the public in the development of capital punishment. This chapter forms part of an ongoing project regarding dialogue pamphlets in the period, which should eventually be able to situate this trend more firmly.
8. [Anon.], *La Journée des Dupes* (n.p.: n. pub., 1790); [Anon.], *Le Martyre de Marie-Antoinette d'Autriche, Reine de France* (Amsterdam: n. pub., 1794); M. J. C., *Le Cri de l'innocence, ou le tribunal coupable* (Avignon: Bonnet fils, n.d.). Further references to these three plays are given after quotations in the main text.

9. See n. 2 above. See also Angelica Gooden, *Actio and Persuasio* (Oxford: Clarendon, 1986), and Paul Friedland, *Political Actors: Representative Bodies & Theatricality in the Age of the French Revolution* (Ithaca, NY: Cornell University Press, 2002).

10. *La Déclaration des droits de l'homme et du citoyen*, article 6, <http://www.elysee.fr/la-presidence/la-declaration-des-droits-de-l-homme-et-du-citoyen/> [accessed 7 December 2016].

11. Maximilien Robespierre, *5ᵉ lettre à ses commettants*, in *Œuvres complètes*, ed. by Eugène Déprez, 10 vols (Paris: E. Leroux, 1910–67), V, 60.

12. *Le Théâtre en France*, ed. by Jacqueline de Jomaron, 2 vols (Paris: Armand Colin, 1988), I, 244.

13. Jean-Pierre Perchellet, 'Les Spectacles parisiens et leur public', in *L'Empire des muses: Napoléon, les arts et les lettres*, ed. by Jean-Claude Bonnet (Paris: Belin, 2004), pp. 153–73.

14. Janie Vanpee, 'Performing Justice: The Trials of Olympe de Gouges', *Theatre Journal*, 51.1 (1999), 47–65 (p. 52). This decree quickly led to a new version of censorship, which targeted all reminders of the monarchical past (Robert, *Dramatic Justice*, pp. 236–38).

15. David Bell, *The Cult of the Nation in France: Inventing Nationalism, 1680–1800* (Cambridge, MA: Harvard University Press, 2001).

16. Philippe Bourdin, 'Les Factions sur les tréteaux patriotiques (1789–1799): combats pour une représentation', in *Représentation et pouvoir: la politique symbolique en France (1789–1830)*, ed. by Natalie Scholz and Christina Schröer (Rennes: Presses universitaires de Rennes, 2007), pp. 23–37.

17. Robert, *Dramatic Justice*, pp. 23-48.

18. On the link between the *drame* and historical plays, see James Johnson, 'Revolutionary Audiences and the Impossible Imperatives of Fraternity', in *Re-Creating Authority in Revolutionary France*, ed. by Bryant T. Ragan and Elizabeth Ann Williams (New Brunswick, NJ: Rutgers University Press, 1992), pp. 57–68, Pierre Frantz, 'Les Genres dramatiques pendant la Révolution', in *Convegno di studi sul teatro e la Rivoluzione francese*, ed. by Mario Richter (Venice : Accademia Olimpica, 1991), pp. 49–63, and Éric Négrel, 'Le Théâtre au service de la Révolution: une rhétorique de l'éloge', in *Une expérience rhétorique: l'éloquence de la Révolution*, ed. by Éric Négrel and Jean-Paul Sermain (Oxford: Voltaire Foundation, 2002), pp. 147–60. For more on the interaction between *sensibilité* and politics, see Cecilia Feilla, *The Sentimental Theater of the French Revolution* (Farnham: Ashgate, 2013).

19. Yann Robert, 'The Everlasting Trials of Jean Calas: Justice, Theatre and Trauma in the Early Years of the Revolution', in *Representing Violence in France, 1760–1820*, ed. by Wynn, pp. 103–19.

20. Robert argues elsewhere that this was actually a symbiotic relationship: as theatre harnessed spectacular politics, the courtroom became more theatrical, increasingly focusing on oratory style, emotion, and the public presence of the accused and their witness, even using theatrical staging and language to describe the judicial process. See Robert, *Dramatic Justice*, pp. 191-225, and Laura Mason, 'The "Bosom of Proof": Criminal Justice and the Renewal of Oral Culture during the French Revolution', *Journal of Modern History*, 76 (March 2004), 29–61.

21. Robert, 'The Everlasting Trials of Jean Calas', p. 115.

22. Sylvain Maréchal, *Le Jugement dernier des rois*, in *Théâtre de la Révolution; ou, choix de pièces de théâtre qui ont fait sensation pendant la période révolutionnaire*, ed. by Louis Moland (Paris: Garnier, 1877), pp. 299–325.

23. Sanja Perovic, 'Death by Volcano: Revolutionary Theatre and Marie-Antoinette', *French Studies*, 67.1 (2012), 15–29 (p. 27).

24. Maréchal, *Le Jugement dernier des rois*, p. 310. See also Mark Darlow, 'Staging the Revolution: the *Fait historique*', *Nottingham French Studies*, 45 (Spring 2006), 77–88 (pp. 80–83), which underlines the instantaneous transformation of general will into action, and Jean-Marie Apostolidès, 'La Guillotine littéraire', *French Review*, 62.6 (May 1989), 985–96 (p. 991), which argues that the revolutionary authorities appealed to an imagined future reaction to encourage the public to accept violent actions as just and necessary.

25. Victor Hugo, *Les Misérables*, ed. by Marius-François Guyard, 2 vols (Paris: Garnier Frères, 1957), I, 26.

26. Arasse, *La Guillotine et l'imaginaire de la Terreur*, p. 102.

27. Perovic, 'Death by Volcano', p. 22.

28. Arasse, *La Guillotine et l'imaginaire de la Terreur*, pp. 52–62, 141–210, and Maxime Du Camp, 'La Guillotine', in *Paris, ses organes, ses fonctions et sa vie dans la seconde moitié du dix-neuvième siècle*, 6 vols (Paris: Hachette, 1972), III, 331–405.

29. Pierre Jean Cabanis, 'Note sur le supplice de la guillotine', in *Œuvres complètes de Cabanis*, 5 vols (Paris: Dossange, 1823–25), II, 161–84 (p. 181).

30. Arasse, *La Guillotine et l'imaginaire de la Terreur*, pp. 96–97, and Paul Friedland, *Seeing Justice Done: The Age of Spectacular Capital Punishment in France* (Oxford: Oxford University Press, 2012), pp. 239–65 (pp. 248–59).

31. Arasse, *La Guillotine et l'imaginaire de la Terreur*, pp. 100–02, 165–66.

32. Ironically, Robespierre accused the English Cavaliers of having done precisely this with respect to the death of Charles I, which was, he claimed, simply one tyrant using the executioner to kill another tyrant (*Archives parlementaires de 1789 à 1860: recueil complet des débats législatifs & politiques des Chambres françaises*, ed. by J. Madival and others, 101 vols (Paris: Librairie administrative de P. Dupont, 1862–), LIV, 75).

33. See Thomas Wynn's discussion of Sade's rarely performed theatre in his *Sade's Theatre: Pleasure, Violence, Masochism* (Oxford: SVEC, 2007), p. 7.

34. Friedrich-Melchior Grimm and others, *Correspondance littéraire, philosophique et critique* [1747–1793], 16 vols (Paris: Garnier Frères, 1877–82), XVI, 552–53. See also Eleanor F. Jourdain, *Dramatic Theory and Practice in France, 1690–1808* (Oxford: Clarendon Press, 1912), pp. 205–21.

35. Wilda Anderson, 'Is the General Will Anonymous? (Rousseau, Robespierre, Condorcet)', *MLN*, 126.4 (2011), 838–52 (p. 848).

36. François Charbonneau, 'Institutionnaliser le droit à l'insurrection: l'article 35 de la constitution montagnarde de 1793', *Tangence*, 106 (2014), 93–112.

37. Anderson, 'Is the General Will Anonymous?', p. 848. On the use of *poissard* elsewhere in the period, see Alexander Parks, *The Genre Poissard and the French Stage of the Eighteenth Century* (New York: Columbia, 1935), and Carla Hesse, *The Other Enlightenment: How French Women Became Modern* (Princeton, NJ: Princeton University Press, 2002), pp. 10–27.

38. Pierre Frantz, 'Violence in the Theatre of the Revolution', in *Representing Violence in France, 1760–1820*, ed. by Wynn, pp. 121–35 (pp. 128–29).

39. Jourdain, *Dramatic Theory and Practice in France, 1690–1808*, p. 221.

40. On her trial and execution see Lynn Hunt, 'The Many Bodies of Marie-Antoinette: Political Pornography and the Problem of the Feminine in the French Revolution', in *Marie-Antoinette: Writing on the Body of a Queen*, ed. by Dena Goodman (New York: Routledge, 2003), pp. 117–38.

41. Perovic, 'Death by Volcano', p. 20.

42. See for example William Hamilton's vulnerable *Marie-Antoinette conduite à son exécution* (1794) now held at the Musée de la Révolution française, Vizille. This sympathetic presentation was crystallized in the Goncourts' *Histoire de Marie-Antoinette* (Paris: Didot Frères, 1858). It is not dissimilar to the stoic and virtuous manner in which Mary, Queen of Scots, was presented after her execution, see John D. Staines, *The Tragic Histories of Mary Queen of Scots, 1560–1900: Rhetoric, Passions, and Political Literature* (Farnham & Burlington, VT: Ashgate, 2009).

43. Martineau de Soleinne, *Bibliothèque dramatique de Monsieur de Soleinne*, 6 vols (Paris: Administration de l'Alliance des Arts, 1843–1845), II, 333.

44. For a full account, see Le Chanoine Saurel, *Un sanglant épisode sous la Terreur à Montpellier, l'affaire dite des Galettes* (Montpellier: Firmin & Montane, 1895). The judgement appears in the *Jugement du Tribunal criminel du Département de l'Hérault, du 19 germinal de l'an deuxième de la fondation de la République française [...] (Affaire dite des Galettes)* (Montpellier: Bonnariq and Avignon, an II).

45. Saurel, *Un sanglant épisode sous la Terreur à Montpellier*, p. 5. 'La liberté ou la mort' was the motto of the first republic in the early years after the Revolution.

46. See *Réseau des médiathèques*, Montpellier, <https://mediatheques.montpellier3m.fr> [accessed 10 January 2017].

47. J. F. Georgel, *Mémoires pour servir à l'histoire des événements de la fin du XVIIIe siècle depuis 1760 jusqu'en 1806–1810*, 6 vols (Paris: Eymery, 1820), V, 77.

48. Neither the title nor its probable author is mentioned in Pierre Jourda's repertoire of Montpellier

theatre in the period, based on theatre archives and local press sources (*Le Théâtre à Montpellier, 1755–1851* (Oxford: Voltaire Foundation, 2001). It is nonetheless interesting to note that the book records a series of plays relating to contemporary events that were censored in the early nineteenth century (pp. 204–06). Further information may be revealed in the course of the THEREPSICORE project on regional theatre, see Philippe Bourdin and others, 'Le programme THEREPSICORE: personnels dramatiques, répertoires et salles de spectacle en province (1791–1813)', *Révolution française*, 367 (2012), 17–48.

49. See *Le Cri de l'innocence*, p. 35.

50. See the subtitle of Marie-Joseph de Chénier's 1793 Calas play, *Jean Calas, ou L'École des juges* (Paris: Moutard, 1793).

51. Saurel, *Un sanglant épisode sous la Terreur à Montpellier*, pp. 7–9.

52. Though 'son trépas' in context refers to Constance's husband (hence my translation 'his') the syntax also makes it possible to read it as potentially applying to the 'peuple' itself ('its'): an implication, perhaps, that the true meaning of the people has been murdered by the revolutionary authorities, and it now seeks revenge.

53. Saurel, *Un sanglant épisode sous la Terreur à Montpellier*, pp. 11–12.

54. Arasse, *La Guillotine et l'imaginaire de la Terreur*, pp. 29, 51, 124–28.

55. See Cesare Beccaria, *Dei delitti e delle pene*, ed. by Franco Venturi (Turin: Einaudi, 1965), p. 64, which argues that disdain and compassion, rather than terror, tend to be the prime reactions of a spectator of an execution.

56. Henriette Lucie Dillon, marquise de la Tour du Pin Gouvernet, *Journal d'une femme de cinquante ans (1778–1815)* (Paris: Chapelot, 1913), pp. 312–13. Cited in Arasse, *La Guillotine et l'imaginaire de la Terreur*, p. 202.

57. Robert, 'The Everlasting Trials of Jean Calas', p. 119.

58. Scott S. Bryson, *The Chastised Stage: Bourgeois Drama and the Exercise of Power* (Saratoga, CA: ANMA Libri, 1991), pp. 112–13.

59. See Michael Hawcroft, *Reasoning With Fools* (Oxford: Oxford University Press, 2007).

CHAPTER 4

Listening for a Man Swinging:
A Prisoner Witnesses in Oscar Wilde's
'The Ballad of Reading Gaol'

E. S. Burt

> The shed in which people are hanged is a little shed with a glass roof, like a photographer's studio on the sands at Margate. For eighteen months I thought it *was* the studio for photographing prisoners. There is no adjective to describe it. I call it 'hideous' because it became so to me after I knew its use.
>
> Oscar Wilde, letter to Robert Ross, 8 October 1897

> Et cette confidence horrible chuchotée
> Au confessionnal du cœur.
>
> [And that horrible confidence whispered
> In the heart's confessional.]
>
> Charles Baudelaire, 'Confession'

Oscar Wilde's autobiographical 'Ballad of Reading Gaol' (1897) stands out among poems bearing witness to the public executions and gibbeted corpses of the past as the rare testimony to a death learned about indirectly, from signs and whispers — a hanging as a quasi-secret event. Through its treatment of the suffering of one prisoner's imagination, it offers a chance to investigate the effects of shrouding executions both on a community and on witnessing, where it is the ear that registers the extinction of life. The prisoner's experience is delivered in a ballad, a narrative poem often set to music. By means of its cadences readers too are placed within reach of an event they cannot help but imagine.

In the first epigraph cited above, Wilde likens the spectacle of the state terminating a man's life, to the hidden work of a photographer taking a picture. The shed becomes a symbol for the change in death protocols. Whatever state functionaries turned it into a hanging shed are responsible for this likeness, which the poet remarks upon rather than invents. In contrast to Wordsworth's freed imagination at the outset of *The Prelude*, Wilde's is fettered to an obsessive image he gets wind of second-hand, in this case, one that substitutes for a picture a prisoner's neck as the thing being snapped. The shift from eye to ear also entails a change in circumstances for the imagination. To understand these changes, this chapter will first link reforms in the death penalty in Victorian England to a shift from Kantian arguments about punishment to John Stuart Mill's utilitarian arguments on suffering, with their discursive performative footing. It will then show Wilde's critique of the performative, with the poet going on to consider the problem raised by the morbid imagination for the penal system and to suggest new limits, or even an end, for the death penalty.

First, a few generalities. 'The Ballad of Reading Gaol' is the sole substantive work that Wilde wrote after emerging from two years of hard labour in prison, part of it spent in Reading Gaol as prisoner C.3.3 — the 'name' under which the ballad first appeared in 1898. The poem's witnessing is autobiographical, inspired partly by an execution carried out in Reading Gaol some months before Wilde's release, the hanging of trooper Thomas C. Wooldridge for the murder of his wife. The speaker knows about the hidden execution only indirectly, but can bear witness first-hand to its effects as a member of the prison population.

Wilde has made use of the ballad form, often appearing on the broadsides that, from the fifteenth century down to the early nineteenth century, brought political questions and sensational events to the public.[1] Broadside accounts of executions, besides a third-person narrative of events, often included a ballad called a 'goodnight' that purported to give the condemned's confession, generally ending on a note of repentance. Wilde's poem abolishes the distance between third- and first-person perspectives with a 'we' capacious enough to capture not just the prisoners with the I in their midst, but also the reader-judges with whom the speaker also makes common cause. The mixture of an inclusive 'we' (I and my readers) and an exclusive 'we' (I and the prisoners), with the shifting perspective that it involves, is one reason the poem has incited queasiness. Among other critics, W. B. Yeats has faulted the poem as insufficiently unified in tone and as exhibiting the exaggerations of late Victorian sentimentality. Indeed, before including it in his 1936 *Oxford Book of Modern Verse*, Yeats pruned the poem severely, from 109 stanzas to 38, to give it a 'stark realism akin to that of Thomas Hardy'.[2] It is difficult to see how Wilde could have avoided the mixed tone, given that his speaker is both a man condemned and one not condemned to death. In his poem, the differences between guilt and innocence, convict and judge are not absolute and every statement must have a confessional aspect, as the I does not simply witness an execution, but is a guilty fellow.

Changing Death Penalty Arguments

Behind the reforms taking place in the British penal system over the century were shifts in the philosophical arguments undergirding it. Wilde's poem taps into an ongoing philosophical argument, as represented by the giving way of the still lingering idealist positions of Kant with his decisive influence on the Romantics, and the emerging utilitarianism of Mill, whose arguments in Parliament in 1868 affected England's decision to maintain execution, while taking it indoors.

Jacques Derrida's discussion of Kant's arguments about the death penalty is helpful in bringing out their strong rationale for giving visibility to execution.[3] In Kant's *Metaphysics of Morals*, a talionic principle reliant on likeness looks for equivalents between crime and punishment. The 'eye for an eye, tooth for a tooth' works best with murder, where the visible likeness of crime to punishment is most striking. Even where, as with Hegel, the equivalence is a matter of reason, with one life made equivalent to another by reference to a common value such as humanity, the aim is to approximate in punishment an image of the crime.[4] Justice demands the representation of its talionic principle in a code of punishments; from there to spectacles of retributive justice used to awe the public is a quick step. One side of what it is to witness, that is, to be present at an event that lays down a memorable impression, emerges in connection with this model.[5] The spectacle exhorts the public to see and abhor the crime in the punishment.

Derrida points out a second Kantian rationale for public spectacles that can also be related to testimony, but this time as the act of bearing witness made theatrical. For Kant, the members belonging to a rational community acquiesce in advance to just punishment even up to loss of life. The dignity of the individual member who submits to the law is deserving of respect, so punishment, especially capital punishment, must be carried out with rigorous attention to human worth. Death must be dignified, light, and easy; the public must not see humanity degraded to animal condition by suffering. Again, Kant's theory presses toward public execution. By its quiescent presence, the public certifies that the punishment was not — as modern law has it — 'cruel and unusual', in a bearing witness that is moreover an act of renewed faith in the common undertaking.[6] In sum, the spectacle is advisable, so that the public will see and remember, and necessary, so that it can bear witness to the state's respect for human dignity in its exercise of authority.

For executions to become quasi-secret in Britain, some of the Kantian-style arguments on capital punishment that helped justify the public hangings of late Georgian and early Victorian times had to have fallen into disrepute under the attacks of the British abolitionists in the early part of the nineteenth century.[7] The abolitionist strategy was to whittle away at the ideal picture of rational punishment that Kant provides with a barrage of pragmatic arguments. One major effect was to reorient arguments about justice away from retribution, which left salvation to the afterlife, towards the rehabilitation of criminals in the here and now. As noted by historian of abolition James Gregory, the arguments put forward in the 1820s by the Society for the Diffusion of Information on the Subject of Capital Punishment, or, a bit later, by the re-formed 1846 Society for the Abolition of Capital Punishment, shifted the emphasis from atonement to earthly redemption.[8]

The utility of public execution as deterrent also came under review. In articles in *Fraser's Magazine* and the *Daily News*, William Thackeray and Charles Dickens doubted that the public could distinguish a crime motivated by passion from the impersonal putting to death by the state.[9] The execution, with its fair-like atmosphere favouring ribaldry and black humour, would certainly not act as a warning. Indeed, Dickens went so far as to speculate on the reverse: if, 'to a bad mind contemplating violence', you represent 'the spectacle of his own ghastly and untimely death [...] out of the depths of his own nature you shall assuredly raise up that which lures and tempts him on'.[10] The tit-for-tat thinking of the talion could even favour murder: to see the state killing is to aspire to its likeness. The ideal state also went under attack in those debates; Britain's 'greatness' was felt to be owed less to its rational constitution than to a working alliance between the commercial interests of the nation and the law, even down to its accounting practices in the penal code.[11]

The utilitarian cast of arguments for reform or outright abolition is evident. In 1856, after conducting a study confirming that of 167 hanged for murder, only three had never attended a hanging, the Wilberforce Committee concluded that public hangings did not deter.[12] With the programme of transporting undesirables to the colonies formally ended (1868), and in the belief that souls might be redeemed by Christian education, the government built more prisons and devised the harsh correction system Wilde knew as a prisoner. At the same time, the reach of capital punishment was being curtailed. By 1861, the over 220 capital crimes under the Bloody Code had been trimmed to a few.

Reforms were enacted, but the pragmatic arguments of the abolitionists had not completely undermined the death penalty. When the abolitionists brought the matter to a vote in April 1868, proposing to abolish capital punishment in an amendment to the Capital Punishment Within Prisons Bill, the death penalty found a strong proponent in John Stuart Mill. In his Parliamentary speech, Kant's ideal justice is set aside in favour of utilitarian policies tending toward the maximum of public happiness and the minimum of suffering. It is human feeling that is sacred, so 'to deter by suffering from inflicting suffering is [...] the very purpose of penal justice'.[13] Because the state works less to punish crimes than to decrease their future number, ascertaining whether the criminal is corrigible is paramount. Death is justified 'when the attendant circumstances suggest no palliation of the guilt, no hope that the culprit may even yet not be unworthy to live among mankind, nothing to make it probable that the crime was an exception to his general character rather than a consequence of it' (p. 267). Kant's requirement that executions respect human dignity is dealt with by subordinating everything to one consideration: execution is less painful than life imprisonment:

> What comparison can there really be, in point of severity, between consigning a man to the short pang of a rapid death, and immuring him in a living tomb, there to linger out what may be a long life in the hardest and most monotonous toil, without any of its alleviations or rewards — debarred from all pleasant sights and sounds, and cut off from all earthly hope, except a slight mitigation of bodily restraint, or a small improvement of diet? (p. 268)

Comparing durations of suffering lets Mill recommend the death penalty: to the unending pain of premature entombment is compared the piercing 'pang' of sudden death. The incorrigible must be dealt the lesser of two agonies, 'as beyond comparison the *least cruel mode* in which it is possible *adequately to deter* from crime' (p. 267, my emphasis). Having thus manifested its general respect for human worth, the state has only to choose the most expeditious death within its accepted practices.

Technical improvements can be sought in delivery, such as the long drop introduced in 1872, not long after Mill's speech.

Mill confines himself to speaking against the amendment to abolish and does not speak directly to the point of the main bill to place execution within prison. However, comments on the effect made on the public imagination suggest that, except perhaps on one point to be taken up below, he has no disagreement with the proposed reform. It is to be desired that an execution 'should seem more rigorous than it is, for its practical power depends far less on what it is than on what it *seems*' (p. 268, my emphasis). With this comment about the appearance of great suffering as a deterrent, Mill leaves room for removing executions from view. The abolitionists have proved that the imagination is not deeply touched by the sight of hanging; perhaps a curtained execution will maintain public focus on one moment of suffering, magnifying it by their fear of the unknown.[14]

This theory of hiding capital punishment to increase its power on the imagination returns the performative to speech. The public is to witness in silent awe as the state solemnly reaffirms its authority over the lives of its citizens through the carrying out of a promise for which only linguistic evidence is provided them. The subsequent protocols make verbal performatives central.[15] The public learns of the solemn pronouncement of a death sentence; it hears the church bell ringing in the fifteen minutes leading up to the execution; it hears the clock strike eight and the silence that follows; it reads the terse announcement posted on the prison gates certifying that the sentence has been carried out. The whole is calculated to impress on the public that the state will be deliberate, solemn, and swift in keeping its promises.

Suffering is to be inflicted on the public's imagination and on the condemned's physical body. But Mill does not want the state to be unnecessarily cruel and to pile suffering on suffering. Placing the punishment where it seems most terrifying to the public, behind the curtain and among convicts, also installs an aesthetic, one might say anaesthetic, distance that reassures the public of its own present security. Similarly, the condemned is to suffer only the physical pang allotted. As he has been deemed incorrigible, there is no need to visit upon him the ordinary rigours by which others are to be corrected. He has access to a chaplain to help reconcile himself to death through repentance and creature comforts like tobacco and beer are allowed. However, there is a third 'audience' receiving the execution, the audience of the prisoners who, like the condemned, are under sentence, but who, like the public, are not sentenced to die by hanging. This third public will also be affected by the decision to execute within prison. It is in considering the prisoners' suffering that we discover a cruelty that does not appear susceptible to alleviation by the compartmentalization of suffering Mill attempts.

Mill claims that only the long duration of pain works to correct prisoners (p. 268). That pain consists in monotonous toil while being deprived of everything that makes life pleasant. To Mill, the prisoner's hopes and fears should be confined to small mitigations of penal life. Reformers agreed with the point. Prisoners take pleasure in individuality and in human converse, so to feel monotony and their anonymity more keenly, they must be deprived of news of the outside world, contact with friends and family, communication with one another. Working for

CONVICTS EXERCISING AT PENTONVILLE PRISON.

FIG. 4.1. 'Convicts exercising at Pentonville Prison', *The Criminal Prisons of London, and Scenes of Prison Life* (London: Griffin, Bohn, 1862)

uniformity in treatment, Victorian reformers devised the 'separation system' that placed prisoners alone in cells where they worked out their sentences of hard labour under numbers instead of names, and the 'silent system', whereby prisoners were forbidden to speak with one another, even during the daily hour of recreation, when they walked in a circle, with each one holding a knot at a regulation distance on a rope that had to be kept taut.[16]

Figure 4.1 shows prisoners at exercise under these systems, wearing the ingenious masks that made conversation difficult and fellow prisoners faceless. Obviously, executions carried out in proximity to a population living under such rules would have different effects than on the public or the condemned. The prisoners would be missing the condemned's prospect of a sharp pang quickly over. But they would be invited by their likeness as convicts under sentence to close imaginative participation. Even with conversation and news forbidden, their proximity to the execution would open them to countless reminders. Their imaginations once jolted into operation, the days would provide no respite to the mind, which would return obsessively to the execution. Given the randomness of the signs the prison public receives, it would be unable to perceive the stages of an ordered ritual and would lack the public's sense of awe as well as its protective distance. Both the pains of the public and of the patient will be experienced by the prison population in a panoply of mixed forms, then. In testifying to the excessive pain of the prisoners, Wilde testifies to state cruelty as well.[17] It is on this point that Mill might have had qualms about placing executions inside prisons. He wants the suffering that will favour correction; he wants to starve the prisoners' imaginations, not shock them to life.

Living Execution Up Close

Before writing the ballad, Oscar Wilde had taken up the question of cruelty to prisoners in two 1897 letters to the *Daily Chronicle*, denouncing the incarceration of children and the 'system of silence and cellular confinement',[18] and suggesting improvements in the treatment of prisoners.[19] In 'The Ballad of Reading Gaol', he witnesses the suffering of the prisoners in proximity to the execution. In setting up the scene of punishment, Wilde seems to have accepted the Millian view on the compartmentalized suffering of public and patient. Thus, the warders, figures for the public with its active imagination, wonder at the condemned man's placidity. They are awed when the prisoners in the cells fall to their knees the night before the execution, as if persuaded of the majesty of the law in correcting the prisoners. The equanimity of the man accused of murder is translated into a 'light and gay' step (l. 6).[20] Once condemned, comforts alleviate his pain: 'And twice a day he smoked his pipe, | And drank his quart of beer' (ll. 193–94).[21] So anaesthetized is he that the night before his execution 'He lay as one who lies and dreams | In a pleasant meadow-land' (ll. 253–55).

The suffering not apparent in the condemned is transferred to the prisoners. The I's pain disappears, cauterized and replaced by that of the condemned:

> The sky above my head became
> Like a casque of scorching steel;
> And though I was a soul in pain,
> My pain I could not feel. (ll. 27–30)

Terror and sleeplessness are displaced onto the convicts, too: 'So [...] through each brain on hands of pain | *Another's terror crept*' (ll. 259–64, my emphasis). Worse still, a logic of persecution is installed in which every stray idea becomes a 'hunted thought' (l. 31). Every thought of innocent pleasure is followed by (*per-secutare*) a thought of the hanging. One light-filled morning, the speaker remembers spring-time trees: 'For oak and elm have pleasant leaves | That in the spring-time shoot' (ll. 133–34); but then follows another tree: 'But grim to see is the gallows-tree, | With its adder-bitten root' (ll. 135–56). The rhymes found in the short lines act as a poetic equivalent for this obsessive return, as in one stanza where the speaker recalls ambition, 'The loftiest place is that seat of grace | For which all worldlings try' (ll. 139–40), but is returned by the rhyme to the 'lofty place' as a scaffold:

> But who would stand in hempen band
> Upon a scaffold high
> And through a murderer's collar take
> His last look at the sky? (ll. 141–44)

Even where the poem self-reflexively meditates on the pleasure of formal symmetry, this logic of persecution comes into play, as the remembrance of art is quickly followed by its hanging equivalent. Thus, the memory of soft pleasures, 'It is sweet to dance to violins | When Love and Life are fair' (ll. 145–46), leads by an anaphoric antithesis to 'But it is not sweet with nimble feet | To dance upon the air!' (ll. 149–50).

This persecuted imagination cannot stop trying to get away from the thought that hunts it by remembrance of innocence and cannot help but return to it by way of poetry's shackling rhymes and figures. Even when the silent prisoners take their exercise, they are participating in this pattern not only by their recurrent thoughts, and the ring that their bodies travel, but also — palpably for the reader — by way of the refrains and anaphora of the ballad:

> Silently we went round and round
> The slippery asphalte yard;
> Silently we went round and round
> And no man spoke a word.
>
> Silently we went round and round
> And through each hollow mind
> The memory of dreadful things
> Rushed like a dreadful wind (ll. 435–42)

The hidden execution distances the public; the prisoners are brought close enough to 'see' the execution in detail, to 'feel' the rope, to 'hear' the scream:

> And as one sees most fearful things
> In the crystal of a dream,
> We saw the greasy hempen rope
> Hooked to the blackened beam,
> And heard the prayer the hangman's snare
> Strangled into a scream. (ll. 385–90)

The two temporalities of suffering that Mill tried to purify and assign to separate publics are both felt by the prisoners. They have already to endure long punishment, but now time slows further under the chill of terror: 'So still it [terror] lay that every day | Crawled like a weed-clogged wave' (ll. 229–30). Wilde's line, with its assonances, voiced [w]s and throttling stops [k], slows the poem's rhythm for readers, too. As for the short pangs of death, they are delivered over and over. Just as time, like Terror, 'was lying still', a sign shocks the convicts into remembrance:

> And we *forgot* the bitter lot [...]
> Till once, as we tramped in from work
> We passed an open grave. [...]
> And we *knew* that ere one dawn grew fair.
>   (ll. 233–40, my emphasis)

The poem turns the rhymes and cadences native to the ballad into talionic equivalents as a means to get across the 'hunted thought' particular to the prisoners.

It could be argued that the prisoners' excessive suffering is useful in their correction. Wilde takes a different view. It is not just that 'every stone one lifts by day | Becomes one's heart by night' (ll. 587–88), but that the execution orients all thought in the same direction:

> We watched him day by day,
> And wondered if each one of us
> Would end the self-same way. (ll. 152–54)

Instead of admiring the law's majesty and abhorring the criminal, the prisoners wonder at the death they may replicate and are fascinated by the condemned: their suffering compels them not to correction but imitation.

There is something going awry with the process of justice as imagined along the reformist principles of Mill. The punishment system is misfiring: the death penalty is not helping to correct the prisoners; the laws are 'strawing' the wheat and 'saving' the chaff (l. 545); the state builds prisons to hide its cruelty to individual prisoners (ll. 535–52). The critique of the Millian-style death penalty passes through prison as a place where the performative model is under attack as dysfunctional. We have now to examine whether those misfires, which are evident in the poem's rhetorical excesses, are incidental or rather indicative of systemic failures of the performative model, with its assumptions about responsible agents or speakers, closed contexts, and appropriate speech acts.

Serving a Sentence: Misfires in Performance

Wilde said that he first conceived of the poem while in the dock awaiting his sentence, long before Wooldridge committed his crime. Sentences must be considered in unpacking Wilde's critique of Victorian penal justice with its linchpin of capital punishment, then. We will look closely at a sentence pronounced, considering its context and the person speaking it, all elements of the discursive situation that J. L. Austin delineates.[22] In order to do anything felicitous with words, one must be the right person in the right context using the right form of words.

The sentence soliciting attention is easily discovered. Pronounced in the right words, under the right circumstances, and by the right official, the phrase concluding the poem's fourth stanza would have the force of a death sentence. The surrounding verses establishing the context must be quoted:

> He did not wear his scarlet coat,
> For blood and wine are red,
> And blood and wine were on his hands
> When they found him with the dead,
> The poor dead woman whom he loved,
> And murdered in her bed.
>
> He walked amongst the Trial Men
> In a suit of shabby gray;
> A cricket cap was on his head,
> And his step seemed light and gay;
> But I never saw a man who looked
> So wistfully at the day.
>
> I never saw a man who looked
> With such a wistful eye
> Upon that little tent of blue
> Which prisoners call the sky,
> And at every drifting cloud that went
> With sails of silver by.

> I walked, with other souls in pain,
> Within another ring
> And was wondering if the man had done
> A great or little thing,
> When a voice behind me whispered low:
> 'That fellow's got to swing.' (ll. 1–24)

The context is one of 'Trial Men' and judgement, but the man's guilt is not in question. Although the poem presumably opens when he is on remand, awaiting trial (the cricket cap, not prison issue, establishes this), the speaker does not allow for the man's innocence.[23] He has murdered the 'poor dead woman whom he loved'. The premature 'sentencing' of one who has not yet stood trial exposes the exceptionality of the context, which is 'outside' England where, as Mill says, the legal system assumes innocence and is slow to judgement.[24] To the speaker, everyone in prison has done something. His doubt is solely over whether the deed is 'a great or little thing'. The favourite Wildean term, 'thing', synonymous with 'feat' here, means that the speaker is not judging the deed as a crime. Instead, he *wonders* about it. To wonder in this case is to desire knowledge one may never get. That is the situation of the prisoner kept from all reliable news in prison, just as it could be that of an author contemplating murder from the point of view of myth or of aesthetics, as Thomas De Quincey did in his essay 'On Murder Considered as One of the Fine Arts'. Facts, evidence, knowledge are not available so one can only ask whether the deed can be called heroic, whether it is tragic or comic in nature, etc.

It thus looks as though there is a sharp border dividing the context outside, where sentences are determined according to legal evaluation, and the context inside the jail, where access to facts is so restricted that evaluation can only be made in fictional terms. The distinction between the contexts does not hold, however. Consider ll. 15 and 16 where Wilde seems to be making a final effort to close the two contexts off from one another by referring to the term indicating the beyond, and thus the master language governing the context within prison and outside its walls. The separate rings of prison — reminiscent of Dante's Hell — are surrounded by walls, except at the top where there is 'the little tent of blue | Which prisoners call the sky'. That phrasing defines the language used by prisoners for what lies beyond, over and against the language of the outside context.

The limiting term refers to the transcendent realm that shelters and encloses the prison. However, a problem arises. Prisoners call it the beyond by one name in their language, and non-prisoners call it by another. But which is which? What is the primary name for the space above the prison and what is the secondary name? How to make grammatical sense of the utterance? Do prisoners call the sky 'tent of blue', or do they call the tent of blue 'sky'?

Common sense prefers the first answer. The mastering term comes from the referential language of the outside world where the space above is normally called 'sky', while prisoners call it 'little tent of blue'. 'Tent' for 'sky' is then a classical metaphor exchanging conventional names to express the prisoners' feeling of immurement, and perhaps too the mournful thought that heaven is closed to them. This reading is possible because 'which' can be read restrictively in British English, as introducing a clause determining a noun where careful American English would use 'that' (the tent of blue that is what prisoners call the sky). Since in prison one wonders without knowledge, whereas outside there are facts to be referred to, this reading is indeed commonsensical. 'Sky' seems the right name for the extent overhead and 'tent of blue' to be good for prisoners.

However, the same clause can be read non-restrictively — a use of 'which' usual in careful American English and possible in British English, especially where there is a break such as a comma or, here, the end of a poetic line. The sense would be that in their language prisoners call the tent of blue by the term 'sky'. 'Tent of blue' would be the more original name, and 'sky' would be substituted for it. In this case, Wilde would not assume that figures are secondary ornaments to a conventional language. 'Tent' would be an inventive, catachrestic name providing a temporary handle for the blue extent that is, and must remain, fundamentally nameless, insofar as it is an opening in, pointing to a beyond to, the walls of a language system.[25] Here, prisoners are speakers who accredit the term 'sky' as conventional and do not understand that the name for the space beyond is missing and can only be filled in temporarily by a catachresis. Wilde's long pre-prison training in paradox would argue in favour of this reading.

In the 'Ballad', the primary effect of this move, which relies on a Romantic tradition setting wild metaphor at the origin of language, is to challenge the closure of context. That challenge is evident first in the extension of the class of prisoners to include all for whom English is foremost a conventional language that names presentable things. The 'tent of blue' also breaches the prison context insofar as it is a fresh figure, reminiscent of a time before the walls of law were built, when humans were nomadic and the world was still to be named. Among the corrupt prisoners, one witnesses an innocent infraction before and beyond 'innocence' and 'guilt' as the law defines them.

One consequence of the breakdown of boundaries is the introduction into the poem of a universalizing tendency due to the fact that the poet, convicted by law, has to name what is outside and before its establishment. The lines that state that 'each man kills the thing he loves' can best by understood by reference to this double position. If everyone is guilty of killing what he or she loves, it becomes a matter of determining which are to pay for it by death. The poet has to ask: on what basis ought this one who killed with a knife die on the scaffold, but not this one who killed with kiss, word, look, or sword? He has also to ask about the community: '*all* men kill the thing they love' (l. 649; my emphasis). What is it that a group loves when it sets apart one killer for killing?[26]

The first-person witness of the performative situation is also problematic.[27] We have noted already that the 'Ballad's' 'we' muddles an inclusive and an exclusive first-person plural. But it is also the I's interiority that is affected. Obviously, once a prisoner has been stripped of name and personal effects, put in a uniform and masque, confined to a solitary cell in silence, and made one of a community of property-less outcasts, it will be hard to find a credible witness to an experience. Where the experience is of entombment (ll. 245–46), moreover, in what present and to what moment can the witness swear? No doubt, Wilde has the privilege Baudelaire accorded the poet: 'il peut à sa guise être lui-même et autrui' [he can be himself and someone else, as he chooses].[28] Wilde's speaker acknowledges this imaginative occupation of others' predicaments, for example, when he says:

> And the wild regrets, and the bloody sweats,
> No one knew so well as I:
> For he who lives more lives than one
> More deaths than one must die. (ll. 393–96)

However, the imaginative occupation of others assumes a projection from a stable position. We assume the I visits and is not the spot being visited. The poet-convict lacks that position, as Wilde says in a letter to Robert Ross:

> I used to rely on my personality: now I know that my personality really rested on the fiction of *position*. Having lost position, I find my personality of no avail. [...] I feel very humble, besides feeling very indignant: the former being my intellectual realization of my position, the latter an emotion that is a 'survival' of old conditions.[29]

In theory, a witness can be tested. But Wilde's speaker's utterances are hardly out of the lordly side of his mouth as assertions of personality before they are denied on the side of intellectual awareness. The I of the 'Ballad' is sometimes a vivid personality propped up on the remnants of authority, and other times an emptied fiction of position known to be such. The result is a speaker as unsteady on his feet as his six-line stanzas are uneven in theirs.

This unsteadiness permeates every aspect of the I's testimony. Consider as one example the contradictions in what Wilde says about the poem. In a letter to his editor Leonard Smithers he explains that he refers to executions in general: 'I was not present at the Reading execution, nor do I know anything about it. I am describing a general scene, with general types'.[30] To another correspondent, however, he claims to represent his experience: 'I, of course, feel that the poem is too autobiographical and that *real* experiences are alien things that should never influence one, but it was wrung out of me, a cry of pain, the cry of Marsyas, not the song of Apollo'.[31] Elsewhere, Wilde confesses its divided aim:

> The poem suffers under the difficulty of a divided aim in style. Some is realistic, some romantic: some poetry, some propaganda. I feel it keenly, but as a whole I think the production interesting: that it is interesting from more points of view than one is artistically to be regretted.[32]

Given the contradictions in point of view, our witness might want to plead the insanity defence known as the 'M'Naghten Rules' (1843). This is the post-prison Wilde critics deplore. The old funambulist testing verities on the tightrope of paradox now appears to be falling flat into contradiction.[33]

And yet, from the opening stanzas of the poem we are discussing, this unsteadiness of position is part of the action, an unsteadiness that the readers of the poem have to be alert to as one of the effects on the discourse of the suffering psyche. The speaker provides a description of the accused, his crime, and the prison context.

This description is very precise, and treated with authority by one who appears possessed of considerable knowledge. From the point of view of the facts, however, it is made up out of whole cloth. The speaker represents that the man did not put on his scarlet soldier's coat to commit the murder, but Wooldridge's regiment did not wear scarlet, so the coat he did not put on for the murder — if indeed he made a conscious wardrobe choice — would have been blue.[34] The murder, the speaker says, took place in the bedroom; the jealous husband lay in wait and killed his wife on the street.

What a poem's speaker says has to be believed, and if he says that the sky is really a tent, and that everyone is mistaken in thinking that the man did not consider wearing a scarlet coat on the day he committed a murder in the bedroom, well, those are the facts so far as the poem, with its claim to represent types and its obedience to rules of form, is concerned. This is Wilde's pre-prison posture, familiar from 'The Decay of Lying', among other places. 'The Ballad of Reading Gaol' is not about the particular, referential execution, but about execution in general. When the speaker tells us that the accused man's step 'seemed light and gay', he means to reveal himself as supreme artificer of this typical murderer. Here is an I forcing himself upon us with all the weight of personality.

Yet, as the term 'seemed' also suggests, the speaker may be attesting to a perception. In fact, the artificer is knocked from his perch by hearing a sentence not of his own making: 'a voice behind me whispered low | "That fellow's got to swing"'. What does it mean that the sentence is reported as overheard? Humiliation, for one thing, since it dethrones the speaker as sovereign personality. The sentence interrupts the poet inventing to remind him that he is not the authoring instance.

The voice disrupts too because its source is unknown. Who whispers and what does the voice mean to say? The referential context of Reading Gaol may seem to fix things: one can suppose it to be the voice of one walking behind C.3.3 on the rope of exercising prisoners, either a recent arrival bringing the news of the execution about to take place. But if we want to rely on the referential situation, we must ask: does this prisoner speak into Wilde's good left ear, or into his bad right ear suffering from chronic middle ear disease, compounded in prison by a perforated eardrum and untreated abscess that likely killed him? Does the speaker hear, or just think he hears, a death sentence? Where in the ring did the rumour of an execution start? The circle evokes the game of telephone, or Chinese whispers, where one child whispers a sentence to another until it reaches the last one, who speaks it aloud so as to compare it to the first speaker's sentence. But with this sentence, a reality check is impossible. A voice pursues the I with a sentence that starts and ends who knows where. Here are a few suggestions, not quite pell-mell, as they may have pressed around the I, each one taking the term 'swing' differently, each evoking a different context, speaker and meaning direction.

First, the sentence may be a bit of noise in the I's head, a personal memory that he hears as if pronounced outside, that he may have even said out loud and then heard as it catches up with him from behind. It is a version of what a judge might say, a deformed memory of the sentence to two years of hard labour that Wilde heard pronounced over him in the 'black dock's dreadful pen'. ('Swing', said by a parent to a child in 'you'd better swing to it', is synonymous with 'do something, put one's will behind it'. It bears some of the term's now obsolete meaning of 'labour, toil', *OED*.) Or maybe, since the whisper from behind is reminiscent of a sexual position often adopted in homosexual congress, it is the voice of Wilde's lost lover, Lord Alfred Douglas. It reminds the speaker of what he is in for, for being 'the centre of a circle of extensive corruption among young men of the most hideous kind',[35] for loving a man, for swinging, i.e. loving freely.[36] Or perhaps, while remembering Douglas, the prisoner could not avoid remembering the voice of his father, the pugilistic Marquess of Queensberry, who goaded the writer into a libel trial he could neither avoid nor win, and who was locked in a deadly struggle with his son in which punches were swung and guns went off — a battle in which Wilde felt 'the mere cat's paw'.[37] To swing is 'to strike a blow with a sword, to come together with blows, to deliver a blow at', or 'to flourish, brandish, wave about; to wield (a weapon or instrument)' (*OED*).[38]

Second, the sentence may be sourced in a collective memory. For the nineteenth-century propertied Englishman, 'swing' was synonymous with labour riot. 'To swing' is 'to flail or thresh wheat by hand', and 'Captain Swing' was the fictional name attached to the threatening letters that the agricultural workers of the 1830s 'Swing Riots' in southern England sent out to announce the destruction of the threshing machines that were taking their livelihoods. 'That fellow's got to swing' would express a collective fear of, or urging to, unrest.[39] In a moment we will see that Wilde's 'The Soul of Man under Socialism' gives a basis to this supposition of revolt.

Third, a further source might be found in the literary memories of voices that intervene at crucial moments to advise, warn, or urge. Consider St Augustine. 'To swing' is 'to change direction, to turn, or cause to turn in alternate directions [...] to pivot', and thus 'to repent, to convert, or to cause to do so'. A voice outside his study saying 'tolle, lege' brought Augustine to long-deferred conversion, and this voice that Wilde hears might similarly warn of imminent conversion.[40] Already a brilliant scholar of Greek at Trinity, Wilde would also have known about Socrates, whose demon regularly warned him against misguided speech or courses of action. As Socrates remarks in his *Apology*, his demon was strangely silent on the day that he went before the tribunal that condemned him to death. The English tradition provides other possible demons. Putting things in the ear is the theme of *Hamlet*. The father's ghost tells his son he has been poisoned in the ear, and with those words, pours poison into that of his tormented son. Hamlet wavers as to what and whether the ghost's words command: to retaliate or not to retaliate. To swing is 'to waver, to vacillate, to change from one condition or position to the opposite' (*OED*).

Three literary works closely associated with Decadence feature demons whispering in the ear. Edgar Allan Poe's story of compulsion, 'The Imp of the Perverse', is suggested by 'got to'.[41] The speaker could be getting echoes of a voice like one that might have urged the prisoner Wooldridge to put an end to the torments of jealousy in a kill-or-be-killed, kill-to-be-killed suicide.[42] In Baudelaire's 'Assommons les pauvres!', the poet's demon also urges action. What Baudelaire's speaker heard can be divined from the beating he administers to a beggar. The demon must have whispered (in French): 'got to swing'. 'Swing, archaic: "to scourge, whip, flog, beat (a person); to strike with a weapon or the hand", "to beat (the flesh) from, (the blood) out of"' (OED).[43] In 'Le Démon de l'analogie' by Mallarmé, one of Wilde's favourite French poets, the meaningless sentence 'la Pénultième est morte' [the Penultimate is dead] comes out of nowhere to obsess the poet who can trace one word, pénultième, back to a treatise on English linguistics he is writing, without managing to dispel the phrase's mysterious hold.[44] Wilde's sentence similarly hits a chord he can exorcize only by writing a poem about it.

Fourthly and finally, in keeping with Mallarmé's idea that a sentence without a source calls for a poem, to swing is 'to move along rhythmically', and also, said of a bell, 'to send forth a peal of sound'. 'That fell-low's got to swing' seems to resonate with the speaker's own fall and pendulum swings; it solicits the poet as bearing some secret that pertains to him, one sourced elsewhere than in his intelligence, one whose mystery and appeal he has yet to work out. Wilde rhymes 'swing' with several important terms in the poem, 'thing', 'ring', 'wing' (ll. 211–12, 239–40, 345). Not accidentally, it rhymes with a term absent from the poem but that is the sentence served by every poet: 'sing!'.

I bring to an end this incomplete list of sources and directions of meaning, all of them woven into the poem's 'web of gloom' (l. 327), to draw two obvious conclusions with respect to the witness and the overheard sentence. First, the witness speaking of one fallen low is himself a much-fallen fellow. Neither present to himself nor credible, he is indeed most (in)credible in bearing witness to just that. Second, there are insurmountable difficulties in determining which is the right sentence being served. That is not the case only because, as we have seen, 'swing' is polysemous and the sentence does not say what kind of swinging it anticipates or commands, or to whom it is said, or by whom. The biggest obstacle comes from the fact that it is both a constative about compulsion (that fellow cannot do anything but swing), and a compelling performative (that fellow is hereby ordered to swing).

Trouble is at hand for Mill's idea that the state can promote the general happiness by maintaining a limited death penalty within the prison precincts. The public is to believe that further suffering of the body politic can be deterred by a sharp pang suffered by a single offending member, inflicted with due solemnity. But from the poem's representation, there is every reason to doubt that the machinery is well regulated, the suffering carefully dosed, and the prisoners learning the right lesson. The imagination vacillates between acute terror, set off by sudden signs that remind of the approaching execution, and the dull pain of recognizing over and over the scaffold as their own likely fate. And, since in Wilde's idea the supposedly closed prison in fact takes in the larger context, the assumption that the cruel effects of the execution have been distanced and limited is wrong. Prison is a petri dish where these effects on the community are magnified. As for the whispered sentence that compels and speaks of compulsion, since each prisoner will hear it differently, some may hear it as a personal invitation to the exceptional death of execution. Indeed, compulsion, with its obsessive, persecutory rhythms that tap into a fascination with death, would foster that understanding.

'The Less Punishment, the Less Crime'

A word remains to be said about what model for capital punishment Wilde proposes in the face of the failed performative model. Wilde was not one to arrogate with Shelley the role of legislator for poets. The poem's breaches of context, its operations on voice and unity of speaker, its erasure and multiplying of sources and addresses, imply that it renounces legislative aspirations, for poetry is not a performative genre so much as a means for exploring the excesses and deficiencies of the performative.[45] There is no positive programme recommended.

And yet, to investigate the misfires of the death penalty within the punishment system, the poem has had to lay out a landscape within which they can be defined otherwise than as errors to be corrected by the will. It has given up on a correction system where 'some grow mad, and all grow bad' (l. 569) to consider the morbid psyche instead. The ballad looks ahead to a death penalty limited in keeping with the findings of the new science of psychoanalysis.

The most direct reference to the psyche as the arena where punishment will require redefining comes from Wilde's anarchist essay, 'The Soul of Man Under Socialism' (1891). There, Wilde contemplates the abolishment of private property and the winding up of state sovereignty as means to get rid of much crime and the habit of disobedience as an attitude of one in thrall to authority. Again, it is paradox, with its negation and inversion of the doxa, that lets Wilde state the suspicion that crimes are not misdeeds to be punished but rather the inverse: acts incited by state interdiction and punishment. The stronger the interdiction, the heavier the punishment, the greater the temptation to engage in the forbidden activities. This paradox once conceived, Wilde can then propose the abolishing of authority and property as a means to psychic health. Forgoing acts of sovereignty, the state will administer only, with consequent reduction in crime and punishment:

> With authority, punishment will pass away. This will be a great gain — a gain, in fact, of incalculable value. As one reads history [...] one is absolutely sickened [...] by the punishments that the good have inflicted; *and a community is infinitely more brutalized by the habitual employment of punishment, than it is by the occasional occurrence of crime.* It obviously follows that the more punishment is inflicted the more crime is produced, and most modern legislation has clearly recognised this, and has made it its task to diminish punishment as far as it thinks it can. [...] The less punishment, the less crime. When there is no punishment at all, crime will either cease to exist, or if it occurs, will be treated by physicians as a *very distressing form of dementia, to be cured by care and kindness.*[46]

Crime is an illness requiring medical diagnosis and treatment. The state is not to assert its sovereignty or to inflict suffering in the name of public happiness. Rather, by incremental steps it is to put itself out of the punishment business. In getting rid of private property, it will also get rid of murderous passions like jealousy (Wooldridge's motive). Then, it will send in doctors in lieu of executioners, 'experts who understand brain-disease', to the sick souls who still commit crimes.[47]

By means of the witness with his persecuted and persecuting imagination, the 'Ballad' shows the prisoners in the grip of a compulsion. It allows the hypothesis that the one who has *'got to swing'* has been driven to the scaffold by a perverse masochism that places guilt before the crime, as its psychic motivator, and not after, as its consequence. That is the model Theodor Reik proposes in *The Compulsion to Confess* (1925) following Freud, and Derrida discusses as part of 'the psychoanalytic revolution',[48] which accelerates the progress toward the end of the death penalty, affecting as it does the law in its fundamental principles.[49] We saw that compulsion and persecution were evident in the circularity of the path the prisoners trace, followed by fear as they are, and following it also: 'Horror stalked before each man, | And terror crept behind'. Morbidity is the state of the psyche under punishment as exacerbated by the proximity of the hanging. Varying symptoms develop, starting with the revolt indicated by the voice whispering a sentence where speech is not allowed, and leading on to a host of other psychic troubles, from nightmares, hallucinations, tears, and cries, to superstition and despair. In the final verse of the poem, lines which can be read as expressing acceptance of the death penalty — 'The man had killed the thing he loved | And so he had to die' — can also be read, once one remembers that 'each man kills the thing he loves', as drawing a logical conclusion: the man had to die because he had killed the thing he loved, that is himself. The death penalty then appears as a means the state offers those who will accept no substitutes to accomplish their goal of self-murder.

In the situation of psychic trouble, punishment would seek cure, or at least alleviation, of the worst symptoms. Here Wilde also looks ahead toward the psychoanalytical revolution by his practice, and suggests that he agrees with Reik that confession may answer the psyche's paradoxical needs. For Reik, confession provides a good punishment in the torments of public shame; it also provides the psyche with an acceptable crime, an outlet for the guilt that drives to deeds meant to bring on punishment.[50] The operation of this logic can be seen in what has been said of the performative: in confessing infractions the speaker has also to confess, beyond past misdeeds, the excesses and misfires in the act of confessing. The confessions of the split I can then function as both crime and punishment. Wilde provides a foretaste of the arguments by Reik, recently recalled by Derrida, that limit capital punishment only to those whose sickness has so far progressed that they cannot accept the substitute for self-torture that is confession.

In what we have said so far, the 'Ballad of Reading Gaol' appears as primarily an oral language directed to the ear. But a more radical poetic argument for the abolition of the death penalty emerges that instead involves writing and reading, and is set up in the second crossing of the paths of the condemned man and the prisoners. The first crossing had established a clichéd likeness: all are 'doomed ships' (ll. 164–66), living out the monotonous days. The second crossing gives the prisoners a sign of difference, a slit in the earth, to be read:

> Till once, as we tramped in from work,
> We passed an open grave.
> With yawning mouth the yellow hole
> Gaped for a living thing [...]
> And we knew that ere one dawn grew fair
> Some prisoner had to swing. (ll. 233–40)

The indeterminate qualifiers 'one' and 'some' indicate the self-referential interpretation of the prisoners: the prisoner scheduled to fill the hole is anyone under the clock of a sentence. The likeness can be recognized as allegorical because it is found despite obvious differences, such as the fact that a hole will open for most prisoners into life, while the one for the condemned opens into the grave. The likeness is not sourced in some property assumed essential to humans, or even the roughly similar shapes of door and grave, but the timetable of the sentence, and the fact that it will be executed under conditions the prisoners know but do not control. This likeness is not available to perception and requires reading.[51]

The allegory of the open grave can be read in different ways. In its undecidability, as well as through the thematics of opening and closure, it seems the temporal equivalent of 'the tent of blue | Which prisoners call the sky'. According to one reading, the literalizing one it has in prison, the empty grave awaits the hanged man. Soon no more figurative swinging will be possible, no more vacillation, no more dancing, loving, turning, rebelling, or converting: time for the last, the literal swing of the hanging, toward which all the others have pointed as preparations or substitutes. This swinging prisoner can stand for all, because execution hyperbolizes the deprivation under which all suffer: one who has already lost all the rights and duties of a subject, loses, too, the right to his own death. It is not just that he is compelled to die by an inescapable, mechanical logic. It is also that he has lost the right to live with the moment of his death hidden by the possibility of another substitute. One dies one's own death when one receives one's best-kept secret, unknown even up to the last breath, that it would be the last.[52] This mystery has been taken away by the state, which has given him 'three weeks of life' and decreed the day and moment: 'ere one dawn grows fair'. To die before the day has become fair is to die before the light, but it is also to die the most unjust, unfair of deaths, one that kills the soul by snatching hope away ahead of time, and one that shows the state as barbaric, since it deprives the psyche of the hope that constitutes its interiority. In Wilde's view, execution makes the prisoners despair; taking away hope does not lead to correction but drives them faster to the desperate measures of the incorrigible.

The second reading for the allegory of the open grave is Christian. Wilde's relations with Christianity are not easy to parse, including as they do a lifelong flirtation with Catholicism and a dubious deathbed conversion, along with numerous indices of heterodoxy. Questions of Wilde's beliefs aside, however, the poem makes use of Christ's tomb, with all that it vehicles about resurgent hope and life precisely *because* it is emptied and left open. We saw that the 'tent of blue' was not to be construed as a figure substituted for the conventional name of 'sky', but as an original naming by figure, a stop-gap term temporarily naming a beyond which is susceptible to other baptisms. Similarly, the empty tomb of the executed Christ stands as a signal not of the ineluctable end, but rather of a surprise suspension and thus of resurgent hope, the possible impossibility of ending. The empty grave does not demand a literal body to fill it but has meaning precisely because it is filled with Christ's body only temporarily, on a three-day visit. The open tomb denotes a place of disruption of the legal programme. The yellow hole is a signal that Reading Gaol and the idea of justice it stands for may be under dismantlement.

Wilde's 'Ballad' contributes in several ways to arguments on the death penalty. To begin with, it provides a testimony to the suffering of prisoners, not just on a thematic level, but also through its imitation in form of some of prison's methods. As a musical poem centred on mouth and ear, moreover, it criticizes the ideal model of the performative underlying the Victorian model of capital punishment. Still in its function as oral language, it begins to lay out the situation for penal justice that the psychoanalytic revolution will bring and, diagnozing crime as illness, even proposes confession as substitute for capital punishment. The psyche whispering the secret motives driving verbal acts makes self-witnessing more than a kind of evidence for Wilde. It becomes a possible substitute even for the death penalty by the blows it deals the I and the claims of sovereignty of the state over the space and parts of the performative.

But, finally, it is through allegory and a call to read signs otherwise than as signifiers with determinate meaning that Wilde makes his strongest argument against the death penalty. The psyche lives in not knowing the moment of death, in hoping for a grave left empty, for a sentence that does not end at the prescribed time and in the prescribed way, for a reading that has not been anticipated. This argument against the death penalty comes less from the internal rhymes and obsessive rhythms of the 'Ballad of Reading Gaol' than from its allegories, which point to places where the inevitable literalization will not have occurred to complete a programme, but a new possibility of reading, a new substitute will instead in-complete it. The Christ figure, like the 'tent of blue', is a temporary fix standing for the surprise interruption of the end programmed by the death penalty with its belief in the end of substitution and final solutions. Wilde's stop-gap solutions are wild figures, poetically-principled arguments against the death penalty.

Notes to Chapter 4

1. A recent essay by Tara Burk, ' "A Battleground around the Crime": The Visuality of Execution Ephemera and Its Cultural Significances in Late Seventeenth-Century England', in *Studies in Ephemera: Text and Image in Eighteenth-Century Print*, ed. by Kevin D. Murphy and Sally O'Driscoll (Lewisburg, PA: Bucknell University Press, 2013), pp. 195–218, investigates a Foucaldian struggle in the woodcuts of the broadsides between the state and the people over the representation of execution. Literary influences for the 'Ballad' include Kipling's 'Danny Deever', where a soldier witnesses the public execution of a fellow soldier, and poem IX in Housman's *A Shropshire Lad*, where a singer compares a modern prison hanging to the older, public mode. Wilde's poem is unusual in making the singer a prisoner.

2. W. B. Yeats, *The Oxford Book of Modern Verse, 1892–1935* (Oxford: Clarendon Press, 1936), p. vii.

3. Derrida, *The Death Penalty*. See especially Session 4, *The Death Penalty*, II.

4. Geoffrey Bennington, 'Ex Lex', *Oxford Literary Review*, 35.2 (2013), 143–63.

5. See Jacques Derrida, '"A Self-Unsealing Poetic Text": Poetics and Politics of Witnessing', in *Revenge of the Aesthetic: The Place of Literature in Theory Today*, ed. by Michael Clark (Berkeley: University of California Press, 2000), pp. 180–207 (pp. 188–89). For hanging as spectacle, see Friedland, *Seeing Justice Done*; and, as a didactic theatre of punishment, see Harry Potter, *Hanging in Judgment: Religion and the Death Penalty in England from the Bloody Code to Abolition* (London: SCM Press, 1993).

6. See Derrida, '"A Self-Unsealing Poetic Text"', p. 197.

7. Kant's work quickly made its way to England, with *Die Metaphysik der Sitten* (1797), which discussed the death penalty, translated as early as 1799. For the importance of Kant to English philosophical tradition, see René Wellek, *Immanuel Kant in England, 1793–1838* (Princeton, NJ: Princeton University Press, 1931), pp. v, 242. Wilde, an Irishman who belonged to the University Philosophical Society at Trinity, and an Oxonian who read 'Greats', would have been familiar with the latest philosophical movements of the time.

8. James Gregory, *Victorians Against the Gallows: Capital Punishment and the Abolitionist Movement in Nineteenth-Century Britain* (London: I. B. Taurus, 2012), pp. 4, 185.

9. William Makepeace Thackeray, 'Going to See a Man Hanged', *Fraser's Magazine*, 22 (July–December 1840), 150–58.

10. Charles Dickens, 'Letter', *Daily News*, 16 March 1846.

11. Gregory, *Victorians Against the Gallows*, p. 182.

12. Potter, *Hanging in Judgment*, pp. 82–83.

13. John Stuart Mill, *Public and Parliamentary Speeches, November 1850–November 1868*, ed. by John Robson and Bruce Kinzer (Toronto: University of Toronto Press, 1988), p. 270. Subsequent references are in the main text.

14. That was Home Secretary Garthorne Hardy's claim when the Capital Punishment Within Prisons Bill was first read in 1867. See John Hostettler, *A History of Criminal Justice in England and Wales* (Hook: Waterside Press, 2009), p. 188.

15. See the Capital Punishment Amendment Act 1868, <http://www.legislation.gov.uk/ukpga/Vict/31-32/24/section/7> [accessed 17 August 2017]. Friedland suggests that 'drawing' the condemned attached to a hurdle through the centre of town functioned to lengthen and 'spectacularize' death (*Seeing Justice Done*, pp. 57–58). It would also have the same function as ringing a bell: namely, that of announcing a hanging.

16. Readers are referred to Wilde's letters to the *Daily Chronicle* for a description of these two systems as he experienced them. For an earlier description, see Henry Mayhew's *The Criminal Prisons of London and Scenes of Prison Life* (London: Griffin, Bohn, 1862), pp. 101–06. See also Richard W. Ireland, *'A Want of Order and Good Discipline': Rules, Discretion, and the Victorian Prison* (Cardiff: University of Wales Press, 2007), p. 106.

17. See *The Complete Works of Oscar Wilde*, ed. by Russell Jackson and Ian Small, 6 vols (Oxford: Oxford University Press, 2000–07), IV, 197.

18. *The Complete Letters of Oscar Wilde*, ed. by Merlin Holland & Rupert Hart-Davies (New York: Henry Holt, 2000), p. 852.

19. For Wilde's views, including his attack on the policies of prison administrator Sir Edmund du Cane, see *The Complete Letters of Oscar Wilde*, ed. by Holland & Hart-Davies, pp. 847–55, 1045–49. See also Du Cane's own work, *The Punishment and Prevention of Crime* (London: Macmillan, 1885), p. 156–57.

20. Oscar Wilde, 'The Ballad of Reading Gaol', in *The Complete Works of Oscar Wilde*, ed. by Jackson & Small, I, 195–216. All subsequent references to this work are in the main text.

21. For a description of death row conditions at the model Pentonville prison, see John Laurence Pritchard, *A History of Capital Punishment* (New York: The Citadel Press, 1960), pp. 142–45.

22. J. L. Austin, *How to Do Things with Words* (Cambridge, MA: Harvard University Press, 1962), pp. 8–9.

23. For the non-pertinence of the legal distinction between presumed innocence and guilt to the psyche of a child, see *The Complete Letters of Oscar Wilde*, ed. by Holland & Hart-Davies, p. 849.

24. See Mill, *Public and Parliamentary Speeches*, p. 271.
25. A catachresis is an abusive figure in which a thing is named by metaphor. In 'normal' metaphor, there is an exchange of already awarded names between two things. For Aristotle's exemplary analogy on the question of metaphor, see Derrida's 'White Mythology', in *Margins*, trans. by Alan Bass (Chicago, IL: University of Chicago Press, 1982), p. 242. For Paul de Man's discussion of the origin of language in catachresis in Rousseau, see 'Metaphor', in *Allegories of Reading: Figural Language in Rousseau, Nietzsche, Rilke and Proust* (New Haven, CT: Yale University Press, 1979), pp. 135–59.
26. In defining killing as an act of love, Wilde also proposes state killing as interested, even desirous. The community has to elect one sacrificial lamb, the Isaac it loves best, to construct its walls.
27. For a discussion of Wilde's approach to the performative in literature, as well as its development over time, see Heather Marcovitch, *The Art of the Pose: Oscar Wilde's Performance Theory* (Bern: Peter Lang, 2010), p. 211.
28. Charles Baudelaire, *Le Spleen de Paris (Petits poèmes en prose)*, in *Œuvres complètes*, ed. by Claude Pichois, 2 vols (Paris: Gallimard, 1975–76), I, 291.
29. *The Complete Letters of Oscar Wilde*, ed. by Holland & Hart-Davies, p. 1138.
30. Ibid., pp. 982–83.
31. Ibid., p. 1025.
32. Ibid., p. 956.
33. Oscar Wilde, *The Picture of Dorian Gray*, in *The Complete Works of Oscar Wilde*, ed. by Jackson & Small, III, 202.
34. When taxed with the fault, 'Wilde replied that it would have been impossible to open his poem "He did not wear his azure coat | For blood and wine are blue"'. Hesketh Pearson, *The Life of Oscar Wilde* (London: Methuen and Co., 1954), p. 349.
35. Judge Wills, at the sentencing, as reported in the *Star*, 27 May 1895. Cited in Michael Foldy, *The Trials of Oscar Wilde: Deviance, Morality and Late-Victorian Society* (New Haven, CT: Yale University Press, 1997), p. 47.
36. This use of 'swing' is anachronistic. The first uses recorded by the *OED* for 'swing' as 'to engage in [promiscuous] sexual partners', and, for 'swing both ways', as 'to enjoy both heterosexual and homosexual relations', date to the sexual revolution of the 1960s and 70s. However, some earlier examples connote pleasure with erotic overtones: see William Cowper's poem 'Epitaph on a Hare' of 1793, or *Harper's Magazine* (1883), which describes swinging as a pleasure of dancing. The rigadoons, arabesques, and pirouettes of the phantom masque in the 'Ballad' can be read as spinoffs of 'swing' in this sense (ll. 290–305).
37. Oscar Wilde, *Epistola: In Carcere et Vinculis*, in *The Complete Works of Oscar Wilde*, ed. by Jackson & Small, II, 89.
38. *Epistola: In Carcere et Vinculis* is the crucial text here, although the 'Ballad' has evidence of a father-son struggle in the Christ story and evokes parricide (l. 366).
39. The law that 'straws the wheat and saves the chaff' (l. 545) remembers the context of threshing and the swing as flail. The cries during the execution are menacing, as the keeping close of the prisoners suggests (ll. 381–84, 397–405).
40. The prisoners fall to their knees, ll. 275–78.
41. For the claim that Wilde met Poe through Baudelaire, see Brynjar Björnsson, 'Oscar Wilde and Edgar Allan Poe: Comparison of *The Picture of Dorian Gray* and "William Wilson"' (unpublished essay, University of Iceland, 1987), <https://skemman.is/handle/1946/10612> [accessed 18 August 2017].
42. Wilde has been reproached for paying little attention to Wooldridge's victim; see Karen Alkalay-Gut, 'The Thing He Loves: Murder as Aesthetic Experience in *The Ballad of Reading Gaol*', *Victorian Poetry*, 35.3 (Fall 1997), 349–66. It is worth noting that the poet leaves the condemned man unvisited too, as part of a strategy of focusing testimony on the psychological effects of the experience.
43. 'Swing' as 'blow' surfaces in the smiting of air by the prison clock (l. 380), as metonym for 'slaying' (l. 361), and in the scourged and flogged prisoners (l. 567).
44. Stéphane Mallarmé, 'Le Démon de l'analogie', in *Œuvres complètes*, ed. by Bertrand Marchal, 2

vols (Paris: Gallimard, 1998–2003), I, 416–17; *Divagations*, trans. by Barbara Johnson (Cambridge, MA: Harvard University Press, 2009), pp. 17–18.

45. Andrzej Warminski, 'As the Poets Do It...', in *Material Events: Paul de Man and the Afterlife of Theory* (Minneapolis: University of Minnesota Press, 2001), pp. 3–31.

46. Oscar Wilde, 'The Soul of Man Under Socialism', in *The Complete Works of Oscar Wilde*, ed. by Jackson & Small, IV, 295. The first emphasis is Wilde's, the second is mine.

47. *The Complete Letters of Oscar Wilde*, ed. by Holland & Hart-Davies, p. 854.

48. Derrida, *The Death Penalty*, II, 185.

49. On confession as accelerating the end of the death penalty see *The Death Penalty*, II, Fifth Session, pp. 127–33; on confession, see also pp. 227–28, 264.

50. Derrida, *The Death Penalty*, II, 182.

51. The next verse drives home the resemblance between cell and crypt: 'each man trembled as he crept | Into his numbered tomb' (ll. 245–46).

52. See Derrida on the finitude of death as paradoxically establishing a relation of undecidability to death that capital punishment takes away, *The Death Penalty*, I, 256–57.

CHAPTER 5

❖

Merging Sovereignty and Meaning in Capital Punishment: Franz Kafka's *Der Proceß* and Bertolt Brecht's *Die Maßnahme*

David Pan

Historically, a key justification for capital punishment has been that it is necessary for the survival of a state, indicating that capital punishment is linked to state sovereignty itself. Such a justification implies that capital punishment may not be merely one particular aspect of a legal system, but rather a core around which an entire legal and political order is built. This reasoning has continued into the present day, and has been used to justify prominent executions such as those of Alfred Rosenberg and other high-ranking Nazis at the end of World War II, or that of Saddam Hussein at the end of the Second Iraq War. This argument about the link between capital punishment and sovereignty leads to its corollary, advanced by Friedrich Nietzsche, who states that such punishment is only important when the state is weak; when a state increases in power, morality becomes internalized into a guilty conscience and the state is able to dispense with death sentences.[1] The examples of Rosenberg and Hussein buttress this argument: both of those executions were partly justified as political moves, used to make a return to a previous regime more unlikely. The execution of the monarch was similarly important for the French Revolution. Such reasoning indicates, though, that the issues of capital punishment and of sovereignty are not purely issues of power, but also of representation. The execution is not just a punishment, but a performance of a narrative about what the state stands against, as well as an attempt to eliminate an alternative narrative of the state.

Sovereignty, then, is not just an issue of power, but also of meaning, and the twentieth-century treatments of capital punishment by Franz Kafka in *Der Proceß* [The Trial] (1925) and Bertolt Brecht in *Die Maßnahme* [The Measures Taken] (1930) both emphasize this connection, depicting capital punishment as the culmination of the individual subject's attempts to establish meaning in the world. Their accounts are thus similar in the way in which they intervened in the particular debates on the relationship between law and sovereignty of the early twentieth century, debates in which the importance of meaning for justice and sovereignty was in dispute. Though both texts end with executions, there is no sense in which they call into question the legitimacy of capital punishment. This is because both texts are constructed as trial proceedings that culminate with both protagonists, Joseph K. in *The Trial* and the Young Comrade in *The Measures Taken,* themselves agreeing to their own executions. If, in the beginning, the protagonists are confused by their condemnation and resist their execution, they both gradually begin to see its meaning and importance. By detailing this process, and by depicting the death sentence as integral to the individual's and the state's constructions of meaning, Kafka's and Brecht's texts offer explanations for the persistence of capital punishment.

Both Joseph K.'s and the Young Comrade's acceptance of their executions coincides with the construction of individual meaning. The texts progress towards a situation in which the final execution can make sense to the protagonist as a kind of self-fulfilment. Because the trials of both texts begin with a kind of mystery about the causes of guilt, but end so definitively with an acceptance of death, both texts function as legitimations for those executions. Self-fulfilment in death occurs because both protagonists come to understand the execution as a kind of sacrifice, in which their own lives can only gain meaning through their subordination of their lives to some outside purpose. Such a subordination of the individual is the movement that is displayed in the moment of execution, and, further, the moment of the sacrifice of the individual is the point at which meaning is established for all. These two texts are similar, then, in the way that they treat capital punishment as part of a representational staging of meaning. Not only does capital punishment need such a meaning in order to become legitimate, but, in these texts, meaning itself requires capital punishment in order to construct itself.

However, the way in which execution leads to meaning indicates a divergence in the functioning of the two texts, a divergence that also provides an insight into the different ways in which Kafka and Brecht relate to the situation of law and justice in early twentieth-century Europe. Both texts are products of a context in which the foundations of law in a transcendent authority had been undermined, leaving no clear replacement for such authority. But the trial process of Kafka's novel never gains legitimacy as a set of public proceedings. Rather, K.'s self-fulfilment remains on a private level, and, in fact, it disappears as soon as it is established, in an execution that remains a secret, private event without an audience. By contrast, *The Measures Taken* consists precisely of the theatrical staging of the execution as a public event. The execution itself takes place secretly in an abandoned quarry while the communist Agitators are on the run, but the play does not depict these events directly. Rather, the play stages a play within the play, in which the surviving Agitators perform the events in China before the chorus of judges. We, as the audience of *The Measures Taken,* are, in fact, witnessing not simply the execution, but also the way in which the subsequent performance of the execution becomes itself integral to a process of legal and political legitimation. To the extent that the chorus of judges publicly affirms the legitimacy of the execution after seeing the performance, Brecht's play establishes in Communism a new political basis for meaning that is simultaneously a new basis for sovereignty. Taken together, Kafka's and Brecht's texts lay out both a private and a public explanation for the enduring existence of capital punishment. On the one hand, *The Trial* indicates that the private construction of meaning requires some larger context to which the individual might be subordinated, even to the point of death. *The Measures Taken* extends this idea by suggesting that such a private meaning cannot be maintained individually, but must be publicly affirmed in order to maintain its significance for the individual. This public affirmation establishes both a vision for the basis of sovereignty and a context for individual meaning.

Insofar as these two texts link the question of capital punishment with sovereignty, they were reactions to the twentieth-century European crisis of meaning. This crisis arose in legal theory with the attempt to use reason to replace religious justifications for the authority of a legal system. One of the most prominent legal thinkers to tackle this problem was Hans Kelsen, who attempted to imagine a legal system that refuses all substantive notions of justice. Instead, his system remains within a framework that only recognizes the positive functioning of law as a pure mechanism without meaning. But, if Kelsen's work lays out the context for understanding Kafka's and Brecht's approaches to capital punishment, both texts ultimately move towards a conception that requires a new metaphysical grounding of law. As Paul Alberts points out, Kelsen's mode of thinking was probably familiar to Kafka. They were both German Jews born in Prague, Kelsen just two years before Kafka, and they both went on to study law. Kelsen began publishing his ideas on law in 1911, in his *Hauptprobleme der Staatsrechtslehre,* just at the time when Kafka was beginning his own career as both a lawyer and a writer.[2] Even if there was no direct connection between the two, the key point is that Kafka's studies and work as a lawyer indicate that he was confronting the same issue of the metaphysical status of law as Kelsen.[3]

But, as opposed to Kelsen's attempt to construct a law without metaphysics, *The Trial* depicts the general problems that arise when law functions as a mechanism that has no clear connection to any overarching metaphysical meaning that could be the basis of justice. In fact, this absence of substantive meaning actually prevents K. from arriving at justice. At the same time, the absence of meaning brings with it both a deterioration of sovereign authority and an erosion of values — to the point where desire and self-interest become the only motivating factors for action in the world of the novel. The only way out of this desperate world without values is for K. to accept a subordination of his own self-interest to some higher value, by affirming his own guilt in previously denying any mode of sacrifice. However, the only way in which he can credibly affirm this guilt is by accepting his execution as the kind of sacrifice that he previously refused to make. The dismal character of K.'s execution, in spite of his self-transformation into a person who accepts the validity of his execution, stems from the private nature of this transformation. *The Measures Taken* stages a similar transformation in the self-understanding of its protagonist, who also embraces capital punishment, but, by contrast, it does so in a way that leads, through the public enactment of the execution, to a new mode of sovereign authority that can serve as the public basis for law and justice. If *The Trial* focuses on the individual's struggle for meaning in sacrifice, *The Measures Taken* affirms a new metaphysical basis for order that is grounded in Communism. In both texts, though, the issue of capital punishment brings Kafka and Brecht to a view of justice that affirms both the need for sovereign authority and the dependence of law on the authority of an overarching metaphysical framework.

The Metaphysical Crisis of Law as Context for Kafka's and Brecht's Depictions of Capital Punishment

In an earlier era, the legitimacy of capital punishment depended on a higher authority, ultimately God, who could justify an execution as an act that goes beyond murder.[4] By the twentieth century, the idea of a divine source of legitimacy for laws had declined, to the point where the jurist Hans Kelsen could reject all theories of law based on absolute norms. He carefully excludes any recourse to absolute authorities such as God or natural law as a justification for law because they do not have any rational justification.[5] Since the absolute value of a particular order cannot be determined rationally, Kelsen excludes this question of the underlying order for law from the discussion of law itself. For Kelsen, transcendent authorities such as God and natural law can only be considered as ideologies rather than truths. Consequently, they can no longer provide a consistent point of reference for a legal system. Rather than looking beyond laws to the ethical or political considerations that might justify the laws, Kelsen focuses on the functioning of laws as a closed system.[6]

The difficulty then becomes the proper justification for capital punishment, which cannot be left up to any arbitrary act of will, but must, in fact, be properly justified as legitimate beyond an individual wilful act. Kelsen first approaches this problem by pointing to the way in which a death sentence is no different from a political assassination, when one considers the facts of the situation.[7] The process of condemning to death can have the 'subjective' appearance of law, but if the process is not integrated into a system of law, then it is not 'objective' and therefore only a false law. But the fact of being integrated into a system of law depends upon there being a context outside of the law that would, in turn, create the integration into a system, which can only occur if the process is linked to a norm that provides meaning to the act.[8] According to Kelsen, the norm itself attains its validity through the authorization of a previous legal act, which thereby functions as the higher norm that authorizes the subsequent norm.[9] This hierarchy of norms establishes the entire system on the basis of the procedural connections between norms. Rather than relying upon a transcendent absolute authority or a pre-existing sense of justice, Kelsen sees this system of norms as the true creator of law. At the same time, however, the norm is also a construct that ultimately depends upon an initially presupposed basic norm, one that dictates that coercion is justified by the historical existence of a founding constitution.[10] That basic norm is the presupposition of the validity of an initial act of will that founds the state. Though he emphasizes the importance of norms, therefore, the hierarchy of norms that he constructs (without any transcendent authority) actually ends up establishing a founding human will as the ultimate authority and source of law, without any regard for the legitimacy of this will.

Kelsen's theory of norms consequently sets up norms as independent of the typical moral schemas by which humans interpret actions. Because the law in Kelsen's theory has a purely formal character, the content of the law is of no importance. His idea of meaning must reduce itself to a mechanistic concept that leaves out any substantive meaning or any sense of understanding, and neither the judge nor the accused need have any understanding of the law for it to have legitimacy.[11] Indeed, Kelsen insists that any basis of law is as legitimate as any other, so long as it has been codified in a set of positive laws. No social reality can be said, based on its content, to be incompatible with this legal category, and he grants equal legal status to the Soviet Union, fascist Italy, and democratic-capitalist France. He sees this equivalence as a consequence of the purity of law as a rational discipline that does not involve itself in substantive issues, which would lead into ideology rather than truth.[12] Kelsen attains a kind of objective mechanism of analysis, but only at the cost of giving up on any substantive meaning, as well as on any basis for distinguishing between morally valid and invalid laws.

Law Without Meaning in Kafka's *The Trial*

Kelsen's basic attempt to separate law from such metaphysical questions as the meaning of justice is founded on the idea that the ultimate meaning of justice is impossible to arrive at scientifically or rationally.[13] The modernity of Kelsen's project coincides here with the modernity of Kafka's text. In both cases, they are working with a system of law that must come to terms with an inability to accept any underlying metaphysical conception of justice. If Kelsen's solution to this dilemma is to move toward a pure theory of law that no longer concerns itself with the question of justice itself, Kafka's *Trial* translates this type of law (one without regard to justice) into a fictional reality. If Kafka is, in this sense, following Kelsen's lead, it is not because he particularly agrees with Kelsen's arguments, but because of a common starting point: the decline of metaphysical systems that could ground law in an absolute truth and morality. The aesthetic effect of Kafka's move stems from his recognition of the spiritual situation of law once a metaphysical conception of justice has been delegitimized. As Alberts describes, *The Trial* can be read as a parodic realization of Kelsen's positivist vision of law as a mere mechanism.[14]

However, the novel is not a direct parody, since Kafka is not so much reacting to Kelsen's vision as depicting a modern situation of law, in which a decline of metaphysical authorities coincides with the continuation of those legal processes already predicated on them. As a number of commentators have outlined, many of the seemingly irrational characteristics of the trial process in Kafka's text — particularly its different stages, including a pre-ascertainment (*Vorerhebung*) and a pre-investigation (*Voruntersuchung*) which precede a primary investigation (*Hauptuntersuchung*), as well as the secret nature of the preliminary investigations — were, in fact, part of the Austro-Hungarian legal practices of the time. These were, however, established over a century earlier and retained many remnants of the Catholic-based Inquisition — thus grounded in divine law — in its ability to begin investigative proceedings based merely on an accusation.[15] Theodore Ziolkowski contends that Kafka's novel parodies Austro-Hungarian practices in order to critique them, and to implicitly support the shift to the more modern German legal practices that did not link law so directly to morality, punishing deeds rather than evil intent.[16] Yet, it may be that the key task of the novel is not to critique traditional practices, but to address the difficult question of sovereignty in the Austro-Hungarian Empire, in which the Catholic Church still competed with the Empire for jurisdiction over legal matters. Arnold Heidsieck documents how Heinrich Singer, one of Kafka's primary teachers in law school, focused much of his research on the competing claims of sovereignty over legal matters by the Empire and the Church from the eighteenth into the twentieth century. Not only does the existence of such competing metaphysical frameworks for law provide a model for the kind of parallel legality of the court in the novel, but also the lack of clear lines of authority and clear procedures leads the protagonist into a fundamental moral questioning of his own life.[17]

The Trial's depiction of the court — and Joseph K.'s reaction to it — highlights the frustration of the expectation that legal proceedings must be grounded in a context of substantive meaning. If every legal decision requires the possible application of a norm, and therefore an interpretation of that norm's meaning, the question is whether it would also require an interpretation of the meaning of the metaphysical authority that is embodied in the norm. If so, every judgment would also imply an interpretation of the metaphysical basis of the sovereignty that the laws display in their power to condemn. Though Kelsen tries to sever the link between law and such a metaphysical basis, The Trial is driven by a refusal to accept such a severing even as it is occurring, indicating that if there is an implicit critique in the novel, it would be of the kind of modernizing procedures advocated by Kelsen. In insulating the legal system from any consideration of a metaphysical basis, Kelsen turns it into a mechanism that simply carries out the commands of the legislator, even as it denies such a structure by referring to a basic norm rather than a legislative command. The result is that there is no longer any difference between justice and human will. David Dyzenhaus points out that if one stays within Kelsen's positivist framework, the result is arbitrary decisions by administrative officials,[18] and it is this mode of arbitrary legal decision-making that seems to be dominant in The Trial.

The Trial's structure is shaped by this problem of a 'headless' legal system. Rather than having any transcendent authority, justice in The Trial is indistinguishable from human will, and there is no clear independent basis for sovereignty. To the extent that sovereignty requires a transcendental power and authority of the commonwealth, this detachment of justice from sovereignty in The Trial becomes the corollary to a crisis of meaning. Both meaning and sovereignty become empty placeholders in a situation in which the protagonist's primary quest seems to be to attain them. On the one hand, if Kelsen imagines a system of justice that does not question the basis of norms, the functioning of the court realizes such a system in the guise of an autonomous process without any overall meaning. On the other hand, K. is thrown upon himself in the attempt to find justice, and capital punishment is no longer linked to the sovereignty of the commonwealth, but becomes an individual sacrifice without a communal meaning.

The Decline of Meaning and the Breakdown of Sovereignty

There is a long tradition of commentators who have placed the problem of meaning at the centre of Kafka's work. Not only do his protagonists seem to be engaged in a vain search for meaning, Kafka's texts themselves are constructed in such a way as to deny readers the experience of unified meaning, trapping them within what Theodor Adorno calls 'a parabolic system the key to which has been stolen'.[19] Yet, the particular structure of meaninglessness that incites a search for meaning is not the point of *The Trial*, but rather a symptom, and not just of a decline of metaphysical authority. For the crisis of meaning is linked to a crisis of sovereignty. *The Trial* demonstrates how meaning and sovereignty are intertwined, each unable to exist without the other. The breakdown in the relationship between law and meaning is perhaps the consequence of the detachment of law from sovereignty, leading, then, to the social and spiritual isolation of the individuals caught up in this system.

The clearest indication of a problematic breakdown of sovereignty is the deterioration of authority figures. If a key aspect of any legal system is the way in which its authority can ultimately be traced back to a sovereign authority, such as a monarch, or the 'people' in a republic, the fundamental defining characteristic of the court in *The Trial* is the absence of such a final legitimating authority. The mysteriousness of the different levels of authority of the court is not just an obfuscation of the real power behind the proceedings but turns out to be a consequence of the absence of any overarching sovereignty. There is no point in the novel where we are finally initiated into the ultimate source of power in the court, and this absence defines the novel's peculiar dynamic.

This absence of sovereign authority correlates with Joseph K.'s general resistance to authority in *The Trial*. K. resembles, in both his personal traits and social position, Georg Bendemann from 'The Judgement'. Both begin in their respective narratives as young men who have, through their own efforts, attained success in their careers. Unencumbered by familial or political constraints, they oversee their affairs as educated individuals, rather than as members of an existing group. Both embody the hope of a modern bureaucracy that such self-made individuals could form the basis of an objective, neutral, and well-functioning institution that would be free of the irrational prejudices, rivalries, and favouritism of traditional cultures. Like Kelsen's system of laws, the objective basis lies purely in the system of relationships that exist without any clearly articulated substantive meaning, but also without apparent figures of authority. If Georg Bendemann's ultimate downfall is linked to his return to family ties, with his intention to marry after having previously rejected familial authority, Joseph K.'s family ties are minimal throughout.[20] He seems to have freed himself from these links to community life, and this lack of cultural roots ultimately supports his tendency to reject almost all forms of higher authority that he encounters.

The text repeatedly points out K.'s neglect of family ties. His most prominent relative is the uncle who served as his guardian and whom K. refers to as 'das Gespenst vom Land' [the ghost from the country], a ghost of his past whom he only sees occasionally and unwillingly.[21] He also forgets his niece's birthday, keeps her waiting in vain to see him when she comes to visit him at the bank, and finally also decides that it is pointless to go and visit her (pp. 96–98). K. then rejects his uncle's assistance when he walks out on the lawyer Huld and the chief clerk in order to be with Leni. He does so as soon as he feels slighted by feeling that they do not properly acknowledge him, noting he 'diente den alten Herren nur als Zuhörer' ['served merely as an audience to the old gentlemen'] (p. 110; 106). This aggravation with being subordinated to the older and more experienced men around him stems from K.'s general difficulty with recognizing authority figures. While the main chapters do not mention his parents at all, the fragmentary chapters link his poor behaviour in the face of authority directly to his weak relationship to his parents. We find, as an explanation for his reluctance to accept the advice of the bank president, that K. never had the benefit of his father's guidance, because he died when he was young, and that he had always rejected the tenderness of his mother, whom he has not seen in at least two years (p. 260).

Such rejection of authority, even at the cost of missing an opportunity for assistance in his trial, hampers K.'s dealings both with the court and colleagues at his bank. Not only is he outraged by receiving advice from the guard Willem at his arrest, which he treats as 'Schulmäßige Lehren [...] von einem vielleicht jüngern Menschen' ['lessons in manners by a man probably younger than himself'] (p. 21; 12), he also refuses to accept the authority of the court at the first inquiry, without even having paused to hear anything from the examining magistrate (pp. 51, 56). While this attitude can be read as a form of justified rebellion against an unjust system, in K.'s case the lack of respect for authority is linked to an excessive focus on his own self-interest; we can further see his self-interest in his own description of his plan to finally visit his mother, not for her sake but his own (pp. 272–74).

More significantly for the structure of the novel, K.'s self-interested rejection of authority reproduces the dominant modes of interaction of the court, in which authority is not maintained through an appeal to principles, but rather through the abuse of power in an administrative hierarchy. *The Trial* offers a perspective on the logic of bureaucratic institutions by setting up K., not in a family business like Georg Bendemann, but as a bank executive. He thus finds himself at the middle levels of a hierarchy that closely resembles the kind of bureaucracy embodied by the court that has accused him. His dual position both as a middle-ranking executive within a bank bureaucracy and as the accused object of an administration within the court serves to demonstrate that the kinds of irrationalities that he complains of within the court are in fact also a part of his daily practice at the bank. Like the 'höhere Beamten der untern Grade' ['higher officials of subordinate rank']

(p. 122, 117) who might be able to help him and to whom he seeks in vain to gain access at the court, Joseph K. demonstrates a high-handed, even predatory, attitude towards those over whom he has some power, such as his landlady, Frau Grubach, whom he castigates for suspecting his feelings about Frau Bürstner (pp. 31–32, 246–48), Frau Bürstner herself, whom he sexually assaults with his kiss 'wie ein durstiges Tier' ['like some thirsty animal'] (p. 48; 29),[22] and the bank's clients, whom he leaves waiting in vain for his attention (pp. 144–45). Moreover, his interactions with other bank employees already follow the same rules of power that he discovers later at the court. On the one hand, he treats lower-level employees such as Rabensteiner, Kullich, and Kaminer with an almost sadistic disdain, requiring them to go and retrieve his hat when he is ready to leave his apartment (p. 24), nearly ridiculing Kaminer's facial deformation (pp. 24–25), and tearing up a letter that Kullich has prepared for him (p. 274). On the other hand, K. uses his relationships to his peers and superiors at the bank as part of a game of power and influence. He is proud of his development of a personal relationship with the bank president through car trips and dinner parties (p. 26) and immediately appreciates that the assistant manager must humble himself in inviting K. to his yacht party (p. 42).

This same quickness to change his behaviour according to his role in a hierarchy occurs within the court system when his own status as accused turns into accuser; this happens at the point where the guards about whom he complains during the initial court inquiry end up being punished by the flogger before his very eyes on the basis of his accusations (p. 87).[23] Indeed, as Graham Fallowes demonstrates, the entire language of the court's proceedings functions without any orientation toward truth and meaning but purely as an expression of power.[24] Just as Kelsen describes law as a system of action and punishment without regard to the addressees of law, the court's proceedings are impervious to K.'s attempts at understanding and interpretation, functioning purely as a power mechanism to control his behaviour. The novel thus enacts the kind of separation of meaning from power that Kelsen's theory suggests.

The incident with the flogger, in addition to demonstrating how the roles of people in the court bureaucracy become determining for their behaviour and possibilities, provides a first indication of the only alternative the novel offers to the power dynamics of the court. After failing to bribe the flogger not to carry out the punishment, K. abandons the guards Franz and Willem to their fate once two bank assistants are attracted by Franz's cries of pain. Feeling guilty about abandoning the guards, K. insists that it was not his fault and justifies this view by noting:

> Aber in dem Augenblick, wo Franz zu schreien angefangen hatte, war natürlich alles zuende. K. konnte nicht zulassen, daß die Diener und vielleicht noch alle möglichen Leute kämen und ihn in Unterhandlungen mit der Gesellschaft in der Rumpelkammer überraschten. Diese Aufopferung konnte wirklich niemand von K. verlangen. Wenn er das zu tun beabsichtigt hätte, so wäre es ja fast einfacher gewesen, K. hätte sich selbst ausgezogen und dem Prügler als Ersatz für die Wächter angeboten.

> [But at the moment when Franz began to shriek, any intervention became impossible. K. could not afford to let the dispatch clerks and possibly all sorts

of other people arrive and surprise him in a scene with these creatures in the lumber-room. No one could really demand such a sacrifice from him. If a sacrifice had been needed, it would almost have been simpler to take off his own clothes and offer himself to the Whipper as a substitute for the warders.] (p. 92; 88)

While he is upset that he has allowed the guards to be flogged, K. nevertheless points out that he was in no way willing to risk his position at the bank in order to save the guards. In equating such a loss of status to the idea of allowing himself to be flogged instead of the guards, K. indicates the fragility of his temporary role as accuser, which might immediately switch into the role of accused victim once his position at the bank is threatened. Moreover, in immediately rejecting such an act of sacrifice, K. points to the behaviour that is excluded by the entire bureaucratic apparatus. Sacrifice does not belong to the range of actions within this institutional context because sacrifice would involve the kind of value judgment and personal commitment that is prevented by a bureaucratic system divorced from an overarching meaning.

Rather than a personal sense of responsibility, which at no point appears as a motive for action either at the bank or at the court, self-interest dominates K.'s behaviour and decision-making. Consequently, he generally does not consider the trial to be an issue of values or of guilt but only of a kind of business project:

> Der Proceß war nichts anderes, als ein großes Geschäft, wie er es schon oft mit Vorteil für die Bank abgeschlossen hatte, ein Geschäft, innerhalb dessen, wie dies die Regel war, verschiedene Gefahren lauerten, die eben abgewehrt werden mußten. Zu diesem Zwecke durfte man allerdings nicht mit Gedanken an irgendeine Schuld spielen, sondern den Gedanken an den eigenen Vorteil möglichst festhalten.

> [This legal action was nothing more than a business deal such as he had often concluded to the advantage of the Bank, a deal within which, as always happened, lurked various dangers which must simply be obviated. The right tactics were to avoid letting one's thoughts stray to one's own possible shortcomings, and to cling as firmly as one could to the thought of one's advantage.] (p. 132; 127)

His own personal advantage becomes the focus of his attention, and, in thinking through his strategy for his trial, K. never considers the possibility of his own guilt until the very end. Though he feels compelled to recall 'das ganze Leben in den kleinsten Handlungen und Ereignissen' ['the whole of one's life down to the smallest actions and accidents'] (p. 134; 128) in order to prepare his brief for the court, he does not engage in any form of self-reflection at this point. Instead, he reduces the whole process to the same type of business activity that he carries out at the bank and in which self-interest is the only consideration.

Similarly, in his relations with women, K. is guided purely by desire and not by any sense of commitment that would also entail sacrifice or any need to consider values. His assault on Fräulein Bürstner is not only crude in its immediate display of animal-like desire, but K. also remains completely oblivious to its moral implications. Later, as Leni tries to become his lover, she asks K. about his current lover, Elsa, whom K. at first denies. When he finally shows Leni a photograph of her, Leni asks 'Würde sie sich aber für Sie opfern können?' ['Would she be capable of sacrificing herself for you?'] (p. 115; 109). K. responds by indicating that she would not make any sacrifices for him and that he had never demanded such a thing (p. 115). He reduces his relationships with women to a logic of pure desire without commitment, mirroring again the way personal relationships develop at the court, for example in the treatment of the washerwoman by both the student and the examining magistrate (pp. 61, 69–70).

In *The Trial*, the imperatives of objectivity and neutrality, in leading away from ideological commitment and sacrifice, result in a system of justice that no longer seems connected to a substantive law but is dominated by fear and desire. In this sense, both K.'s actions and the court's mechanisms present examples of the functioning of the unified system that would exist if one could really cut off all legal judgments from an overarching moral and theological context. If such a context is indeed an external imposition on the pure functioning of a legal system, the heterogeneity of this context also links law to a meaning that would go beyond the dynamics of self-interest and desire. As Gilles Deleuze and Félix Guattari have outlined, the functioning of the court, but also K.'s actions, conform to a logic of pure desire and will, in which there is a univocal adherence to self-interest and desire, without the heterogeneous intervention of any kind of moral authority that would limit this logic of desire.[25]

Understood in this way, Kafka's depiction of the court is not a general critique of bureaucracy nor of totalitarian systems, but rather a demonstration of the way a bureaucracy degenerates into a system of self-interest when a context of sovereignty recedes.[26] For, as Richard Posner emphasizes, the key characteristic that separates the court of *The Trial* from totalitarian justice is the 'lack of any *political* point. Joseph K. has no politics and the mysterious court that condemns him has no political mission'.[27] This missing political element indicates that, as opposed to a totalitarian state in which everything is politicized, in the court of *The Trial* there are no politics, even to the point where there does not seem to be anyone in charge. Consequently, desire and will are unchecked by any kind of higher authority, and there is nothing to limit the play of self-interest and desire.

Execution as Sacrifice

Dyzenhaus, in his interpretation and revision of Kelsen's ideas, suggests that a transcendent authority may not be necessary for law to regain a moral component. Retaining Kelsen's idea of a merging of law with the state and supplementing it with Lon Fuller's idea of the inner morality of law,[28] Dyzenhaus returns to the idea of natural law as the underlying moral basis of all legal systems.[29] In bringing back natural law as the basis for law, he discards the element of theology as well as of a transcendent sovereignty. In doing so, he lays out the possibility of dispensing with capital punishment as the point where meaning and sovereignty coincide. Instead of a result of an existential conflict, Dyzenhaus understands sovereignty and the state as themselves constituted by law.[30] By linking the inner morality of law with Kelsen's idea that the entirety of a legal system itself constitutes sovereignty, Dyzenhaus attempts to save Kelsen's project of eliminating sovereignty as a representational excess that goes beyond law.

However, Dyzenhaus's approach still cannot avoid Kafka's implicit critique. Dyzenhaus contends that the idea of natural law might substitute for a metaphysical meaning. But the concept of self-preservation upon which natural law is based still leaves unanswered the question of individual meaning, which, in Kafka's text, can only be attained with the individual's acceptance of sacrifice. If the key issue of both morality and meaning in *The Trial* is the way in which K. must consent to a sacrifice (a sacrifice that affirms some principle that transcends his own self-interest), then natural law, as a system that is ultimately based on the principle of self-preservation rather than self-sacrifice, cannot suffice to establish a substantive meaning. Consequently, if sovereignty and meaning have disappeared in the mechanisms of the court, the only way for them to reappear in the context of *The Trial* is through a return to sacrifice as that which can re-establish a transcendent authority, without which meaning and morality remain absent.[31]

The execution is the point where K. finally attempts to consider some kind of principle other than fear or desire as a motivator for his actions. In agreeing not to resist his executioners, K. admits the errors of his previous behaviour, noting: 'Ich wollte immer mit zwanzig Händen in die Welt hineinfahren und überdies zu einem nicht zu billigenden Zweck. Das war unrichtig, soll ich nun zeigen, daß nicht einmal der einjährige Proceß mich belehren konnte?' ['I always wanted to snatch at the world with twenty hands and not for a very laudable motive, either. That was wrong, and am I to show now that not even a year's trial has taught me anything?'] (p. 238; 225–26). K. berates himself for his previous pursuit of questionable goals and draws attention to the way that he has, up to this point, only pursued his own self-interest without a thought for any higher principle. This is essentially the same critique that the father of 'The Judgment' uses against Georg Bendemann,[32] except that, in this case, K. notes 'daß man es mir überlassen hat, mir selbst das Notwendige zu sagen' ['that I have been left to say to myself all that is needed'] (p. 239; 226), and he assents to his execution as something necessary, realizing even 'daß es seine Pflicht gewesen ware, das Messer, als es von Hand zu Hand über ihm schwebte, selbst zu fassen und sich einzubohren' ['that he was supposed to seize the knife himself, as it travelled from hand to hand above him and plunge it into his own breast'] (p. 241; 228). K.'s consent to his own execution is crucial as the moment when capital punishment returns in *The Trial*, not as a state mechanism, but as the decision of an individual who links meaning in life with the sacrifice of that life. This connection between meaning and sacrifice in the moment of execution establishes a modern basis for capital punishment: not directly, as the affirmation of a transcendent authority, but due to the dependence of individual meaning on a structure of sacrifice.

The difficulty of the execution in *The Trial*, though, is that, without a communal context of sovereignty, the death sentence is stripped of meaning; it becomes an individual event, still detached from an overarching context of meaning. Though K. sees it as his responsibility to kill himself, he then realizes that he does not have the strength to do this:

> Aber er tat es nicht, sondern drehte den noch freien Hals und sah umher. Vollständig konnte er sich nicht bewähren, alle Arbeit den Behörden nicht abnehmen, die Verantwortung für diesen letzten Fehler trug der, der ihm den Rest der dazu nötigen Kraft versagt hatte.

> [But he did not do so, he merely turned his head, which was still free to move, and gazed around him. He could not completely rise to the occasion, he could not relieve the officials of all their tasks; the responsibility for this last failure of his lay with him who had not left him the remnant of strength necessary for the deed.] (p. 241; 228)

Though he assents to the decision and thereby sets up the situation for a self-sacrifice, he is unable to execute himself. If the execution were to rely only on his individual actions, such a self-execution would subvert itself. Instead of demonstrating the way in which he should look outside of his own desire and will for meaning, it would imply that K. might somehow be self-sufficient in his judgment, rather than dependent on a larger context of meaning that would justify both his actions and his judgments.

In forcing the representatives of the court to carry out the execution, he shifts the focus onto the court and the legitimacy of its authority. But because the court's authority does not rely on any substantive values either, and there is no public representation of such values, the execution does not in fact attain the representational quality of a sacrifice that could affirm some vision of sovereign authority. Instead, K.'s death is carried out without an audience, and he cries out 'Wie ein Hund!' [Like a dog!], with the narrator indicating: 'es war, als sollte die Scham ihn überleben' ['it was as if the shame of it must outlive him'] (p. 241; 229). His death serves no purpose except to underline the error of his life, and the court offers no other ideal that would create some kind of transcendence of his material life. Consequently, he does not die as a human within a context of collective ideals, but as a dog with only his mere life. Even the shame, which could only refer to collective ideals in their negation, is presented in the sentence as a hypothetical.

This missing aspect of political representation is a continual problem in the novel. While at the first inquiry K. demands 'die öffentliche Besprechung eines öffentlichen Mißstandes' ['the public ventilation of a public grievance'] (p. 53; 42–43), the lawyer Huld later explains 'daß das Verfahren nicht öffentlich sei, es kann, wenn das Gericht es für nötig hält, öffentlich werden, das Gesetz aber schreibt Öffentlichkeit nicht vor' ['that the proceedings were not public; they could certainly, if the Court considered it necessary, become public, but the Law did not prescribe that they must be made public'] (p. 120; 115). The secret nature of the court elicits K.'s insistence on a public legitimacy from the beginning, and this legitimacy is the first thing that K. tries to attack when confronted by the court. He first attempts to treat his arrest as a joke (p. 12), then demands some kind of legitimation for the guards' authority (p. 20). His eventual recognition of the court stems at first from the way in which others immediately accept its legitimacy. His uncle knows about the court when K. mentions it (p. 100), and he recommends the lawyer Huld as someone who specializes in such cases (pp. 102–03). Once K. meets Huld, he goes on to speak with several other figures, Leni, Tintorelli, Block, and the court chaplain, who are related to the court and grant it an implicit legitimacy. They accept the court's continuing existence and procedures as a kind of unavoidable fate rather than as the outgrowth of particular ideological decisions. Only K. himself asserts at the first inquiry that the court's procedures undermine its legitimacy, voicing the possibility of a dissent that would lead to an overthrow or transformation of the system. When he does this, though, he is not able to offer any principle or programme for justifying this transformation beyond his own feeling of outrage.

This lack of a substantive principle undermines K.'s ability to resist the court's eventual judgment, even though its own legitimacy remains in question until the end. When he is being escorted to his execution, the question of the legitimacy of the court arises when K. asks the executioners, 'An welchem Theater spielen Sie?' ['What theatre are you playing at?'] (pp. 236; 224), and, later on, they encounter a policeman who finds them to be 'eine nicht ganz unverdächtige Gruppe' ['a not quite harmless-looking group'] (p. 239; 226). But in each such case of a possible questioning of the court's authority in the novel, K. ultimately acknowledges its legitimacy. When the guards and Aufseher prepare to leave in the first chapter, K. 'hatte die Absicht, falls sie weggehen sollten, bis zum Haustor nachzulaufen und ihnen seine Verhaftung anzubieten' ['had the intention, if they were to leave, of running after them to the front door and challenging them to take him prisoner'] (p. 23; 14). Even though he insists at the first inquiry that the legitimacy of the court depends upon his consent, he ultimately grants this recognition. He claims 'es ist ja nur ein Verfahren, wenn ich es als solches anerkenne. Aber ich erkenne es also für den Augenblick jetzt an, aus Mitleid gewissermaßen' ['it is only a trial if I recognize it as such. But for the moment I do recognize it, on grounds of compassion, as it were'] (p. 51; 40). Finally, when the executioners hesitate before the policeman, K. is the one who pulls them onwards so as to escape the policeman (p. 239). In spite of the court's lack of clear public legitimacy, K. feels an inner need to recognize it and to accept its judgment.

But this clearly cannot be an affirmation of some kind of ideal, as the court remains without meaning. Instead, there is only a kind of fatefulness of the court's existence and procedures, which becomes a replacement for its truth. When the priest in the cathedral remarks, 'man muß nicht alles für wahr halten, man muß es nur für notwendig halten' ['it is not necessary to accept everything as true, one must only accept it as necessary'], K.'s response is: 'Trübselige Meinung [...] Die Lüge wird zur Weltordnung gemacht' ['A melancholy conclusion [...] It turns lying into a universal principle'] (p. 233; 220). K. perceptively notes that the affirmation of necessity, when it is not connected to any kind of overarching principle, leads to an abandonment of the hope of an absolute truth. Every world order is then a kind of lie, which does not have any metaphysical claim to legitimacy.

But this insight does not have to be a paralyzing one, as it is for the perspective of *The Trial*, in which there is no alternative way of viewing necessity and fate from the way they are structured by the court. Because the lie that is the court is also the hidden structure of the world in the novel (in which no alternative forms of authority are offered), the consciousness of fatefulness that emerges in the sacrifice is also an abandonment of higher absolute principles; thus, the novel remains dismal throughout. But this despair is not the only alternative that remains. *The Trial*'s death sentence, without any ideals and without a sense of sacrifice, can fruitfully be contrasted with the execution in Kafka's 1919 'In the Penal Colony'. This story's attempt to re-integrate law with substantive values through sacrifice lays out the alternative of a law that tries to retain sovereignty, even as the metaphysical basis has disappeared. While sacrifice is studiously excluded from law in *The Trial*, it is the centre of attention for the apparatus of 'In the Penal Colony', to the point that the Officer does exactly what K. avoids: he offers himself up for punishment in place of the condemned man. In addition, if the lawyer Huld emphasizes that 'das Verfahren nicht öffentlich sei' ['the proceedings were not public'] (p. 120; 115), the officer of the penal colony is at pains to point out the public nature of his judgment system: 'Um es nun jedem zu ermöglichen, die Ausführung des Urteils zu überprüfen, wurde die Egge aus Glas gemacht' [In order to allow everyone to examine the execution of the judgement, the harrow is made of glass].[33] If secret inquiries and hidden court officials are the characteristics of the legal bureaucracy in *The Trial*, public sacrifice is the form for an alternative type of judgment that tries to integrate sovereignty into the legal process. The distorted form that this justice takes in 'In the Penal Colony' highlights again, however, the obstacles that Kafka's texts mark out for such a unified conception of meaning and sovereignty when a metaphysical basis for it has disappeared.[34]

Capital Punishment as Sacrifice in Brecht's *The Measures Taken*: Re-affirming Sovereignty

If Kafka's texts are unable to find their way out of this dilemma of establishing meaning in the absence of an overarching metaphysical framework, Bertolt Brecht offers a solution. In fact, Brecht's solution has become the most frequent path taken in a world that, in its return to a firm connection between meaning and sovereignty, has become increasingly ideological. Brecht's attempt to establish a new form of Communist community ends up following the same plan that Kafka lays out in 'In the Penal Colony'. In the face of a Communist party structure that threatens to turn the law into a bureaucratic procedure, Brecht's *The Measures Taken* tries to redeem the party by staging its judgments as a form of public sacrifice. In doing so, Brecht treats Communism as a particular political ideology that, since it is in competition with other ideologies, needs to be brought to the masses in a convincing way. Significantly, the Young Comrade of *The Measures Taken* faces the same problem as K. in *The Trial*. The most grievous error he makes in the play is, like K., to assert his own individual will. Disregarding the objections from the party Agitators, he breaks with party discipline and removes his mask: 'Weil ich recht habe, kann ich nicht nachgeben. Mit meinen zwei Augen sehe ich, daß das Elend nicht warten kann' [Because I am right, I cannot give in. With my two eyes I see that the misery cannot wait].[35] Relying on his own individual judgment, the Young Comrade no longer acts as part of the party but in his own name. Such action is problematic, not because the party is always right, but because the unity of the collective is the first priority. As the Agitators insist:

> Zeige uns den Weg, den wir gehen sollen, und wir
> Werden ihn gehen wie du, aber
> Gehe nicht ohne uns den richtigen Weg
> Ohne uns ist er
> Der falscheste.
> Trenne dich nicht von uns! (p. 67)

> [Show us the path that we should follow, and we
> Will follow it with you, but
> Do not take the correct path without us
> Without us it is the most incorrect one.
> Do not separate yourself from us!]

Even if the party is wrong, the individual must remain subordinate to it, in order to gradually move the party toward a collective recognition of the truth. If the individual breaks with the party simply because the party is wrong, this only leads to a breakdown of the community, whose preservation is a more important priority than the objective truth of its perspective. Sovereignty becomes the measure for meaning.

After disobeying the orders of the Agitators and being forcibly carried out of the city, the Young Comrade comes to realize his error in removing his mask and again identifies with the group. He 'öffnete die Augen, erfuhr, was geschehen war, sah ein, was er getan hatte, und sagte: Wir sind verloren' [opened his eyes, saw what had happened, and realized what he had done, and said: We are lost] (p. 75). Realizing the negative consequences of his actions, he once again identifies with the rest of the party and assents to his execution. As with K., individual meaning can only come with the acceptance of sacrifice, but, also like K., his decision is combined with an inability to carry it out himself. When the Agitators asks 'Willst du es allein machen?' [Do you want to do it alone?], the Young Comrade responds 'Helft mir' [Help me] (p. 83). Though the Young Comrade's assent is crucial for the affirmation of Communism, he also lacks the strength to carry out the execution himself. Like K., he will not release the executioners from the task. The individual in both *The Trial* and in *The Measures Taken* requires the judicial apparatus to carry out the execution, thereby compelling the legal system to be linked to an act of collective will. Brecht's innovation, however, is to insist on the public nature of such an act of will, which would hopefully provide the transcendent foundation that would transform the execution from an act of arbitrary wilfulness into an act of sovereignty.

Brecht's linking of *The Measures Taken* with *The One Who Says Yes* and *The One Who Says No* is important to remember here because the possibility of dissent emphasizes how the decision regarding sacrifice is constitutive for the ideology.[36]

Even though the Agitators emphasize that the resistance of the Young Comrade would not have changed their decision, his assent provides the legitimation for the sacrifice — a sacrifice that needs to be reproduced by the Control Chorus in order for it to have a defining significance for the collective. Since the assent has to be staged in *The Measures Taken* for the Control Chorus, it is not primarily a moment of courage that affirms individual sovereignty. Instead, it is a moment in which all participants assent to the subordination of the individual to the specific collective goals that are expressed in the situation of sacrifice; this assent needs to be made public in order to achieve its full effect as a defining decision. The play does not just depict the sacrifice directly. Rather, the play stages the process whereby the Agitators re-enact the scene for the Control Chorus, resulting in a public assent of all the participants to the sovereignty of the collective. The sacrifice is consequently not staged as an individual tragedy but rather as a cultural-political necessity with emblematic significance.

The theatricality of the assent to the sacrifice, in which the execution will be carried out regardless of whether there is assent or not, indicates that both the assent and the sacrifice have a ritual character. The ritual is not simply a submission, but an experience that allows for an aesthetically mediated process of assent. The moment of sacrifice comes about through a conflict between a set of values and a set of circumstances that oppose these values. The potential threat to these values leads to the need to establish the particular ritual whereby the sacrifice must be embraced in an act of courage: before killing him, the Agitators ask the Young Comrade if he agrees with their judgment (pp. 94–95). It might be supposed that this moment of assent provides the individual with the opportunity to evaluate the legitimacy of these demands. However, the individual's decision-making power is limited to agreeing or disagreeing with the execution, which will be carried out regardless of whether the individual agrees. The degree of assent only has significance in terms of the representational value of the assent for the spectators, which include the other Agitators and the Control Chorus. The moment of assent is crucial, not so much for its demonstration of individual courage, but for its consequences for the collective's adherence to the value system that holds it together.

Accordingly, the Young Comrade shifts attention away from the individual sovereignty involved in the sacrifice and towards its public character by drawing attention to the ideological goals of the sacrifice. As the Young Comrade dies, he does not simply lament the loss of his own dignity, as K. does, but rather affirms the specific goals of the sacrifice and the character of the community for which the sacrifice is made:

> Im Interesse des Kommunismus
> Einverstanden mit dem Vormarsch der proletarischen Massen
> Aller Länder
> Ja sagend zur Revolutionierung der Welt. (p. 95)

> [In the interests of Communism
> In agreement with the advance of the proletarian masses
> Of all countries
> Saying yes to the revolutionizing of the world.]

By linking his sacrifice to Communist goals, the Young Comrade embeds its violence within the collective's self-understanding. The community's goals are linked directly to the necessity of the sacrifice, which, in turn, only gains significance in relation to these goals. The centrality of the goals demonstrates that the specific definition of the collective conceptually precedes the violence, and, in fact, violence has no meaning here except in terms of how it threatens or supports the ideals of this collective.

The defining of ideals begins with the decisions of the Young Comrade and the Agitators. But the final affirmation can only take place once a larger audience has a chance to assent to this first decision. Halfway through *The Measures Taken*, the Control Chorus, which had been sitting in judgment over the actions of the Agitators, changes its role by stating: 'Lange nicht mehr hören wir euch zu als Urteilende. Schon als Lernende' [For quite some time we have no longer been listening to you as judges. We have become learners] (pp. 85–86). Instead of acting as the representatives of the ideals and the arbiters over the specific situation, they have now taken the role of learners who must cede authority to those who make decisions in the specific situation of sacrifice. The primary task of *The Measures Taken* is not to propagandistically enforce adherence to communist ideology from above, but to establish a situation in which an existential decision in a specific situation might become defining for the ideology. The act of sacrifice, though enacting a subordination to the collective, also has a defining function within the cultural order. On a fundamental level, this acclamation requires the supporters of the political order to be willing to sacrifice themselves in defending it against alternative orders. Since this commitment to self-sacrifice cannot be imposed from above, Brecht's staging of sacrifice as political representation illuminates the way in which political order and individual action must merge in order to establish and stabilize the sovereignty of a particular order against competing ones.

The play's understanding of justice in terms of a dynamic of sacrifice creates the aesthetic structure for a Communist ideology that takes political representation to be a key element. The success of this representation can only be measured by the extent to which it increases the capacity of Communists for self-sacrifice. By linking political ideology to individual sacrifice, *The Measures Taken* draws out the aesthetic consequences of Kafka's critique of bureaucracy, doing so in a way that establishes public representation as the basis for a law that would ground sovereignty in the will of the people, yet also create an objective basis for this will.

Kelsen's denial of the objectivity of such a structure still remains valid, however. The grounding of law in the sovereignty of the people only retains objectivity within the community that is established by the political representation. There is no absolute objectivity, but only a representationally mediated one. The killing of the Young Comrade only becomes a necessity if the values of Communist ideology are affirmed as the highest ones, which must be pursued at all costs. Within a different value system and concomitant structure of sovereignty, the necessity of this execution would fall away, even if capital punishment might still be an essential aspect of such an alternative basis for sovereignty. The definition of a situation of necessity always involves a corresponding affirmation of a particular set of values, and the task of the political representation is to establish the objectivity of these values for a political community.

As Brecht's play shows, the delegitimation of bureaucracy and of an absolute truth does not have to lead to an affirmation of the lie as a world without ideals. Instead, *The Measures Taken* establishes the truth of its ideology, not as an absolute one, but as a constructed one that can be traced back to a set of sacred texts. The affirmation of these texts in the sacrifice finds its justification in the community assent that establishes the texts' legitimacy, not on an absolute level but a representational one. What K. describes as a lie has been reinterpreted by *The Measures Taken* to be ideology, a textual construction that has no absolute validity, but whose truth is legitimated by a process of popular assent. This process does not so much establish a lie as provide a textual tradition with a legitimate source of authority that is grounded in an aesthetic response of the collective.

Taken together, *The Trial* and *The Measures Taken* lay out the connection between meaning and sovereignty in the death sentence. The vain search for meaning in Kafka's text culminates in the wilful acceptance of the execution, not as something foreign but as necessary for K.'s own ability to construct his life as meaningful. However, the sought-for meaning remains elusive, as the execution remains a private and individual event due to the secret and non-public nature of the court. Meaning, though dependent on the capacity for sacrifice, cannot constitute itself without a context of political sovereignty that could link individual sacrifice into a greater totality. *The Measures Taken* depicts the representational structures that could establish such a totality, not as part of a divinely justified truth, but as the consequence of the representational context of the execution itself. The link between legitimacy and representation that Brecht lays out leads to a kind of sovereignty — one that depends upon a popular will that is formed through the spectacle of sacrifice itself. As such, capital punishment becomes a performance that must extend itself across a community, becoming the basic form of political sovereignty. Not only do all members of the community become the targets of capital punishment, but they all also become the witnesses and the executioners.

Notes to Chapter 5

1. Friedrich Nietzsche, *Zur Genealogie der Moral*, in *Sämtliche Werke: Kritische Studienausgabe*, ed. by Giorgio Colli and Mazzino Montinarie, 15 vols (Berlin: de Gruyter, 1967–1977), IV, 308–09, 324–25.
2. Paul Alberts, 'Knowing Life Before the Law: Kafka, Kelsen, Derrida', in *Philosophy and Kafka*, ed. by Brendan Moran and Carlo Salzani (Lanham, MD: Lexington Books, 2013), pp. 179–97 (pp. 185–86).
3. See Arnold Heidsieck, *The Intellectual Contexts of Kafka's Fictions: Philosophy, Law, Religion* (Columbia, SC: Camden House, 1994), pp. 114–20.
4. Francisco de Vitoria, *Political Writings*, ed. by Anthony Pagden and Jeremy Lawrance (Cambridge: Cambridge University Press, 1991), pp. 11–12.
5. Hans Kelsen, *Reine Rechtslehre: Einleitung in die rechtswissenschaftliche Problematik* (Leipzig: Franz Deuticke, 1934), p. 15.
6. Ibid., p. 33.

7. Ibid., p. 4.
8. Ibid.
9. Ibid., p. 5.
10. Hans Kelsen, *Reine Rechtslehre, mit einem Anhang: das Problem der Gerechtigkeit*, 2nd edn (Vienna: Deuticke, 1960), pp. 203–04; *Pure Theory of Law*, trans. by Max Knight (Berkeley: University of California Press, 1967), p. 201.
11. Kelsen, *Reine Rechtslehre* (1934), p. 24.
12. Ibid.
13. Ibid., p. 14.
14. Alberts, 'Knowing Life Before the Law', pp. 185–86.
15. Heidsieck, *The Intellectual Contexts of Kafka's Fictions*, pp. 115–16. Theodore Ziolkowski, *The Mirror of Justice: Literary Reflections of Legal Crises* (Princeton, NJ: Princeton University Press, 1997), pp. 226–31. Maximilian Bergengruen, 'Im "gesetzesleeren Raum": Zur inquisitorischen Logik von Rechtssätzen und Rechtssprichworten in Kafkas "Proceß"', *Zeitschrift für Deutsche Philologie*, 134.2 (2015), 217–49 (pp. 222–30).
16. Ziolkowski, *The Mirror of Justice*, pp. 234–40.
17. Heidsieck, *The Intellectual Contexts of Kafka's Fictions*, pp. 105–06.
18. David Dyzenhaus, 'Positivism and the Pesky Sovereign', *European Journal of International Law*, 22.2 (2011), 363–72 (p. 364).
19. Theodor W. Adorno, 'Notes on Kafka', in *Prisms*, trans. by Samuel and Shierry Weber (Cambridge, MA: MIT Press, 1997), pp. 245–71 (p. 245). See also Hans Dieter Zimmermann, for whom *The Trial* stages an 'endless search for meaning', 'Die endlose Suche nach dem Sinn: Kafka und die jiddische Moderne', in *Nach erneuter Lektüre: Franz Kafkas Der Proceß*, ed. by Hans Dieter Zimmermann (Würzburg: Königshausen und Neumann, 1992), pp. 211–22 (pp. 211–13). Similarly, Walter Sokel argues that the difficulty of meaning establishes the main conflict of *The Trial* as one between worldly power and desire on the one hand and the demands of a sphere of mysterious depth opened up by the court on the other hand, *Franz Kafka: Tragik und Ironie: Zur Struktur seiner Kunst* (Munich & Vienna: Albert Langen Georg Müller Verlag, 1964), p. 143.
20. David Pan, 'The Persistence of Patriarchy in Franz Kafka's "Judgment"', *Orbis Litterarum*, 55 (2000), 135–60.
21. Franz Kafka, *Der Proceß: Textband*, ed. by Malcolm Pasley (Frankfurt am Main: Fischer, 1990), p. 95. English translations are based upon Franz Kafka, *The Trial*, trans. by Willa and Edwin Muir (New York: Schocken, 1984), p. 92. Subsequent references to these books are in the main text.
22. On the power that K. exercises over Fräulein Bürstner, see Elizabeth Boa, *Kafka: Gender, Class, and Race in the Letters and Fictions* (Oxford: Clarendon Press, 1996), pp. 198–200; Graham Fallowes, 'Power and Performativity: "Doing Things With Words" in Kafka's *Proceß*', *Oxford German Studies*, 44.2 (2015), 199–225 (p. 222); and Britta Maché, 'The Bürstner Affair and Its Significance for the Courtroom Scenes and the End of Kafka's *Prozeß*', *German Quarterly*, 65.1 (1992), 18–34 (pp. 19–20).
23. On the inversion of roles in this scene, see Henry Sussman, 'The Court as Text: Inversion, Supplanting, and Derangement in Kafka's *Der Prozeß*', *PMLA*, 92.1 (1977), 41–55 (pp. 41, 44–45).
24. Fallowes, 'Power and Performativity', pp. 213–15.
25. Gilles Deleuze and Félix Guattari, *Kafka: Toward a Minor Literature*, trans. by Dana Polan (Minneapolis: University of Minnesota Press, 1986).
26. For a version of this reading, see J. P. Stern, 'The Law of The Trial', in *On Kafka: Semi-Centenary Perspectives*, ed. by Franz Kuna (London: Elek Books, 1976), pp. 22–46 (pp. 33–34).
27. Richard Posner, *Law and Literature* (Cambridge, MA: Harvard University Press, 1998), p. 138.
28. Lon L. Fuller, *The Morality of Law* (New Haven, CT: Yale University Press, 1969).
29. Dyzenhaus, 'Positivism and the Pesky Sovereign', p. 367.
30. Ibid., p. 369.
31. On the structure of sacrifice, see David Pan, *Sacrifice in the Modern World: On the Particularity and Generality of Nazi Myth* (Evanston, IL: Northwestern University Press, 2012).
32. Franz Kafka, *Drucke zu Lebzeiten: Textband*, ed. by Wolf Kittler (Frankfurt am Main: Fischer, 1994), p. 60.

33. Kafka, *Drucke zu Lebzeiten*, p. 215.

34. David Pan, 'Kafka as a Populist: Re-reading "In the Penal Colony"', *Telos*, 101 (Fall 1994), 3–40.

35. Bertolt Brecht, *Die Maßnahme: Kritische Ausgabe mit einer Spielanleitung von Reiner Steinweg* (Frankfurt am Main: Suhrkamp Verlag, 1972), p. 67. Subsequent references are in the main text.

36. Klaus-Dieter Krabiel, 'Die Maßnahme', in *Brecht Handbuch in fünf Bänden*, ed. by Jan Knopf, 5 vols (Stuttgart: Metzler, 2001), I, 253–66 (p. 253). David Pan, 'Sacrifice as Political Representation in Bertolt Brecht's *Lehrstücke*', *Germanic Review*, 84.3 (2009), 222–49.

PART III

Lyric and Law

CHAPTER 6

Dreadful Forms:
The Romantic Ballad and the
Death Penalty

Mark Canuel

In William Wordsworth's ballad 'The Thorn', first published in *Lyrical Ballads*
in 1798 (this collection was a collaboration with Samuel Taylor Coleridge), the
narrator contemplates the story of a young woman, Martha Ray, who has possibly
murdered and buried her child born out of wedlock. Rehearsing various rumours
that swirl among the townspeople concerning the poem's central character, the
narrator then claims that 'some had sworn an oath that she | Should be to public
justice brought' (ll. 232–33).[1] It is clear enough from the context of the entire poem
that the narrator is not one of these people: he instead invites the reader to 'trace'
the mysterious tale and ponder its details (227). And thus, by placing the urge for
'public justice' — a trial and possibly a hanging of the criminal — in the words
and thoughts of others, Wordsworth distinguishes the aims of his own ballad from
centuries of literary history that had forged a seemingly indissoluble connection
between the genre of the ballad and narratives of crime and punishment. From
the most ancient of English ballads to criminal broadsides or 'street' ballads of the
poet's own day, ballads had become the preeminent genre for representing treason,
murder, and theft, along with the just deserts that fall upon criminal offenders.
This is something that Wordsworth and his audience would have known all too
well. 'The Thorn' daringly asks for the reader's curiosity and wonder, not for her
vengeance.

   In this essay, I show that 'The Thorn' is in fact one of many instances of Romantic
ballads that register a profound awareness of the connection between balladry and
penal laws or practices. Early English and Scottish ballads, many dating from the
seventeenth century or before, rendered the crimes of offenders in sensational
details, followed by retributive punishments that were often sanctioned by a king,
by God, or both. Closely connected to this tradition, popular 'execution broadsides'
or 'criminal broadsides' — anonymously authored, cheaply printed, and sold for
one penny or less — creatively drew upon ancient balladry's forceful narratives,
powerful imagery, and strangely menacing formal effects. The Romantic poets

I discuss, primarily Robert Southey and William Wordsworth, create innovative contributions to the ballad genre that were keenly aware of the grisly sensationalism and stern moralizing of modern execution ballads and their progenitors in ballads from previous centuries. But I argue that these poets did not merely reflect or continue this tradition; instead, they thoughtfully and inventively intervened in it. To clarify the stakes of this intervention, I briefly provide a political context for the work of Romantic poets by glancing at the contributions of important penal reformers of the late eighteenth century, but my argument focuses more intently on the extraordinary formal work of ballads themselves, which waged their battle against the logic and expectations reinforced by, and imagined within, the literary genre. In works ranging from Southey's 'Jaspar' (1798) to Wordsworth's 'The Thorn', writers mobilized the ballad form within a project of critique and revision. Although ballads for many generations had merely defended violent retributive punishments, Romantic poets employed the form as the means of registering anxieties about penal authority and hopes for more rehabilitative postures toward criminal subjects.

Ballads, Executions, and Uncertain Authority

The ballads most cherished by British Romantic writers, and best known to today's students of literature, were transcriptions of poems from generations of oral tradition (perhaps predating publication by centuries), edited and compiled within influential collections by the likes of Thomas Percy, Joseph Ritson, and Walter Scott. Many of the most beloved ballads from these collections touch on, or combine, related themes of greed, theft, trespass, treason, murder, and retributive justice. Literary histories of the ballad tend to treat this long-standing connection between form and subject matter somewhat laconically, as a matter of fact: the oldest English ballads, it is said, are often about outlaws.[2] And it is most certainly worth noting that the earliest ballad in F. J. Child's celebrated collection of English and Scottish ballads was the tale of an early and particularly famous outlaw: 'Judas', that is, a ballad that recounts Judas's betrayal of Christ for 'thritti platen of selver'.[3] Even this one early instance begins to indicate the somewhat more expansive evaluation made in *The Princeton Encyclopedia of Poetry and Poetics*: just as significant as the religious or 'supernatural' subject matter in the ballad's development over several centuries is its corresponding emphasis on 'sensational and violent' subject matter and 'domestic crimes' (although obviously the case of 'Judas' is one of many instances demonstrating that crimes treated in the ballad are frequently of national or world-historical, rather than 'domestic', significance).[4] The purpose of this essay is not to speculate too broadly about the causes for the early established connection between balladry and criminality, but even the most casual form of sociological analysis would be inclined to connect the repetitions and other 'mnemonic' devices of the ballad with both sacred and secular ritual functions.[5] So many instances of the ballad, in other words, convey not simply an isolated story but a rehearsal and repetition of a shared set of legally-sanctioned social relationships: these are relationships broken by outlaws and retributively addressed and rebuilt by either human agents, divine forces, or often a complex, even confusing, combination of both.

Numerous examples could help us to explore these connections among ballads, outlaws, and juridical authority further. But I concentrate on one of the most frequently praised of them in the English tradition, 'The Children in the Wood', also known (among other titles) as 'Babes in the Wood'. I take this example to be a particularly interesting one precisely because the poem displays both the urgency and ambiguity in the treatment of retributive justice in the ballad genre as a whole. As with most ballads, the author of this work is unknown: early printed examples of it date back to the late sixteenth century, although its subject matter, Sharon Turner has argued, appears to place it in the time of Richard III, who reigned from 1483 to 1485 (and possibly to refer to him).[6] Joseph Addison praised the poem for its combination of inspired 'genius' and 'natural' mode of expression.[7] It was repeatedly featured in ballad collections throughout the eighteenth and nineteenth centuries; and it even appeared in a staged version with a mangled happy ending — a 'musical piece' by Thomas Morton, performed at the Haymarket Theatre in 1793.[8] No doubt suppressing its theatrical associations, Wordsworth fondly notes the poem (by the title 'Babes in the Wood') in his 1800 Preface to Lyrical Ballads when he searches for a mode of writing that adequately conveys 'feeling' to the reader.[9]

In the poem, a wicked uncle is entrusted with the care of his dead brother and sister-in-law's children; he is charged with the executorship of the young heirs' estate. After caring for the children for only a year, greed gets the better of him. He 'bargain[s] with two ruffians strong' (l. 73) to kill the children in the forest so that he can take their fortune for himself.[10] Once the hired assassins have the children alone in the wood, the one with 'milder mood' tries to avoid killing them: in an argument with the second assassin, he kills him. The first hired killer leaves the children to go to town, with a promise to 'bring you bread | When I come back again' (ll. 111–12), but this moment never comes. The children wander and die. The uncle is reduced to 'want and misery' (l. 140), ultimately dying in debtor's prison. The remaining ruffian confesses the 'truth' of his involvement in the children's death before he is hanged for a separate robbery (l. 149).

The general themes of crime and punishment would connect this ballad with many other celebrated examples of the genre, from the heart-wrenching 'Gilderoy' (whose hero is hanged under strict laws for stealing livestock) to 'The Outlaw Murray' (whose hero is mercifully excused by James V for his rebellious possession of Ettrick Forest). But I focus on 'The Children of the Wood' above all others not simply because of its great popularity but because of its intriguing ways of treating juridical authority as a problem rather than as an accomplished fact. Such authority is both absolutely central for asserting social order, and yet the forms and operations that enact that authority are utterly incoherent and obscure. The obscurity of authority within the poem's juridical subject matter in an uncanny sense echoes the obscurity of authorial agency so familiar to readers of all ancient ballads — is it a poem by any one person? Is it by several people? And who? What counts as a definitive version of the ballad? 'The Children in the Wood' in analogous ways points to an authoritative juridical agency for the supposedly just punishments meted out for the uncle's and the killers' crimes; but it also frustrates any confidence that we might have in the wisdom and coherence of that agency by making punishments appear confused in their intent or inscrutable in their design.

Consider, for instance, the strange multiplication of authority figures in the poem, the implications of which deepen when we further consider that the trusting father and murderous uncle may be stand-ins for Edward V and Richard III, respectively. Whose words and deeds represent the law? The writer of the will (the father) or the executor of it (the uncle)? Surely the way that the ballad looks to 'God's blessed will' as a foundation for penal sanctions appears to clear up the picture, but it also makes that 'will' look faulty and irrational. God's will authorizes the distribution of punishments whereby the uncle is deprived of all he owns, and even of his two sons, and then dies, while the surviving ruffian is also 'judged to die' (l. 147). The last stanza in particular reinforces the idea of God as the ultimate source of authority for earthly punishments, thus encouraging us to adopt a sense of satisfaction with the justice and probative value of those punishments:

> You that executors be made,
> And overseers eke,
> Of children that be fatherless,
> And infants mild and meek,
> Take you example by this thing,
> And yield to each his right,
> Lest God with suchlike misery
> Your wicked minds requite. (ll. 153–60)

The lines certainly do convey a sense that the penalty of death is appropriate for the crime and also has a deterrent value. According to that logic, the reader/auditor is supposed to accept the just punishment and use it has a guide for her actions. But even these seemingly sure-footed lines do not quite make sense. Is the ballad saying that 'wicked minds' will be punished whether they act or not? And is the punishment for a wicked mind the same as the punishment for a wicked deed? What about the line 'And yield to each his right'? Who determines right? Does the uncle have any 'right', and with that right would he have been furnished with a portion of the estate (which he apparently did not have)?

Upon further inspection, other claims about the mechanisms of punishment in the poem begin to look equally murky. The working of authority seems conspicuously inexact and even unjust. The uncle dies in prison, which might perhaps approximate a form of retributive punishment, although it is certainly lighter than the bloody deaths meted out to the ruffians he employs. The deaths of the uncle's sons carry vengeance well beyond the expected bounds and punishes even those who do not seem to deserve it: this punishing of sons for the crimes of the father presumes a version of what the common law defined as 'corruption of blood', the crimes of the father extended to his progeny.[11] Why did they need to die, and in what sense were they yielded a 'right'? The first ruffian appears not to have committed nearly as great an offence as the second. We are simply told that the children did not 'see the man | Approaching from the town' (ll. 115–16), making it unclear whether he did or did not return to help them. But there is a troubling formal equivalence between the punishments: both die, that is, at the hands of a vengeful but imprecise human agency. The insistent connecting of these earthly punishments to divine will, in other words, is accompanied by a frustrating and confusing sense that there is no exact patterning of punishments in relation to offences. Whatever is just from God's perspective is nonsensical or even random from a human one, or (far more likely) a nonsensical collection of punishments is simply described as divine in order to disguise its flimsiness.

It is impossible to extricate this thematization of punishment in ancient ballads from the mobilization of the ballad genre within criminal broadsides. These broadsides (single sheets of paper printed on one side only) were often produced and sold in areas around Seven Dials and Covent Garden in London, and usually consist of an account of, or speech by, a criminal, followed by an account or anticipation of his or her punishment — usually a hanging. They were written in prose, poetry, or a combination of the two. The majority of the broadsides that have been collected in archives (some of them very helpfully digitized) date from the sixteenth to the nineteenth centuries, with a lapse between the Revolution of 1642 and the Restoration of Charles II.[12] They were sold by printers to the large audiences attending the transportation of the body from prison to scaffold, and, in many cases, they were written with the suggestion of a popular tune to which the words would be sung. Removing executions from public view in the late eighteenth century, and eliminating a vast number of capital offences in the early decades of the nineteenth century, contributed to the end of this practice in England.

By saying that it is impossible to extricate the themes of crime and punishment in ancient ballads from the emergence of the 'street ballad' broadside, I refer in one sense to the empirical facts of print culture. Ancient ballads were distributed as broadsides even as broadsides featured tales of criminals (along with many other subjects as well). Poems in the Jersey Collection (or 'Osterley Park' Collection) of Ballads, for instance, include a reissue of 'Gilderoy' along with 'Captain Johnson's Last Farewell' (Johnson was executed at Tyburn in 1690 as an accessory to kidnapping).[13] The republication of ancient ballads in cheap broadsides alongside more topical ballads (that is, ballads sold at executions) was a common practice throughout the nineteenth century. The endurance of this practice suggests that a distinction between 'ancient' and topical 'street' ballads can be made with careful modern scholarly research, but this was not an accepted division in the practices of ballad publication or collection. Beyond the publication facts, it is worth noting that the close connection in both form and content between the ancient ballads and their low-culture counterparts could be seen as a supple one, in which the ballad form is not simply imposed upon its content but instead invites or summons it because of balladry's long-accumulated associations between literary form and juridical content. It would not be overly extravagant to claim that the story of the ballad is the story of modern crime and law: this is not to say that ballads simply represent legal apparatuses, but that they creatively engage with them. The ritualistic, repetitive, rhythmic, mnemonically-driven aspects of the ballad form — so congenial for bringing the singular into the fold of community, particularly when we consider the conscription of balladry into execution songs sung by executioner and audience — seems in the most abstract description of its form to describe the features of the law. Thus, the antique ballad is not simply a literary influence on street ballads; the latter is an extension of the formal and political possibilities explored in the former.

Many of the criminal broadsides published from the seventeenth to the nineteenth centuries were entirely composed in ballad form, although others consisted of prose narratives followed by ballads. The publications were largely anonymous, and when they contained speeches by executed criminals, those speeches were of doubtful authorship. In many cases, broadsides make it clear that the ballad is 'on' or 'concerning' the dying words of a criminal, rather than an exact transcription of the outlaw's dying words. The obscurity surrounding the authorship of ballads and accompanying text in crime broadsides capitalizes on, and in fact aggrandizes, the questions about origin and authority in the history of balladry in general. The status of the broadside texts as ephemeral accompaniments to staged events — these are executions succeeded by still other executions and their textual accompaniments — is tacitly acknowledged in their composition. Equally crucial to this fragile design, however, is their oft-repeated claim (echoing the terms of the ancient ballads) to be absolutely definitive in their account of the workings of a regal or divine authority that exercises power above and beyond the ephemerality enacted in the cheap and evanescent broadsides.

How do we 'read' these broadsides? In many of them, there is certainly a great deal of attention to the criminal's own character, attracting the potential sympathy of the audience member or reader. This is, of course, a quality to be found even in the most ancient of ballads, and 'Gilderoy', told in the voice of the criminal's lover and speaking in the most plaintive terms of the beauty and kindness of the condemned man, provides an early precedent. Indeed, the ballad, based upon the life of Rob Roy, is more or less continuous in form and effects with more topical and ephemeral broadsides. Such attention to the criminal's side of the story dilates still further when broadsides feature the supposed words of criminals themselves. In the account of Captain Thomas Green, for instance, executed for piracy in Edinburgh in 1705, the act of confession for 'youthful sins' would seem to make an audience partial to his side, and this is typical of such dying statements.[14]

Michel Foucault's work in *Discipline and Punish* is particularly interested in this phenomenon in broadsides because of the 'equivocal' ways in which the criminal's supposed last dying words portrayed him or her not merely as a justly punished offender but rather as a 'sort of saint'.[15] This reversibility obviously contests the ways in which the entire scene of execution, on Foucault's terms, is designed as a theatrical display of sovereign power. What interests me just as much, or perhaps more, is the broader confusion around issues of authority that occurs even within these works, an extension of the confusion and uncertainty regarding juridical authority to be found in ballads like 'The Children in the Wood'. In repeated instances in the criminal broadside ballads, we encounter the invocation of a cruel vengeance that is the result of a human penalty but also occasionally God's, although the connection between the two sources of authority is intriguingly unclear. In many ballads, to be sure, there simply is no contradiction between the will of God and human punishments: the criminal 'commends | His spirit' to God in the process of the execution in 'A Warning to Murtherers', based on the execution speech of John Gower, a coachmaker who murdered his wife.[16] But there is often a great deal of uncertainty about the status of the penal process and whether it is something that we as readers are inclined to believe in or ratify. God is the God of 'Mercy', as one ballad about Janet Riddle, a child murderer executed in 1702, declares. But God is also the one who causes Riddle's crime to be discovered by a 'Witness', and for her ultimately to be executed.[17] The conflict might be said to advance the confusions in the ancient ballads a step further: rather than a vague or imprecise authority for retributive punishments, such punishments seem estranged from and contradictory to the divine authority that simultaneously sanctions them. The confusion appears everywhere in criminal broadsides. Even in the shortest of ballads, as in the account of the arsonist James Butler, divine authority is internally divided, simply confused. There is a God of 'mercy', but also a God of vengeance: 'Providence could not permit | He should unpunished be'.[18]

Things are still more tangled in a broadside ballad from 1775 on John Bolton, who murdered a young woman apprenticed to him (once she became pregnant with his child). God in this ballad is the God of 'grace' and stands above the world of 'all mortal men' who do violence to each other. There is a real sense, moreover, in which the crimes and punishments of the world are proportioned according to their own logic: 'Murder prepense it is the worst of crimes, | And calls aloud for vengeance at all times'. The God of grace, however, does not simply stand aside from the world of crimes and punishments but actively intrudes in it: the entire plot of crime depends upon a struggle with 'the Tempter'; 'Providence' intrudes in the criminal's plans and directs him to strangle his victim rather than poison her, the better to lead to a 'train of proofs' that will convict him. Is Providence a kind of criminal that uses Bolton as an agent, just as the uncle uses the ruffians in 'The Children in the Wood'? Finally, the operations of justice (whether we call those operations human or divine) are undermined or at least troubled by the criminal's suicide — 'my last vile crime'. According to the logic and rhetoric of the poem, the criminal's final act wins out over other contending sources of authority, and it is not even clear whether Providential authority itself is free of criminal intent.[19]

We can now see that the multiple determinations of penal authority in early modern ballads and criminal broadsides tend to reinforce each other. There is a sovereign source of authority in these works — God or a king, or both — but the actual reach of that authority seldom goes unquestioned and is often radically unclear. The result is that the entire penal structure represented in and supported by balladry is troubled by numerous contradictions. Punishing is divine but also human; it is merciful but also vengeful; it is impeccably just but also frustratingly incoherent; its authority is eternal but also ephemeral and unpredictable.

The tensions and contradictions inhabiting the ballad's representations of crime and punishment have some connection to observations that Susan Stewart and others have made about ballads and their origins, and I want to provide a sketch of those recent arguments here. While acknowledging the criminal subject matter of ballads, Stewart's primary argument is that ballads were repeatedly employed throughout the eighteenth century to typify a lost national culture, even though that entire project depended upon repetition and artificiality that undermined, or at least troubled, claims of authenticity.[20] This essentially deconstructive interest in the ballad form — it is natural but also constructed — has been taken into various other directions: Maureen McLane, for instance, has pointed out how the ballad depends upon notions of oral culture but must construct the oral through writing, hence the positioning of the ballad at an 'oral-literate conjunction'.[21] In my own take on the ballad tradition, I have little reason to argue against the suggestion that these works are highly artificial mediations. Still, my focus on a particular strain of ballad writing and the functionality of that strain within penal discourses allows us to see that the uncertain constructions of authority are not merely an abstract concern about the construction of poetry or a national public. They compose the juridico-political logic according to which the punishment of death was constructed as a necessary but troubling part of the order of the world.[22]

The Romantic Ballad: Southey and Penal Formalism

The route that we have taken through both ancient and popular ballads about crime and execution helps us to appreciate the degree to which Romantic poets writing in the ballad genre, with their own stories of crime and punishment, were profoundly aware of the modes in which ballads had traditionally constructed a relationship with the power to punish. Linda Venis has suggested that it is difficult to find direct lines of influence from popular broadsides on the poems in *Lyrical Ballads*, but, as I have already suggested, it is not possible to examine eighteenth- and nineteenth-century printing practices and easily assume that audiences themselves made strong distinctions between popular and ancient texts.[23] More to the point, however, I am less intent on showing specific influences or echoes than on showing points of contention that expose intertwined poetic and political resistances against the regime of punishment imagined within the ballad tradition.

I have written elsewhere about the importance of penal reform in the Romantic age, and about the largely neglected context of the campaign against the death penalty, carried out in the work of reformers such as Jeremy Bentham, Basil Montague (a close friend of Wordsworth and Coleridge), and Samuel Romilly. The work of these reformers pre-dated but informed the concrete changes in the criminal law in the Criminal Law Act of 1826, which consolidated the penal code and eliminated the death penalty for numerous offences. I will briefly rehearse these interconnected arguments here. In England, eighteenth-century penal reform in general, and opposition to the death penalty in particular, was argued on two fronts that sought to address the confusion, violence, and imprecision perpetuated by the frequent but highly irregular use of capital punishment to punish a range of crimes from petty theft to murder. On the one hand, reformers pointed to the arbitrary and unpredictable aspects of punishments that were the result of 'judge-made law'. Reformers sought to replace a cruel, unpredictable, and unsystematic application of violent and bloody penalties with a clearly graduated series of punishments that would be minutely calibrated to the severity of offences. On the other hand, reformers just as often pointed to the *utility* of punishments as the impetus for reforming them: punishment was not merely about the visible system of penalties but about the effect of such penalties on an offender (of which the visible system was certainly a part). Thus, it was remarked that if a fine as small as a shilling could deter a potential offender from the crime of murder, then such a penalty would be sufficient. The two rationales were uncomfortably but inseparably positioned together in the work of reformers and in the literary texts of the day. But what is worth particular emphasis here — and what will be of importance for understanding some poems in *Lyrical Ballads* — is that the discourse of utility, which stressed the impact of punishment on the subject, carried within it a powerful impulse toward reform. It challenged the purpose of any pattern of punishments with questions or outright scepticism about the effects of those punishments on individuals and social groups.[24]

Considering both facets of the reformist sentiments together with the long history of ballad writing that I have now addressed, we can begin to discern the impact of Romantic writing on the close alliance between ballad writing and the death penalty. The Romantic remaking of ballad forms, I want to argue, is inseparable from an increased self-consciousness about the death penalty and other forms of punishment. Still more, however, the examples of Southey and Wordsworth amply demonstrate how poetic vantage points on reform, while certainly recognizable in relation to the 'context' I mention above, employ literary form in ways that demonstrate contrasting alignments within the existing reformist juridical discourse. Ballads (and other literary works) do not simply occupy a context; they contribute to it and shape it.

The ballads I discuss actually participate in a larger literary discourse on punishment: they are part of a more general reforming sensibility that touches all forms of corporal punishment, imprisonment, and transportation.[25] One of the most powerful claims of Southey's 'Botany Bay' eclogues, for instance, is that the severity of transportation as a punishment (most often for theft) has made the criminal insensitive even to death: 'the dart of death | Has lost its terrors to a wretch like me', the speaker in 'Elinor' says (ll. 53–54).[26] It is clear that the point here — repeated by many in the Romantic age — is that the punishment of transportation violates the key reformist doctrine that penalties should be organized in a carefully calibrated system in which lesser crimes are paired with lesser punishments. Wordsworth and Coleridge similarly pitch their poems in *Lyrical Ballads* as imaginative contributions to a reformist agenda, eloquently complaining about the harsh treatment and miserable conditions in prisons. Coleridge's poem 'The Dungeon', extracted from his drama *Osorio* (revised for performance as *Remorse*) laments the poor condition of prisons; the speaker wishes that the prisoner, the 'wandering and distempered child' addressed in the poem, would be able to benefit from the 'benignant touch of love and beauty' to be found in nature's 'ministrations' (ll. 30, 20).[27] Also looking to nature as a healing presence, something I will discuss at length later in this essay, Wordsworth's speaker in 'The Convict' extends compassion to an 'outcast of pity' locked in a dungeon (l. 12); at the end of the poem, he addresses the prisoner with a wish that he (the poet) might 'plant thee where thou might'st blossom again' (l. 52).[28] John Thelwall's *Poems Written in Close Confinement* attacked the practices of both prison and transportation. He ironizes the British government's attempt to rid the country of political prisoners, whose hopes and dreams — no matter how harsh the sentencing — would live on as the 'seeds of freedom'.[29]

Robert Mayo some years ago made it clear that this reformist bent in poetry in general and in ballads in particular was not unusual in the years during and following the French Revolution, and his argument about the pervasiveness of various forms of protest needs to be kept in mind particularly in light of more recent claims about the avoidance of politics in Romantic writing.[30] What Mayo was not able to show, however, was the finer-grained manoeuvring around the issue of penal law, and specifically around the issue of capital punishment, which had been so central to the history of the ballad. Many of Southey's ballads self-consciously comment on the ballad genre's traditional obsessions with crime and punishment; but, more than this, they assert the power of the poetic form itself as a construction of penal authority. Never content merely to imitate antique ballads or their heirs in popular street ballads, Southey frames his works as decisive advances on them.[31] A poem with a seemingly archaic subject matter like 'A Ballad of a Young Man' from 1798 presents a compelling first case in point. It tells the tale of a young man who reads the works of Cornelius Agrippa and is then punished by the Devil for his curiosity; but the poem is really only superficially reminiscent of an antique ballad. Agrippa is closely connected to a line of Romantic thinking dating back at least to William Godwin's novel *St Leon* of 1799 (and forward to Mary Shelley's *Frankenstein* of 1818) that became fascinated with the hazy connections and disconnections between occult, forbidden knowledge, and visionary schemes of metaphysical and social thinking. The entire premise of the poem is that reading leads to dangerous knowledge:

> The young man, he began to read
> He knew not what, but he would proceed,
> When there was heard a sound at the door
> Which as he read on grew more and more.
>
> And more and more the knocking grew,
> The young man knew not what to do;
> But trembling in fear he sat within,
> Till the door was broke and the Devil came in. (ll. 21–28)

The ballad ends with the Devil tearing the young man's heart from his body, an act of violence which serves as a warning to other 'young men' who should 'take heed | How in a conjurer's books they read' (ll. 49–50). The resonance of the scenario with the Faust legend is not nearly as striking as its clear distinction from it: this is a ballad that is not about a scholar's quest for forbidden knowledge. It is a ballad about right and wrong reading material (a subject dear to Hannah More, among many other reformers of Southey's day), and that punishes wrong reading with death. The fact that the ballad addresses the subject of reading in a charged political situation in which revolutionary publications invite legal suppression and imprisonment enhances our appreciation for Southey's project. Immersed in a media culture saturated with novel political and literary ideas, the poem anxiously situates itself as a sternly punitive form of novelty. While bravely throwing itself into the current of novel ideas, it also seeks to work as a novelty against novelty.

The strenuous exertions of Southey's decidedly modern take on the ballad are further accentuated formally by the curious interest that the poem takes in ballad meter itself. The fact that the Devil's knocking on the door — with the words 'more' repeated exactly four times — corresponds to the poem's rollicking tetrameter. It would not be going too far to suggest that the poem employs its own knocking as an accompaniment to the Devil's, knocking some sense into us about the dangers of those 'horrible leaves of magic' to be found in other threateningly revolutionary writings (l. 17).

What, however, is the precise connection that Southey wants to draw between the knocking of poetry's meter and the violence of the Devil? Is the poem endorsing violence as a response to sedition, or does it offer an alternative to it? Other poems, such as 'Lord William' and 'Mary, Maid of the Inn', both appearing in the 1799 edition of Southey's *Poems*, can help us to answer such questions. They represent equally violent penalties on criminals. They also continue, although somewhat more uneasily, to connect the work of the poetry with violent modes of punishment. In 'Lord William', a murderer mysteriously drowns even after he is tortured by his own guilty conscience: the drowning seems like a fitting, but also redundant, punishment. 'Mary' is even more ambivalent about violent punishment: a young woman learns that her betrothed is a murderer who is eventually hanged at the end of the ballad. The tone of the poem is grimly comic because Mary, coaxed by the townspeople to spy on her beloved, eventually finds out what everyone else knew all along: that her husband is a criminal sure to be hanged. But what is particularly striking about the poem is that its apparent alignment with vengeful public judgment is not entirely complete. Mary becomes a 'poor maniac' as a result of the narrated events: this is not simply because her would-be husband is a murderer but because he was put to death for it. Whereas 'The Children of the Wood' makes 'corruption of blood' part of the process of punishment, 'Mary' draws attention to the death penalty as a producer of uncontrolled suffering for which the poem mournfully attempts to account.

We see, then, that Southey manages to pursue a delicate political balancing act on the issue of punishment. On the one hand, his poetry sternly warns against revolutionary philosophies of the day and aligns itself with a violent use of force to quell them. On the other hand, a poem like 'Mary' also registers uneasiness about violent and bloody punishments, exciting sympathy for the 'poor maniac' suffering in their wake. I think this is why 'Jaspar' — perhaps one of Southey's most beautiful and intriguing ballads — is a poem so profoundly invested in establishing a formal commitment to the idea of answering crime with controlled, but not entirely violent, suffering. The poem was published anonymously (as 'Jasper') in the *Morning Post* on 3 May 1798; it is particularly intriguing that Southey had sent the poem to Charles Williams-Wynn, a moderate reformer who would eventually side with Romilly's penal reform efforts about a decade later.[32] In the ballad, Jaspar, a poor young man who is envious of those with greater wealth, kills a man, steals his money, and dumps the body in the river. His friend Jonathan is a poor 'labouring man' (l. 63) whose family has come on especially hard times with his wife's sickness. 'Now the sufferer found himself | Of everything bereft', we are told, since his landlord has seized all of his property (ll. 79–80). Jaspar encourages Jonathan to kill his landlord, but, taken to the brink of his crime, Jonathan desists as he grows 'sick at heart' at the very thought of the murder (l. 143).

At the end of 'Jaspar,' we are left with the image of Jaspar wandering in the woods alone:

> And fearful are his dreams at night
> And dread to him the day;
> He thinks upon his untold crime
> And never dares to pray.
>
> The summer suns, the winter storms,
> O'er him unheeded roll,
> For heavy is the weight of blood
> Upon the maniac's soul. (ll. 173–80)

Here again, Southey closely connects the telling of the tale with the 'untold' crime of the murderer and the punishment he is to receive for it. The ballad tells what is untold, in other words, and thereby strengthens the connection between its own form and a public attention to or exposure of offences. But we also see that this version of the ballad form, as in 'Mary', has shifted its alliances somewhat: rather than connecting itself with a scene of spectacular violence, Southey's poem subscribes to a form of 'conscience' (l. 142) that inflicts a mental and physical pain and isolation falling short of death.

The link between lyric poetry and conscience is truly powerful, and one of Romantic poetry's most significant contributions to the history of punishment consists in its dramatizing of conscience as a response to criminal action. In Mary Robinson's 'The Haunted Beach' (1800), a murderer is tortured by his own guilty conscience. Coleridge explores emotions connected with guilt and gives them a powerful ethical force in his drama *Osorio* (from which, as I explained earlier, 'The Dungeon' is extracted).[33] What is remarkable about Southey's representation of conscience in this ballad is that conscience is not solely a mental or psychological phenomenon; it is rigorously externalized and identified with a juridical and aesthetic formal order and clarity. Conscience is like a prison. When Jaspar says 'Nor eye below, nor eye above, | Can pierce the darkness here', the point is not that God sees Jaspar's crimes, but that the poem, acting on behalf of a pain-inducing conscience, most certainly does with unforgiving rigour (ll. 155–56).

Wordsworth's 'The Thorn' and Utilitarian Critique

Southey's ballads, we now see, traffic in the violent forms of justice that are inherited from the ballad tradition, but they also collectively convey an uneasiness about that tradition and an impulse to devise a formal intervention within it. Wordsworth's poem 'The Thorn' takes that uneasiness about the severity of penal sanctions so far that the poem conveys a virtual indifference toward the particularity of crime. Past actions, criminal or not, are less important in their call for specific retributive responses and more important for their production of consequent effects: 'misery', suffering, and other emotions or practices that place the claims of the present over those of the past. Thus, rather than decisively committing the poem to depending upon one kind of penalty or another — as Southey does even by aligning 'Jaspar' with a retributive 'weight of blood' on Jaspar's 'soul' — it surprisingly suggests that the work of poetry could be a substitute for punishment even more complete than Southey's. Whereas Southey's reformism makes the ballad genre co-produce but soften the violence of punishment, Wordsworth's reformism makes poetry, and the salutary influences of the natural world it describes, entirely supplant punishment's place. Poetry represents and encourages rehabilitation.

The narrator of Wordsworth's poem has long been a subject of critical discussion, in part because of the poet's note appended to the 1800 edition of the text: there, he clarifies, among other things, that the speaker is meant to be a person, perhaps a retired sea captain, who is 'not a native' of the region described in the poem. Such a person, 'having little to do', becomes 'credulous and talkative from indolence', and displays 'superstitious' habits of mind. Superstitious minds have 'slow faculties', 'deep feelings', and 'imagination', he claims, rather than 'fancy', which he defines as the mind's ability to adjust to new situations.[34] I understand part of the significance of Wordsworth's note to lie in an attempt to underline the narrator's distance from empirical facts. These facts include a possible murder, and thus the distance from that fact also entails a distance from the punishment that might be required as retribution for it.

The ballad, as I mentioned at the beginning of this essay, tells the tale of a woman who may (or may not) have murdered her child. Although we are told late in the poem that 'some had sworn an oath that she | Should be to public justice brought' (ll. 232–33), the narrator clearly separates himself from these people. We only know from the speaker that the woman regularly visits a particular spot, 'high on a mountain's highest ridge' (l. 23), which he describes in loving detail at the beginning of the poem. High on this ridge is a thorn overgrown with lichens, next to a muddy pond and a 'beauteous heap' of moss (l. 36):

> Now would you see this aged thorn,
> This pond and beauteous hill of moss,
> You must take care and chuse your time
> The mountain when to cross.
> For oft there sits, between the heap
> That's like an infant's grave in size,
> And that same pond of which I spoke,

> A woman in a scarlet cloak,
> And to herself she cries,
> 'Oh misery! oh misery!
> Oh woe is me! oh misery!' (ll. 56–66)

The narrator later identifies the woman as Martha Ray, and tells her story. She was going to marry Stephen Hill, but he 'had sworn another oath' to another woman, and he marries the other woman instead (l. 125). The narrator knows very little else beyond these bare facts about her life and that she has been seen visiting the spot (he has seen her himself). There is some speculation that a child was born, and that the hill of moss is the child's grave, but these are conveyed as the beliefs of others. After asking what the thorn, pond, and moss mean to her — that is, why Martha Ray visits the spot crying in 'misery' — he explains:

> I cannot tell; but some will say
> She hanged her baby on the tree.
> Some say she drowned it in the pond,
> Which is a little step beyond,
> But all and each agree,
> The little babe was buried there,
> Beneath that hill of moss so fair. (ll. 214–20)

The stanza insists upon delineating the specific outlines of, and complexities within, an interpretive community by specifying both the areas of disagreement (over how the child was murdered) and the area of agreement (the place of burial). But the supposed consensus conveyed here is contradicted by an earlier statement: no one 'ever new' what became of the child:

> And if a child was born or no,
> There's no one that could ever tell;
> And if 'twas born alive or dead. (ll. 158–60)

The narrator's inability to tell a tale that he then proceeds to tell has struck more than one reader as cause for some annoyance: Coleridge eventually criticized the work in his *Biographia Literaria* (1817) insisting that representing 'dulness and garrulity' in a narrator could only result in dullness and garrulity in the poem.[35] Still more lately, the speaker's combination of loquacity and blockage has struck critics as an exploration of the limits of language more generally.[36] But neither view can entirely account for how and why the ballad amounts to a tactical avoidance of the grisly details of crime and punishment that had stood for centuries at the centre of the ballad tradition. Implied within the telling of this tale is that, if there had been a child (dead or not), Martha would be guilty of infanticide without a witness to the birth. William Blackstone in his *Commentaries on the Laws of England* had pronounced the 1623 Act with this stipulation unduly harsh, since it makes 'concealment of the death almost conclusive evidence of the child's being murdered by the mother'.[37] What is striking about 'The Thorn', then, is that it taps into the long history of the ballad's fascination with violent crimes and violent penalties, but frames this association, as we have seen, as a particular belief in the idea that Martha Ray should be brought to trial and perhaps punished for her offence, although the balladeer (who has obviously been unable to witness the birth or even verify whether a child was born or not) refuses to endorse such an idea. The garrulous narrator of the 'The Thorn' in this sense provides a surprising instance of what Saree Makdisi identifies as the modernizing spirit of the *Lyrical Ballads*, in that he relegates a barbaric form of punishment to the margins. What needs to be acknowledged, however, in contrast to Makdisi's argument, is that this gesture is not easily viewed as a politically conservative one.[38] The ballad's modernizing spirit consists of a distance from retributive violence.

We might also now revisit Mayo's striking and informative suggestions about the literary precedents for various poems in *Lyrical Ballads*. 'The Thorn' in particular was most likely inspired by numerous other ballads about murdering mothers, among them 'The Cruel Mother', a Scottish ballad that Wordsworth copied into his commonplace book, and Gottfried August Bürger's 'Des Pfarrers Tochter von Taubenhain', translated by William Taylor as 'The Lass of Fair Wone' in the *Monthly Magazine* in 1796 (the latter is of particular interest to Mayo).[39] 'The Cruel Mother', interesting though it may have been to Wordsworth, only recounts the tale of the mother killing her child. Bürger's ballad is far more rich and detailed. Even so, the German poet's orientation toward his subject matter is entirely different from that of Wordsworth. His ballad matter-of-factly tells the tale of a parson's daughter who is seduced, bears a child, kills the child, and is hanged for her crime. After her death, her ghost haunts the desolate place of the hanging. The poem is more similar in scope to criminal broadsides: it attracts sympathy for the unfortunate woman but does not raise serious doubts about her actions and does not quite suggest that hanging her was unjust. Indeed, making the scene of her hanging into the focal point for the end of the poem might permit a certain level of identification with capital punishment rather than an outright criticism of it.

When we turn back to the 'The Thorn', we see how important it is, in contrast to Bürger's poem, that the 'spot' originally attracting the speaker's notice is a place of mystery. It is a place that is magnified in terms of the questions, rather than the answers, that it provokes and generates. The overwhelming point of the narration of 'The Thorn', in fact, is that the spot on the mountain-top is of greater significance than speculations about what Martha did or did not do, or at least the speaker surprisingly suggests that 'Perhaps when you are at the place | You something of her tale may trace' (ll. 110–11).[40] This is not because of the 'shadow of a babe' that some can 'trace' in the pool of water — this is once again a belief that is not shared by the speaker. What the speaker means by tracing the tale is something far more reduced in scope: he means simply that we must witness, and in a sense participate in, its importance to Martha, who regularly comes to the spot (we are reminded of this over and over again) and cries 'Oh misery! oh misery!'. Whatever has happened to Martha — whatever chain of events led to the present moment — is less important than her present suffering. And with a utilitarian spirit, that is, the narrator focuses his interest on the pain that she demonstrates as a result of her experiences, even as the regularity of her visits to the spot for two decades conveys a kind of reformed consciousness. The spot, moreover, is not simply a place of pain for Martha, but a place that incites, at least for the narrator and for us, a general sense of aesthetic pleasure: the narrator continually talks about the beauty of the particular spot, and also how Martha's visits are connected to the beauty of the world — to its stars, the moon, the winds, the surrounding green hills. Wordsworth thus makes 'The Thorn' into a crime ballad that drifts toward a nature lyric, making the spot, with all of its beauty, into a focal point for individual and social reformation.[41] Because of its emphasis on the aesthetic pleasures to be enjoyed from this place of possible crime, the poem and its privileged spot act as alternatives to retributive punishment altogether.

After the Ballad, after Retribution

Even when we look at Southey's poetry, we can get a glimpse of this logic. In 'Jaspar', Jonathan's conscience is awakened through his connection to nature: to the calm night, the still air, and the sweet song of the nightingale (ll. 129–30). Nature does not quite overtake 'Jaspar', however. And what must be emphasized about 'The Thorn' is how far the meditation on nature mangles the familiar narrative form of the ballad. The shift of poetic alliances away from penal apparatuses to interpretations, emotions, and other attachments to the natural world defiantly argues against the secure authority of penal structures in favour of the authority of viewing and reading subjects. For those subjects, a poetic meditation on nature does not furnish a perfectly calibrated pattern, but rather a focal point for collective, wondering contemplation. Another way of putting this would be to say that Wordsworth paradoxically constructs a ballad, among the most ancient of literary forms, that argues against the authority of literary and juridical forms with which the genre of the ballad had so anxiously and uneasily aligned itself.

Any examination of Wordsworth's longer career — he died in 1850 and became a passionate supporter of the established church and a range of other traditional institutions — would reveal that the poet was hardly secure in his resistance to capital punishment and other forms of juridical violence. In fact, his *Sonnets Upon the Punishment of Death* from 1841 nearly reversed his early position, and thus we must be cautioned against taking 'The Thorn' as an example of his work as a whole. Still, it is worth noting that the very first sonnet in the terribly grim *Punishment of Death* series concentrates on a 'spot' on the road to Lancaster Castle (the castle itself was the site of over 100 executions for murder, theft, and other crimes) and asks for the reader to identify not with the place of execution but with the criminals' 'showers' of tears before their hangings.[42] The natural 'spot' here is closely connected with the seemingly repentant and reformed criminal. And thus, the defence of the death penalty in these sonnets oddly makes capital punishment seem overly cruel, excessive, and even extraneous. We find, in other words, that this much later defence of capital punishment oddly repeats the topoi of 'The Thorn', suggesting the survival of the earlier poem's somewhat radical positions on the issue even in their apparent overturning.

'The Thorn', then, completes our picture of three vastly different but related ways of thinking about the ballad's connection with the death penalty. From its origins, the ballad is connected with a violent, intractable, and unpredictable force. Southey's extraordinary contribution is to think of the work of the poet as an artful harnessing, controlling, and taming of this force. In *Lyrical Ballads*, the work of the poet is not identified with the stern but moderated application of retributive justice, as it is in Southey's writing: retributive justice is a belief that cannot be identified with poetry at all. Poetry's relation to justice is still the issue, however: what we observe is a complex shift in juridical perspectives from a retributive to a restorative account. The work of poetry achieves a potent connection to the natural spot as a site of restoration and rehabilitation in Wordsworth's famous ballad, for the poem, like the natural spot, fulfils Coleridge's definition of poetry as that to which we return with pleasure.[43] If there is any force in the narrator's claims about the pleasure and wonder in natural beauty to be found in the mysterious spot on the mountain-top, it might be possible to think of Martha someday finding some pleasure there as well.

The shift in gears from crime ballad to nature poetry, and the suggestion that poetry might take the place of punishment, could be considered alongside attempts in our own day to think beyond the logic of retributive justice. Although not explicitly framed as utilitarian arguments, contemporary views are often infused with a utilitarian spirit in that they tend to point out the futility of retributive forms of justice — whether in the form of capital punishment or prisons — and they tend to argue for the individual and social benefits that accrue from rehabilitation. Rehabilitation launches a strong claim for the power of acculturation. It insists that people can be remade if placed in a different set of conditions, and the effort of that theory is always to imagine what those conditions might look like. In Angela Y. Davis's important work, for example, the alternatives to the prison industrial complex are envisioned on the model of rehabilitation facilities and community assistance programmes in order to enhance systemic equality. These, Davis soberly cautions, require 'radical transformations of many aspects of our society'.[44]

Part of what is at stake in the shift from the ballad to the nature lyric in Wordsworth's 'The Thorn' — and also in related poems in *Lyrical Ballads* like 'The Dungeon' and the 'The Convict' — is that nature becomes a rehabilitative environment, although of a very unique and complex kind. If the shift from retribution to restorative nature is indeed a large-scale cultural shift, the very notion of nature's restorative possibilities cannot be considered apart from its unscripted, unpatterned quality. Trees, after all, are not laws or rehabilitation clinics. Instead, the thorn in nature, and 'The Thorn' in *Lyrical Ballads*, provokes regular contact that invites acculturation beyond culture. For in 'The Thorn', the varieties of misery, wonder, pleasure, and other modes of mental operation suggest the possibility of restorative, imaginative contact without the burdens of routinization, normalization, and discipline.

Notes to Chapter 6

1. William Wordsworth, 'The Thorn', in William Wordsworth and Samuel Taylor Coleridge, *Lyrical Ballads*, ed. by W. J. B. Owen, 2nd edn (Oxford: Oxford University Press, 1979).

2. 'Ballad', in *Women and Gender in Medieval Europe: An Encyclopedia*, ed. by Margaret Schaus (London: Routledge, 2006), pp. 58–59; Robert Mayo, 'The Contemporaneity of the *Lyrical Ballads*', *PMLA* (1954), 486–522.

3. *The English and Scottish Popular Ballads*, ed. by Francis James Child, 5 vols (New York: Houghton Mifflin, 1898), I, 243–44.

4. 'Ballad', in *The New Princeton Encyclopedia of Poetry and Poetics*, ed. by Alex Preminger and T. V. F. Brogan (Princeton, NJ: Princeton University Press, 1993), p. 117.

5. Ibid., p. 116. On the connection between poetry and ritual, see Jonathan Culler, *Theory of the Lyric* (Cambridge, MA: Harvard University Press, 2015), p. 131.

6. Caroline A. Halsted, *Richard III as Duke of Gloucester and King of England* (Philadelphia: Carey and Hart, 1844), p. 17.

7. Joseph Addison and others, *The Spectator*, 6 vols (London: H. D. Symonds, 1796), II, 21.

8. [Anon.], *The Children in the Wood: A Musical Piece* (Dublin: John Rice, 1794).

9. Wordsworth & Coleridge, *Lyrical Ballads*, p. 176.

10. 'The Children in the Wood', in Thomas Percy, *Reliques of Ancient English Poetry*, 3 vols (London: Cassell, Petter, and Galpin, 1866), III.

11. William Blackstone, *Commentaries on the Laws of England*, 4 vols (Chicago, IL: University of Chicago Press, 1979), IV, 373–79.

12. Prominent collections include those at Harvard University, University of California San Diego, and the National Library of Scotland, all of which are acknowledged in my notes.

13. *Broadside Ballads of the Restoration Period from the Jersey Collection Known as the Osterly Park Ballads*, ed. by F. Burlington Fawcett (London: John Lane, 1930).

14. 'Captain Thomas Greene's Last Farewell' (Edinburgh, 1705), National Library of Scotland, <http://digital.nls.uk/broadsides/broadside.cfm/id/15814> [accessed 3 August 2018].

15. Michel Foucault, *Discipline and Punish: The Birth of the Prison*, trans. by Alan Sheridan (New York: Random House, 1977), p. 67.

16. 'A Warning to Murtherers' (1684–86), UC Santa Barbara English Broadside Ballad Archive, <http://ebba.english.ucsb.edu/ballad/21374/xml> [accessed 3 August 2018].

17. 'Last Speech and Confession of Janet Riddle' (21 January 1702), UC Santa Barbara, <http://ebba. english.ucsb.edu/ballad/34335/image> [accessed 3 August 2018].

18. 'Particulars of the Trial and Execution of James Butler, for Arson' (1829), Harvard Crimes Broadside Project <http://iiif.lib.harvard.edu.manifests/view/drs:478771658i> [accessed 3 August 2018].

19. 'A True and Tragical Song, concerning Captain John Bolton' (1775), UC Santa Barbara Archive, <http://ebba.english.ucsb.edu/ballad/31133/xml> [accessed 8/3/2018].

20. Susan Stewart, 'Scandals of the Ballad', *Representations*, 32 (1990), 134–56.

21. Maureen McLane, *Balladeering, Minstrelsy, and the Making of British Romantic Poetry* (Cambridge: Cambridge University Press, 2008), pp. 212–52.

22. My argument explores an aspect of the ballad tradition that lies somewhat closer to Steve Newman's conception of the political resonance of ballads in *Ballad Collection, Lyric, and the Canon: The Call of the Popular from the Restoration to the New Criticism* (Philadelphia: University of Pennsylvania Press, 2004), although I delineate a more specific area in which political negotiation occurs.

23. Linda Venis, 'The Problem of Broadside Balladry's Influence on the *Lyrical Ballads*', *Studies in English Literature*, 24 (1984), 617–32.

24. Canuel, *The Shadow of Death*, pp. 11–33.

25. 'Transportation' refers to the practice in England of transporting, by ship, convicted criminals from 1790 to 1823 to a penal colony in New South Wales, Australia.

26. Robert Southey, 'Elinor,' in *Joan of Arc and Minor Poems* (London: Routledge, 1853).

27. Samuel Coleridge, 'The Dungeon', in Wordsworth & Coleridge, *Lyrical Ballads*.

28. William Wordsworth, 'The Convict', in Wordsworth & Coleridge, *Lyrical Ballads*.

29. John Thelwall, 'Stanzas Written on the Morning of Trial,' in *Poems Written in Close Confinement* (London: John Thelwall, 1795), l. 31.

30. Mayo, 'The Contemporaneity of the *Lyrical Ballads*'. For a recent account of the silencing of

political protest in early Romantic writing, see John Bugg, *Five Long Winters: The Trials of British Romanticism* (Stanford, CA: Stanford University Press, 2014).

31. David Fairer discusses the connection between English literary history and English law in Southey in 'Southey's Literary History', in *Robert Southey and the Contexts of English Romanticism*, ed. by Lynda Pratt, Vincent Newey, and Joanne Shattock (London: Ashgate, 2013), pp. 1–18.

32. See <http://www.historyofparliamentonline.org/volume/1790–1820/member/williams-wynn-charles-watkin-1775–1850> [accessed 3 August 2018].

33. For a discussion of conscience and its relation to punishment, see Canuel, *The Shadow of Death*, pp. 115–41.

34. Wordsworth & Coleridge, *Lyrical Ballads*, p. 139.

35. Samuel Coleridge, *Biographia Literaria*, ed. by James Engell and Walter Jackson Bate, 2 vols (Princeton, NJ: Princeton University Press, 1983), II, 49.

36. Susan Wolfson, '*Lyrical Ballads* and the Language of (Men) Feeling: Wordsworth Writing Women's Voices', in *Men Writing the Feminine* (Albany: SUNY Press, 1994), pp. 29–57.

37. Blackstone, *Commentaries on the Laws of England*, IV, 198. The connection to child murder is also explored in Josephine McDonagh, *Child Murder and British Culture, 1720–1900* (Cambridge: Cambridge University Press, 2003).

38. Saree Makdisi, *Making England Western: Occidentalism, Race, and Imperial Culture* (Chicago, IL: University of Chicago Press, 2014), pp. 87–130. Makdisi's postcolonial argument repeats the feminist argument about the *Lyrical Ballads*. For a particularly compelling account of the narrator's questionable uses of his female subject, see Karen Swann, 'Martha's Name, or The Scandal of 'The Thorn', in *Dwelling in Possibility: Women Poets and Critics on Poetry*, ed. by Yopie Prins and Maeera Schreiber (Ithaca, NY: Cornell University Press, 1997), pp. 60–79.

39. Wordsworth & Coleridge, *Lyrical Ballads*, p. 141; Gottfried August Bürger, 'The Lass of Fair Wone', trans. by William Taylor, *Monthly Magazine*, 1 (1796), 223–24.

40. In an extreme version of this argument, Stephen Maxfield Parrish argues that the poem is 'about a man (and a tree)', in ' "The Thorn": Wordsworth's Dramatic Monologue', *ELH*, 24 (1957), 155.

41. The fact that Wordsworth began his writing of the poem in the form of couplets further demonstrates the degree to which this ballad represents a struggle against the ballad tradition.

42. William Wordsworth, 'Suggested by the View of Lancaster Castle', in *The Poems. Volume 2*, ed. by John O. Hayden (Harmondsworth: Penguin, 1977), ll. 1, 13.

43. Coleridge, *Biographia Literaria*, II, 13.

44. Angela Y. Davis, *Are Prisons Obsolete?* (New York: Seven Stories Press, 2003), p. 108.

CHAPTER 7

❖

A Song Before Execution:
José de Espronceda's 'El reo de muerte'

Michael Iarocci

> Only one who hears the voice of humankind in the poem's solitude can understand what the poem is saying.
>
> T. W. ADORNO, 'On Lyric Poetry and Society' (1957)

Madrid, 1833. After years of exile from Spain, the radical Romantic José de Espronceda (1808–42) returns to the capital. He is among a cohort of Spanish political exiles who return to their home country with high political expectations as constitutional liberalism establishes itself after years of absolutist oppression. Among the most politically progressive of those returning, Espronceda has participated in revolutionary politics abroad, and the poetry he pens after his return takes a decidedly social turn. During the 1830s he will compose the poems that subsequently contribute to his canonization as Spain's premier Romantic poet, and, among them, 'El reo de muerte' [The Convict Condemned to Death] (1837) is arguably his most powerful statement on Spain's death penalty.[1] It continues to fascinate readers today for its trenchant indictment of capital punishment, its innovative poetics, and its national and transnational resonances. In a broadly European context, Espronceda's poem dialogues with Victor Hugo's renowned *Le Dernier Jour d'un condamné* (1829), the popular, fictionalized diary of a convict as he awaits his execution, which circulated widely across Europe, both in the original French and in translation.[2] Within a more national context, 'El reo de muerte' engages the specific socio-political moment of Spain's emerging liberal order.

In what follows, I take up Espronceda's famous poem in order to elucidate these various levels of engagement, and in order to ask the broader generic question of poetry's particular mode of engagement with the issue of execution. On the one hand, intertextual dialogue and cross-cultural adaptation loom large. As we will see, 'El reo de muerte' reworks Hugo's paradigmatic text in fascinating ways. At the same time, however, the recasting of the Hugolian narrative of a condemned man's last hours *as poetry* brings the particularities of lyric discourse (the respective roles of voice, figure, meter, rhythm, rhyme, etc.) to the fore. The work thus raises fundamental questions concerning the roles of stylization and aesthetic distance within Romantic social critique. What does it mean to confront impending execution in poetic form? What is particular to the way poetry indicts the violence of the state and the social order that sustains it? What tensions obtain between the writing and reading of poetry on the one hand, and the subject of execution on the other? These are among the key questions I will engage in what follows as I take readers through the poem in order to probe its intricacies, its resonance for the Spanish reading public of the 1830s, and its continuing purchase on readers today. After a brief historical overview of the political and literary context in which the work appeared, I develop a close reading of the poem in order to highlight the complex relationship between sense and sound in the poem. I put my analysis of the poem into dialogue with key notions from T. W. Adorno's 'On Lyric Poetry and Society' (1957) in order to underscore the political charge that stylization and aesthetic distance acquire in Espronceda's work.

Aesthetic Distance as Critique

'El reo de muerte' first appeared in 1837 in the pages of the newspaper *El Español*.[3] It has conventionally been grouped with a handful of other poems from the same period — 'Canción del pirata' [The Pirate's Song], 'El mendigo' [The Beggar], 'El canto del Cosaco' [The Cossack's Song] — that together represent an overtly contemporary, socio-critical turn in Espronceda's work. The poems are also traditionally considered to represent a more mature, more fully Romantic moment within the poet's *oeuvre*. Espronceda's early writing was strongly marked by the neoclassical norms that the poet learned under the tutelage of Alberto Lista (1775– 1848), while the poems of the 1830s develop a new idiom in which Byron and Hugo, among others, become important reference points. Beyond its place in Espronceda's literary biography, however, 'El reo de muerte' must also be situated at the particular juncture of Spanish political history to which I have alluded briefly.[4]

In the wake of Napoleon's misadventures in Iberia (1808–14), monarchic absolutism was re-established in Spain in the person of Ferdinand VII, who, with the exception of the brief constitutional hiatus known as the Liberal Triennium (1820–23), ruled as an absolute monarch until his death in 1833. Ferdinand's reactionary reign was marked by the repression, imprisonment, and execution of liberals who favoured constitutionally limited monarchy. This was particularly the case during the last ten years of his reign, the so-called 'ominous decade'. As a consequence, considerable swathes of the Spanish liberal lettered class, Espronceda among them, went into exile. Primarily residing in England and France, these Spaniards became intimately familiar with the culture and politics of their host countries, and the impact of their years abroad is not difficult to detect in their writing.

Following the death of Ferdinand VII, the Queen Regent María Cristina was forced to conclude a pact with Spanish liberals in order to ensure the succession of her daughter, Isabela II. With the definitive end of absolutism in the 1830s, formerly exiled Spanish liberals were granted amnesty, and they returned to Spain eager to participate in the emerging political order. New political fault lines, however, now divided progressive, revolutionary liberals, the *exaltados,* from their more conservative counterparts, the *moderados*. Such is the political milieu in which Espronceda, an avowed *exaltado*, publishes 'El reo de muerte' for the first time, and in this sense politics are at once the catalyst for Espronceda's exile and return, the ground that makes possible the poem's publication, and also the object of its intervention.[5]

Divided into two equal sections, Espronceda's poem focuses on the experiences of a convict the night and early morning preceding his execution. It is a narrative poem comprised of a total of twenty-one stanzas of varying type, including a refrain that recurs at irregular intervals. (I reproduce the full poem, with facing translation, at the end of the chapter.) There are few, if any, traces of the juridical proceedings that have presumably lead to the moment. Readers do not know what the convict has been accused of, how long he has been imprisoned, or if he is, in fact, guilty or not. In contrast to Hugo's protagonist in *Le Dernier Jour d'un condamné*, whose guilt emerges in glimpses over the course of his writing, the convict's guilt or innocence here remains an unknown, and there are other striking differences as well. Rather than the simulacrum of a first-person diary, the condemned man's plight in the poem comes to readers through lyrical third-person narration. In addition, Espronceda carries out an extraordinary compression of time vis-à-vis Hugo's narrative: from six weeks of prolonged psychological suffering in *Le Dernier Jour d'un condamné*, to less than twenty-four hours in Espronceda's poem; from the reading experience of a short novel, to 146 verses. If the dilatory quality of suffering emerges in part through the act of reading the journal entries that mark the passage of time in Hugo, Espronceda privileges the closing moments of that narrative, the intensity of the condemned man's very last hours.

For Spaniards of the day, the convict in the poem would quickly be recognized as being 'en capilla' [in chapel], the period immediately preceding the execution of the sentence. A time set aside with a chaplain in order to square away spiritual matters, in Spain it traditionally involved a night of vigil before morning executions. It was, in this regard, a threshold moment that ritualistically marked a shift away from the more quotidian experience of imprisonment. Suspended between darkness and light, the night and the dawn, and, more tellingly, between the last remaining hours of the convict's life and the moment of death that awaits him, the poem in its entirety unfolds in the in-between time spent 'en capilla'. The judiciary and sociological detail of Hugo's narrative (exchanges with lawyers, encounters with *gendarmes*, movement through the carceral system, conversations with other convicts, the encounter with the crowds) is almost entirely absent in what amounts to a poetic distillation of the situation. Space is restricted to the convict's makeshift chapel-cell throughout. The lyric intimacy and intensity brought to the narrative seemingly eclipse other concerns.

As readers imaginatively enter this space in the first stanza, however, they also move into a highly stylized verbal structure. Rather than the confessional style and diction of a journal writer, in 'El reo de muerte' Espronceda makes no effort to hide the dexterity and poetic artifice of the narrating lyric voice. His formal innovations, including the use of more than one meter in a single composition, were considered radically modern, experimental gestures that purposefully flouted longstanding conventions. *Polimetría*, or multiple meters within a single poem, was one of the signatures of formal rebellion within his poetics.[6] Across the genres, Romantic literary innovation was broadly perceived as part and parcel of the liberal revolution, much as Hugo had described in his famous 1827 *Préface de Cromwell.*[7] Readers come to know the convict, his environs, and his memories in an overtly innovative poetic language that abjures any of the pretence of the tradition of poetic realism. There is, in this regard, an early verbal performance of aesthetic distance, and the gesture is central to the way Espronceda's poem mounts its critique. Along with its overtly socio-critical content, the poetic form of the work will itself be a mode of indictment, functioning along the lines of Adorno's observations in 'On Lyric Poetry and Society' (1957): 'The work's distance from mere existence becomes the measure of what is false and bad in the latter. In its protest the poem expresses the dream of a world in which things would be different'.[8] Russell Berman offers an instructive gloss on Adorno's conception of the relationship between aesthetic autonomy and history:

> No twentieth-century critic was a more stalwart defender of aesthetic autonomy than Theodor W. Adorno, and yet none insisted more vociferously on the hidden or as he sometimes put it, 'subterranean' reverberations between the world of art and society. Hence his famous designation of lyric verse as a *geschichtsphilosophische Sonnenuhr,* a philosophical sundial of history, somehow indicating — albeit negatively, in the mode of a sundial's shadow — the temporal and categorical constitution of the social condition. However one understands the precise functioning of that metaphorical sundial, there is no doubt that, for Adorno, the poem, or more generally, the successful work of art, has this indicative capacity — the capacity to designate its historical moment and therefore articulate its criticism — due precisely to the distinctiveness of art, its autonomy. In other words, his critical vision rests on the dialectical paradox that the proximity of art and society, the societal character of the aesthetic, is premised on their separation.[9]

Through Espronceda's initial extended hyperbaton, for example, readers traverse a series of 'floating' adverbial clauses in the first three verses before the convict makes his grammatical appearance as the subject of the sentence in the fifth verse:

Reclinado sobre el suelo	[Reclined on the ground,
Con lenta amarga agonía,	With slow, bitter agony,
Pensando en el triste día	Thinking of the sad day
Que pronto amanecerá	That soon will dawn,
En silencio gime el reo	In silence moans the convict
Y el fatal momento espera	And awaits the fatal moment
En que el sol por vez postrera	When the sun for the last time
En su frente lucirá. (ll. 1–8)	Will shine on his brow.]

When he does so, it is between the main verbs of the stanza, 'gime' and 'espera', and hyperbaton emphasizes the convict's isolation by making 'reo' the last word of the verse. Physical abjection, a slow agony, and the condemned man's fixation on death qualify both the moan and the waiting, such that suffering and the passage of time converge. At the same time, the convict's moan, the acoustic core of the scene, offers an early cue to the importance of sound in the poem. A wordless utterance of suffering, the moan is, on the surface at least, a sign of raw affect, and it stages an intriguing tension that will inform much of the poem: the tension between the voice of the poet-narrator, on the one hand, and the world of his agonizing protagonist on the other.

At the level of the scene depicted, the only sound in the chapel is the convict's moan, but the vehicle that has delivered this scene is anything but inarticulate, and anything but quiet. Much of the poem is written in the meter of the *octavilla aguda*, an eight-verse octosyllabic stanza with a markedly sonorous rhyme scheme. The *octavilla* organizes almost continuous rhyme — of the eight verses, only the first and the fifth remain open — and it delivers a rhythmic punch with final accents in assonant rhyme in verses four and eight. In addition, the poem will often play with the conceptual links between rhyming words, such that 'agonía' [agony] in the first stanza, for instance, finds its rhyme with 'día' [day], the source of the agony. (Other examples of antithetical rhyme pairings include, for example, 'cielo' [heaven] and 'duelo' [sorrow] in stanza 3, 'bacanal' [bacchanalian] and 'infernal' [infernal] in stanza 8, and 'expirar' [to expire] and 'despertar' [to awaken] in stanza 12.) The sounds of the poem consequently maintain a rich and complex relationship with sounds within the convict's world. If this is generally true of the relationship between sound and sense in most poems, it becomes especially charged in 'El reo de muerte' because, as we will see shortly, sounds also play an important role within the narrative that unfolds. The poem is full of sounds, but the story it delivers is also very much about sounds. The drama of the convict's plight as time brings him ever closer to the moment of execution is largely figured by the arrival of sounds. In addition, the question of sound will often point to the difference between what the convict hears and what readers 'hear' in the poem, which consequently becomes charged with meaning. In place of the seeming transparency of a confessional voice, the poem structures a reading experience in which the artifice of the discourse (in the form of hyperbatons, enjambments, metric experimentation, and rhyme) highlights the poetic mediation of the convict's story.

Movement into the second stanza proceeds metonymically: from the convict, to the space he inhabits, to the friar by his side; and, again, hyperbaton momentarily suspends verbal fragments before the full picture emerges. 'Un altar y un crucifijo' [an altar and a crucifix], and then, panning out, 'la enlutada capilla' [the darkened chapel] all make their appearance before the main subject and verb, 'Lánguida vela amarilla | Tiñe en su luz funeral' [A languid yellow candle | Stains in its funereal light]. When the image coalesces grammatically, the adjectives 'enlutada' (as well as 'darkened' this can also mean 'mournful', or 'dressed in black'), 'lánguida' and 'funeral' make clear that if a sickly yellow candlelight stains the chapel ('teñir' is 'to stain' but also 'to colour', or 'to dye') so does the idea of death itself. Then, next to the convict, there is another sound: the garbled voice of the friar who has been charged to pray for him. There is no counsel to be had, and the friar is himself described as 'agonizante' [agonizing], a word that becomes an ironic reprise of the convict's earlier 'agonía', insofar as the friar's suffering is little more than the tedium of having to pray. In a visual echo of the half-pronounced words he mumbles, the friar's face is half covered, and the image of the muffled, unintelligible recitation of prayer again stages sounds that, like the convict's moan, perform their distance from the carefully crafted sounds of the poem. In effect, the wordless sounds of the convict's world reverberate against the sounds of the words in the poem, creating an awareness of the poem's aesthetic distance from the world it represents.

In the next three stanzas, sounds within the convict's world fall into the background as the narrative turns to a brief account of the protagonist himself, his thoughts, and his memories. First the convict appears to adopt the classic supplicant's pose:

El rostro levanta el triste	[The sad one lifts his face
Y alza los ojos al cielo:	And raises his eyes to heaven;
Tal vez eleva en su duelo	Perhaps in his sorrow he sends up
La súplica de piedad:	A plea for mercy:
¡Una lágrima! ¿es acaso	A tear![10] Is it a tear of fear
de temor o de amargura?	Or bitterness perchance?
¡Ay! ¡¡a aumentar su tristura	Oh! To increase his sadness
vino un recuerdo quizá!! (ll. 17–24)	Came a memory perhaps!!]

The scene is almost ekphrastic in its citation of the iconography of saints and martyrs, but its meaning is deeply ambiguous. The narrator carefully frames what readers see with adverbs of uncertainty, and the emotional content of the supplicant's pose remains undecidable. At stake in such a question is the moral psychology of the convict, who is either fearful of divine judgment or, conversely, embittered and resentful as he looks up at the heavens. In a more theological framework, the question is whether the scene is the visual *imitatio Christi* it appears to be or its opposite, a quasi-diabolical recrimination of divine providence. Before such matters are resolved, however, the narrative turns elsewhere.

Readers learn that the condemned man has scarcely emerged from childhood — 'aún el lloro | de la niñez no enjugó' [childhood's tears he has yet to dry] (ll. 27–28) — and that what has interrupted his heavenly gaze are thoughts of his mother. Remembrance of her love and her imagined grief at the prospect of his death intensify the convict's despair. The 'tristura' of that memory, amplified in the third stanza, becomes full-blown despair in the fifth as the convict, 'sin esperanza' [without hope], sees clearly that death awaits him. Even as hopelessness tortures the convict's psyche, however, the body marches on: 'Su corazón en su pecho | Siente con fuerza lartir' [In his chest he feels | his heart beating strongly] (ll. 35–36). The heart is seemingly reduced to its purely physiological dimensions.[11] It beats strongly, despite the despair, and whatever solace the friar might have offered disappears as the convict notes that his putative spiritual counsellor, a man much older than he who will nevertheless outlive him, has fallen asleep.

It is precisely at this moment of despair, in many regards the emotional nadir of the first section of the poem, that sounds enter the picture once again; not in the form of a moan or a muffled prayer, but rather the sounds of revellers outside of the prison:

¿Mas qué rumor a deshora	[But what sound unexpectedly
rompe el silencio? Resuena	Breaks the silence?
Una alegre cantinela	Happy singing spills out
Y una guitarra a la par,	And at the same time a guitar
Y gritos y de botellas	And shouts, and the sound
Que se chocan, el sonido,	Of bottles clinking,
Y el amoroso estallido	And the amorous burst
De los besos y el danzar. (ll. 41–48)	Of kisses, and dancing.]

Polysyndeton links the various sounds and suggests the energy of their accumulation as sound-images of the happiness the convict will never enjoy again. In a fascinating turn, however, a second, very different song is evoked from within the very midst of this one. Interrupting the description of the revellers' merrymaking, the narrative voice interjects:

Y también pronto en son triste	[And soon too in a sad sound
Lúgubre voz sonará:	A lugubrious voice will resound:
'¡Para hacer bien por el alma	'To do good for the soul
Del que van a ajusticiar!' (ll. 49–52)	Of the one they will put to death!']

Spanish readers of the day would have recognized in these verses the citation of a traditional appeal for prayers and charitable contributions. Members of lay religious associations often made such calls in sing-song fashion as crowds gathered to view the spectacle of execution, and donations were used in support of prayers for the condemned.

The narrative interruption of the revellers' song thus juxtaposes their merrymaking with a foretaste of the song to come: a lugubrious call for charity that the convict will presumably hear just prior to his execution. A change in meter accentuates the interruption as the poem shifts from the *octavilla* to the four-verse *quarteta asonantada,* also known as the *tirana,* which contains the call to charity. The stanza, which has strong associations with oral tradition, is characterized by assonant rhyme in verses 2 and 4, but the *verso agudo* [acute verse] continues, such that the punch of a last accented syllable present in the earlier *octavillas* persists despite the change in meter.[12] In effect, readers hear the change from one song to the other, turning the revelry outside the prison into a mockery of the convict's misery by evoking the very different melody the convict will soon hear. Within the reading process, the call to charity is also a repetition of the poem's opening epigraph.[13] It now becomes clear that those words are returning as a refrain. The narrative juxtaposition (the convict does not yet hear this song, but the reader does) again underscores the difference between what readers experience on the one hand, and what the convict has heard on the other.

As the first section of the poem comes to a close, the poet-narrator returns to the sounds of merriment that had been interrupted by the aside:

Y la voz de los borrachos	[And the voice of the drunkards
Y sus brindis, sus sueños	And their toasts, their dreams,
Y el cantar de las ramera	And the signing of the harlots
Y el desorden bacanal	And the bacchanalian disorder,
En la lúgubre capilla	Penetrate the mournful chapel

Penetran y carcajadas	And loud laughter
Cual de lejos arrojadadas	As if hurled from afar,
De la mansión infernal. (ll. 53–60)	From the infernal mansion.]

Polysyndeton, this time arranged as anaphora, accentuates the accumulation of sounds again, and the repetition of 'y' links this stanza to the earlier description of the merrymaking. The acoustic footprint of the party, however, has acquired new tones. The 'alegre cantinela' now becomes 'la voz de los borrachos', and, as the party progresses into inebriated excess, the earlier dancing and kissing reveal themselves to be moments of sexual commerce with harlots.

The sound of the revelers no longer 'resounds' as it did it initially, but now 'penetrates' the chapel, a penetration which the poem emphasizes by placing the verb in initial position. Syntactic violence echoes the violence of the penetration itself, and the sexual connotations are difficult to overlook. The song of debauchery implicitly becomes figured as a kind of sound-rape, a sexualized, sonic mockery of the solemnity of the convict's vigil, with hellish, diabolical laughter to boot. As this sacrilege literally hangs in the air, however, the *tirana* returns a second time.

The refrain now contrasts not with a generic image of revelry but, more pointedly, with its sexually diabolical tenor. It pointedly juxtaposes the orgiastic sins of *cupiditas* with the call to *caritas*, a contrast that highlights the fact that the revelers' singing is, both in its lascivious content and in its torturous effects on the convict, antithetical to the sounds of Christian charity. Once more, it is the readers of the poem rather than the convict who hear the words of the refrain and experience the effects of the juxtaposition. Within the convict's world, the call to charity has not yet arrived, and the narrator's prolepsis is a fine example of the way the poem exploits the differences between the poet-narrator and the convict. The former is visibly at work, orchestrating meters, rhythms, rhymes, acoustic contrasts, and thematic juxtapositions, while the latter, imprisoned in a cell, suffers the anguish of the wait.

In the last stanza of Section I, the narrator recounts the convict's reaction to the revelers' song. Returning to the *octavilla* form again, we read:

¡Maldición! Al eco infausto	[A curse! To the unfortunate echo,
El sentenciado maldijo	The sentenced man cursed
La madre que como hijo	The mother who like a son
A sus pechos le crió;	Raised him at her breast,
Y maldijo el mundo todo,	And he cursed the whole world,
Madijo su suerte impía	He cursed his pitiless fortune
Maldijo el aciago día	He cursed the bitter day
Y la hora en que nació. (ll. 65–72)	And hour in which he was born.]

With Byronic defiance, the repetition of 'maldijo' four times in eight verses underscores that the convict's despair has, in fact, turned to outright spiritual rebellion. The question of the convict's moral character, which was left hanging in the third stanza, is definitively resolved here. Exacerbated by the sounds outside of the prison, his despair (itself considered a sin within Catholic theology) has undergone a crescendo of sorts, turning into a generalized malediction that spares none. In effect, the convict responds to his condemnation and the singing outside his cell with a condemnation of his own. The earlier, ambiguous *imitatio Christi* gives way to rebellious quasi-Satanic recrimination, and the stanza performs what it says. The convict puts together his curses 'al eco' of the revellers' hellish tune, and the stanza itself echoes that tune through anaphora, which was one of the key rhetorical figures of the stanzas describing the revellers' song. The repetition of 'y' in those stanzas now finds an analogue in the repetition of 'maldijo'. This formal echo in turn suggests that the diabolical song of the revellers, which penetrated the convict's cell, is now resonating within the word-thoughts of his curses themselves. The sound of the revellers becomes the template for the convict's own form of sounding off.

As Section I comes to a close, the protagonist's moral and spiritual trajectory becomes clear. On his final night 'en capilla', no solace is to be found. The friar's prayers, muttered before he dozes off, offer no consolation. The convict's heavenly gaze finds no relief in the transcendent. His memories do not comfort, and the sound of merrymaking, an insult to his condition, slowly takes possession of both the cell and his psyche, turning his despair into open rebellion against the world and its values. What seems most lacking throughout is any trace of empathy for the convict's plight; that is, precisely the *caritas* for which the refrain calls. Nothing around the convict is, in fact, doing any 'bien por el alma | Del que van a ajusticiar' as called for in the *tirana*. Such is the condition that becomes 'infernal', both in the sense of inflicting suffering on the convict, and in the sense of prompting him to a blasphemous, anti-Christian malediction of his world. In effect, Section I charts the way the convict's sentence, coupled with his experience of incarceration, has turned him into a Satanic outcast.[14]

Social Indifference and the Politics of *Caritas*

Section II opens with a stark contrast: from the hellish recriminations of the previous section's closing, readers turn to the tranquillity of a moonlit night over Madrid. The sounds of Section I have abated, and the shift from Section I to Section II has involved a leap forward in time. It is still the night before the execution, but the silence that has settled over the city suggests that we are well into the early morning hours. The first stanza conveys the idea both through its placid nocturnal imagery and, formally, by means of a momentary adjustment to the stanza's meter. It maintains the *octavilla* form, but now with shorter hexasyllabic verses, as if to quieten the earlier, octosyllabic version. More pointedly, individual sources of sound from Section I (voices, shouts, and musical instruments) are evoked once more in order to emphasize that they have fallen mute. Anaphoric polysyndeton, which marked the revellers' song and the convict's curses, appears once again, but this time as the negation of sound:

Ni voces se escuchan   [No voices are heard
Ni ronco ladrido   Nor harsh screaming,
Ni tierno quejido   Nor the tender plaint
De amante laud. (ll. 77–80)   Of an amorous lute.]

If the sounds around him were a source of anguish for the convict in Section I, however, the silence of the early morning hours offers little consolation. The quiet hours of the night signal that he is closer to the moment of death, and there is still no empathy to be found. The city's slumber becomes a figure of collective indifference to his fate: 'El hombre duerme y no cuida | Del hombre que va a expirar' [Man sleeps and cares not | for the man who is going to expire] (ll. 83–84). Exploiting the ambivalence of 'el hombre', which can mean 'man' generically, or conversely 'the man', the repetition of the word at the beginning of each verse highlights the contrast between the collective and the individual. The refrain now appears a third time, but with a different introduction:

Que sin pena ni cuidado	[For without pity or care
Los hombres oyen gritar:	Men hear the cry:
'¡Para hacer bien por el alma	'To do good for the soul
Del que van a ajusticiar!' (ll. 89–92)	Of the one they will put to death!']

Logically speaking, the call to charity would not be sounding in the darkness of the early morning, and, in this regard, its evocation here is not yet an event within the convict's world. Once more, it is a narrative aside to readers, a commentary on the generalized indifference of the populace.

As the focus shifts from the bird's-eye view of the city to the officers involved in the execution, sound interrupts the condemned man's night once more. While the judge and executioner sleep without a worry, the sound of the gallows under construction is a reminder of what awaits. Significantly, its entry into the poem is marked by precisely the same expression that had introduced the revellers' song in Section I. Compare '¿Mas qué rumor a deshora | Rompe el silencio?' [But what sound unexpectedly | Breaks the silence?] (ll. 41–42) in the sixth stanza to 'Tan sólo rompe el silencio' [All that breaks the silence] (l. 97) in the fourteenth. The gallows under construction is thus linked to the song that so perturbed and transformed the convict in Section I. Both are figures of the way the external world's sounds permeate the convict's psyche as part of his agony.

Whereas the sounds of the revellers lead to the convict's cursing of the world, however, the still of the night finds him in a different state. In the hours that have elapsed he has fallen into uneasy sleep, and repetition of the same verb, 'envolver' [to envelop], in the descriptions of Madrid's repose and the convict's, respectively, underscores the chasm between the two. Untroubled slumber envelopes the city, while feverish dreams envelop the convict's psyche. Paralleling the turn to his interior in Section I, the poem now probes the anguished content of his dreams, a transition marked by three asterisks and a shift from the *octavilla* stanza to a hendecasyllabic *cuarteto* or quatrain:

Loca y confusa la encendida mente,	[His fiery mind mad and in a blur,
Sueños de angustia y fiebre y devaneo	Anguished dreams, and fever and delirium
El alma envuelven del confuso reo	Envelop the dazed condemned man
Que inclina al pecho la abatida frente.	Who drops his dejected brow to his chest.]
(ll. 101–04)	

If infernal imagery in Section I intimated that the death sentence was a living hell for the condemned, here the poem takes up the question in a more decidedly psycho-social register, suggesting that the mental torture of awaiting execution can in fact lead to madness.

Following the quatrain, readers move into a meter of Espronceda's own invention: an eight-verse stanza comprised of seven three-syllable verses, followed by a final verse of six syllables. With three quick beats per verse, the stanza markedly picks up the poem's tempo:

Y en sueños	[And in dreams
Confunde	He confuses
La muerte	Death,
La vida.	Life.
Recuerda	He remembers,
Olvida	He forgets,
Suspira	He sighs,
Respira	He breathes
Con hórrido afán.	With hideous effort.]

The accelerated meter conveys the fits and starts of the condemned man's mind as he dreams, but, tellingly, the only sounds within the scene are again non-verbal markers of suffering (sighs and effortful breathing) of the sort we first encountered in the convict's opening moan. There is consequently a divergence once more between the sounds and rhythms of the poem, and the sound-world of the convict.

The narrative then turns to the two dreams with which the poem closes. They are variations on well-known Romantic topoi. In the first, the man imagines the moment of his execution in the form of a noose that tightens implacably:

Y cuanto más forcejea	[And the more he wrestles
Cuanto más lucha y porfía	The more he struggles and grapples
Tanto más en su agonía	The more in his agony
Aprieta el nudo fatal. (ll. 118–21)	The fatal knot tightens.]

The sighs and effortful breathing of the previous stanza turn out to be the physical manifestations of a dream of asphyxiation, highlighting the bodily consequences of psychological duress. In the midst of the dream, the refrain returns a fourth time, again with a different introduction:

Y oye ruidos, voces, gentes	[And he hears noises, voices, people
Y una voz que dirá:	And a voice that will say:
'¡Para hacer bien por el alma	'To do good for the soul
Que van a ajusticiar!' (ll. 122–25)	Of the one they will put to death!']

The moment of truth arrives acoustically, first as noise, then as voices, and finally as the words of the refrain. It is the first time that the protagonist plausibly hears these words, and they come to him in a dream. The future tense that introduces it, however, suggests that even within the convict's delirium, the sound of the call remains anticipated. It haunts his dream-world as a marker of the moment that has yet to arrive.

The second dream, extended over the last two *octavillas* of the poem, stages a variant of the love-death motif. For brief moments the convict:

libre se contempla,	[imagines himself free,
Y el aire puro respira,	And he breathes pure air,
Y oye de amor que suspira	And he hears that the woman
La mujer que un tiempo amó,	He once loved is sighing with love,]
(ll. 126–29)	

The scene takes place in the *locus amoenus* of a spring meadow, but, when the convict reaches for his beloved, the dream dissipates, revealing the stark fate that awaits him: 'Y halla un cuerpo mudo y frío | Y un cadalso en su lugar' [And he finds a cold mute body | And a gallows in her place] (ll. 140–41).[15] That the image of the beloved should yield to a scene on the gallows is in keeping with the acoustic logic of the poem. Once again, an external sound has made its way into the convict's mind; he has slept to the sound of the gallows going up, and, like the revellers' song in Section I, it has infused his dreaming with its presence.

The refrain now returns to close the poem:

Y oye a su lado en son triste	[And next to him in sad sounds
Lúgubre voz resonar:	He hears a mournful voice resound:
'¡Para hacer bien por el alma	'To do good for the soul
Del que van a ajusticiar!' (ll. 142–46)	Of the one they will put to death!']

No longer an anticipated future, the words sound as his dream dissipates, because the actual call to charity, with everything it means, has finally arrived just beyond his cell. The last verses evoke the liminal state of consciousness between sleep and waking, when ambient sounds seep into dreams, with the added rub that for the convict, as the poem informs early on, to awaken is to arrive at the moment of his execution.

The poem has, in this regard, been a voyage toward the convict's acoustic encounter with the refrain, which only late in the poem insinuates itself into his dreams, and then into his waking. As in Hugo, rather than execution itself, the torturous effects of knowing that execution awaits have been at the core of the narrative, and the refrain is the harbinger of that knowledge. It is telling in this regard that the call to charity does not appear with standard periodicity. Its five manifestations across the poem are in stanzas 7, 9, 13, 18, and 21, and it is embedded within a *tirana* whose first two verses often vary. Rather than the consistent regularity of a standard refrain, the call to charity is in fact characterized by the unpredictability of its entrance into the poem and the varying contexts of its appearance, as if to figure the way the thought of impending death recurs with a rhythm of its own.

The opening verses of the poem also offer a twist on the conventional functions of the refrain. The call for charity is an epigraph, and technically speaking the story has not yet begun. The words appear directly, without narrative contextualization, free of the *tirana* form. The words are simply there, at the beginning of the poem, and, in this sense, they tacitly speak directly to the reader, posing an ethical question. How are we to hear these words in light of the world utterly devoid of compassion that will follow? To return to them via the poem's circular itinerary (these are the poem's first and last words) is no doubt to note the refrain's biting ironies, but it is also to ask oneself what would, in fact, 'do good for the soul of the one they will put to death'? Compassion for the man's plight would be a point of departure, but the poem also suggests something else. It intimates that there is a contradiction within the question itself, insofar as the death sentence (the 'van a ajusticiar' of the second verse) is, in fact, what has been undoing the convict's soul all along.

In retrospect, each section of the poem has limned the dismantling of the good in a slightly different register. Section I tracks its undoing in terms of religious morality, charting the 'diabolical' transformation of the convict, while Section II traces the condemned man's alteration in terms of psychological and physical suffering. The humanitarian conclusion that there can be no 'good for the soul' so long as 'they will put to death' is, in this regard, difficult to avoid. Without calling for it openly, abolition is the poem's unspoken moral centre. At the same time, the poem raises the question of the reader's relationship to the collectivity depicted. The poem unveils the complicity of a social order that not only tolerates execution but also inflicts further harm through its everyday activities, whether in revelry or in sleep. In this sense, readers (who 'hear' the call to charity) are prompted to reflect on whether they are, in fact, any different; that is, whether they too are inured to the call, and whether the quotidian unfolding of their own lives does not unwittingly contribute to the kind of moral travesty depicted. True *caritas* would involve more than a few coins for the convict's soul at his execution. Rigorously speaking, it would call for a juridical and social order in which capital punishment could not be inflicted to begin with.

Against the backdrop of the triumph of constitutional liberalism in Spain in the mid-1830s, the poem can consequently be read as a disillusioned commentary on the persistence of capital punishment beyond absolutism. Ferdinand VII had been merciless in his execution of liberals in the preceding decade, and many of those returning to Spain saw capital punishment as a vestige of an *ancien régime* that would soon be abolished by the new liberal state.[16] It is in this regard no coincidence that much of the poem is cast in gothic light — a world of moans, candles, mumbling friars, diabolical bacchanalia, and nightmares — as if to suggest that the death penalty belongs to a pre-modern, barbarous political world. At the same time, the poem's transnational, intertextual dialogue with Hugo is in effect an instantiation of the international humanitarian universalism that informed the French author's campaign against capital punishment, an assertion that the criticism of state killing is as apposite to Madrid as it is to Paris.

History would, of course, subsequently prove Espronceda and liberals of his kind sanguine about liberalism's relationship to capital punishment. Modern liberal nation-states did not, by and large, do away with state killing until much later, if at all. In Spain the political struggles of the 1830s between progressive *exaltados* and conservative *moderados* would eventually be decided in favour of the latter, and their agenda, which did not question capital punishment, would stretch well into the second half of the nineteenth century. As for the death penalty, it would persist in Spain, intermittently, until the Constitution of 1978, a scant seven years before its abolition in France.[17]

If 'El reo de muerte' is an intriguing example of the internationalization of literary interventions against the death penalty, however, it is also a fascinating rewriting of Hugo's paradigm. While many of the commonplaces of the *Le Dernier Jour d'un condamné* make their appearance (an emotionally distant chaplain, dreams of childhood, memories of a beloved, imagining the moment of death, etc.), there are also pronounced cultural and aesthetic differences. The more overtly Christian, metaphysical dimensions of Section I, the religious call to charity of the refrain, and the setting of the poem in its entirety within the time and space of 'en capilla', for example, might be understood productively as a kind of cultural translation aimed to capitalize on Spanish Catholic sentiment. Similarly, the interpellation of readers primarily in terms of *caritas* in the refrain not only incorporates a recognizably local practice, but may also have been a deft attempt to mobilize well-meaning Spaniards through the invocation of familiar Catholic theological categories.[18]

As significant as such cross-cultural rewriting might be, however, Espronceda's work also poses a fundamental aesthetic question, for, in effect, the poet's artistic gambit involves rendering key features of Hugo's narrative in the mode of lyric. Espronceda's intuition, I think, was that the 'idée fixe' that so tortured Hugo's convict was a lyrical concept at its core.[19] Insofar as the conventions of verse poetry (the rhyming and alliterative repetition of sounds, the repetition of meter from verse to verse, the repetition of stanzas, the repetition of refrains) are predicated on recurrence, there is a generic predisposition toward phenomena that are themselves steeped in repetition. Espronceda exploits these potentials to great effect in his poem, and it seems no coincidence that many of the key rhetorical figures, such as polysyndeton and anaphora, are also figures of repetition. In this sense, the poem re-figures the preoccupation with impending execution as song, as a macabre, ironic melody that comes and goes, literally echoing with other sounds of the convict's world: the moan, the mumbled prayer, the construction of the gallows. Espronceda makes the 'idée fixe' sing, and he turns the poem into the echo chamber of its foreboding.

There is also, however, one last, very different song. It is the song that is the poem itself, a song that stages a profound reversal vis-à-vis the injurious songs it contains. Espronceda offers a song in service of the suffering convict, a song that is in fact a plea for something different. In this sense, the poem's sounds are more than merely signs of the convict's suffering. In their excess, they contain within them both an ethical reflection on the representation of suffering and a foretaste of a different, future soundscape. We have seen repeatedly that 'El reo de muerte' often marks its distance, and our own, from the world it represents. It may seem a strange gesture within a project that aims to elicit sympathy for the convict, but it reminds readers of the limits of sympathetic identification, underscoring that whatever we might feel, we do not walk fully in the convict's shoes. The repeated differences between his sound-world and our own points to an ethical reflection on the perils of belief in full understanding when the suffering of others is the subject.[20] The distance, however, is not simply put to the service of ethics. There is also a tacit insistence throughout the poem on aesthetic distance, on the fact that we have no access to the convict and his plight other than through the artistic mediation of the poem. As a form of sound-art that acknowledges its degree of separation from the world, the poem, which presents itself as *a different song* and affords its own acoustic pleasures, might thus be said to contain utopian intimations of a less violent world to come. If one of Espronceda's major achievements in 'El reo de muerte' is to make the 'idée fixe' of impending execution sing as poetry, the converse is equally true. The poet's song is also thinking. It is reflecting on itself and on a future in which the sounds of execution can no longer be heard, and it asks its readers to do the same.[21]

El reo de muerte	*The Convict Condemned to Death*
¡¡Para hacer bien por el alma Del que van a ajusticiar!!	To do good for the soul Of the one they will put to death!!
I	I
[1] Reclinado sobre el suelo Con lenta amarga agonía, Pensando en el triste día Que pronto amanecerá, En silencio gime el reo Y el fatal momento espera En que el sol por vez postrera En su frente lucirá.	Reclined on the ground, With slow, bitter agony, Thinking of the sad day That soon will dawn, In silence the convict moans And awaits the fatal moment When the sun for the last time Will shine on his brow.
[2] Un altar y un crucifijo, Y la enlutada capilla Lánguida vela amarilla Tiñe en su luz funeral, Y junto al mísero reo, Medio encubierto el semblante, Se oye el fraile agonizante En son confuso rezar.	An altar, and a crucifix, And the darkened chapel A languid yellow candle Stains in its funereal light; And next to the wretched convict, His face half covered, One hears the suffering friar Pray in garbled sounds.
[3] El rostro levanta el triste Y alza los ojos al cielo: Tal vez eleva en su duelo La súplica de piedad: ¡Una lágrima! ¿es acaso De temor o de amargura? ¡Ay! ¡¡a aumentar su tristura Vino un recuerdo quizá!!	The sad one lifts his face And raises his eyes to heaven; Perhaps in his sorrow he sends up A plea for mercy: A tear! Is it a tear of fear Or bitterness perchance? Oh! To increase his sadness Came a memory perhaps!!
[4] Es un joven y la vida Llena de sueños de oro, Pasó ya, cuando aún el lloro De la niñez no enjugó: El recuerdo es de la infancia ¡¡Y su madre que le llora Para morir así ahora Con tanto amor le crió!	He is a young man and life Full of golden dreams, Has already passed, while Childhood's tears he has yet to dry: The memory is of childhood And his grieving mother, Who raised him with so much love, To see him die this way now!!

[5]
Y a par que sin esperanza
Ve ya la muerte en acecho,
Su corazón en su pecho
Siente con fuerza latir,
Al tiempo que mira al faile
Que en paz ya duerma a su lado,
Y que ya Viejo y postrado
Le habrá de sobrevivir.
[6]
¿Mas qué rumor a deshora
Rompe el silencio? Resuena
Una alegre cantinela
Y una guitarra a la par,
Y gritos y de botellas
Que se chocan, el sonido,
Y el amoroso estallido
De los besos y el danzar.
[7]
Y también pronto en son triste
Lúgubre voz sonará:
'¡Para hacer bien por el alma
Del que van a ajusticiar!'
[8]
Y la voz de los borrachos,
Y sus brindis, sus quimeras,
Y el cantar de las rameras,
Y el desorden bacanal
En la lúgubre capilla
Penetran, y carcajadas,
Cual de lejos arrojadas
De la mansion infernal
[9]
Y también pronto en son triste
Lúgubre voz sonará:
'¡Para hacer bien por el alma
Del que van a ajusticiar!'
[10]
¡Maldición! Al eco infausto
El sentenciado maldijo
La madre que como a hijo
A sus pechos le crío;
Y maldijo el mundo todo,
Maldijo su suerte impía,
Maldijo el aciago día
Y la hora en que nació.

II

[11]
Serena la luna
Alumbra en el cielo,

And while hopeless
He sees death lie in waiting,
In his chest he feels
His heart beating strongly,
While he looks at the friar
Who in peace now sleeps beside him,
And who old and prostrate
Is sure to survive him.

But what sound unexpectedly
Breaks the silence?
Happy singing spills out
And at the same time a guitar
And shouts, and the sound
Of bottles clinking,
And the amorous burst
Of kisses, and dancing.

And soon too in a sad tone
A lugubrious voice will resound:
'To do good for the soul
Of the one they will put to death!'

And the voice of the drunkards,
And their toasts, their dreams,
And the singing of the harlots,
And the bacchanalian disorder,
Penetrate the mournful chapel,
And so does loud laughter
As if hurled from afar,
From the infernal mansion.

And soon too in a sad sound
A lugubrious voice will resound:
'To do good for the soul
Of the one they will put to death!'

A curse! To the ill-fated echo
The sentenced man cursed
The mother who like a son
Raised him at her breast;
And he cursed the whole world,
He cursed his pitiless fortune
He cursed the fateful day
And hour in which he was born.

II

Serene the moon
Shines in the sky,

Domina en el suelo
Profunda quietud;
Ni voces se escuchan,
Ni ronco ladrido,
Ni tierno quejido
De amante laud.
[12]
Madrid yace envuelto en sueño,
Todo al silencio convida,
Y el hombre duerme y no cuida
Del hombre que va a expirar;
Si tal vez piensa en mañana,
Ni una vez piensa siquiera
En el mísero que espera
Para morir, despertar;
[13]
Que sin pena ni cuidado
Los hombres oyen gritar:
¡Para hacer bien por el alma
Del que van a ajusticiar!
[14]
¡¡Y el juez también en su lecho
Duerme en paz!! ¡¡y su dinero
El verdugo placentero
Entre sueños cuenta ya!!
Tan solo rompe el silencio
En la sangrienta plazuela
El hombre del mal que vela
Un cadalso al levantar

On the ground
Deep stillness reigns,
No voices are heard,
Nor harsh screaming,
Nor the tender plaint
Of an amorous lute.

Madrid lies enveloped in slumber.
Everything invites silence,
And man sleeps and cares not
For the man who is going to expire.
If he thinks perchance of tomorrow
Not once even does he think
of the wretch who waits
to awaken, in order to die;

For without pity or care
Men hear the cry:
'To do good for the soul
Of the one they will put to death!'

And the judge in his bed
Also slumbers in peace!!
And pleased, the executioner
Counts his money in his dreams!!
All that breaks the silence
In the small bloody plaza
Is the wicked man who stays awake
as he builds the scaffold.

★   ★   ★   ★   ★

[15]
Loca y confusa la encedida mente,
Sueños de angustia y fiebre y devaneo
El alma envuelven del confuso reo
Que inclina al pecho la abatida frente.
[16]
Y en sueños
Confunde
La muerte,
La vida.
Recuerda,
Olvida,
Suspira,
Respira
Con hórrido afán.
[17]
Y en un mundo de tienieblas
Vaga y siente miedo y frío,
Y en su terrible desvarío
Palpa en su cuello el dogal;

His fiery mind mad and in a blur,
Dreams of anguish, fever and delirium
Envelop the soul of the dazed convict
Who tilts a dejected brow to his chest.

And in dreams
He confuses
Death,
Life.
He remembers,
He forgets,
He sighs,
He breathes
With hideous effort.

And in a world of shadows
He roams and feels fear and cold,
And in his terrible madness
He touches the noose on his neck;

Y cuanto más forcejea	And the more he wrestles
Cuanto más lucha y porfía	The more he struggles and grapples,
Tanto más en su agonía	The more in his agony
Aprieta el nudo fatal.	the fatal knot tightens.
[18]	
Y oye ruido, voces, gentes,	And he hears noise, voices, people
Y aquella voz que dirá:	And the voice that will say:
¡Para hacer bien por el alma	'To do good for the soul
Del que van a ajusticiar!	Of the one they will put to death!'
[19]	
O ya libre se contempla,	Or he imagines himself free,
Y el aire puro respira,	And he breathes pure air,
Y oye de amor que suspira	And he hears that the woman
La mujer que un tiempo amó,	He once loved is sighing with love,
Bella y dulce, cual solía,	Beautiful and sweet, the way she oft
did,	did,
Tierna flor de primavera,	A tender spring flower,
El amor de la pradera	The love of the meadow
Que el abril galán mimó.	That gallant April indulged.
[20]	
Y gozoso a veral vuela,	And happy he flies to see her,
Y al canzarla intenta en vano,	And in vain he tries to reach her,
Que al tender la ansiosa mano	For as he tends his eager hand
Su esperanza a realizar,	To realize his hope,
Su ilusión la desvanece	The pitiless dream suddenly
De repente el sueño impío,	Dispels its illusion,
Y halla un cuerpo mudo y frío	And he finds a mute cold body,
Y un cadalso en su lugar.	And a gallows in her place.
[21]	
Y oye a su lado en son triste	And next to him in sad sounds
Lúgubre voz resonar:	He hears a mournful voice resound:
¡Para hacer bien por el alma	'To do good for the soul
Del que van a ajusticiar!	Of the one they will put to death!'

Notes to Chapter 7

1. For a history of the death penalty in Spain, see Pedro Oliver Olmo, *La pena de muerte en España* (Madrid: Los Libros de la Catarata, 1995). Other noteworthy Spanish cultural figures of this period who criticized capital punishment include the artist Francisco de Goya (1746–1828) and the writer Mariano José de Larra (1809–37). All translations are my own.

2. The first Spanish translation of *Le Dernier Jour d'un condamné* dates from 1834. That Espronceda knew Hugo's work is widely acknowledged within the critical literature. For early source-study scholarship on Hugo's influence within Spanish literature see A. A. Parker and E. Allison Peers, 'The Vogue of Victor Hugo in Spain', *Modern Language Review*, 27.1 (January 1932), 36–57. See also by the same authors, 'The Influence of Victor Hugo on Spanish Poetry and Prose Fiction', *Modern Language Review*, 28.1 (January 1933), 50–61.

3. Section I of the poem appeared by itself on 17 January 1837. Section II was added, and the poem in its entirety was republished on 11 July 1837. See José Espronceda, *Obras completas*, ed. by Diego Martínez Torrón (Madrid: Cátedra, 2006), p. 1374, n. 38.

4. For the most extensive study of Espronceda's life, work, and historical moment, see Robert Marrast, *Espronceda et son temps: littérature, société, politique au temps du romantisme* (Paris: Klincksieck, 1974).

5. Spain's first liberal constitution of 1812 had sought to systematize and unify the legal system. The Penal Code of 1822, drafted during Spain's Liberal Triennium, was the most important criminal code during the first half of the century in Spain, but it was suspended with the return of absolutism in 1823. Absolutist juridical proceedings were neither transparent nor systematic, and the next legal code would not be approved until 1848. Hangings and execution by garrote were the most common forms of capital punishment, and the latter slowly became the preferred mode over the course of the century. The penal system at the time Espronceda wrote the poem was without a unified code, and was implemented irregularly.

6. A classic formal analysis of Espronceda's work and its innovation is Domingo Ynduráin, *Análisis formal de la poesía de Espronceda* (Madrid: Taurus, 1971). Within Spanish Romantic poetics, metric variation became an expressive phenomenon in its own right. A more recent overview of meter in Espronceda is Justo Agudo Martínez, 'Métrica de *Poesías líricas y fragmentos épicos* de José de Espronceda', *Rhythmica*, 11 (2013), 13–43.

7. Victor Hugo, *Préface de Cromwell*: 'Il y a aujourd'hui l'ancien régime littéraire comme l'ancien régime politique. Le dernier siècle pèse encore presque de tout point sur le nouveau' [There is today a literary *ancien régime* like the political *ancien régime*. The last century still weighs on the new one at almost every point] (in *Oeuvres complètes*, 45 vols (Paris: Ollendorff, 1904–52), XXIII, 49). For a synthetic discussion of the relationship between political liberalism and Romanticism in Spain see Ricardo Navas Ruiz, *El romanticismo español* (Madrid: Anaya, 1990), pp. 47–49. Appraisals of the complex interplay of liberal political ideology and Spanish Romantic subjectivity include Susan Kirkpatrick, *Las románticas: Women Writers and Subjectivity in Spain* (Berkeley: University of California Press, 1989), pp. 37–55, and Michael Iarocci, *Properties of Modernity: Romantic Spain, Modern Europe, and the Legacies of Empire* (Nashville, TN: Vanderbilt University Press, 2006), pp. 1–52.

8. Theodor W. Adorno, 'On Lyric Poetry and Society', in *Notes to Literature* (New York: Columbia University Press, 1991), pp. 37–54.

9. Russell Burman, *Literature Sets You Free: Literature, Liberty and Western Culture* (Iowa City: University of Iowa Press, 2007), pp. 208–09.

10. For analysis of the trope of the single tear within Spanish Romantic literature, see Russell Sebold, '"Una lágrima, pero una lágrima sola": sobre el llanto romántico', in *Trayectoria del romanticismo español* (Barcelona: Crítica, 1983), pp. 185–94.

11. Hugo's convict similarly contrasts psychic distress with physiological wellbeing: 'Pas malade! en effet, je suis jeune, sain et fort. Le sang coule librement dans mes veines [...] je suis robuste de corps et d'esprit, constitué pour une longue vie; oui, tout cela est vrai; et cependant j'ai une maladie, une maladie mortelle, une maladie faite de la main des hommes' [Not ill! The truth is I am young, healthy and strong. The blood runs freely in my veins [...] I am strong in body and spirit, I was made to live long; yes, this is all true, and yet I have a malady, a mortal malady, a malady made by the hand of man] (*Le Dernier Jour d'un condamné* (Paris: Gallimard, 2000), p. 126).

12. In the original publication, the *tirana* was appended to the preceding *octavilla* in what appears to be a non-traditional twelve-verse stanza. Modern editions vary on the presentation, sometimes printing the *tirana* independently and other times attaching it to the *octavilla*. I will discuss the *tirana* as a separate stanza in order to highlight the import of its various entries into the poem.

13. The early modern dramatist Agustín Moreto made use of the saying with almost identical wording in his play *El valiente justiciero y el rico-hombre de Alcalá*. Martínez Torrón observes that it is the most likely literary source from which Espronceda took the phrase. Espronceda, *Obras completas*, p. 1374, n. 38.

14. Espronceda's assimilation of and intertextual rapport with Byron is well documented. See for example, Esteban Pujals, *Espronceda y Lord Byron* (Madrid: Centro Superior de Investigación Científica, 1951). Of particular interest in this context is Byron's own intervention on the death penalty, for which see Canuel, *The Shadow of Death*, pp. 1–10. For recent work on the metaphysical in Espronceda's writing, see Elizabeth Scarlett, 'The Metaphysics of Espronceda's Romanticism in *El Estudiante de Salamanca*', *Bulletin of Hispanic Studies*, 93.1 (2016), 29–44.

15. The dream shares interesting parallels with Chapter XXXIII of Hugo's work, in which the

convict reminisces about a youthful dalliance with a young Spanish girl, Pepita (*Le Dernier Jour d'un condamné*, pp. 206–09). The fleeting image of love followed by the gallows finds another fascinating possible intertext in the famous ending to the fourth movement of Berlioz's *Symphonie fantastique*, which was performed for the first time in Paris in 1830 and left strong traces in Espronceda's longer, fantastical poem, *El estudiante de Salamanca*.

16. At the age of fifteen Espronceda had witnessed the absolutist regime execute General Rafael Riego y Nuñez (1784–1823), the liberal icon who had ushered in the Liberal Triennium. Seven years later, Espronceda enlisted in an unsuccessful attempt to overthrow Ferdinand VII. The leader of the rebellion, Joaquín Romualdo de Pablo y Antón (1784–1830) was captured and executed, prompting the poet to write 'A la muerte de Joaquín de Pablo (Chapalangarra)' [On the death of Joaquín de Pablo (Chapalangarra)]. While 'El reo de muerte' deliberately excludes political references from its discourse, its implicit relationship to Espronceda's progressive politics is clear. A useful history of Ferdinand's reign is Rafael Sánchez Mantero, *Fernando VII: un reinado polémico* (Madrid: Temas de Hoy, 1996). In a more biographical register, see María Pilar Queralt, *Fernando VII* (Barcelona: Planeta, 1997). For a history of repression under Ferdinand immediately following the Liberal Triennium, see Pedro Pegenaute, *Represión política en el reinado de Fernando VII* (Pamplona: Universidad de Navarra, 1974).

17. The last executions in Spain took place in 1975 under the ailing dictatorial regime of Francisco Franco (1892–1975), prompting mass protests across Europe. The Constitution of 1978 outlawed capital punishment with the exception of military crimes during times of war. In 1995 the death penalty was removed from the Spanish military penal code. The constitution continues to allow the reinstitution of military capital crimes should the military penal code be amended.

18. Within Catholicism *caritas* is considered the greatest of the theological virtues and encompasses both the common sense of 'charity' and the more robust notion of love of God and neighbour. See Joseph Sollier, 'Love (Theological Virtue)', in *The Catholic Encyclopedia*, <http://www.newadvent.org/cathen /09397a.htm> [accessed 9 August 2018]. Curiously, although far less overt in the journal entries of Hugo's work, Christian ethics figure prominently in the closing lines of his 1832 'Préface': 'La douce loi du Christ pénétrera enfin le code et rayonnera à travers. On regardera le crime comme une maladie [...]. On traitera par la charité ce mal qu'on traitait par la colère. Ce sera simple et sublime. La croix substituée au gibet. Voilà tout' [The sweet law of Christ will penetrate our legal code and shine through it. We will look upon crime as a malady [...] We will treat with charity the ill that we used to treat with anger. It will be simple and sublime. The cross substituted for the gallows. That is all] (*Le Dernier Jour d'un condamné*, pp. 52–53).

19. In Chapter VI, Hugo's convict evokes the 'idée fixe' as part of his explanation of the impetus to write his journal: 'Cette idée fixe qui me possède ne se présente-t-elle pas à moi à chaque instant, sous une nouvelle forme, toujours plus hideuse et plus ensanglantée à mesure que le terme approche? Pourquoi n'essaierai-je pas de me dire à moi-même tout ce que j'éprouve de violent et d'inconnu dans la situation abandonnée où me voilà?' [Doesn't this fixed thought that possesses me present itself before me at every instant under a new form, more hideous and bloody as the end approaches? In my abandoned situation, why not try to tell myself all that feels violent and unknown to me?] (*Le Dernier Jour d'un condamné*, p. 105).

20. For discussion of the ethics of representation in relation to images of atrocity, see Susan Sontag, *Regarding the Pain of Others* (New York: Picador/Farrar, Straus & Giroux, 2003). Of particular interest is her insistence on the difference between experience and its representation. Those who have not actually experienced atrocities, she argues, 'can't understand, can't imagine the experiences that those images represent' (p. 126). While there are important phenomenological differences between poetic images and photographs, the general ethical framework pertains.

21. My comments on singing concepts and thinking songs are meant to resonate with Adorno's conception of lyric in 'Lyric Poetry and Society'. Robert Kaufman has suggestively glossed one of Adorno's central concerns in 'Adorno's Social Lyric, and Literary Criticism Today: Poetics, Aesthetics, Modernity', in *The Cambridge Companion to Adorno*, ed. by Thomas Huhn (Cambridge: Cambridge University Press, 2004), pp. 354–75 (p. 363): 'How, spontaneously yet rigorously, to make thought sing and to make song think? [...] Lyric dramatizes with special

intensity modern aesthetic quasiconceptuality's more general attempt to stretch conceptual thought proper; this special intensity arises from lyric's constitutive need musically to 'stretch' objective conceptual thought's very medium, language — to stretch it all the way toward affect and song, but without relinquishing any of the rigor of conceptual intellection'.

PART IV

Poetics and Politics

CHAPTER 8

Putting Pain to Paper:
Victor Hugo's New Abolitionist Poetics

Ève Morisi

Tu veux être poète —
— Sais-tu quelle pensée agite
Une tête qui va tomber?

[You want to be a poet —
— Do you know what thought agitates
A head about to be cut off?]

VICTOR HUGO, fragment from 1825 found in
the manuscript of *Odes et ballades* (folio 127)

The death penalty was both familiar and repulsive to Victor Hugo (1802–85) from a very young age. He reportedly caught sight of the remains of hanged men suspended from trees in Italy in 1807, and saw a terrified Spanish man who had been condemned to death walking to the scaffold in 1812, the year his own godfather, General Lahorie, was executed.[1] In 1820, Louis Pierre Louvel, the murderer of the duc de Berry, was also led to the scaffold before his eyes. These experiences, and the greasing of the guillotine he witnessed before the execution of a young man guilty of a crime of passion in 1827, allegedly led Hugo to write a short novel that focuses exclusively on capital punishment: *Le Dernier Jour d'un condamné* [The Last Day of a Condemned Man] (1829).[2]

Hugo arguably developed the most extensive portrayal of and ethical reflection on state killing of the European nineteenth century through a myriad of fictional, poetic, and visual works.[3] As he became increasingly committed to social progress and the defence of all *misérables*, capital punishment also found itself at the centre of his most forceful political speeches.[4] The one he delivered before the Constituent Assembly on 15 September 1848 famously called for 'the pure, simple, and definitive abolition of the death penalty' — as opposed to the abolition of the death penalty for political crimes only. In 1851, he spoke against capital punishment at the Seine Assizes when his own son Charles was put on trial and sentenced to six months in prison for criticizing an execution. In addition, Hugo intervened publicly and in private in favour of men condemned to death, such as John Charles Tapner, the English criminal he defended in vain before his botched hanging in 1854, the

American abolitionist John Brown, executed in 1859, and the condemned men of the Paris Commune.

Le Dernier Jour d'un condamné, which Hugo tellingly nicknamed 'the book of the severed head' (*OCH*, IX, 1275), stands out within this rich corpus and tireless activism because of its literary originality and previously unequalled focus on the 'capital experience'. Causing quite a stir upon the novel's publication, these characteristics subsequently made it a landmark for such writers as Fedor Dostoevsky, Gustave Flaubert, and Albert Camus. First published in February 1829, during the reign of Charles X (1824–30), a period of extreme penal severity, this early novel in the first person relates the painful stream of consciousness of a man condemned to death, from his sentencing to the day of his decapitation.[5] Some reviewers, past and present, have argued that the novel was initially intended less as an abolitionist plea than as an opportunistic and sensationalistic piece in keeping with the trend of the day.[6] The narrative may not appear to function as a plea insofar as it does not seek to develop explicit arguments in favour of the abolition: Hugo would go on to do so in a famous militant preface he added to his novel in 1832.[7] Yet it would be erroneous to question the abolitionist nature of the narrative itself. In the *post scriptum* that closes a letter to his editor Gosselin of 3 January 1829, a passionate Hugo insisted that *Le Dernier Jour d'un condamné* be published before the debate that was to occur on 28 February 1829 in the Chambre des Députés about the possible reconsideration of counterfeiting as a non-capital crime.[8] In addition to this epistolary evidence, the abolitionist efficacy of Hugo's novel lies in its new poetics, as this chapter argues. *Le Dernier Jour* undoes representation, stages a crisis in communication, and sets in motion an innovative expressive regime. Together, these strategies result in a poetic activism that annihilates the legitimacy of modern state killing.

Undoing Classical Representation

Once an ultra-conservative whose writing soon came to be marked by 'frenetic' aesthetics and whose political sensibility became increasingly progressive, Hugo sided with the literary Moderns in 1823, when he gushingly praised an anti-death penalty poem by Jules Lefèvre-Deumier. He commended its 'strong and daring imagination [...] often rough and reckless in its conceptions', its 'expression, new and picturesque [...] frequently bizarre', its 'colours', and the 'torture' it sometimes imposed on poetic language.[9] This 'new and pure school', Hugo now claimed, was the necessary corollary of the French Revolution. At the time, a number of French Romantics such as Lefèvre-Deumier represented capital punishment critically. The proponents of Classicism deemed both the topic chosen and the manner used to be iconoclastic and undesirable.[10] First published anonymously, *Le Dernier Jour d'un condamné* was to display even more radically revolutionary features than the writing of these Romantics: it went so far as to unpick time, space, events, and character.

Dead time prevails in *Le Dernier Jour.* Forty-nine concise chapters providing glimpses into the condemned man's consciousness are bracketed between the pronouncement of a death to come (the exclamation 'Condemned to death!'

inaugurates and punctuates the novel) and death itself: an interrupted ending and the capitalization of the condemned man's final words 'FOUR O'CLOCK' point to the imminent moment of the legal killing. Spatially, the novel is also locked in: enclosure reigns in the courtroom, the cell, and, above all, the mind. The condemned man is 'en prison dans une idée' [imprisoned in an idea], that of the death sentence, 'courbé sous son poids' [bent over under the weight of it] (I, 657). An embedded incarceration, judicial and mental, therefore frames the narrative. It functions as a peculiar tragedy in which little room is left for action.

Except for writing, no significant deed marks the condemned man's experience. Rather, he inhabits a world of fearful thoughts and micro-events, and, even when it comes to these modest happenings, he is unable to partake in them fully or actively. In his recollection of his trial, he remains inert despite his desire to speak; during most of his captivity, he finds himself reduced to watching the walls of his cell and interacting superficially with the prison guards and his fellow convicts. This inactivity clearly distinguishes the protagonist from Hugo's other famous, and always dynamic, convicts, from Claude Gueux, to the man in the iron mask, to Jean Valjean. Here, the knowledge that all the other characters (his peers, the judicial and state authorities, and the people) are shown to have of the condemned man's status and the repeated reminders of his impending execution bring home his inescapable passivity.

Instead of relating a dynamic sequence of events, the novel foregrounds the protagonist's moral and emotional wandering through internal focalization. This results in a relative diegetic discontinuity within the narrative's dead time: analepses, prolepses, and digressions alternate in the condemned man's prose as his mind races to come to terms with his sentence. As a wounded psyche takes centre stage, the narrative breaks with the conventions of early nineteenth-century French fiction, which did explore the interior life and subjectivity of characters in depth but was still concerned with the unfolding of a plot or a particular destiny — from Chateaubriand to Constant, de Staël, Stendhal, or the early Balzac. In contrast, Hugo stages a nameless and, even more strikingly, story-less protagonist.

Indeed, the chapter meant to reveal the condemned man's life and misdeed (XLVII) is left blank. Contrary to what some critics have asserted, his identity and history are not erased entirely, however.[11] Several cues suggest that he is educated (III, 662) and belongs to a relatively privileged social sphere: his knowledge of Latin, his manners, his disgust when he wakes up on a pallet bed in the prison infirmary (XIV, 674), and his clothing, elegant and unworn (XXIII, 689), for instance. The condemned man's portrayal therefore constitutes what might be called a 'counter-sketch': it is minimalistic, but provides enough information to turn him into the counterpoint to the stereotypical nineteenth-century criminal. Hugo thereby reverses the figure of the irredeemable proletarian gangster found in contemporary medical and criminological discourses.[12] And while the narrative is structured as a tragedy, the represented subject is not an aristocratic or heroic figure. Hugo replaces these forms of characterization imposed by deterministic sociology or rigid literary genres with a suffering silhouette into which the bourgeois reader is absorbed.

The overlap created between character and reader is furthered by the occasional confusion of voices and other modes of conflation between character, author, and audience. The injunctive formula 'Condemned to death!' that inaugurates the text and recurs throughout cannot be assigned to a single voice, for instance, although that of the condemned man otherwise predominates. Rather, it makes us wonder: is this a performative utterance emanating from the judicial institution? The whisper of the alienated condemned man's interior voice — he does claim, after all, that 'une voix a murmuré à [s]on oreille' [a voice has whispered in [his] ear] (I, 658)? Or a collective hateful shout (p. 661)? With this opening phrase whose source remains unclear and whose repetition in the first chapters gives it a chorus-like quality, an instability pertaining to who speaks sporadically surfaces in the novel. It raises the question of who is responsible for the death sentence, as an utterance and as a reality. It disorients us as readers, all the more so as we ourselves quickly become the possible doppelgänger of each of the actors liable to utter these ominous words: the judge, hearing and assessing the protagonist's case; the stunned protagonist himself, into whose shoes we are put; and the people, reacting with passion and voyeurism to a criminal's condemnation.

Symmetrically, doubts arise regarding the text's recipient. For if, in theory, the condemned man's writing in the first person comes across as self-addressed and diaristic, several moments of interpellation trouble this logic. He repeatedly hints at the presence of some possible readership or witness. Firstly, he envisages the future publication of his story in Chapter VI and, later in the same chapter and in Chapter XXXIV, considers its reception by 'ceux qui condamnent' [those who condemn] (p. 664) and by a wider, indefinite audience: an all-embracing 'on' [they] (p. 698).[13] Secondly, the frequent use of exclamations and rhetorical questions calls for outside sympathy or indignation, in the present time of his writing:

> Depuis l'heure où mon arrêt a été prononcé, combien sont morts qui s'arrangeaient pour une longue vie! Combien m'ont devancé qui, jeunes, libres et sains, comptaient bien aller voir tel jour tomber ma tête en place de Grève! Combien d'ici là peut-être qui marchent et respirent au grand air, entrent et sortent à leur gré, et qui me devanceront encore!
> Et puis, qu'est-ce que la vie a donc de si regrettable pour moi? (III, 662)

> [Since the hour when my sentence was pronounced, how many have died who were all set for a long life! How many have preceded me, young, free, and healthy, who were fully expecting to go and see me lose my head this or that day on the Place de Grève! Before that time comes, how many are there walking and breathing in the open air, coming and going as they please, who might yet still die before I do!
> And besides, what is there about my life that I will regret so much?]

Such apostrophic rhetoric de facto forces us into the fictional space of the novel.

Likewise, the author occasionally brings himself into the diary. He is the implicit figure who proves the condemned man wrong when the protagonist declares himself unable to 'voir un être humain qui [l]e croie digne d'une parole et à qui [il] le rende' [see any human being who believes [him] worthy of being either spoken to or about] (III, 662). Hugo also injects an italicized citation from his own early novel *Han d'Islande* (1823) into the condemned man's prose in Chapter III and, throughout, distils analogies between himself and his protagonist. While the first edition of *Le Dernier Jour d'un condamné* was anonymous, subsequent editions were not and capitalized on Hugo's name, which was hardly unknown after the publication of his *Préface de Cromwell*, the manifesto of French Romantic drama (1827).[14] More importantly, a passage superimposes writer and character independently of Hugo's identity: Chapter VI thematizes the question of writing and conjoins the condemned man penning his ordeal and, at the meta-fictional level, the author crafting his novel. After the condemned man questions the use of transcribing his thoughts and feelings onto paper, he concludes that his enterprise is indeed legitimate and ends up justifying the very form and agenda that Hugo adopted for his book:

> Ce journal de mes souffrances, heure par heure, minute par minute, supplice par supplice, si j'ai la force de le mener jusqu'au moment où il me sera physiquement impossible de continuer, cette histoire, nécessairement inachevée, mais aussi complète que possible, de mes sensations, ne portera-t-elle point avec elle un grand et profond enseignement? N'y aura-t-il pas dans ce procès-verbal de la pensée agonisante, dans cette progression toujours croissante de douleurs, dans cette espèce d'autopsie intellectuelle d'un condamné, plus d'une leçon pour ceux qui condamnent? Peut-être cette lecture leur rendra-t-elle la main moins légère, quand il s'agira quelquefois de jeter une tête qui pense, une tête d'homme, dans ce qu'ils appellent la balance de la justice? Peut-être n'ont-ils jamais réfléchi, les malheureux, à cette lente succession de tortures que renferme la formule expéditive d'un arrêt de mort? Se sont-ils jamais arrêtés à cette idée poignante que dans l'homme qu'ils retranchent il y a une intelligence; une intelligence qui avait compté sur la vie, une âme qui ne s'est point disposée pour la mort? Non. (VI, 664)

> [This daily record of my sufferings, hour by hour, minute by minute, ordeal by ordeal, if I have the strength to carry on with it until the moment when it will be physically impossible for me to continue, this story of my sensations, necessarily unfinished, but as complete as possible, won't it contain a great and profound teaching? Won't there be, in these minutes of agonizing thought, in this increasing progression of pain, in this sort of intellectual autopsy of a condemned man, many a lesson for those who condemn? Maybe this reading will make them less heavy-handed in the future, when it comes to throwing a thinking head, a man's head, into what they call the scales of justice? Maybe, poor them, they have never thought about this slow succession of ordeals contained in the expeditious formula of a death sentence? Have they ever paused to consider this poignant idea that, in the man they are removing, there is a mind; a mind that had counted on life, a soul that did not prepare itself for death? No, they have not.]

Some of the terms used here possess a manifesto-like quality and anticipate those Hugo will choose for his preface of 1832. They thus challenge the text's internal focalization. As if by means of ventriloquism, the character accounts for the author's enterprise of laying bare the psychic reality behind capital punishment.

As it destabilizes spatio-temporal coordinates, atomizes plot under the pressure of the obsession of death, empties out character, represents an unexpected subject, intermittently conflates protagonist, author, and audience, and blocks off the possibility of a denouement by making the spectacle and narrative of (his own) decapitation inaccessible to the protagonist, *Le Dernier Jour d'un condamné* deliberately undoes key tenets of classical representation. It undermines and, at times, even abolishes the existence and relation of a substantial storyline, contained within a specific space-time, composed of prominent actions, centred on an identifiable protagonist distinct from the writer and reader, and an ending that coincides with some form of closure. Instead, what prevails is a discourse disorganized by fear and which does away with the text's very fictional status.

Further Disorder: Narrative Inconsistency and De-fictionalization

Indeed, there is more to the literary disorder orchestrated by Hugo. His novel goes so far as to undermine narrative consistency, verisimilitude, and its own status as fiction. The book's very title, when confronted with its actual content, creates an aporia. Several time markers point to a duration that far exceeds the twenty-four hours it promises to the reader: 'Voilà cinq semaines que j'habite avec cette pensée' [I've been living with this thought for five weeks now] (I, 657); 'ce sera dans six semaines' [it will take place in six weeks] (II, 661). The reader witnesses the last week of the condemned man's existence, not just his last day, and the month and a half subsequent to his condemnation is also related. The text oscillates between retrospection and contemporaneity, and the latter does not take over until the chilling wake-up call of Chapter XIX: 'C'est pour aujourd'hui!' [Today's the day!] (p. 679). As Dostoevsky has noted, Hugo 'has recourse to an even greater improbability by assuming that a man sentenced to death is able (and has the time) to keep a diary not only on his last day, but also during his last hour and, literally, his last minute'.[15]

Contrary to what one might expect, however, these breaches of the narrative ethos do not generate mistrust in the speaker or a *Verfremdungseffekt* pointing to the illusory nature of the condemned man's story. While they do fulfil the Brechtian agenda of making the audience a 'consciously critical observer', led to ponder socio-political matters, the opposite of a distancing occurs, in fact: the discontinuities and incoherence of *Le Dernier Jour d'un condamné* lead to the reader's full adhesion to the protagonist's experience, as they appear to both reveal and be produced by the irresistible violence and inner turmoil triggered by the sentence pronouncement that launches the book's inexorable race to the scaffold. The condemned man's prose enforces a peculiar realism anchored in the immediate life of a threatened psyche, and thereby creates an effective sense of disorder and a literature that refuses to regulate anguish.

The genre of *Le Dernier Jour* partakes in this peculiar removal from the realm and rules of fiction. Jean Rousset has argued that the text marked the invention of the 'roman-journal' [novel-diary].[16] Combining a single protagonist, a single locus (the prison), and a single, auto-centric discourse allowed Hugo to deepen the sense of intimacy characteristic of writings based on self-expression, such as first-person narratives, autobiographies, or epistolary novels, which, from Rousseau to Laclos, had flourished during the French eighteenth century. The *faux* diary also suppresses the minimal distancing found in the published poems, novels in the third person, short stories, and memoirs that addressed the issue of capital punishment in the 1820s. Instead, it exposes a speaker's experience and subjectivity as unaffected by the social codes and intersubjective dynamics present in some of these other highly popular genres, pushing to its limits the sense of veracity and privacy they strived to achieve.

What further 'de-fictionalizes' the novel–diary is the context in which it was produced and the paratext with which Hugo envelops the condemned man's account. As an early reviewer did not fail to notice, the book came out after contemporary periodicals published first-person narratives relating the *in extremis* experience of actual men condemned to death.[17] One such publication was the diary of a Corsican convict who starved himself to death all the while reporting on his slow and painful demise.[18] Another was the testimony of an Englishman who miraculously survived his hanging. Published in *Le Globe* in January 1828, this piece is strikingly similar to the novel in several respects. Not only is the title of the article in which it is inserted, 'Dernières sensations d'un homme condamné à mort' [Last Sensations of a Man Condemned to Death], an obvious echo of Hugo's novel, but the framing, descriptions, and analytical quality of the Englishman's diary, which *Le Globe* summarizes as 'everything he felt from the verdict until his execution', are also the same as those of *Le Dernier Jour d'un condamné*. What is more, the core of Hugo's fiction seems to take up the very traits of this testimony that *Le Globe* highlights: 'the gradual extinction of all moral thought, sensory perceptions becoming clearer and more distinct as the faculties of the soul grow weaker, the almost-absolute impossibility of turning to religious ideas'.[19] The repeated anticipation of the execution, visions, hallucinations, and alterations of the condemned man's consciousness that pervade *Le Dernier Jour* likewise structure this British source text. Hugo complemented these testimonies, presented as genuine, with accurate or colourful depictions of the realities of carceral life with which he sought to become familiar through direct and indirect examination, including visits to the Bicêtre prison.[20]

Le Dernier Jour reinforces this hyper-reality effect through an efficient paratext. The book's first edition of 1829, as well as the following one, comprised two elements: a preface suggesting that the condemned man's story may (or may not) have been transcribed from a 'bundle of discolored papers of various sizes' (p. 641); and, more remarkably, a fold-out facsimile of the *argot* song heard by the condemned man, reportedly annotated by him, and found in his papers following his death (p. 712; Figure 8.1).

The process that underlies these multiple devices of de-fictionalization is one of recording. More specifically, the novel stages the exhaustive logging of the condemned man's mental, physical, and social experience. Its ambition of exhaustiveness was perhaps best diagnosed by Dostoevsky, who argued that, just like the short story entitled 'A Gentle Creature' (1876), it had a 'fantastic element'

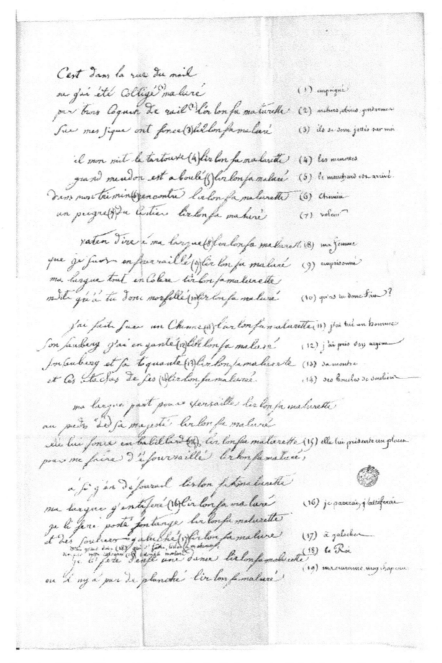

FIG. 8.1. Victor Hugo, Fold-out facsimile insert included in the first edition of
Le Dernier Jour d'un condamné, 1829, in: Maison de Victor Hugo.

to it that paradoxically made it 'one of the most realistic and most truthful [novels the Frenchman] ever wrote'. In the Russian writer's opinion, the novel functions as if the transcription of a 'psychological sequence' in its totality could be carried out by a 'stenographer' while a character would tell 'a story, interrupted by all sorts of digressions and interludes [...] in a rather rambling way [...] sometimes [...] speaking to himself, sometimes [...] addressing an invisible listener, a sort of judge'.[21]

The fact that *Le Dernier Jour d'un condamné* inserts itself into a lineage of documents presented as genuine, and that it resorts to a hybrid scientific-administrative procedure of comprehensive *enregistrement* that brings realism to border on the unreal, may account for the label that Hugo attributed to his fiction in a play-preface ('A Comedy about a Tragedy') he came to add to the novel: that of 'nouveau roman' (p. 647). He coined this now-familiar phrase long before Émile Henriot proposed it in 1957, and before Alain Robbe-Grillet subsequently adopted it to describe the enterprise of twentieth-century French writers themselves eager to break away from the consecrated genre of the novel.[22] The negative critiques published shortly after *Le Dernier Jour* first came out emphasize the unacceptability of its new generic and poetic features, which have also puzzled twentieth-century critics.[23] Hugo's own sales-oriented publisher Charles Gosselin expressed reservations about the unique genre of *Le Dernier Jour*. But Hugo responded that he wished to publish an 'analytical' novel devoid of antecedents (pp. 1242–43).[24]

The 'drame intérieur' of *Le Dernier Jour* thus appears to actualize deliberately, in the realm of (de-fictionalized) prose fiction, what his radical *Préface de Cromwell* of 1827 prescribed for the theatre: a liberated form, a drama redefined as a kind of complete and modern poetry that renders reality in its aesthetic variety and tensions. The narrative inconsistencies, hyper-realism, and de-fictionalization used to better render and dissect an 'agonizing thought' seal the novel's break away from what Jacques Rancière has called 'representative poetry': 'Representative poetry was composed of stories submitted to principles of concatenation, characters submitted to principles of verisimilitude, and discourses submitted to principles of decorum'.[25] By contrast, Hugo shows conventional representative poetics to be unable to tell a story of life and (state-imposed) death.

Crisis of Communication

The question of speech and communication prolongs that of a deliberately troubled and de-fictionalized representation in *Le Dernier Jour d'un condamné*. A profound crisis of linguistic exchanges pervades the novel. Not only does it feature, as previously mentioned, a speaker with a blurred identity. It also problematizes the very articulation of language and key functions of verbal communication — expressive, conative, phatic, and referential.

The condemned man's phonation apparatus fails upon the pronouncement of his sentence: his tongue is petrified, his breath short, and a single bodily motion and a monosyllable become a cipher for the words he cannot voice.

> J'aurais eu, moi, tout à dire, mais rien ne me vint. Ma langue resta collée à
> mon palais [...] mille émotions [...] se disputaient ma pensée. Je voulus répéter

> à haute voix ce que je lui avais déjà dit: Plutôt cent fois la mort! Mais l'haleine me manqua, et je ne pus que l'arrêter rudement par le bras, en criant avec une force convulsive: Non! (II, 661)

> [I myself would have had so much to say, but nothing came to me. My tongue remained stuck to the roof of my mouth [...] a thousand emotions [...] were competing for my thoughts. I wanted to repeat out loud what I had already told him: I'd rather die a hundred times! But I didn't have enough breath left, and all I could do was stop him briskly with my arm, shouting with convulsive force: No!]

This incapacity to utter more than a syllable is at once symbolic and proleptic. It signals the impossibility of calling upon common language in a complex manner within a life-threatening context. Unspeakable or unsatisfactory, such language is repeatedly disqualified as a tool capable of expressing the existential condition of the condemned man caught between life and death.

Mirroring this dictional difficulty is the metaphorical deafness of the protagonist's interlocutors. In Chapter II, immediately after he leaves the courtroom, we are told that two young women show their excitement in anticipation of the day of the execution. Their exclamation, 'ce sera dans six semaines!' [it will take place in six weeks!], and, even more patently, the body language one of them displays, clapping her hands out of impatient enthusiasm, indicate that the phrase 'Condamné à mort' can take on a jubilatory quality for some auditors. On several occasions, the text emphasizes this process of loss or perversion of meaning, following a gradation that culminates in the description of a voluble crowd whose voice becomes 'plus vaste, plus glapissante, plus joyeuse encore' [even more vast, more yelping, more joyful] once the execution is imminent (XLVIII, 711).

The priest, the very actor whose task is to comfort the condemned man, prepares the ground for such uninhibited *contre-sens*. His logorrheic speech has:

> Rien de senti, rien d'attendri, rien de pleuré, rien d'arraché à l'âme, rien qui vînt de son cœur pour aller au mien, rien qui fût de lui à moi. Au contraire, je ne sais quoi de vague, d'inaccentué, d'applicable à tout et à tous; emphatique où il eût été besoin de profondeur, plat où il eût fallu être simple; une espèce de sermon sentimental et d'élégie théologique. [...] Et puis, il avait l'air de réciter une leçon déjà vingt fois récitée, de repasser un thème, oblitéré dans sa mémoire à force d'être su. Pas un regard dans l'œil, pas un accent dans la voix, pas un geste dans les mains. (XXX, 693)

> [Nothing heartfelt about it, nothing tender, nothing tearful, nothing torn from the soul, nothing coming from his heart to mine, nothing from him to me. Quite the opposite, something vague, flat, applicable to everything and everyone; emphatic when he would have needed to be deep, plain when he should have been simple; a sort of sentimental sermon and theological elegy [...] Besides, he seemed to be going over a lesson that he had already recited twenty times, to rehearse a theme, obliterated in his memory because he knew it like the back of his hand. Not a look in his eye, not a stress in his voice, not a gesture with his hands.]

The mechanical rhetoric described here jeopardizes the expressive function of language.[26] It is no surprise that, correspondingly, the reception of such messages should be hindered, if not nullified. The condemned man cannot establish true contact with or hear the words of his interlocutors from the religious and judicial orders without some reticence: 'Mais ce bon vieillard, qu'est-il pour moi? que suis-je pour lui? un individu de l'espèce malheureuse, une ombre comme il en a déjà tant vu, une unité ajoutée au chiffre des exécutions' [But this good old man, what is he to me? What am I to him? An individual of the desperate kind, a shadow like the many he has already seen, a simple unit added to the number of executions] (XXX, 694). One also thinks of the 'paroles caressantes' [caressing words] of the gaoler, 'prison incarnée' [prison incarnate] whose 'œil [...] flatte et [...] espionne' [eye [...] flatters and [...] spies] (XX, 680), or the cynicism that lies behind judicial transcription as it appears in Chapter XXIII: 'nous ferons les deux procès-verbaux à la fois, cela s'arrange bien' [we will complete the two certificates at the same time, that's quite convenient] (p. 686). While the mechanical, duplicitous, or cynical use of language may be a common trait of human communication, the condemned man's critical situation appears to systematize it and to associate it closely with cruelty, intentional or otherwise. It morphs into a marker through which his interlocutors disavow his individuality, minimize the value of his existence, and contribute actively but inconspicuously to his fate.

What about the condemned man's language itself, then? It has difficulty being in touch with the outside world. On the one hand, this struggle manifests itself in a disconnect from factual reality: the protagonist's writing alternates between segments that refer to and then shut out actual events. His alienated consciousness, shocked upon hearing the death sentence, only pays attention to his objective environment in a discontinuous manner before returning to the obsession of his execution. So much so that actuality repeatedly takes him by surprise, such as when he gets off his cart and seems to catch sight of the guillotine: 'Entre les deux lanternes du quai, j'avais vu une chose sinistre. Oh! c'était la réalité!' [Between the two lanterns on the quay, I had seen a sinister thing. Oh! T'was reality!] (XLVIII, 711).[27]

On the other hand, the words of the man condemned to death sometimes come across as inoperative. He is unable to make the bailiff and the priest realize that the bad news of the day is his beheading (XXII), does not manage to talk an old gendarme into exchanging clothes with him (XXIII), and, even in the course of a most elementary conversation with the prison's clerk, he is unsuccessful at making himself truly heard:

> — Il fait beau, dis-je au guichetier.
> Il resta un moment sans me répondre, comme ne sachant si cela valait la peine de dépenser une parole; puis avec quelque effort il murmura brusquement:
> — C'est possible. [...]
> — Voilà une belle journée, répétai-je.
> — Oui, me répondit l'homme, on vous attend. (II, 659)

> ['Lovely weather,' I said to the desk clerk.
> A moment went by without him responding to me, as if he didn't know if it was worth his wasting a word; then, with some effort, he muttered abruptly, 'Could be.' [...]

'Today's a fine day,' I repeated.
'Yes,' the man answered, 'they are waiting for you.']

In this instance, the attempt at bringing the other closer by way of a phatic, innocuous chat fails. Beyond the fact that scathing irony colours the protagonist's tentative small talk about the nice weather on the very day he is sentenced to death, a dismissive reply is obtained at the cost of self-repetition. The state employee is also quick to send the main character back to the cold institutional reality that awaits him and to signal that he can no longer enjoy the status of legitimate interlocutor even before the condemnation has been pronounced. He has already become a paradoxical figure, both invisible and over-exposed, undeserving of the most trivial words and acting as society's absolute centre of attention. All surround and watch him, the 'juges chargés de haillons ensanglantés [...] trois rangs de témoins aux faces stupides [...] deux gendarmes aux deux bouts de mon banc [...] les têtes de la foule [...] [l]es douze jurés' [judges in bloodied rags [...] three rows of witnesses with stupid faces [...] two gendarmes at either end of my bench [...] the heads of the crowd [...] the twelve jurors] (XIII, 659). His hybrid position, at once subaltern and 'royal' — 'vous serez seul dans votre loge comme le roi' [you will be alone in your own box like the king] (XIII, 670) — largely compromises the possibility of basic social contact with the Other through language.

Communication is thus aborted in many ways in *Le Dernier Jour d'un condamné*. This breakdown goes so far as to affect the heart of human linguistic exchanges, namely the message itself. While there are moments of relative linguistic transparency in the novel-diary, such as when the condemned man clinically recounts his pre-mortem grooming (XLVIII) and other dehumanizing processes, Hugo intermittently inflects or suspends the immediate intelligibility of such prose. As if corroborating the impossible elementary linguistic interactions noted above, the idioms of the speaker and the judicial institution at times reject literal meaning, highlight paradoxes, and point to the duplicity of the sign. The protagonist wields dark humour when he leaves the sick room, for example: 'Malheureusement, je n'étais pas malade' [Unfortunately, I wasn't unwell] (XV, 676). Later on, he underlines the linguistic hypocrisy of the prison director who, careful to show concern for the condemned man, emphatically calls him 'monsieur' and, against all expectations, asks, on the day of the execution, whether he slept well with the most courteous turns of phrase (XIX, 679–80). Here, as in the scene where the protagonist officially finds out about the rejection of his appeal, the satire of the paternalistic and falsely gracious masquerade that drapes the death penalty is denounced through the exhibition of a language centred on form and devoid of much content. The elaborate and dignified rhetoric with which the condemned man mockingly mimics the bailiff's wooden speech, or what Hugo's preface of 1832 will later name 'les entortillages sonores du parquet' [the Attorney General's loud circumlocutions] (*OCH*, IV, 480) underscores this critique:

> — Monsieur, m'a-t-il dit avec un sourire de courtoisie, je suis huissier près de la cour royale de Paris. J'ai l'honneur de vous apporter un message de la part de monsieur le procureur général. [...]

— C'est monsieur le procureur général, lui ai-je répondu, qui a demandé si instamment ma tête? Bien de l'honneur pour moi qu'il m'écrive. J'espère que ma mort lui va faire grand plaisir? car il me serait dur de penser qu'il l'a sollicitée avec tant d'ardeur et qu'elle lui était indifférente. [...]

— L'arrêt sera exécuté aujourd'hui en place de grève [...] Nous partons à sept heures et demie précises pour la Conciergerie. Mon cher monsieur, aurez-vous l'extrême bonté de me suivre? (XXI, 681)

['Sir,' he said to me with a courteous smile, 'I am a bailiff for the Royal Court of Paris I am honoured to deliver a message to you on behalf of his honour Attorney General.' [...]

'Is his honour Attorney General,' I answered, 'the one who requested so insistently that I be decapitated? Honoured indeed that he should write to me. I hope that my death will greatly please him? For it would pain me to think that he requested it with such ardour and that it left him indifferent.' [...]

'The decision will be carried out today on the place de Grève [...] We are leaving for the Conciergerie at seven and a half sharp. My dear Sir, will you be so very kind as to follow me?']

Civility here paradoxically reveals barbarity. The 'message' presented on behalf of 'le procureur général' is a pure formality denying the condemned man's status as an interlocutor. As the 'arrêt' then confirms, both as a thing (an irrevocable judicial decision signifying his death) and as a telling noun (evocative of termination), what is presented as a 'message' masks pure violence and may indeed constitute such violence itself.

Irony, grating overtones, deceptive ornamentation: the signified is subject to caution in the condemned man's account. So is the signifier, whose gratuitous nature is underscored by the text. The protagonist twice evokes the mysterious combinations of letters that could be fatal or providential to him: 'guillotine' (XXVII, 691), with its ten graphemes portrayed as repulsive — 'leur aspect, leur physionomie est bien faite pour réveiller une idée épouvantable' [their appearance, their physiognomy is indeed made to conjure up a dreadful idea] — and 'Charles' (XL, 701), the name of the king who can grant pardon, with its seven letters. Despite their anodyne appearance, the two signs have the formidable power to make fundamental and contrasting realities exist: death and life. 'Il suffirait qu'il écrivît avec cette plume les sept lettres de son nom au bas d'un morceau de papier, ou même que son carrosse rencontrât ta charrette!' [It would suffice for him to write with this quill the seven letters of his name at the bottom of a piece of paper, or even for his carriage to come across your cart!] (p. 701). This insistence on the arbitrariness inherent in the signifier and in the occurrence of the king's name or appearance points to another arbitrary reality: that of the death penalty, which they can either bring into being or cancel.

By thus staging the vanity, fraudulence, or randomness of the sign along with failing intersubjective relationships, Hugo designs a poetics of dysfunctional, if not impossible, communication. In this light, the complete silence — the blank — by which the speaker's 'story' is engulfed (XLVII) seems as much caused by the lack of time before his execution (as indicated by an 'editor's note') as it symbolizes communicational failure. Another suspension of speech adds to this silence: that of all the executed men unable to testify about the experience of beheading. The 'rusted' and 'fragment[ed]' written traces they are reduced to leaving on the walls of the protagonist's cell make their silencing perceptible, as does the following unbeatable objection:

> Ils disent que ce n'est rien, qu'on ne souffre pas, que c'est une fin douce, que la mort de cette façon est bien simplifiée [...] Qui le leur a dit ? Conte-t-on que jamais une tête coupée se soit dressée sanglante au bord du panier, et qu'elle ait crié au peuple: Cela ne fait pas de mal! (XXXIX, 700)

> [They say that it is nothing, that you don't suffer, that it is a gentle end, that death in this way is made much easier [...] Who told them this? Is it told that a severed head ever sprang up all bloody on the edge of the basket, and that it shouted to the people: It doesn't hurt!]

The condemned man here disqualifies the late eighteenth-century discourse on the painlessness of the guillotine used to legitimize its adoption in the context of humanitarian penal reforms. A sudden hush is that on which his writing itself closes. After writing down the time of the day at which he is taken out of his cell for the last time, 'QUATRE HEURES' [FOUR O'CLOCK] (XLIX, 711), he seems noiselessly driven to death. This forced silence marks a final climax in the indistinction and unverifiability of language to which the narrative has previously pointed. It also underlines the limits of literature which the text seeks actively to resist by giving voice to the soon-to-be-executed prisoner.

If language and its uses undergo various processes of suspension, what *Le Dernier Jour d'un condamné* ultimately reveals is the possibility of absolute inaudibility, be it that of the loudest cries. 'Je ne distinguais plus les cris de pitié des cris de joie, les rires des plaintes, les voix du bruit; tout cela était une rumeur qui résonnait dans ma tête comme dans un écho de cuivre' [I could no longer tell the cries of pity from the cries of joy, the laughter from the wailing, the voices from the noise; all that was a rumour resounding in my head like in a brass echo] (XLVIII, 710), says the condemned man on his way to the execution. *His* ultimate cry, the one likely to be uttered out of fear on the scaffold, is also obliterated from the narrative. Nevertheless, the cry as a sound does occupy a prominent place in Hugo's text, from the vociferation that opens and traverses it, to the impatient clamour of the crowd (II, XXII, XXVI, XLVIII), the *forçats*'s shouts (XIII), and more centrally, the condemned man's own screaming against his condemnation (II) and the ghastly visions that form in his imagination (XIII).[28] While the latter occurrences seem absorbed by the text's overarching narrative (the reduction of man to silence by lethal justice), the novel-diary preserves the properties of the *condamné*'s cry: its violence, power of interpellation, and immediate intelligibility. Indeed, it exacerbates them by forging an expressive poetry.

Towards Expressive Poetry

The contraventions of conventional dramatic and novelistic representation and of human communication that Hugo stages periodically find a point of contact and contrast in a language able to realize immediate and potent expression; 'expressive poetry', as Jacques Rancière defines it, in opposition to representative poetry:

> The new poetry — expressive poetry — is made of sentences and images, sentence-images that have inherent value as manifestations of poeticity, that claim a relation immediately expressive of poetry [...]. In opposition to the primacy of fiction, we find the primacy of language. In opposition to its distribution into genres, the anti-generic principle of the equality of all represented subjects. In opposition to the principle of decorum, the indifference of style with respect to the subject represented. In opposition to the ideal of speech in action, the model of writing.[29]

Following in Gustave Planche's footsteps, Rancière identifies *Notre-Dame de Paris* (1831) as the literary work that, 'much more than *Hernani*, symbolizes the scandal of the new school'.[30] *Le Dernier Jour* is already exemplary of this shift, in fact. Not only does it ignore the rules of Aristotelian representation, as shown earlier, but it also establishes the primacy of language and repeatedly produces meaningful 'sentence-images' as described by Rancière. They enable the telling of the unique realities and sensations experienced by the condemned man as his horizon narrows and decapitation looms larger.[31]

The primacy of language constitutive of expressive poetry may emerge surreptitiously, through the combination of the literal and the figurative, word plays, or prosodic modulations. These devices allow a number of sentences to conjure up the existential questioning and exceptional violence inherent in capital punishment. Marie, the condemned man's young daughter, visits him in his cell without recognizing him and tells him that her father is (already) dead, describing his position as follows: 'Il est dans la terre et dans le ciel' [He is in the ground and in heaven] (XLIII, 705). Imbricating the prosaic and the poetic, the material and the spiritual, her observation captures the totality of his fate and interrogations (XLI). Other passages likewise bring together the metaphorical and the literal. The condemned man calls the thought of his death 'l'horrible idée à se briser la tête au mur de son cachot!' [this idea so awful as to make you want to smash your head against your cell wall] (VII, 665), using a predicate that points to the actual beheading that awaits him. Later on, he also employs a telling adverbial phrase to underline the popular excitement, and the commercialization, that surround his imminent execution: 'Des marchands de sang humain criaient à tue-tête' [dealers in human blood were shouting their heads off] he notes, about the people who hire places from which to see the scaffold (XLVIII, 709).[32] Read literally, 'à tue-tête' transposes the image of the impending decapitation onto those eager to watch it, or suggests that they themselves provoke it. In the same chapter, as the condemned man's cart passes by them on its way to the scaffold, the people shout 'Chapeaux bas! Chapeaux bas' [Hats off! Hats off!] and ask that he be greeted like the king. 'Eux les chapeaux, moi la tête!' [Off with their hats and off with my head!] he replies (p. 709). The appropriation of the idiom 'Chapeau bas!' through this added image of head severance juxtaposes a symbol of deference — not devoid of irony — and one of butchery, an idea highlighted by the name of a tower about which the condemned man enquires while his cart passes by it: 'Saint-Jacques-la-Boucherie'. In these instances, the poetic properties of language, including the ability to move from one level of meaning to another and to multiply and inflect images, make them the guarantor and reminder of a peculiar reality.

Repeatedly in the novel, prosody and rhythm alone also convey meaning with immediacy. The dilation or interruption of a syntagm, the repetition of a term or phoneme make sense by virtue of the sounds produced:

> Hé bien! avant même que mes yeux lourds aient eu le temps de s'entr'ouvrir pour voir cette fatale pensée écrite dans l'horrible réalité qui m'entoure, sur la dalle mouillée et suante de ma cellule, dans les rayons pâles de ma lampe de nuit, dans la trame grossière de la toile de mes vêtements, sur la sombre figure du soldat de garde dont la giberne reluit à travers le cachot, il me semble que déjà une voix a murmuré a mon oreille: — Condamné à mort! (I, 658)

> [Well then! before my heavy eyes even had the time to half open to see this fatal thought written into the horrible reality around me, on the wet and oozing paving stone of my cell, in the pale rays of light of my night lamp, in the coarse weft of the cloth of my garments, on the sombre face of the watchman whose cartridge pouch gleams through the dungeon, it seems to me that a voice has already whispered in my ear: — Condemned to death!]

In this sentence-stanza, rugged [r], liquid [l], and whistling [s] sounds partake in the deliquescence that the condemned man describes in his environment. His distorted perception, which affects the surface, texture, chromaticism, grain, and light of the setting, also shows through a stretched, hypotactic construction. Here, prose is poetic in its musicality in addition to its images. It confirms that *Le Dernier Jour d'un condamné* is a proto- 'roman-poème', in Henri Meschonnic's words.[33] The signifier, or a combination of signifiers, sporadically shortcuts the signified and the incommunicability that prevails in the condemned man's world. In fact, the signifier may become a self-sufficient signified, giving access to the protagonist's inner state. This use of language helps fulfil the agenda he sets out for his text: making his daughter and us 'sa[voir] par [lui] [s]on histoire' [know [his] story through [him]] (XLVI, 706).

Hugo's expressive poetry may also take on a more overt, and indeed spectacular, form: that of the *argot* used by the convicts in Chapter V, and re-emerging in Chapters XVI and XXIII, for example.[34] This idiom radically counters the disembodied speech of the judicial, penitentiary, and religious authorities that encircle the condemned man.[35] It even shows itself to be fully aware of the duplicity of the conventional language previously mentioned: the condemned man reports that, in slang, 'la langue' (both 'language' and 'tongue') is called 'la menteuse' [the liar]. While its traits are coarse, vaudevillian, or grotesque — '[c]'est toute une langue entée sur la langue générale comme une espèce d'excroissance hideuse, comme une verrue' [it is a whole language grafted onto general language, like some kind of hideous excrescence, like a wart] (V, 663) — and while its words sound 'difformes et mal faits, chantés, cadencés, perlés' [misshapen and badly formed, sung, rhythmic, pearl-like] (p. 678) as in the young woman's song, this *argot* allows for a newfound dynamic orality thanks to its 'énergie singulière' [singular energy] (p. 663), phonic and metaphorical. For the first time, it also establishes an exchange and ruptures the competing monologic dynamics of lethal justice and of the condemned man's stream of consciousness: the sociolect is taught by the convicts and learnt by the speaker, who then rephrases it so that the reader, the other learner of this language, can assimilate it.

A certain brutality accompanies this regained life and transitivity of language. With its discordant and sordid character, the convicts' dizzying lexical *copia* about capital punishment entertains a mimetic relationship to its referent and environment: this language that 'fait l'effet de quelque chose de sale et de poudreux, d'une liasse de haillons qu'on secouerait devant vous' [feels like something dirty and dusty, a bundle of rags being shaken in front of you] (V, 663) mirrors the unappealing appearance of executions, as well as that of crime and social misery. The aural and imagistic harshness of the *argot* appears to be necessary, however: it exposes the reality of state killing in contrast to the various *langues de bois* that conceal it.[36] It makes palpable for the reader and the condemned man the fact that the death penalty is about leaving traces of blood behind oneself ('du raisiné sur le trimar', p. 663), about an eerie intimate union with the noose ('épouser la veuve' [marrying the widow]), and about turning a rational mind, '*la sorbonne*,' into a mere head, '*la tronche.*'

As rare as it is in the novel-diary, a positive intersubjective relationship emerges from this ruthless and dissonant renaming of the world. Although the condemned man does not feel like he belongs to the community of the convicts, he receives a message of sympathy from them: 'ces hommes-là me plaignent, ils sont les seuls. Les geôliers, les guichetiers, les porte-clefs, — je ne leur en veux pas, — causent et rient, et parlent de moi, devant moi, comme d'une chose' [those men feel sorry for me, and they're the only ones. The gaoler, the counter clerks, the guards with the keys — I am not cross with them — chat and laugh, and talk about me, in front of me, as they would of a thing] (p. 663). In addition to overturning the linguistic concealment of lethal justice by making its violence perceptible to the mind's eye and ear, *l'argot* thus constitutes the language of those who resist the blindness of this same justice and sometimes display the capacity to perceive and, for a moment, preserve the condemned man's human status.

A second kind of manifest poetic expressiveness complements the imagistic and aural freedom of *l'argot*. It is born from the numerous hallucinations that pervade the novel-diary. Within the metaphor of mental incarceration that frames *Le Dernier Jour d'un condamné* (I) and the condemned man's tentatively lucid account of his wait for and obsession with his execution, one repeatedly finds fantastic 'sentence-images' through which these hallucinatory visions come into being.[37] They include the 'pensée infernale' [infernal thought] of the death sentence, 'comme un spectre de plomb à mes côtés, seule et jalouse [...] dans mes rêves sous la forme d'un couteau' [like a spectre of lead next to me, alone and jealous [...] in my dreams in the shape of a knife] (I, 658); the 'fantasmagorie des juges, des témoins, des avocats, des procureurs du roi' [phantasmagoria of the judges, witnesses, lawyers, king's prosecutors] in addition to 'deux masses de peuple murées de soldats' [two masses of people walled in by soldiers] and their 'faces béantes et penchées' [gaping and tilted faces] that seem moved by threads converging towards the condemned man (II, 658, 659); the mental picture of a severed head spinning around in a limbo-like landscape after the execution (XLI); and the ghastly dream of a witch-like incarnation of death, 'petite vieille, les mains pendantes, les yeux fermés [...] sans voix, sans mouvement, sans regard' [little old lady, with lolling hands, her eyes closed [...] voiceless, motionless, with no gaze] (XLII, 703). These nightmarish apparitions depend on a performative power of language that conjures them up, makes them as real to the reader's mind as they are to the speaker's, and dissolves them.

Chapter XII provides both one of the most forceful illustrations of this process and its figuration *en abyme*. The phantasmagoria it features turns the wall of the protagonist's cell into a palimpsest. After he has symbolically torn off the spider's web that covers their names, anonymous and well-known beheaded criminals ('Jacques', 'Papavoine', 'Bories', 'DAUTUN', 'POULAIN', 'MARTIN', 'CASTAING') come to converse in a free cacophony that culminates in an apocalyptic vision: the severed bodies of these 'hommes de meurtre et de sang' are brought back to life:[38]

> Il m'a semblé tout à coup que ces noms fatals étaient écrits avec du feu sur le mur noir; un tintement de plus en plus précipité a éclaté dans mes oreilles; une lueur rousse a rempli mes yeux; et puis il m'a paru que ce cachot était plein d'hommes, d'hommes étranges qui portaient leur tête dans leur main gauche, et la portaient par la bouche, parce qu'il n'y avait pas de chevelure. Tous me montraient le poing, excepté le parricide.
>
> J'ai fermé les yeux avec horreur, alors j'ai tout vu plus distinctement. (XII, 669)
>
> [It seemed to me all of a sudden that these fatal names were written with fire on the black wall; an ever-hurried chiming burst out in my ears; a reddish glow filled up my eyes; and then it became apparent to me that this dungeon was full of men, strange men who carried their heads in their left hands, and carried them by the mouth, because there was no hair. All of them showed me their fists, except for the parricide.
>
> I closed my eyes with horror, then saw everything more distinctly.]

The views of the imagination only become visible through a language that cultivates spectacularity, hyperbolism, and supernaturalism here. As though through a self-reflexive movement, the names of fire on the prison cell point to the ability of a violent distortion of language to produce potent images that help the reader understand the condemned men's distress and fate.

If these 'sentence-images' (Rancière) emerging from an internal perspective may give a vivacious, dramatic life to the impalpable, they may, conversely, erase reality. In Chapter II, the *condamné* envisions the world that surrounds him with new eyes following the pronouncement of his sentence. By way of a metaphor, his surroundings undergo a sudden metamorphosis. While a warm chromaticism and luminosity initially characterize the scene, this landscape is abruptly obscured once the clerk of the court utters the death sentence: 'Ces larges fenêtres lumineuses, ce beau soleil, ce ciel pur, cette jolie fleur, *tout cela était blanc et pâle, de la couleur d'un linceul*' [These large, luminous windows, this beautiful sun, this pure sky, this pretty flower, *all of that was white and pale, the colour of a shroud*] (II, 661, my emphasis). Here, objective reality in its stereotypical beauty is anaesthetized, the world discoloured and made uniform in a hallucinatory vision. Henri Meschonnic (p. IX) has also signalled such radical transformations as men ceasing to be fully animate and the jail ceasing to be inanimate to become an all-encompassing vigorous, smothering hybrid in the novel. All these metamorphoses largely rely on metaphors that present the unimaginable as real, through the strong, stative verb 'to be' and the presentative turn of phrase 'c'est' [this/it is] in particular: 'ces guichetiers, c'est de la prison en chair et en os. La prison est une espèce d'être horrible, complet, indivisible, moitié maison, moitié homme. Je suis sa proie, elle me couve, elle m'enlace de tous ses replis' [these counter clerks, 'tis prison made flesh and blood. The prison building is a sort of horrible being, complete, indivisible, half-house, half-man. I am its prey, it overwhelms me, it wraps its folds around me] (XX, 680). As the text progresses, the condemned man's prose crafts, revisits, or annihilates the same object through figuration, be it the yellow hue of light, the jail, or the thought of death. Reality comes to be annexed or subverted by poetic language just as it is appropriated by his anguished subjectivity. At times, through this expressive poetry, it no longer seems that language is in charge of conveying his perception in the diary, but rather that it is live perception itself.

★　　★　　★　　★　　★

Directly accessing the intimate obsession with, and fear of, a programmed death: such is Hugo's tour de force when approaching capital punishment in *Le Dernier Jour d'un condamné*. The novel serves the abolitionist cause through a writing that infiltrates and prolongs the condemned man's existential crisis in the face of execution. Literary creation, as if pushed by the gravity of its subject matter, here goes against the grain of established codes to create a voice that sounds eminently real in the alternately lucid and shocked perception of its environment and its desperate attempts to cling to life. Before Hugo, Chateaubriand, the Catholic writer he so revered, and, more lengthily, Pierre-Simon Ballanche, had both asserted that the crucifixion of Christ constituted an exceptional and sufficient bloody expiation of man's sins, which lethal justice was therefore not to replicate; the eighteenth-century jurist Cesare Beccaria, and the numerous French and European philosophers who followed his lead, had tended to insist on the useless, if not counter-productive, character of the death penalty by focusing on a cost-benefit calculation that pointed to the negative political consequences of capital justice. With his early novel, Hugo goes down a different path to question state killing. He creates an indefectible solidarity between, if not a superimposition of, his life-begging protagonist and the reader through the cultivation of a representational disorder that explodes classical conventions and the rules of fiction. *Le Dernier Jour* refuses, as Flaubert noted, to 'faire des réflexions [...] sur la peine de mort' [offer reflections [...] on the death penalty].[39] Indeed, its power stems from the way its unique narrative and dramatic tactics instead force the reader into the inescapable grip of capital punishment so that his voyeurism morphs into his living the sentence himself. The novel thereby turns around the popular spectacle of the execution, during which the condemned man is usually keenly watched from the outside. The understanding, or rather the shared experience of his ordeal, is doubled by that of another rupture that the novel-diary stages: verbal communication and intersubjectivity are shown to fail in numerous ways once death has been decreed. Even the literal cries of the condemned man are fruitless or silenced in the novel. Yet another form of cry sporadically emerges throughout and overturns this incommunicability: a regime of expression through which the fixed idea of death, the execution, and the attempts at escaping them, are conjured up with immediacy and violence through imagistic and phonic plays. 'On ne renverse pas l'échafaud avec des arguments mais avec des mots, des images et des émotions qu'ils font naître' [One does not overthrow scaffolds with arguments but with words, images and emotions to which they give birth], claimed Robert Badinter, the Minister of Justice who obtained the abolition of capital punishment in France in 1981.[40] Himself a former lawyer to men condemned to death, Badinter also pondered in 2007: 'Dans le jury, il suffisait parfois d'une voix pour sauver la tête d'un homme. Combien ont été sauvés parce que les jurés avaient lu *Le Dernier Jour d'un condamné*?' [In the jury, one vote was sometimes enough to save a man's life. How many were saved because the jurors had read *Le Dernier Jour d'un condamné*?].[41] The two remarks may well beg to be connected: *Le Dernier Jour* meticulously fashions not an abolitionist discourse, but a ruthless abolitionist poetics, so that, in an apparent paradox, the novel's political and ethical impact has its origins in formal reinvention. Standing in lieu of overt political argument is a deafening language of pain through which Hugo satisfies the demand implicit in the above-cited epigraph: to earn his title, the poet penetrates — and formulates — the innermost thoughts of a dead man walking, at the border of humanity.

Notes to Chapter 8

1. See Chapters VI, XXI and XXII of *Victor Hugo raconté par un témoin de sa vie*, in Victor Hugo, *Œuvres complètes. Édition chronologique*, ed. by Jean Massin, 18 vols (Paris: Le Club français du livre, 1967–70), I. All subsequent references to Hugo's works are from this edition.
2. *Le Dernier Jour d'un condamné* is included in the third volume of Massin's edition. References to this work are in the main text with the relevant chapter and page numbers only. When other texts by Hugo are cited, the abbreviation *OCH* is followed by the relevant volume and page numbers.
3. For an overview, see for instance: Raymond Jean, *Écrits de Victor Hugo sur la peine de mort* (Maussane les Alpilles: Actes Sud, 1979); *Victor Hugo contre la peine de mort*, ed. by Jérôme Picon and Isabel Violante (Paris: Textuel, 2001); and Paul F. Smets, *Le Combat pour l'abolition de la peine de mort: Hugo, Koestler, Camus, d'autres: textes, prétextes et paratextes* (Brussels: Académie royale de Belgique, 2003). The landmark study analyzing this production in its entirety remains Savey-Casard's *Le Crime et la peine dans l'œuvre de Victor Hugo*. See also 'Dame guillotine', the opening section of Stéphanie Boulard's *Rouge Hugo* (Villeneuve d'Ascq: Presses universitaires du Septentrion, 2014), pp. 21–93.
4. Over thirty years before the publication of the eponymous novel, Hugo uses the term 'misérables' in the preface of *Le Dernier Jour d'un condamné*. For figures establishing a correlation between

misery, the lack of an education, and capital punishment in the 1800s, see Benoît Chabert, 'Sur la peine de mort en France', in *Victor Hugo contre la peine de mort*, ed. by Picon & Violante, pp. 169–73 (p. 173).

5. The Code pénal of 1810 listed thirty-six to thirty-nine offences punishable by death, established that parricides would have their hand cut off, reinstated branding, and made aiding and abetting a capital crime in certain cases. Attempted capital crimes and a number of non-lethal crimes were also subject to the death penalty. A measure adopted in 1825 made capital punishment applicable to acts of sacrilege. See Martin Monestier, *Peines de mort: histoire et techniques des exécutions capitales des origines à nos jours* (Paris: Cherche Midi, 1994), p. 216; Pierre Lascoumes, 'Révolution ou réforme juridique? Les codes pénaux français de 1791 à 1810', in *Révolution et justice pénale en Europe: modèles français et traditions nationales (1780–1830)*, ed. by Xavier Rousseaux, Marie-Sylvie Dupont-Bouchat and Claude Vael (Paris & Montreal: L'Harmattan, 1999), pp. 61–69 (pp. 65, 68–69); and Chabert, 'Sur la peine de mort en France', p. 169.

6. See Edmond Biré, *Victor Hugo avant 1830* (Paris: Jules Gervais, 1883), pp. 473–74; Charles Nisard's review of *Le Dernier Jour d'un condamné* published in *Le Journal des Débats* on 26 February 1829; Henri Guillemin's introduction to *Le Dernier Jour d'un condamné* (Paris: Seuil, 1963), p. 205; and Marie-Claire Vallois, 'Écrire ou décrire: l'impossible histoire du "sujet" dans *Le Dernier Jour d'un condamné* de Victor Hugo', *Romantisme*, 48 (1985), 91–104 (p. 92).

7. This chapter focuses on the narrative as it was available to readers when the book first came out in 1829. For an examination of its multiple para- or pre-texts, see Kathryn Grossman's insightful *The Early Novels of Victor Hugo: Towards a Poetics of Harmony* (Geneva: Droz, 1986), pp. 111–58, and Albert Halsall, '*Le Dernier Jour d'un condamné à mort* [sic]', in *Victor Hugo et l'art de convaincre: le récit hugolien, rhétorique, argumentation, persuasion* (Montreal: Éditions Balzac, 1995), pp. 407–34.

8. See *OCH*, III, 1243. Translations are mine throughout unless otherwise noted. This proposition was supported by the famous abolitionist figure Victor Destutt de Tracy. See Frank Paul Bowman, 'The Intertextuality of Victor Hugo's *Le Dernier Jour d'un condamné*', in *Alteratives*, ed. by Warren Motte and Gerald Prince (Lexington, KY: French Forum Publishers, 1993), pp. 25–45 (pp. 37–38).

9. See *OCH*, II, 51. The two writers had attended the execution of a parricide in 1820. See Yves Gohin, 'Les Réalités du crime et de la justice pour Victor Hugo avant 1829', in *OCH*, III, i–xxv (pp. iv–v). The first epigraph of Chapter XLVIII of *Le Dernier Jour d'un condamné* is an excerpt from 'Parisina', one of Lefèvre-Deumier's poems in *Le Parricide*.

10. *OCH*, II, 50. For an examination of the central role played by the literary representations of capital punishment in the 'querelle des Classiques et des Modernes' and the innovativeness of the Romantic works that dealt with the death penalty, see Guyon, *Les Martyrs de la veuve*, pp. 81–124. On French Romantic aesthetics in its relation to bloody and capital scenes, see Marcandier-Colard, *Crimes de sang et scènes capitales*, pp. 277, 279. Politically speaking, Hugo claims to have been 'libéral-socialiste' as of 1828. See *OCH*, IX, 1019–20.

11. See Nisard's review of *Le Dernier Jour d'un condamné*, for instance.

12. See, for example, Armand Corre, 'À propos de la peine de mort et du livre du Professeur Lacassagne, *Peine de mort et criminalité*', in *Archives d'anthropologie criminelle de médecine légale et de psychologie normale et pathologique*, 23 (Lyon: A. Rey et Cie, 1908), pp. 231, 238. See also Jean-Claude Farcy, 'La Peine de mort: pratique judiciaire et débats', in *Criminocorpus. Revue hypermédia, histoire de la justice, des crimes et des peines* (13 April 2010), <http://journals.openedition.org/criminocorpus/129> [accessed 5 January 2018].

13. Jean Rousset also points to these passages that I call 'moments of interpellation'. See '*Le Dernier Jour d'un condamné* ou l'invention d'un genre littéraire', in *Hugo dans les marges*, ed. by Lucien Dällenbach and Laurent Jenny (Geneva: Éditions Zoë, 1985), pp. 35–50 (pp. 40–41).

14. See Massin, *OCH*, III, 611–13. Hugo expanded on the biographical traits he shared with his character when revising his text.

15. Fedor Dostoevsky, preface to 'A Gentle Creature: A Fantastic Story', in *The Best Short Stories of Fyodor Dostoyevsky*, trans. by David Magarshack (New York: The Modern Library, 2001), p. 216.

16. Rousset, '*Le Dernier Jour d'un condamné* ou l'invention d'un genre littéraire', p. 42.

17. 'Le Dernier Jour d'un condamné, roman; par M. Victor Hugo', Le Globe, 4 February 1829.

18. Giornale, incominciato li 25 Novembre dell'anno 1821 da Luc'Antonio Viterbi, condannato alla pena di morte. Published in its entirety by Robert Benson in 1825, then taken up in the London Magazine, before a passage translated into French came out in the Revue Britannique in May 1826.

19. See 'Dernières sensations d'un homme condamné à mort', Le Globe, 3 January 1828.

20. Hugo visited Bicêtre with David d'Angers in October 1827, and again in October 1828. They also went to the jail of the Conciergerie in 1827. In addition, Hugo relied on reports from the Gazette des Tribunaux and on Vidocq's evocations of the convict's carceral life and argot. See Gustave Charlier, 'Comment fut écrit Le Dernier Jour d'un condamné ?', Revue d'histoire littéraire de la France, 22 (1915), 321–60 (p. 345). This very quest for the picturesque is criticized in the review of Le Dernier Jour published in Le Globe on 4 February 1829.

21. Dostoevsky, preface to 'A Gentle Creature: A Fantastic Story', p. 216. Rousset ('Le Dernier Jour d'un condamné ou l'invention d'un genre littéraire', p. 35) and Victor Brombert (Victor Hugo and the Visionary Novel (Cambridge, MA: Harvard University Press, 1984), pp. 29, 248) briefly mention this Dostoevskyan connection as well.

22. On Le Dernier Jour d'un condamné as a nouveau roman, see also Hélène Lowe-Dupas ('Innommable guillotine: la peine de mort dans Le Dernier Jour d'un condamné et Histoire d'Hélène Gillet', Nineteenth-Century French Studies, 23 (1995), 341–48 (p. 343)), who follows in France Vernier's footsteps ('Cela "fait mal et ne touche pas"', La Pensée, 245 (mai–juin 1985), 41–58), and Guyon (Les Martyrs de la veuve, pp. 115–20). In one of the best, although unfinished, studies of Le Dernier Jour ever published, Lucien Dällenbach has argued that the book could have been written by Butor or Robbe-Grillet in the 1950s ('Le Vide plein ou les révélations de l'homme sans tête', in Hugo dans les marges, ed. by Dällenbach & Jenny, pp. 51–90 (p. 52)).

23. See Émilie Bozon, L'Expression du moi dans 'Le Dernier Jour d'un condamné' de Victor Hugo (Paris: Le Manuscrit, 2002), p. 18. For the vehement criticism levelled against Le Dernier Jour by Hugo's contemporaries, see for instance the review by Nisard, who suggested that every breach of fiction and classical representation discussed here be remedied by a more conventional rewriting of the novel.

24. Hugo points to two potential eighteenth-century predecessors, Xavier De Maistre and Laurence Sterne, only to assert the originality of his work with increased emphasis. De Maistre's A Journey Around My Room and Sterne's A Sentimental Journey Through France and Italy differ from Le Dernier Jour in that they mainly resort to retrospection, include an addressee, and are often humorous and playful in their substance and tone.

25. Jacques Rancière, Mute Speech: Literature, Critical Theory and Politics, trans. by James Swenson (New York: Columbia University, 2011), p. 50.

26. See the speaker's unambiguous judgement: 'Les forçats, les patients sont du ressort de son éloquence. Il les confesse et les assiste, parce qu'il a sa place à faire' [Those doing hard labour, the patients come under the remit of his eloquence. He confesses and assists them because he must climb the ladder] (p. 693).

27. See also Chapter II.

28. Henri Meschonnic ('Vers le roman-poème: les romans de Hugo avant Les Misérables', in OCH, III, VII, XII), Brombert (Victor Hugo and the Visionary Novel), and Guy Rosa ('Commentaires du Dernier Jour d'un condamné', in Le Dernier jour d'un condamné suivi de Claude Gueux et de l'affaire Tapner, ed. by Guy Rosa (Paris: Librairie Générale française, 1989), p. 250) have also pointed to the condemned man's cris, which I connect to an extensive poetic strategy here.

29. Rancière, Mute Speech, p. 50.

30. Ibid., p. 42.

31. Charlier's study of the evolution of the manuscript of Le Dernier Jour d'un condamné indicates that Hugo avidly sought to heighten the imagistic quality of his work ('Comment fut écrit Le Dernier Jour d'un condamné ?').

32. Meschonnic has pointed out that 'l'attention que Hugo porte aux puissances du langage est le moteur de ses jeux de mots' [the attention that Hugo pays to the power of language is the driving force behind his word plays] ('Vers le roman-poème', p. VIII).

33. For a detailed examination of the alliterations, echoes, and the play with finals that make up

what Meschonnic terms the chiseled and powerful 'phrasé' of *Le Dernier Jour d'un condamné*, see the section entitled 'La Prosodie' in 'Vers le roman-poème' (pp. XI–XIII).

34. Yvette Parent has shown that a few of the terms that Hugo presents as *argotiques* are in fact *poissards* (another form of popular dialect) and that a small number of his words do not appear in *argot* dictionaries ('L'emploi de l'argot dans *Le Dernier Jour d'un condamné*', published by the Groupe Hugo of Université Paris 7 on 8 February 2003, <http://groupugo.div.jussieu.fr/ Groupugo/03–02–08Parent.htm> [accessed 5 January 2018]). On the re-invention of *l'argot* in Hugo's fiction, see also Boulard, *Rouge Hugo*, pp. 319–20.

35. The *condamné* himself is able to play with this disincarnate speech sporadically: he uses a 'dead' language, Latin, to impress the prison concierge, who does not understand it but perceives its prestige. As a consequence, he allows the convict to go on weekly walks inside the jail (V, 663).

36. The idiomatic phrase 'langue de bois' prolongs the analogy between vegetation and language that Hugo sketches through the metaphor of the grafted tongue — thereby harking back to a long-standing ambition to enrich the French language, as exemplified by Du Bellay's *Défense et illustration de la langue française* (1549). Thus in *Le Dernier Jour d'un condamné*, one finds, on the one hand, the hideous but living grafted plant of the *argot*, and, on the other, the *bois mort* of 'la langue générale' as it is used by officials.

37. For a survey of hallucinations and the guillotine in Hugo's works other than *Le Dernier Jour*, see Boulard, *Rouge Hugo*, pp. 38–44.

38. For an overview of the crimes and executions of these figures, see Gohin, 'Les Réalités du crime et de la justice pour Victor Hugo avant 1829', pp. iv-ix, xii-xiii.

39. Gustave Flaubert, letter to Louise Colet, 9 December 1852, in *Correspondance*, ed. by Jean Bruneau (Paris: Gallimard, 1980), p. 204.

40. Robert Badinter, 'Je vote l'abolition de la peine de mort', *L'Histoire*, 261 (2002), 56–57 (p. 56).

41. Robert Badinter, 'Préface', in *Choses vues à travers Hugo: hommage à Guy Rosa*, ed. by Claude Millet and others (Valenciennes: Presses universitaires de Valenciennes, 2007), pp. 7–10 (pp. 7–8).

CHAPTER 9

❖

Novel Arguments Against Capital Punishment: Plotting Death Sentences in E. D. E. N. Southworth's *The Gipsy's Prophecy* and *The Lost Heiress*

John Cyril Barton

In June of 1829, Edward Livingston, one of America's foremost lawyers and legislators, wrote to James Fenimore Cooper, without question the most influential American novelist of the time. Livingston's letter concerned the burgeoning movement to abolish capital punishment, a campaign to which Livingston himself had significantly contributed with his influential penal reports first presented before the Louisiana State Legislature in 1821 and widely circulated thereafter in pamphlet form. Livingston included copies of his reports with his letter, and in it he solicited Cooper's help in ending 'a practice supported only by prejudice and the fear of innovation which outrages humanity, and disgraces the legislation of the civilized world'.[1] Cooper, Livingston reasoned, was in a unique position to aid the cause, given his critical acclaim and enormous readership: 'You are one of the very, very few', Livingston wrote, 'whose works are not only read in all civilized nations, but by all the reading part of every nation.' It was, however, not merely to Cooper's literary reputation but to the power of literature itself that Livingston appealed:

> The department of literature which you have [...] adopted is one that enables you to impress most forcibly on the mind the truths you may wish to inculcate. The skill with which you embody the passions and exemplify their operation and effects, the genius which enables you to give to fiction all the interest of reality, the knowledge of human nature by which you detect and expose the most secret workings of the mind, and the command of language and descriptive powers you possess, to throw into the most interesting form the incidents your fancy creates, all these fit you in the most eminent degree for the task I propose. (p. 175)

Calling attention to the power of literary narrative and to prose fiction in particular, Livingston went on to outline the 'task' he proposed:

It is that of exemplifying (in a work written expressly with that view) the evils of capital punishment. One of the most prominent among them (its irremediable nature) seems to me to offer the finest field for a display of your powers in describing the effects of an erroneous judgment founded on false or mistaken testimony — the unavailing efforts of conscious innocence; its uncredited association, its despair; the remorse of the mistaken jurors and judge when the falsity of the charge is discovered too late for redress; the chain of circumstances by which guilt was presumed or the motives for the perjury by which it was asserted, in your hand, might be worked up into a picture that would cause the hardiest advocate for capital punishment to pause in his desire to inflict it. (p. 175)

Livingston's letter is remarkable for several reasons. To begin with, it is an early and powerful instance of what scholars today call 'Law and Literature', an inter-disciplinary field or consideration, in this case, of a legal problem on which a literary approach could shed light. Livingston is clearly appealing to the fictive, that property of invention and imagination belonging to any literary form; but it is telling that his appeal is to a novelist and to what we might think of as novelistic discourse or 'Discourse in the Novel', to invoke Mikhail Bakhtin's influential theory of the genre.[2] Indeed, Livingston's appeal suggests the intrinsic aptness of a novel, when compared to a poem or play (the two other literary forms of the day that drew most from the fictive), for exposing what he dubs 'the evils of capital punishment'. For unlike drama, which calls for a staged performance and theatrical audience, a novel could reach potentially any English-speaking reader in the United States (or abroad) with virtually no production cost beyond that of publication. And unlike the verse form and the greater unity of voice associated with poetry (Bakhtin), the prosaic style and protean form of the novel enable the genre more readily to incorporate various voices and professional discourses, as well as to offer a more extended engagement with character and incident than a conventional poem.

The professional discourse Livingston had in mind was obviously the law, and the novel could go beyond not only theatre halls and courtrooms, with their limited audiences, but legal discourse itself, with the restrictive rules governing what constitutes evidence and how it can function. To be sure, with the unrestricted access to evidence afforded through what Livingston calls 'the department of literature', a novelist could manage plot and develop character to expose the limitations of law while revealing a truth perhaps inaccessible through legal means. Literature could thus supplement the law, revealing what Wai Chee Dimock has productively figured as the 'residues of justice', her trope for the commensurate play between law and literature, especially how literary works uncover 'residues unsubsumed and unresolved by any order of the commensurate, residues that introduce a lingering question, if nothing else, into any program of justice, whether corrective, distributive, compensatory, or revolutionary'.[3] It is in the exposure of such 'residues' that Livingston saw a popular novel contributing to the anti-gallows movement. Such a novel, dramatizing the processes and procedures of state killing, could have an incalculable impact on how countless American readers — who were also citizens with a say in the government — might think and feel about capital punishment.

Cooper, as far as scholars know, never directly responded to Livingston's letter; nor did he ever write the kind of work for which the eminent lawyer had hoped — though Cooper's fiction stands in a complicated relation to capital punishment, as I have suggested elsewhere.[4] Even so, from the time Livingston had privately written to Cooper to the eve of the Civil War, hundreds of poems advocating the abolition of the death penalty were printed in national periodicals and especially in *The Prisoner's Friend*, a magazine devoted to the anti-gallows cause.[5] Likewise, dozens of novels and numerous tales would be published during this time that made explicit statements against the gallows or dramatized scenes overtly criticizing the practice. Yet a quarter century would elapse before Livingston's formula for an anti-gallows work materialized in novel form. In fact, not one but two such novels organized around the issue and 'written expressly', as Livingston had proposed, to expose 'the evils of capital punishment' were published in the 1850s. Both were penned by E. D. E. N. Southworth (1819–99), a popular novelist who commanded a readership in her day on a par with that of Cooper's in his.[6] The first of these works, *The Lost Heiress* (1854), centres on the irremediable nature of the death penalty and explores the vexed relation between sovereign authority in relation to civic responsibility that arises in a democratic republic when the state kills. The second, *The Gipsy's Prophecy* (1859), takes shape around a sensational murder, capital trial, and impending death sentence in order to interrogate conceptions of evidentiary value and the exercise of executive authority in the administration of lawful death. Whereas the first of these novels argues against capital punishment primarily from a perspective *behind* the law, the second does so from the viewpoint of the condemned citizen *before* it. Taken together, these novels form Southworth's dyad on the death penalty, the central statement from a writer who likely 'wrote more about the death penalty than any other American novelist of the nineteenth century'.[7]

With Livingston's letter as a heuristic frame, this essay examines Southworth's 'novel arguments', that is, her use of plot, character, incident, as well as empathetic intrigue and investment in ways Livingston suggested, in terms of what I have elsewhere called 'the cultural rhetoric of capital punishment', by which I mean the tropes, arguments, and narratives that animated debates about the gallows in antebellum America.[8] There were several prominent strands within this broader rhetoric. One consisted of appeals to religious authority that featured interpretations of scriptural evidence, such as Genesis 9:6, the parable of Cain and Abel, and principle of *lex talionis*. Related to biblical arguments were appeals to sympathy and sentiment — not only *for* the condemned and his family but *to* private citizens who were asked if they could serve as hangman or approve of capital punishment if one of their family members was sentenced to death. These latter kinds of appeals morphed into more overtly political ones that challenged the right of *any* citizen to take the life of another in a democratic republic.

In addition to biblical narrative and both sentimental and political appeals, arguments in novels and elsewhere drew from infamous cases and executions, taken from the historical archive or ripped from contemporary headlines. However, the trope and narrative combined most frequently in fiction to make such novel arguments was that of condemned innocence, a personification of what Livingston called 'conscious innocence' and an inversion of the fratricide Cain, who personified conscious guilt. No nineteenth-century novelist worked more deliberately with this trope and narrative to make anti-gallows arguments than Southworth. We can begin to see how by looking first at *The Gipsy's Prophecy*, which pits an innocent person before the law to plot out the formula Livingston imagined. Looking at this later novel first reveals a subtle and more 'novel' argument at work in Southworth's earlier *The Lost Heiress*, which seeks to expose contradictions and paradoxes at play in the administration of capital punishment in a democratic republic.

Condemned Innocence and Circumstantial Evidence in *The Gipsy's Prophecy*

Set in England and written for a transatlantic audience, *The Gipsy's Prophecy* tells the story of Gerald Mostyn, a virtuous young aristocrat who is accused, tried, and a convicted of a capital crime based primarily on circumstantial evidence. The narrative itself, however, is told from the perspective of Mostyn's newly-wedded wife, Constance Wynn. The novel's protagonist, Constance, not only remains steadfast and constant (as in her name) to her husband but plays a dramatic role in attempting to prevent his execution. Organized around a sensational murder, a trial, and an impending execution, *The Gipsy's Prophecy* comes close to realizing the anti-gallows plot that Livingston proposed. To quote from Livingston's formula, *The Gipsy's Prophecy* highlights the horrors of an 'irremediable' sentence, turns on a misleading 'chain of circumstances', and demonstrates how 'erroneous judgment founded on false or mistaken testimony' could make the innocent appear guilty, thus pitting 'conscious innocence' against a judicial system susceptible to human error and caprice. That Southworth wrote the novel expressly to criticize capital punishment is evident not only through the work's design but in remarks she made following a staged production of it: 'In the novel,' the author told the play's audience following a performance the year it was published, 'I sought to draw the reader's mind to a closer consideration of the question of capital punishment. If by this work [...] a few thinking men and women may be led to reflect upon [...] the death penalty [...] then the holiest purpose of the writer will have been blessed with success'.[9]

Southworth writes this 'purpose' into the novel's structure. Before the murder and trial take centre stage, the book begins with a prophetic reference to 'the dark form of the — Scaffold!' that will blight Constance's life and that preoccupies the novel's plot.[10] Picking up on this allusion two chapters later, Southworth stages a debate on 'Capital punishment and the recently started question of its abolishment' (p. 54). On one side is Reverend Osborne, a conservative minister who 'took the cautious, conservative view'. The Reverend saw criminals as 'low, uneducated, unregenerate men' who, 'like animals', could 'only be governed by fear'. On the other side is Constance, who 'assumed a more enlightened, liberal, and humane position'. In direct opposition to Reverend Osborne, Constance rejects capital punishment in principle, seeing it as an institution based on 'retaliation' and 'vengeance', what she terms 'the offspring of hate and fear, whence no good could ever come' (pp. 55–56). Placed at the outset of the narrative, this debate thematizes the novel's central question about the expediency of the death penalty — a question then playing out in England, as Southworth's narrator notes, but especially in America, as the author well knew.[11] To be sure, by the time *The Gipsy's Prophecy* was published, hundreds of articles and dozens of legislative reports and extralegal books concerning capital punishment had been published in the United States, and three states had abolished the practice by 1853 — the most recent being Wisconsin, where Southworth herself resided in the early 1840s. For her antebellum American readers, the exchange between Constance and Reverend Osborne would have served as shorthand for debates about the death penalty then raging across much of the country. Constance would have represented a gendered version of the era's leading anti-gallows reformers, exemplified by both John O'Sullivan, the influential editor of the *Democratic Review* and two-term House Democrat from New York who authored a widely-circulated legislative report advocating the abolition of capital punishment, and Charles Spear, the tireless reformer who spearheaded *The Prisoner's Friend*, the nation's first periodical devoted to the anti-gallows cause. Reverend Osborne, in contrast, stands in for many conservative clergymen well known for championing the gallows — the best known of whom was George B. Cheever, a prominent Presbyterian minister who penned *Punishment by Death: Its Authority and Expediency* (1842), what one historian has dubbed 'the most famous and influential defence of the gallows in American History'.[12] Participating in the debate of its day, the exchange between Constance and Osborne also advances the novel's plot by foreshadowing events to come, as Constance later puts her beliefs into practice by trying to overturn her husband's death sentence.

The crime for which Mostyn is convicted is the murder of his rich, elderly grandfather, Hugh Horne, the novel's symbolic patriarch and possessor of the family estate, Horne's Hole. It occurs on Christmas Eve when old Mr Horne, stabbed and mortally wounded, is discovered dying in his bedroom by the young and beautiful Alice Owen, Mr Horne's nurse and housekeeper. Statements are taken by the authorities, and witnesses are later deposed, with the exception of Alice, who disappears the day after the murder. Direct testimony also plays a significant role in the case against Mostyn, but it is primarily because of circumstantial evidence — so crucial in nineteenth-century law and literature, as Alexander Welsh has convincingly shown — that Mostyn is convicted.[13] Those circumstances involve motive, means, and opportunity. For not only was Mostyn present at the time of the murder, but he stood to inherit the bulk of the family fortune from the grandfather with whom he had recently been on bad terms. The most damning evidence against Mostyn, though, comes out at trial: first, the prosecution enters into evidence Mostyn's discovered bloodstained suit; second, Alice, a reluctant witness for the state, acknowledges having seen the back of Mostyn fleeing the crime scene. Through Alice's testimony, not only is Mostyn positively identified, but Mr Horne's dying declaration to Alice is also admitted into evidence: 'O Alice!', Mr Horne exclaims before expiring, 'Gerald Mostyn, my grandson, has done it!' (p. 198).

With the circumstances stacked overwhelmingly against Mostyn, the novel self-consciously turns to an interrogation of legal evidence. Over the course of eight pages, the concept of circumstantial evidence is explicitly broached thirteen times. On two occasions readers hear of 'the proverbial fallibility of circumstantial evidence' (pp. 202, 207), a claim that flies in the face of the equally proverbial 'circumstances cannot lie!' that Welsh has identified as a rallying cry in nineteenth-century courtrooms and novels alike.[14] One occurs during the defence attorney's closing argument, wherein he references 'the well-known trials of Jennings, Crow, Shaw, and several others, all clearly convicted, and incontinently executed, for crimes committed and afterwards confessed by others' (p. 202). This 'citing of several celebrated cases' constitutes a key piece of evidence in the novel's argument against capital punishment, even though — or rather, precisely because — it fails to convince the jury, who convict Mostyn. These citations not only illustrate for readers how lawful evidence can make the innocent appear guilty; they also point to the historical record, documenting actual instances in which individuals have been executed for crimes they did not commit. That Southworth intended readers to take *note* of these cases is evident from the 'note' that she appends to the defence lawyer's citation: 'These cases may be found recorded', Southworth explains, 'under the head of "Circumstantial Evidence" in a book published about twenty years ago, entitled "Celebrated Trials"' (p. 202).

In referencing these cases, Southworth clearly wanted her audience to link the fictive case against Mostyn to the historical ones of Jennings, Crow, and Shaw, thus providing readers with a behind-the-scenes look at how the law can misconstrue the facts. But what we ultimately learn defies belief, as the circumstances logically connecting Mostyn to Mr Horne's murder are not at all what they seem. Mostyn's innocence, in which Constance steadfastly believes and for which readers are encouraged to hope, gradually comes to light through the unconscious agency of Alice and through events involving Dr Horne, an esteemed physician and favoured nephew of the late Mr Horne, who stands to inherit along with Mostyn. For, not long after the murder, readers witness the so-called good doctor proposition Alice and then, when she refuses to comply, frame her for grand larceny. The larceny case against Alice creates a subplot that parallels the central one concerning Mostyn, whose conviction, readers eventually learn, was similarly orchestrated by Dr Horne. Whereas the case against Mostyn primarily shows how circumstances can be manipulated, the one against Alice demonstrates how testimony can be falsified and how class standing can unjustly influence how evidence functions in a court of law. In the face of Alice's conscious innocence, the jury returns a guilty verdict. The shock of the verdict throws Alice into a paraphyletic fit that makes it appear as though she has died. Presuming her death, the court releases Alice's body to the good Dr Heath, a foil to Dr Horne, who becomes Alice's protector and marries her shortly after she is charged with theft. When Dr Heath later discovers Alice to be alive, he arranges a sham funeral to publicize her death, all the while keeping her secretly housed in a country home in close proximity to Horne's Hole. Unconsciously driven by knowledge of her innocence, Alice nightly sleepwalks to Horne's Hole and stands, like an avenging angel, before Dr Horne, commanding him to 'CONFESS' (p. 430). Haunted by these repeated visits, the terrified and guilt-stricken doctor eventually confesses not only to framing Alice but to murdering his uncle for money and leaving evidence behind to suggest Mostyn's guilt.

This cloak-and-dagger novel — featuring a supposed death, somnabulation, and the confession of a murderer who had successfully evaded the law — is certainly designed to entertain through sensation. Yet it is precisely through the preposterous plot that we find a crucial component of the novel's anti-gallows argument. For it is only in a work of fiction that such a scenario could play out. In reality, a case consisting of such iron-clad evidence (like those of Jennings, Crow, Shaw) would undoubtedly lead to the execution of an innocent person, as there would be no *deus ex machina*, or rather ghost in the bedroom in Mostyn's case, to shed light on human error and to resolve an understandable misunderstanding.

Southworth thus presents an important part of her novel argument by managing plot and developing both character and incident. She also draws from sensation, a style that shocks and titillates, to support her stance against the gallows. Literary sensationalism, along with sentimentalism, had its share of practitioners among popular antebellum novelists who used fiction to promote the anti-gallows cause. George Thompson frequently engaged in sensation to critique capital punishment in novels such as *The House Breaker* (1847), *Bristol Bill* (1851), *The Outlaw* (1851), and *The Gay Girls of New York* (1853), as did William Gilmore Simms in many of his 'Border Romances', and George Lippard perfected the practice in works such as *Legends of the Revolution* (1847), *The Empire City* (1853), and his best-selling *The Quaker City* (1845).[15] Without the excessive violence and sexual intrigue of Lippard or Thompson, Southworth employed similar strategies to expose the fallibility of legal evidence, highlighting the absurd proof it would take in some cases to bring out the truth. Taking a page from both Thompson and Lippard, who dramatize in high dudgeon the physical and psychological torments of the condemned, Southworth details the anguish and despair to which Mostyn succumbs while he awaits execution.[16] This drama reaches a high point precisely midway through the novel when Mostyn is forced to go through all the rituals and administrative procedures of Hanging Day. In fact, Mostyn is brought to the brink of lawful death: he is escorted to the gallows and given his last rites; he has the rope fastened around his neck; and he 'stand[s] upon the fatal drop!' as the 'sheriff advance[s] his foot near the spring' of the gallows' trap door before a stay of execution arrives at the very last moment (p. 249). Through such painstaking details, Southworth registers the mental and emotional horrors that condemned subjects face when spending months (or more) confined to a prison cell while anxiously awaiting death — all the while knowing exactly when and by what means they can expect to be killed.

Yet a more substantial argument comes out in one of the (failed) attempts to obtain a pardon or commutation for Mostyn. That scene dramatically unfolds when Constance takes it upon herself to meet with the Home Secretary, the designated executive invested with the power to pardon in England's parliamentary system. It so happens that Constance is on personal terms with the Home Secretary, Lord Starr, an old family friend and a former suitor for Constance's hand. That Constance, as part of Britain's landed aristocracy, has access to the Home Secretary through personal connections and class standing while the vast majority of British citizens do not is part of Southworth's critique. The crux of her criticism, however, comes through Constance's interaction with Lord Starr, who wields authority with caprice and even malice. Far from an impartial state agent, the Home Secretary uses his power to exploit Constance. In fact, during their 'privated' meeting, he propositions her, declaring 'there is one condition upon which I will interfere to save Gerald Mostyn's life'. That condition, though never explicitly stated, becomes clear when the Home Secretary professes his 'love' and all but forces himself upon Constance, thus bartering Mostyn's life for sexual favours or an illicit relationship (p. 230). In this way, Southworth shows how the executive power to pardon can fall into all-too-human hands.

Lord Starr's actions, in this respect, are not much different from the novel's villainous Dr Horne. This scene was obviously written to titillate and to entertain. Nonetheless, it also squarely attacks the executive branch as it relates to the administration of capital punishment, showing how a state agent can act capriciously and maliciously, or wield power for personal gain. Setting the novel in England, as opposed to America, enables Southworth to interrogate longstanding institutions in Anglo-American law, such as the judiciary and trial-by-jury system as well as the pardoning power invested in a single state agent. Derived from British law, these institutions were of course hallmarks of criminal justice in the United States at the time Southworth was writing, a point to which I return to conclude this essay. Here, however, it is important to note that Southworth extends her attack on executive authority from the perspective of two state agents intimately involved with the practice of state killing but with little power to change it. For when news of Lord Starr's rejection of Constance's appeal for clemency reaches the prison holding Mostyn, the following exchange ensues: 'Lor, there shouldn't be nobody hung if *I* was the monarch', the warden laments, to which the turnkey replies, 'No more there shouldn't, sir, if *I* was the Minister' (p. 238). These subjunctive musings imagine a more sympathetic state than those, unlike the Home Minister, who are directly involved with administering lawful death. They also suggest the possibility of ending capital punishment through legislation or executive fiat — a possible solution, given evident problems with the judiciary and executive branches of government.

Sovereignty and Responsibility Behind the Law in *The Lost Heiress*

A secondary concern of *The Gipsy's Prophecy*, questions about executive authority and the pardoning power provide the focus of *The Lost Heiress* (1854), one of Southworth's most popular works published four years earlier in novel form and serialized a year before that in the *Saturday Evening Post*, a venue that exposed the narrative to a wide readership. This novel, like its successor, is also plotted around a central death sentence, thereby offering a critique of capital punishment even as it capitalizes from the drama of the death penalty. Its criticism, however, takes a different form. Whereas *The Gipsy's Prophecy* hinges on a near execution at its structural centre and concludes with a pardon granted in its final pages, *The Lost Heiress* stages an execution that is carried out in its opening chapters. In fact, the novel begins on the eve of the scheduled execution of William O'Leary as the condemned man's family, along with leading citizens of Maryland, are preparing to present final appeals for a pardon or commutation before a newly elected governor assuming office the next day. The novel thus shifts back and forth between the condemned and his family in prison and the new governor and his family in the state mansion. This narrative strategy interlinks the fates of two families on opposing sides of the law, connecting them through the legal power to execute and the responsibility that comes with that authority.

The Lost Heiress, in fact, highlights this vexed relationship between sovereignty and responsibility even before Daniel Hunter, the governor elect, takes office. On the eve of his inauguration, Hunter's wife Augusta marvels at the authority to be invested in her husband, telling him to think how 'by the stroke of [his] pen' he could save a 'fellow creature from the scaffold; what a privilege!'. In response, Hunter promptly replies, 'And a responsibility!'.[17] The soon-to-be governor's response to this *responsibility* (or accountability) to the law structures the entire novel. We can begin to see how by looking more closely at its opening conflict: the race against the clock to prevent an impending execution, a veritable convention of death-penalty narratives from Cooper's *The Spy* (1821) through a diverse range of twentieth- and twenty-first-century Hollywood films.[18] In *The Lost Heiress*, that drama builds over several early chapters and reaches a high point in Chapter Five, 'The Petition'. In it, the new governor is visited by other state figureheads — a Major General, the Bishop of Maryland, a Chief Justice of the State Supreme Court, and a Commodore of the Navy — who present a formal petition 'signed by so large a number of persons', readers are told, 'that the Bishop only turned the pages' to signify the prisoner's overwhelming support (p. 52).

It is here that Southworth presents her strongest argument *for* the death penalty, as Hunter propounds a principled rejection of the suit and responds specifically to objections raised by the dignitaries. 'Thoroughly well acquainted with the case of William O'Leary', Hunter first offers his views on O'Leary's trial and then turns to the underlying question of capital punishment itself:

> I have referred again to the minutes of the trial [...]. The guilt of the prisoner seems to me to be an indubitable fact. [...] Gentlemen, I think that the judge and jury have performed their duty. [...] I am glad that they have done so that no false sentiment of compassion has unnerved the stern hand of justice. Mercy to the guilty is too often cruelty to the innocent. The pardon of a murderer is a deed pregnant with terrible responsibilities. We know not how much the hope of impunity tempts to crime! Let the consequences of crime to the criminal be sure, awful, unchangeable, irresistible, and many a reckless man, who now gives way to his headlong passions, would hold them in some check, and many a plotting villain would hesitate and turn back from the meditated guilt. Tell me, if you please, that the fear of punishment is an improper instrument of reformation — and I will answer you that it is the only motive — also, that the laws do not attempt to reform the guilty, but to protect the inoffensive, not to regenerate the heart, but to restrain its guilty passions from breaking into overt crime. The law is not reformatory but restraining — 'a terror to evil doers'.
> (p. 54)

Anticipating Captain Vere's now classic defence of the death penalty in Melville's *Billy Budd* (1891), Hunter delivers as thoughtful a justification of the death penalty as one might find in pro-gallows literature. Conversant with cultural debates at mid-century, *The Lost Heiress* offers no strawman argument for the gallows, as one might say *The Gipsy's Prophecy* does through both Reverend Osborne's predictable defence of the gallows and Lord Starr's corrupt wielding of state power. On the contrary, the pro-capital punishment position finds an admiral spokesperson in Governor Hunter, a character almost universally championed both within the novel and by critics outside it.[19] Antebellum readers familiar with debates surrounding the death penalty would have heard in Hunter's argument echoes from Cheever's *Punishment by Death* (1842) and *A Defence of Capital Punishment* (1846). For, like Cheever, Hunter rejects the principle of reform while unabashedly embracing retribution and the permanent incapacitation afforded through capital punishment.

Hunter's justification also resonates with that of Leonard Bacon, an influential Congregationalist minister who railed against the anti-gallows movement in 'Shall Punishment Be Abolished?' (1846), an essay published several years before Southworth would pen her governor's defence. Whereas Hunter rules out the 'false sentiment of compassion' that 'unnerve[s] the stern hand of justice', finding in 'fear' a healthy and appropriate consequence of punishment, Bacon discredits the 'religion' of anti-gallows reformers, reducing it to 'a mere sentimentalism'; moreover, he mocks the idea that punishment should be based on reform. 'Punishment, in the administration of justice by civil government, nothing but a reformatory process?' Bacon scoffs. 'Who does not know better?' he responds. 'Punishment is the sanction of law. It is the expression of moral sense of the state against the crime.'[20] Whereas Hunter, who embodies what Bacon calls the 'moral sense of the state', defends the death penalty as a 'necessary terror to evil doers', Bacon supports it being inflicted '*in terrorem*'. Yet while Hunter's argument shares underlying assumptions with Bacon's, his is couched in more measured terms. There is, for instance, no biting sarcasm and little hyperbole in Hunter's defence. Indeed, far from a caricature of the pro-capital punishment position, as progressive readers today might characterize Bacon or Cheever in their zealous defences, Hunter stands for the integrity of the law and its unyielding implementation.

Justifying the death penalty in general, Hunter also approves its particular use in the case at hand, noting the 'due form', 'impartiality', and 'humanity' exhibited during the O'Leary trial. His familiarity with the case clearly demonstrated, Hunter does not merely pass on, or pay lip service to, the previous decisions of the jury's verdict and the judge's sentence. On the contrary, he actively reaffirms them. His decision is therefore not a self-interested or flip one, as Lord Starr's is shown to be. Rather, it is thoughtful and carefully considered, possessing important attributes of what Jacques Derrida has called a 'just decision', his term for a responsible decision a judicial or executive agent might reach, as opposed to one that is automatic and pre-programmed, or a decision that merely rubber stamps a previous decision. 'To be just,' Derrida argues, 'the decision of a judge, for example, must not only follow a rule of law or a general law but must also assume it, approve it, confirm its value, by a reinstituting act of interpretation, as if ultimately nothing previously existed of the law, as if the judge himself invented the law in every case.'[21] Despite its conservative politics, Hunter's response exemplifies such a decision insofar as it constitutes 'a fresh judgment', another term Derrida uses for an interpretation that yields a just decision. For Hunter does not just follow 'the rule of law' and the 'general law', to borrow Derrida's words, in upholding the earlier verdicts; he also 'assume[s]' and 'confirm[s]' the law through a 'reinstituting act of interpretation' that founds the death penalty in general by accepting the specific enactment of it. It is, then, no accident that the governor's affirmation of O'Leary's execution is grounded in a defence of the death penalty itself.

That Hunter is no 'mere calculating machine' but an executive agent responsible to his decision is further illustrated through his response to the state dignitaries who respectfully challenge him.[22] The first to do so is Chief Justice Robert S. Turner, who reminds the governor that O'Leary was found guilty on 'circumstantial evidence alone' (p. 55). Emphasizing the fallibility of such evidence, Justice Turner points to 'the numerous cases in which innocent men had been condemned and executed under circumstantial evidence' (pp. 55–56). Such evidence, as we have seen, plays a key role in *The Gipsy's Prophecy*, not only in the near execution of Mostyn but in the historical cases of actual innocence cited at trial by Mostyn's lawyer and footnoted by Southworth herself.

In *The Gipsy's Prophecy*, Southworth can be seen as shying away from the full force of this argument. Mostyn's death sentence, after all, is ultimately reversed. The state thus avoids assuming the responsibility that would have entailed from the execution of an innocent man. In *The Lost Heiress,* however, Southworth addresses the issue head on by carrying out the death sentence of a potentially innocent man. Justice Turner, in fact, pursues this line of argument when he asks Hunter to 'consider what would be his feelings if he should now persist in refusing to grant a reprieve to the prisoner' only to learn later of his innocence. Sidestepping the question about his personal 'feelings', Hunter here refers back to the court record, noting that this point 'was most eloquently urged upon the consideration of the jury by the able counsel of the prisoner' (p. 56). Siding with the jury, Hunter affirms the verdict and assumes responsibility for it, putting the supposed security of society above the protection of an individual citizen. As he had earlier put it when first propounding his position: 'The pardon of a murderer is a deed pregnant with terrible responsibilities' (p. 54). What Hunter fails to note, however, is that the opposite is also true and rife with 'terrible responsibilities' of its own.

Whereas Justice Turner contests the Governor's decision by attending to evidentiary concerns, Bishop Storr challenges it by invoking religion and the merits of mercy. In reply, Hunter quotes several Christian responses to capital punishment, including *lex talionis* and the need for its impartial administration (p. 57). In distinguishing the moral from the lawful, Hunter advocates an unbiased and unyielding application of law that operates irrespective of one's personal capacity or desire to forgive, while acknowledging the state's monopoly on violence. In response, the Commodore asks, 'But if the condemned were your brother?' to which Hunter promptly replies: 'If guilty, he should suffer, though our mother interceded for his pardon' (p. 57).

Hunter's response to the Commodore reverberates sardonically over the second half of *The Lost Heiress*, and I have worked carefully through the governor's argument *for* the death penalty because it sets up Southworth's novel argument *against* it. For, midway through the work, some eleven years after Hunter rendered his verdict, the former governor and now distinguished statesman is forced to eat his words. Bishop Storr has come to visit Hunter, who has served as a US senator and Secretary of State since their last meeting, in order to share incontrovertible proof of O'Leary's innocence. This time Hunter has nothing to say in his defence, and Bishop Storr is given the final word, pointedly asking Hunter (who 'exercises a mighty influence upon the age') a series of pronounced rhetorical questions:

> A young man, amiable, innocent, exemplary in all the relations of life, is charged with a crime he has never committed — he is overwhelmed by circumstantial evidence — he endures all the torture, suspense, shame and anguish of a long imprisonment, a terrible trial, and a public death! I repeat there has been an awful wrong done! Who is the wrong-doer or the wrong-doers? Not the judge and jury who convicted him! For they went by the law and the testimony, and with the evidence before them they could do no otherwise than condemn him! Not the Governor, for it was his duty to see the laws carried into effect! Who then? Daniel Hunter, I ask you, as a law-maker, a leader among men and nations, upon whose head or heads has fallen the innocent blood of this young man? (pp. 256–57)

Situated near the novel's structural centre, the bishop's statement and questions about responsibility for O'Leary's execution serve as a counterpoint to Hunter's earlier declarative statements unequivocally justifying the institution of lawful death. Through them, Southworth underscores the novel's anti-gallows plot and radically undercuts the position from which Hunter had earlier vigorously defended the death penalty. If the purpose of *The Gipsy's Prophecy* is to get 'a few thinking men and women', as the author herself put it, to question capital punishment, then the primary objective of *The Lost Heiress* is to dramatize the dire need of changing the minds of state and national leaders on the issue. In other words, whereas *The Gipsy's Prophecy* works from the bottom up in promoting its reform agenda, *The Lost Heiress* works from the top down — striving to change the hearts and minds of influential political figures like Hunter who represent what Livingston dubbed in his letter to Cooper, the 'hardiest advocate for capital punishment'.

Framed in part as a series of open-ended, rhetorical questions, the bishop's remarks speak not only to the predicament at hand but to a situation brought into being any time a potentially innocent person is executed. That situation, as Southworth suggests, is fraught with tension when carried out in a republican form of government, wherein the sovereign 'people' lawfully put to death a citizen who constitutes part of that sovereign entity. It was for this reason that several of the nation's Founding Fathers — William Bradford, Thomas Jefferson, John Jay, James Madison, Ben Franklin, and Benjamin Rush among them — saw the death penalty as anathema to republican principles. Rush can be seen as speaking for this group when he denounced 'Capital Punishments' as 'the natural offsprings of monarchical governments' and powerfully equated 'an execution in a republic' to a 'human sacrifice in religion'.[23] Closer to Southworth's own day, Robert Rantoul, Jr., an influential House Democrat and leading spokesperson for the anti-gallows movement in the late 1830s, drew from the earlier writings of Rush and Livingston to bring to fruition what I have elsewhere called the 'republican argument against the death penalty' — a series of interrelated arguments that made the death penalty antithetical to the administration of a democratic republic.[24]

One contemporary of Southworth's who applied this argument was George Washington Quinby. Named after a Founding Father himself, Quinby was a Unitarian minister who published *The Gallows, the Prison, and the Poor-house* (1856), which appeared just two years after *The Lost Heiress*. A progressive work ahead of its time, Quinby's book linked capital punishment and the criminal justice system to economic policies that fostered poverty and violence, conditions that were reproduced, Quinby argued, through the prison system. More than a third of *The Gallows, the Prison, and the Poorhouse* provided a sustained critique of capital punishment, and Quinby built a significant part of his argument around claims found in Southworth's novels. One of them concerned questions of responsibility that accompanied the execution of the innocent. Citing the case of a young man from Louisiana recently hanged for a crime he did not commit, Quinby questions readers, as Southworth does, about who bears responsibility:

> Now permit me to inquire of my reader: '*Who killed* that young man?'. 'Who killed him?' you respond: 'Why the sheriff, the hangman'. No, my friend, you mistake. The hangman acted simply as an instrument of the government. 'Ah, yes,' say you, 'I see how it is, the *government* killed him. The government made the law declaring that he should be killed; described *how* he should be killed, and *who* should be used as an *instrument* in the work of death. Then the *government* strangled the man, simply using the hands of the sheriff to adjust the knot — place the rope — draw down the cap, and let him swing'.[25]

Dialoguing with readers, Quinby provides a civics lesson like the one Southworth propounds, forcing readers to acknowledge their own complicity in state killing. In doing so, he exposes (as Southworth does) a disjunction between sovereignty and responsibility within the criminal justice system, one that highlights an ideological gap or blind spot in a republican form of government that lays claim to the authority to take life while endlessly deferring responsibility for the supreme act. Whereas Southworth lets Bishop Storr's question ring out rhetorically without direct response, Quinby directly answers the question he poses. In doing so, Quinby uncovers 'another question behind all this, in which *you* and *I* should have been specially interested if we had been citizens of Louisiana at that time, viz: *Who, or what, constitutes the government of a State?*' This 'Who or what', of course, refers to 'The people' themselves. 'They are responsible for its laws and institutions', Quinby concludes, 'while the *officers* of government are only responsible for the *execution* of the laws' (p. 59). Yet in making 'The People' responsible for their laws, Quinby denies the authority of any state agent to participate in the killing of another citizen, since that is a 'right which he does not possess' (p. 61). On this point, Quinby draws explicitly from Rantoul's republican argument against the death penalty, which he cites authoritatively and at length in developing his own. This argument is most evident in Quinby's privileged phrase, 'Each Citizen is Responsible', the subtitle of the chapter from *The Gallows, the Prison, and the Poorhouse* from which I have been quoting.

Like Southworth, Quinby complements this line of argument by emphasizing the issue of 'Irremediability', the title of his book's next chapter and the hinge, as we have seen, on which Southworth's *The Lost Heiress* turns. Indeed, Southworth's novel argument works by linking the irreversibility of capital punishment to questions of responsibility. These two interrelated principles are clearly at stake in O'Leary's execution, not only through the dialogue and debate between Governor Hunter and the state dignitaries but also in the later news of O'Leary's innocence. Yet there are other subtle yet significant ways in which these two principles — irremediability and responsibility — work through the second half of the novel to supplement and reinforce its anti-gallows argument. A prime example can be found in the novel's title, which itself is a direct consequence of O'Leary's execution. For 'the lost heiress' to whom the novel's title refers is Maud Hunter: the governor's only child who is kidnapped by Norah O'Leary, the mother of the condemned, in retaliation for the state's execution of her son. The rationale for this act of vengeance is depicted through a private meeting between Norah and Governor Hunter, which immediately follows and doubles the scene dramatizing the state dignitaries' petition for O'Leary's pardon. Whereas Hunter deflects legal and religious objections in the first meeting, the second has him confronted by intense sympathetic appeals from the mother of the condemned. It is through this scene, as Jones argues, that Southworth's sentimental argument is at its strongest.[26] The scene is also significant in that it morally locates responsibility for O'Leary's death upon Hunter, as sovereign, while the formal structure of law limits his liability.

Holding Hunter wholly responsible for the decision over her son's life, Norah exhorts the governor: 'You, and you only, can save my child. You have so much power. Oh, my God! that any human being should have power over my one child's life to take it away at this pleasure!' (p. 69). Echoing but from a different perspective the terms in which Augusta had first marvelled at the authority invested in the governor, Norah reifies Hunter as a veritable king and, like Augusta, calls attention to the uncanny, performative force that would come about simply through his signature: 'You can do it, by only writing your name. Good Heaven, when I think of the terrible power that resides in this hand! this hand of yours!' (pp. 69–70). In emphasizing the power invested in his person, Norah fixes responsibility onto the governor, thus working against the logic of the criminal justice system which strives to uncouple any one agent in the system from the power he or she authorizes, so that no one is held responsible. Yet, as Norah's pleading suggests, and as Jacques Derrida has argued, power is never expressed through sovereignty as such. Rather, that force can only be exercised through a designated sovereign — someone authorized to decide on the exception.[27]

If Hunter — who is variously identified as the 'man of the people' (pp. 18, 32), 'the greatest statesman of the age' (p. 442), and a 'godlike orator' (p. 468) with a 'godlike intellect', as well as a 'majestic benignity' and 'sovereign majesty' (p. 468) — symbolically embodies the just sovereign constrained by the unjust laws of capital punishment, then Norah comes to represent Old Testament retribution and personal vengeance. Southworth drives this point home in depicting how the idea of kidnapping the governor's daughter comes to Norah after she witnesses her son's hanging. Reciting the biblical dictum of *lex talionis*, Norah adds a twist. ' "An eye for an eye, and a tooth for a tooth, and life for life," and a child for a child' (p. 150), Norah muses to herself as she descends into the woods like a beast no longer beholden to civil authority. An expression of personal vengeance, Norah's declaration also speaks to the state's retribution exacted upon her son, thus exposing a logic of give-and-take structurally similar in these two acts of vengeance. In fact, Hunter had cited the same biblical passage when defending the death penalty before the state dignitaries, and the abduction of Hunter's daughter approximates the loss of Norah's son, thereby brokering 'a child for a child', as in Norah's formulation. Yet there is, of course, an obvious and crucial difference between the acts committed against Maude and her family and the one against O'Leary and his. Not only is one perpetuated by the state (according to due process) and the other by a private citizen, but the crime against Maud and the Hunters is *not* irremediable; that is, it can be reversed.

The novel makes this point on several fronts. Perhaps the clearest example unfolds in 'The Restored Daughter', Chapter XXXVII, which stands in stark contrast to the chapter depicting the permanent eradication of Norah's son. Yet there are subtle and more significant ways in which the reversible substitutes or stands in for the irremediable in the second half of the novel. A key example occurs in the wake of O'Leary's execution and the kidnapping (presumed death) of Maud. It involves a chance meeting between Augusta and Ellen O'Leary, the condemned's widow, whose meek and forgiving disposition make her a foil to Norah. The grieving wife and the grieving mother are brought together when the benevolent and charitable Augusta has come to visit a hospital to which Ellen and her children, along with much of Baltimore's poor, have been admitted following an outbreak of pestilence. At the hospital, an exchange of sorts is arranged when Augusta proposes to adopt Ellen's daughter Honoria (of approximately the same age of her lost Maud) and raise her as her own, with all the privilege afforded by wealth and political prestige. Ellen agrees but does so on her own terms, insisting that Honoraria be taken as a 'free gift'. As we learn from Ellen's internal perspective, which Southworth narrates through free indirect discourse, 'Had she accepted any remuneration for her daughter, it would seem to her like selling little Honoria for a price. No, indeed! If she gave the child, it should be a free gift, for the child's good — she could not receive any assistance that might look like pay or what was worse — alms' (p. 194). Articulated in such terms, this negotiation and exchange — a *giving* (rather than *taking*) of a child for nothing in return — cuts against or altogether obviates the logic of give-and-take that underpins both the execution and the kidnapping as mutually retaliatory acts.

That such a transaction is crucial to the novel's plot is evident in the pronounced tautology of 'free gift', a metaphor for Honoria, a child who replaces the irreplaceable, another child. This attempt to replace the irreplaceable suggests an unconscious desire on the novel's part to undo what cannot be done. Augusta, through her role in the scene, helps to bring out this meaning when, in receiving Honoria, she insists that Ellen's decision to give freely 'is not irrevocable — that at any time in the future,' as she tells her, 'if you should feel you could not abide by the terms, you can take back your child' (p. 210). Couched in these terms, Augusta's stipulation that Ellen is free to change her mind calls to mind the irrevocable sentence Hunter essentially pronounced when authorizing O'Leary's execution.

The former governor, likewise, employs this very term, the 'not irrevocable', in scenes that involve not Ellen or her daughter but her fatherless son, Falconer, who has come to age by the end of the narrative. Those scenes also involve Hunter's own daughter and unfold many years after the execution, thus paving the way to the novel's resolution. In the fifteen-odd years between Maud's abduction and restoration, she and Falconer had grown up as intimates and step-siblings, after Norah had given Maud to Ellen to raise as an orphaned relative of the O'Leary family. Near the end of the novel, the two are about to be married shortly after Falconer learns of his father's wrongful execution and just as the Hunters learn of their daughter's existence. In fact, it is on Maud and Falconer's wedding day that the Hunters learn of Maud's true identity. This revelation precipitates a mad rush to the wedding ceremony where Daniel Hunter, laying claim to his legal rights over Maud as a minor, interrupts the nuptials just before Maud completes her vows. This race to prevent the marriage and its last-minute disruption oddly parallels the race to stop O'Leary's execution that had begun the narrative. Only this time, Hunter plays quite a different role, preventing rather than ensuring that a life-altering, performative event take place. Even so, Hunter appears here in the familiar role of sovereign; only this time around, he exercises authority and power in deciding the future of the condemned man's son. And this time, Hunter decides differently. Far from upholding a previous decision and abiding by the letter of the law, Hunter pronounces a verdict intentionally open and subject to change. As Hunter explains to his daughter in the days following her thwarted nuptials: 'I do not pronounce an irrevocable sentence' (p. 369). Hunter, as father and sovereign, reiterates this declaration not long after when writing to an irate Falconer, telling him that 'he [Hunter] pronounced no irrevocable sentence' (p. 380).

These repeated declaratives — framed, indeed 'pronounced', as 'sentence[s]' involving the son of the man over whose execution Hunter presided — are crucial to *The Lost Heiress*'s novel argument against the death penalty. They not only evoke the 'irrevocable sentence' of death but strive symbolically to undo it. Hence, Hunter's pronouncements here are decidedly *not* 'irrevocable', just as the earlier terms on which Ellen gives Honoria are 'not irrevocable', as Augusta had insisted. Coming as they do from the novel's symbolic and (at one point) literal first family, these revocable decisions are haunted by the irrevocability of the enacted death sentence. As such, they signify a displaced desire to undo what cannot be undone, thus underscoring the irremediability that comes into being each time a human('s) being is lawfully put to death. And as performative acts — sentences that try to undo (or provide the possibility of undoing) a previous action — these pronouncements reinforce the thematic of forgiveness that resounds over the second half of the novel, thereby transforming the logic of retribution and the unforgivable epitomized by the death penalty in the first half. Implicit in Ellen freely giving her child to the Hunters, the scene of forgiveness is explicitly staged when Augusta and Daniel Hunter are summoned to an asylum to which Norah O'Leary has been confined for more than a decade, as if she were serving a prison sentence for her crime. There, Norah confesses her deed before the Hunters on her deathbed, readily asking Augusta's forgiveness but withholding that request from Daniel Hunter until the last moment. Augusta freely forgives Norah, just as Ellen had earlier given Honoria as a 'free gift', a symbolic act gesturing toward this later scene of forgiveness. Daniel Hunter, who departs this scene of forgiveness before it unfolds, never explicitly forgives Norah. Nor does he ever overtly ask for forgiveness for his role in O'Leary's execution, although he does pay Ellen a visit shortly after learning of O'Leary's actual innocence 'to make reparation' for what Ellen has suffered, namely by offering to educate and establish Falconer in business. Yet Hunter offers his assistance while insisting that Ellen not, as he tells her, 'look upon me as the executioner of your husband — a young man whom I found ordered for death the day upon which I came to office' (p. 270). This remark, through which Hunter offers reparation while abrogating responsibility, marks another example of the disjunction between sovereignty and responsibility that *The Lost Heiress* brings to light. Even so, Hunter plays an instrumental role in bringing about the novel's resolution which, as we shall see, works through reconciliation and forgiveness.

Jones, in his ground-breaking work on Southworth and the gallows, has identified the author's most famous work, *The Hindered Hand*, as her 'most sophisticated foray in the debate over the death penalty'.[28] While perhaps not her most sophisticated foray, *The Lost Heiress* has my vote for the novelist's most effective and affecting contribution to the anti-gallows cause. If Southworth criticizes capital punishment through a series of oblique and indirect acts, as Jones ingeniously shows in his analysis of *The Hindered Hand*, she provides a direct and straightforward attack through the first half of *The Lost Heiress* — a broader argument supplemented, in ways that I have suggested, through unconscious actions and desires of characters in the second half.[29] This strategy accounts for an important part of Southworth's novel — an argument one finds not only in *The Gipsy's Prophecy* and *The Lost Heiress* but, as Jones has demonstrated, in an array of novels she published from the 1850s through the 1870s. In several of them, Southworth curiously links marriage and the death penalty. In *The Gipsy's Prophecy*, for instance, Gerard Mostyn is arrested for a capital crime on his wedding day, whereas Capitola Black (the heroine of *The Hidden Hand*) shudders in horror and regret when she realizes her wedding day coincides with the day on which the novel's villain, whom she helped to capture, is to be executed. At the end of *The Lost Heiress*, marriage plays a more conventional yet crucial role, as it brings together two families divided by the principle of retribution and the institution of capital punishment. For in the novel's final pages Daniel Hunter, who has secretly served as Falconer's benefactor, revokes his sentence barring the marriage, and Falconer, who has sworn vengeance on the sovereign who decided against his father, eventually comes to see Hunter as the benevolent leader he is consistently portrayed to be. Hunter thus becomes an agent of reconciliation, allowing Maud and Falconer to become husband and wife. In this respect, *The Lost Heiress* resonates with Nathaniel Hawthorne's *The House of the Seven Gables* (1851), a novel similarly plotted around death sentences and also employing marriage to resolve its central conflict in order to unite two families, the Pyncheons and the Maules, in a scene of forgiveness that undoes the primal wrong of Matthew Maule's execution orchestrated by Colonel Pyncheon.

The House of the Seven Gables, as I have shown at length elsewhere, presents its own anti-gallows argument.[30] But Hawthorne's novel does not focus on the death penalty. Nor was it 'written expressly', as Livingston proposed, 'to expose the evils of capital punishment', as *The Lost Heiress* and *The Gipsy's Prophecy* certainly were. In his astute analysis of her work, Jones has emphasized Southworth's sympathetic arguments against the gallows, noting the ways in which readers are encouraged to identify with the sufferings and injustices endured by those sentenced to death. For Jones, Capitola symbolically represents a feminized sentimental state, one intended to replace the stern model of justice embodied by Hunter. A provocative argument, this reading neglects important aspects of Southworth's examination of evidentiary value and sovereign authority. For one thing, it overlooks the role Hunter plays in bringing about the reconciliation by undoing his pronounced sentence in the conclusion of *The Lost Heiress*. For another, it misconstrues the chain of evidence and structure of authority at work in *The Gipsy's Prophecy*. It is not, as Jones indicates, 'the governor [who] relents to Constance's request' that leads to Mostyn's stay of execution.[31] Rather, that act is authorized by the Home Secretary — quite different from a governor in the United States or the Prime Minister, in the British parliamentary system — and it has nothing to do with Constance's plea. Lord Starr instead grants the stay because new evidence potentially proving Mostyn's innocence has come to light: the actual killer who is unknown (Dr Horne, we learn later) confesses to a priest his crime. However, the actual murderer refuses to make his confession public or to allow the priest to breach his sworn confidence. This scenario brings to light another problem with the rules of legal evidence in getting to the truth through a court of law.

While acknowledging the importance of sympathy and sentimentalism, I have attended to other novel aspects of Southworth's anti-gallows argument. Those include her use of sensation as well as her interrogation of evidentiary value and the structure of sovereign authority in the administration of lawful death. Arguably the most important component of Southworth's novel argument comes through Bishop Storr's loaded question — 'Who is responsible?' — which reverberates through the novel's second half and gives rise to what we might call its political unconscious, the desire on the Hunters' part of undoing what cannot be undone. Yet despite this powerful argument, *The Lost Heiress* fails to be 'the *Uncle Tom's Cabin* of the anti-gallows movement', as Jones aptly puts it. It fails to be so, however, not because that argument is 'confined to a single plot about capital punishment', but because the novel fails to address deeper, underlying assumptions of the state's right to kill when citizens are guilty as charged.[32] It is, after all, much easier to condemn a system that condemns to death an innocent person than it is to condemn a system that lawfully kills the guilty. It would be another half century before such an argument would appear in novel form in Clearance Darrow's *An Eye for An Eye* (1905), a work by a lawyer-briefly-turned-novelist who wrote about retribution and revenge from a different perspective, turning the tables on the state and going beyond Livingston's novel idea about how a novel could contribute to the case against capital punishment.[33]

Notes to Chapter 9

1. Edward Livingston to James Fenimore Cooper, 20 June 1829, in *Correspondence of James Fenimore Cooper*, 2 vols (New Haven, CT: Yale University Press, 1922), I, 174. All further references to this letter are in the main text with page numbers only.
2. My understanding of the novel, opposed to poetry in relation to law, is indebted to Bakhtin's influential theory of dialogism and heteroglossia as well as his notion of poetry's 'centripetal force', which pulls toward a unified voice, and the novel's 'centrifugal force', which pulls away from it. See Mikhail Bakhtin, 'Discourse in the Novel', in *The Dialogic Imagination*, trans. by Caryl Emerson and Michael Holquist (Austin: University of Texas Press, 1981).
3. Wai Chee Dimock, *Residues of Justice: Literature, Law, and Philosophy* (Berkeley: University of California Press, 1997), p. 5.
4. See John Cyril Barton, 'Cooper, Livingston, and Death-Penalty Reform', in *James Fenimore Cooper Society: Miscellaneous Papers*, 27, ed. by Steven Harthorn and Shalicia Wilson (Cooperstown: The Society, 2010), pp. 1–5, and *Literary Executions*, pp. 260–68. For a different take on Cooper and capital punishment, see Jones, *Against the Gallows*, pp. 30–32, 40–44.
5. For important work on anti-gallows poetry see Jones, 'The Politics of Poetry', in *Against the Gallows*, and especially Birte Christ, 'Rallying Reformers in Anti-Gallows Poetry of the 1840s and 1850s' (forthcoming book chapter).
6. Southworth's massive popularity has been well noted. Indeed, she is generally considered the most widely read American novelist of the nineteenth century, given the fifty-odd novels she published over five decades. For a recent reassessment of Southworth's work, see *E. D. E. N. Southworth: Recovering a Nineteenth Century Popular Novelist*, ed. by Melissa J. Homestead and Pamela T. Washington (Knoxville: University of Tennessee Press, 2012). For earlier treatment of Southworth, see Fred Lewis Pattee, *The Feminist Fifties* (New York: D. Appleton-Century, 1940); Frank Luther Mott, *Golden Multitudes: The Story of Best Sellers in the United States* (New York: Macmillan, 1947); Mary Noel, *Villains Galore: The Heyday of the Popular Story Weekly* (New York: Macmillan Company, 1954); Herbert F. Smith, *The Popular American Novel, 1865–1920* (Boston, MA: Twayne, 1980); and Mary Kelley, *Private Woman, Public Stage: Literary Domesticity in Nineteenth-Century America* (New York: Oxford University Press, 1984).
7. Jones, *Against the Gallows*, p. 134.
8. See Barton, *Literary Executions*, p. 7.
9. Quoted in Jones, *Against the Gallows*, p. 149.
10. E. D. E. N. Southworth, *The Gipsy's Prophecy* (Philadelphia: T. B. Peterson, 1861), p. 37. Further references to this edition are in the main text.
11. Southworth herself first contributed to the anti-gallows movement in her short story, 'Thunderbolt to the Hearthstone' (1847). See Chapter 4 of Jones's *Against the Gallows*.
12. Philip English Mackey, 'Introduction: An Historical Perspective', in *Voices Against Death: American Opposition to Capital Punishment, 1787–1977* (New York: Burt Franklin, 1977), pp. xi–liii (pp. xxiii–xxiv).
13. As Alexander Welsh demonstrates in *Strong Representations: Narrative and Circumstantial Evidence in*

England (Baltimore, MD: Johns Hopkins University Press, 1992), following the Enlightenment, a new paradigm emerges for the presentation of facts in the discursive practices of both law and literature. Around the turn of the nineteenth century, circumstantial evidence and inferential reasoning derived from it displaced direct testimony (which could be mistaken or perjured) as the basis for persuasive argumentation. Thus, evidence that went unseen but fitted within a larger pattern of corroborating circumstances was often given priority over eye-witness accounts.

14. Welsh, *Strong Representations*, pp. 17, 24.
15. For shock-and-awe strategies, see David S. Reynolds, 'Radical Sensationalism: George Lippard in his Transatlantic Contexts', in *Transatlantic Sensations*, ed. by Jennifer Phegley, John Barton, and Kristin Huston (Farnham: Ashgate, 2012), pp. 77–96. See also Jones, *Against the Gallows*, for a discussion of Lippard's and Thompson's work in an anti-gallows context and Barton, *Literary Executions*, for an analysis of Lippard's and Simms's work in this context.
16. See in particular Christopher Looby's analysis of Thompson's *The House Breaker* in 'George Thompson's "Romance of the Real": Transgression and Taboo in American Sensation Fiction', *American Literature*, 65 (December 1993), 651–72, and Barton's analysis of *The Quaker City* in *Literary Executions*, pp. 114–17.
17. E. D. E. N. Southworth, *The Lost Heiress* (Philadelphia: Deacon & Peterson, 1854), p. 20. Further references to this edition are in the main text.
18. In Chapter 10 of *Pictures at an Execution* (Cambridge, MA: Harvard University Press, 1998), Wendy Lesser discusses this plot device in the Academy award-winning *I Want to Live!*, a convention writ large in more recent films such as *Dead Man Walking* and *Last Dance*. In *Literary Executions*, I trace this convention back to Cooper's *The Spy* and other American novels.
19. For an assessment of contemporary responses to *The Lost Heiress* as well as more recent criticism, see Paul Christian Jones, 'Revising Uncle Tom's Cabin: Sympathy, the State, and the Role of Women in E. D. E. N. Southworth's *The Lost Heiress*', in *E. D. E. N. Southworth*, ed. by Homestead & Washington, pp. 183–204. Jones, in criticizing Hunter, positions himself against the critical reception that has generally viewed Hunter in a positive light. For a recent overview of contemporary reviews of Southworth's work, see Linda Naranjo-Hueble, ' "The Road to Perdition": EDEN Southworth and the Critics', *American Periodicals*, 16.2 (2006), 123–50.
20. Leonard Bacon, 'Shall Punishment Be Abolished?', *New Englander and Yale Review*, 4.16 (October 1846), 563–88 (p. 571).
21. Jacques Derrida, 'Force of Law: The Mystical Foundation of Authority', *Cardozo Law Review*, 11.5–6 (1990), 920–1045 (p. 961).
22. Ibid.
23. Benjamin Rush, *Considerations on the Injustice and Impolicy of Punishing Murder by Death* (Philadelphia: Carey, 1792), pp. 18–19.
24. Barton, *Literary Executions*, pp. 28, 34, 48, 51, 60, 65. For a discussion of Rantoul's work in this context, see *Literary Executions*, pp. 36–40.
25. George Washington Quinby, *The Gallows, the Prison, and the Poor-house: A Plea for Humanity, Showing the Demands of Christianity in Behalf of the Criminal and Perishing Classes* (Cincinnati, OH: G. W. Quinby, 1856), pp. 58–59. Further references to this edition are in the main text.
26. Jones, 'Revising Uncle Tom's Cabin', pp. 187–89.
27. See Derrida building on Carl Schmidt's influential theory of sovereignty, *The Death Penalty*, 1, 85.
28. Jones, *Against the Gallows*, p. 134.
29. *The Hindered Hand* does not focus on capital punishment per se or overtly present an argument for its abolition, as both *The Gipsy's Prophecy* and *The Lost Heiress* do. As Jones shows, however, anti-gallows arguments are indirectly present in the novel ('Revising Uncle Tom's Cabin', p. 151).
30. See Barton, *Literary Executions*, Chapter 4.
31. Jones, *Against the Gallows*, p. 148.
32. Jones, 'Revising Uncle Tom's Cabin', p. 185.
33. For a reading of Darrow's novel in this context, see Barton, *Literary Executions*, pp. 249–54.

❖

Stephen King's Poetic Justice: Seriality, Narrative Framing, and Intertextuality in *The Green Mile*

Birte Christ

During the 1990s and 2000s, execution numbers in the United States peaked after a period of relative decline. The year 1999 broke the tragic record of the highest number of executions — ninety-eight in total — since the reinstatement of capital punishment in many states in the US in 1976. For a variety of reasons, execution numbers dwindled after World War II, and the year 1968 was the first in US history without a single execution. When the US Supreme Court declared the imposition of the death penalty to be in violation of the Constitution in a number of consolidated cases in *Furman v. Georgia* in 1972, many commentators thought that the death penalty was a thing of the past. However, the opposite was the case: states amended their statutes, *Gregg v. Georgia* overturned *Furman* in 1976 and made capital punishment constitutional once again. In fact, the death penalty returned with a vengeance. The number of executions rose steadily throughout the 1980s.[1]

Not least because of its prior, perplexing history, capital punishment was hotly debated in American society in the 1990s. Hollywood took its fair share in making capital punishment a mainstream topic of debate, producing more than a dozen capital punishment-themed films including the critically acclaimed and still best known death row drama *Dead Man Walking*, starring Sean Penn and Susan Sarandon (1995, dir. by Tim Robbins).[2] By contrast, literary treatments of capital punishment in the 1990s were relatively rare,[3] especially when compared to the role that literature played in earlier periods of heightened argument about capital punishment in the US.[4] Yet one of the few death penalty-themed texts of the decade dominated the bestseller lists for most of the summer of 1996: Stephen King's *The Green Mile*. Because it was published on the heels of *Dead Man Walking*'s box office triumph, King's horror thriller, drawing on elements of magical realism as well as the Southern Gothic tradition, could be dismissed as simply exploiting a current political issue for commercial success, as critics like Harold Bloom would most probably claim. A poster child for culturally conservative defenders of literary hierarchies, Bloom found King to be an 'immensely inadequate writer' when the National Book Foundation awarded King the 'Medal of Distinguished Contributions to American Letters' in 2003, and stated that King's books 'do little more for humanity than keeping the publishing world afloat'.[5]

By contrast, I argue that *The Green Mile* fulfils cultural functions beyond 'mere' entertainment and has aspirations beyond commercial success. King's novel makes an important intervention into the public debate about capital punishment in 1996. While cultural conservatives may perhaps grant that popular fiction makes political interventions in the sense of reaffirming the political and social status quo, I argue, rather, that *The Green Mile* embraces a progressive agenda, if ambivalently so. On the one hand, it is indeed conservative and subscribes to a simplistic, Manichean, and, in terms of genre, melodramatic view of the world: good and evil can clearly be differentiated, and murderers are born with the evil inside them. Hence, systemic reasons and a social responsibility for crime — the strongest arguments against any punishment, but irreversible punishment in particular — never enter the novel's belief system. On the other hand, however, like much of nineteenth-century literature dedicated to reformist causes, it works to create empathy with the condemned and, from that affective position, potentially political resistance against capital punishment.

In what follows I will show that the elicitation of empathy — even though ideologically at odds with the assumption of inborn, irremediable evil — is, in fact, what is at the heart of *The Green Mile* in terms of its literary technique. While thematically often dependent on individualist, essentialist explanations for crime, the novel employs a whole range of literary structures to allow the reader to suffer vicariously through the existential pain and terror of awaiting one's own execution and through the violence of total institutions more generally. The irritation that results from the disconnect between ideology and form can be read as the text's invitation to think through each of the positions they represent — the existence of essential evil and the human power of empathy — and their relation to capital punishment.

In creating formal structures designed to invite the reader's empathy with the condemned Other in *The Green Mile*, King implicitly makes the claim that popular literature, as much as 'high' literature, can be an institution of equity vis-à-vis the law and promote greater social justice. Commercial success, then, makes 'popular' literature all the more relevant: if any literary work helped shape public opinion about the death penalty in the 1990s, it was *The Green Mile*, which sold more than 3 million copies in 1996 alone. Admittedly, there is one other popular title of the decade that may be said to rival *The Green Mile*'s cultural significance: John Grisham's 1994 legal thriller *The Chamber*.[6] Based on the lawyer Grisham's knowledge of actual cases and committed to a realist framework, *The Chamber* makes rather straightforward arguments against capital punishment and can be seen as an example of a popular *littérature engagée* with an openly didactic bent.[7] By contrast, *The Green Mile* is a generic hybrid of horror fiction, magical realism, and Southern Gothic, whose complex use of narrative strategies and literary intertexts does not primarily serve as a vehicle for an ideological agenda. Instead, this formal and aesthetic complexity serves as a crucial component of the novel's perspective on capital punishment, which is why I believe it merits particular scrutiny.[8]

The novel *The Green Mile* is a fictional autobiographical account of a series of events that take place in Cold Mountain penitentiary, Georgia, in 1932. The story revolves around the prison's death row, dubbed 'the green mile' because of its green linoleum floor, and around John Coffey, a black man sentenced to death for the rape and murder of twin girls. As the reader learns in the frame narrative, the story is supposedly written down on six consecutive days by Paul Edgecombe, the former superintendent of Cold Mountain's death row (called E block), who is recollecting the events at age 104 in a retirement home. Edgecombe tells the story of how he found out that John Coffey, who hardly talks, can write no more than his name, and has the memory and intellect of a child, has been wrongly convicted. John Coffey, the story has it, possesses supernatural healing powers. He saves the lives of E block's pet mouse Mr Jingles and the warden's wife Melinda, heals Edgecombe from an excruciating urinary infection, and infuses or (in an inversion of what the state and the execution team will be doing to him) '*electrocute[s]*' Mr Jingles and Edgecombe with life: as a result, both the mouse and Edgecombe live well beyond their natural age.[9] Edgecombe and the members of his staff, who become convinced of Coffey's innocence and innate goodness as they witness his magic acts, cannot save Coffey's life. Only his supernatural powers — which would not be admissible as evidence even if there were a chance for an appeal or retrial — can explain why, contrary to appearances, he did not kill the twin girls, but instead held them in his arms trying, but failing, to bring them back to life. Edgecombe and his team eventually execute Coffey. All of them quit their work on death row in disillusionment and disgust afterwards.

At the most basic level, *The Green Mile* can be seen as a conversion narrative that offers the reader a figure of identification in the character of Paul Edgecombe. It charts Edgecombe's development from a supporter of capital punishment who believes in its capacity to deliver justice to a sceptic of the system, and invites the reader to live vicariously through that development, too. While not losing sight of the novel's ideological contradictions, I argue in what follows that a number of formal structures powerfully pull the reader into a position of empathy with the condemned and invite her to think critically about an unjust penal system. Specifically, King's novel does so through the use of a serial narrative structure, through the framing of its historically distant death penalty narrative with a narrative set in the present, as well as with a framing by paratexts and through a play with intertexts, foremost among them Charles Dickens's novels, William Faulkner's *Light in August*, John Steinbeck's *Of Mice and Men*, and Marcel Proust's *À la recherche du temps perdu*.

Because the film version of *The Green Mile* is so well known, as is the criticism on it among scholars interested in the 'cultural life of capital punishment', it should be noted here that my assessment of the novel as profoundly ambivalent differs significantly from important readings of the film that see it as confirming the legitimacy of capital punishment throughout.[10] As Austin Sarat, for instance, has pointed out, the film version reduces King's text to a morality tale: to quote Brian Jarvis, in the film *The Green Mile*, 'a systemic critique of capital punishment is [...] foreclosed by facile moral antithesis', 'cultural anxiety about crime and punishment is directed away from institutional systems towards individuals', and 'institutional violence is hidden behind individual sadism'.[11] This reading of the film is convincing because in the process of the novel's remediation, the morality tale — which, as I have pointed out above, is also part of the novel — is not countered by the formal literary devices that pull the novel's cultural work in the opposite direction: the film is not structured as a serial narrative, the frame narrative is minimized to a few minutes at the beginning and end of a 189-minute film, the novel-specific paratextual framing is missing, and intertextual play revolves, fittingly, around filmic rather than literary predecessors.[12]

Seriality and the Paradoxical Pain of Time

Perhaps the most striking formal aspect of the novel *The Green Mile* is that it originally appeared in six instalments in chap-book style between March and August of 1996.[13] The six small paperbacks also each contained a frontispiece illustration (by Mark Geyer), true to the project's Victorian spirit. In the fictional world, these six instalments correspond with the six day-long sessions during which Paul Edgecombe writes down his memories as well as observations of present events in the sun room of his retirement home, with Paul clearly serving as the author's double. With this publication scheme, King consciously sought to re-create the publishing conditions of nineteenth-century serial publication, and he cast himself in the footsteps of Charles Dickens. The first instalment included, in the place of a foreword, 'A Letter' to his 'Dear Constant Reader', in which King explained the historical origins of the format and stressed that, just like Dickens, he was going to be writing instalments and finishing the story as the first instalments were being published and commented on by readers and reviewers. King indeed worked on the last three instalments during the early summer of 1996 at a time when the first three already occupied three spots on the national best-seller lists.[14]

King's return to the serial format in 1996 coincides with a broader renaissance of serial narration, especially in the form of so-called quality television series, whose (ongoing) 'golden era' arguably was heralded by David Lynch's *Twin Peaks* in 1990 and began in earnest with the production of *The Sopranos* in 1997.[15] Since then, a great number of studies have engaged with the question of seriality's functions and, more specifically, with what might be called the form's ideology, 'from Dickens to Soap Opera', as the title of one study has it.[16] As virtually all studies agree, there are three interrelated formal principles of serial narration that potentially come with ideological implications. One, serial narratives employ repetition with variation or, in Gertrude Stein's words via Sabine Sielke's perceptive reflexions on seriality as an epistemological form, they employ 'insistence'.[17] Second, they allow for heightened complexity, among other reasons because serial narratives' sheer length or *Erzählzeit* (narrating time) can incorporate a large cast of characters and their development, panoramic visions as well as small-grained observations, expanded psychological, and other explorations, and can develop their own figurative language and meta-reflexive discourse.[18] Third, serial narratives share a resistance to closure and constantly defer reader/audience gratification.

The timed release of serial narratives in conjunction with the deferral of closure has often been seen as endowing serial formats with a special capacity to activate readers to reflect critically on the narrative or imagine alternative, even subversive storylines and outcomes — and hence endow them with a certain ideological openness. King notes this when he relates his own serial reading experiences to his 'Constant Reader' at the beginning of the first instalment:

> I have always liked stories told in episodes. [...] I liked [the serial format] because the end of each episode made the reader an almost equal participant with the writer — you had a whole week to try to figure out the next twist of the snake. Also, one read and experienced these stories more *intensely*, it seemed to me, because they were rationed. (p. xv)

More importantly to my argument here, however, King also observes that serial narratives, almost inversely, allow the writer to 'gain [...] an ascendency over the reader which he or she cannot otherwise enjoy: simply put, Constant Reader, you cannot flip ahead and see how matters turn out' (p. xv). In other words, the author of serial narratives has a special power over the reader's reception of the text, specifically over the timing, pace, and order of reception. This power is based in the formal characteristics of serial narratives mentioned above — repetition with variation, length and complexity, deferred gratification, and resistance to closure. They are intimately related to time and pace, especially when viewed from the perspective of the reader and the reading process.

In *The Green Mile*, King employs this power of serial form to the purpose of making the reader vicariously feel what it means to await one's execution on death row, and via such empathy with those sentenced to death, ultimately strives to generate abolitionist sentiment. The pain or, perhaps more precisely, the existential terror of the death sentence is figured in the novel as the terror of time: death itself or dying is not the most excruciating aspect of a death sentence (although the executions related in the text certainly are physically painful, too), but knowledge and anticipation of the exact moment when it will occur is. The novel, in other words, takes on the 'unnatural' heteronomous control of life time as capital punishment's prime terror, pain, and injustice, and uses serial heteronomous control of reading time to make the reader vicariously experience it. A life ended at the state's hands is, of course, a life cut short. A serial narrative's relation to (life) time, by contrast, is that it is overly long, and potentially never ends. King's novel exploits exactly this inversion of the serial novel's and capital punishment's respective relationships to time in order to allow for the reader's affective engagement with the pain of knowing one's end. The death row inmates', specifically John Coffey's, life time and the reader's time of reception, each at the mercy of an ineluctable authority (the state, the author/publisher), are explicitly constructed as parallels through the interplay of serial form, magical realist story elements, and thematic reflexions on the part of narrator Paul Edgecombe. Moreover, different conceptions of time are signified and bound together by the novel's central spatial metaphor, the green mile.

Unlike many narratives that revolve around innocent men on death row, the novel does not take its pace from the protagonist's conventional race against the clock to save the wrongly condemned. Instead, readers learn fairly early on in instalment 1 that Coffey will be executed by Edgecombe and his team. The central function of this inversion of the temporality of the standard narrative is that readers' vicarious experience is not focused on the thrilling ups and downs of potentially saving the innocent, but instead on waiting, with the condemned, for the inevitable: his death at the state's hands at the end of the narrative. Most obviously, this vicarious waiting on the part of the reader becomes waiting in real time as she has to pause her reading until the release of the next serial instalment; her living and waiting with Coffey stretches over at least five months in the summer of 1996. Empathy with the condemned man's situation is thus facilitated by the narrative through placing the reader into a position similarly unfree as that of the condemned: she cannot control her own time, she is forced to wait like Coffey is. Paradoxically the reader, like the condemned man, wishes for the waiting to be over: they both wish for the pain to end, yet that end also means an end to pleasure — an end to the pleasure of life, and an end to the pleasure of the text. This very basic painfulness of waiting in real time, as well as its pleasure, is heightened for the reader text-internally by a number of formal strategies and themes connected with them.

The reader's waiting for the next instalment is filled with tension and, in this sense, becomes 'painful' as the text continuously offers hints but withholds central pieces of information that eventually explain, for instance, John Coffey's innocence and Mr Jingles's and Edgecombe's long life spans. These mysteries can only fully be understood in instalments 5 and 6. King specifically uses the recaps that are built into the frame narrative of instalments 2 to 6 to provide the reader with additional bits of information on these mysteries, even when plot developments in the instalment in question revolve, at least for the time being, around other issues (Sharon Russell has helpfully referred to a multiplicity of 'front burner' and 'back burner' plots, typical of serial narratives, as alternating in King's text.)[19] As King notes in his 'Author's Afterword', he wished to include recaps in the text in an elegant, unobtrusive way (p. 452), one of the reasons why he invented the frame narrative, beginning in instalment 2. The recaps are motivated by the aged narrator/writer Edgecombe reflecting on his writing and processes of memory and struggling to order events at the beginning of each instalment. The narrator's shaky memory, in this sense, becomes the pretext to help out the reader and her memory, which potentially might fail her, too, not because of old age but because of the gap of a month between the release of instalments.

Moreover, cliff-hangers — a central element of traditional serial narratives — heighten the 'pain' of waiting. The end of instalments 2 and 3 feature cliff-hangers in the literal sense of the word: at the end of the instalments, it is not clear whether guard Dean Stanton and the mouse Mr Jingles, respectively, will live or die. At the end of the first instalment, suspense is created more subtly by opening up questions around the story of John Coffey, the major one, which concludes the instalment, being why Edgecombe and his team quit working on death row after Coffey's execution; similarly, the open question at the end of instalment 4 is how Edgecombe came to be convinced of, and can prove (at least to his team), Coffey's innocence. At the end of instalment 5, events right before Coffey's execution pick up pace as Edgecombe and the team of guards take Coffey out of the prison to heal the warden's wife from a deadly brain tumour; the instalment ends before Coffey has been returned to his cell and Edgecombe's last, ominous words state that 'our evening was *far* from over' (p. 422).

As a continuous partial release of the story as well as cliff-hangers heighten the pain of waiting, the reader's increasingly urgent desire to learn the whole story propels her emotionally towards Coffey's execution. Coffey's is the last execution of three around which alternating instalments are structured. In other words, narrative momentum towards Coffey's death is created and then 'painfully' put on hold by the timed gaps of serial release. The detailed descriptions of executions in the electric chair in instalments 2 and 4 build up to render Coffey's execution in instalment 6 as full of horror. The execution of a Washita Cherokee council elder in instalment 2 'went well — if there was ever such a thing as a "good one" (a proposition I strongly doubt)' (p. 110), but the narrative, in fact, does not describe that execution, but dwells on the rehearsal for it during which the prison vendor Toot-Toot, a grotesque, Gothic stock character, plays the condemned man. The detailed account of the execution's rehearsal in place of the real one squarely represents executions as primarily spectacles of power and highlights the inhumanity inherent in them. The execution of Edward Delacroix in instalment 4, then, is intentionally botched by 'evil' guard Percy Wetmore, Edgecombe's antagonist, and ends with the condemned man literally burning to death. Even though Coffey's execution is by far the most 'dignified' one, because it technically 'goes well' and because he is surrounded by the team of guards who have come to love him, the build-up creates a lens of reception through which to understand the execution as the most illegitimate, most inhumane one yet — as the state kills, in Edgecombe's words, a 'gift of God' (p. 488).

While the partial release of information, cliff-hangers, and a build-up of scenes of execution towards Coffey's heightens the pain of waiting for the next serial instalment in terms of the plot set in 1932, King's narrative frame set in the present works to highlight the pain of waiting on a thematic, reflexive level. In doing so, *The Green Mile* not only deepens its discussion of the 'paradoxical pain of time' that knowing the exact date and time of one's own death inflicts and offers more structures of empathy for the reader, but it also makes a broader argument about the violence of total institutions, of which death row is just one.

Narrative Framing and the Violence of Total Institutions

In King's novel, the frame narrative set in the present works to parallel Coffey's and Edgecombe's wait for their deaths. When the aged narrator begins to reflect on his writing and his present circumstances at the opening of instalment 2, he devotes his first paragraph to establishing a parallel between life on death row and life in a retirement home. The retirement home Georgia Pines, he makes clear, is, 'in its way, [...] as much of a killing bottle as E Block at Cold Mountain ever was' (p. 79). In what follows, the text continues to set up Edgecombe's experiences in the retirement home as an eerie mirror of life on the 'green mile' in 1932: Brad Dolan, a staff member at Georgia Pines, cruelly bullies Edgecombe throughout the narrative, and functions as the present-day counterpart to Percy Wetmore, the 'evil' guard on E block, whose only desire is to 'experience [an execution] right up close so he can smell the guy's nuts cooking' (p. 55). Elaine Connelly, Edgecombe's 'ladyfriend' (p. 164) at Georgia Pines, is the female companion that his wife Janice, long dead, used to be.[20] In order to sneak out of the retirement home and visit Mr Jingles in the woods, Edgecombe and Elaine trick Dolan much in the same way the guards trick Percy Wetmore in order to sneak John Coffey out of prison so he can heal the warden's wife. In Edgecombe's efforts at recollection, moreover, the spaces of Georgia Pines and Cold Mountain merge, the long hallways between residents' rooms echoing the green mile and the condemned men's cells on each side of it, and 'the sunroom of this glorious old folks' home', where he sits down to write, '[is] gone, replaced by the storage room at the end of the Green Mile where so many of my problem children took their last sit-me-downs' (p. 336).

The novel's dramatic comparison of death row and retirement home can be read as a criticism of how society deals with its elderly members: just as society locks away its criminals in prisons, condemns them to civil death, and, on death row, robs them of every hope of ever leaving, society similarly places its elderly members in institutions, robs them of a public, self-determined life, and, likewise, those individuals will not leave — except when dead. In this parallel, the retirement home appears as potentially even more problematic than death row in terms of its ethics, since those locked away in old age are innocent with regard to the law, presuming the law generally does its work. In this sense, then, the novel is expressive of a fear of institutionalization in old age that the post-war baby boomer generation, which King and his core of readers in 1996 belong to, was the first to experience on a mass scale.

Yet the novel's focus is less on critiquing the ethicality of institutions for the elderly, but on highlighting the nature of pain that they inflict, a pain that is calculated to inflict a psychological death onto their residents even before the physical body gives in. In paralleling death row and the retirement home, the novel not only expands on what I have called 'the paradoxical pain of time' — the simultaneous desire for the waiting to end and fear of the end of one's life — but adds another dimension to the pain experienced on death row, or during any kind of imprisonment or institutionalization: it highlights the numbing effect of routines, calculated uneventfulness, and other forms of heteronomous control of time. In contrast to death row, the retirement home is an institution the reader potentially knows from first-hand experience as a visitor and, above all, an institution that she is personally terrified by. While hardly a reader of King's novel has to fear ending up on death row, almost all readers are justified in fearing the retirement home. In developing the theme of heteronomous control of time within the context of the retirement home, the text allows the reader to experience the pain of death row vicariously through placing her imaginatively into a similarly structured institution alongside narrator Edgecombe. The pain of the retirement home, then, is employed to make the pain of capital punishment accessible.

Much of Edgecombe's frame narrative is taken up by reflexions on institutional and personal time. At the beginning of the fourth instalment, he reflects on the passing of time since his 'grandchildren Christopher and Danielle more or less forced [him] into Georgia Pines':

> It's been a little over two years. The eerie thing is that I don't know if it *feels* like two years, or longer than that, or shorter. My sense of time seems to be *melting*, like a kid's snowman in a January thaw. It's as if time as it always was — Eastern Standard Time, Daylight Saving Time, Working-Man Time — doesn't exist anymore. Here there is only Georgia Pines time, which is Old Man Time, Old Lady Time, and Piss the Bed Time. The rest... all gone. (p. 249)

Edgecombe, on the one hand, complains about the way in which the retirement home makes him lose track of time, and observes something similar when it comes to the challenge of recollecting the events of 1932: the challenge 'seem[s] to have more to do with *when* than *what*' (p. 81). On the other hand, it becomes clear that one's sense of time is always governed by external authorities or institutions. On the benevolent side, those are governments agreeing on a synchronization of clocks and the rhythms of one's work schedule, and on the malevolent side, one's time is governed by the schedule of institutions like the retirement home, which is separate from active life and marked by degeneration. This degeneration — physical, as implied in 'Piss the Bed Time', yet foremost mental and psychological — is precipitated by the retirement home's control over its residents' time:

> This is a dangerous place. You don't realize it at first, at first you think it's only a boring place [...] but it's dangerous, all right. I've seen a lot of people slide into senility since I came here [...]. They come here mostly all right [...] and then something happens to them. A month later they're just sitting in the TV room, staring up at Oprah Winfrey on the TV with dull eyes, a slack jaw, and a forgotten glass of orange juice tilted and dribbling in one hand. A month after that, you have to tell them their kids' names when they come to visit. And a month after that, it's their own damned names you have to refresh them on. Something happens to them, all right: Georgia Pines Time happens to them. Time here is like a weak acid that erases first memory and then the desire to go on living. (pp. 249–50)

The 'weak acid' that works on people's minds is what first appears as boredom: daily routines that are characterized by their uneventfulness. Yet these are, as Edgecombe asserts, 'dangerous': they are designed to manage and ultimately destroy individual lives in what is made to appear as a rational, humane process for the best for those subjected to it. As Edgecombe's grandchildren tell him, he should be institutionalized 'for [his] own good' (p. 249).

Control of time, of course, is the central method by which 'total institutions', in Goffman's formulation, and 'complete and austere institutions', in Foucault's words, do their work of 'disciplining and punishing'. In *Discipline and Punish*, Foucault establishes the importance of the 'time-table', which in Georgia Pines is explicitly structured by meal times, television time, and bed time, and in Cold Mountain by the guards' shifts and, in a larger temporal dimension, successive dates of execution.[21] Foucault observes, specifically, that 'the administrative and economic techniques of control reveal a social time of a serial, orientated, cumulative type', and that 'the "seriation" of successive activities' must be seen as one of the primary articulations of power.[22]

Edgecombe consciously 'fight[s]' against the retirement home's control of his time — and with it against the slow erasure of memory and the extinction of any hope for the future. He does so by way of his writing (first of a diary and then of the present account of events in 1932), through active recollecting, and through physical exercise, especially when sneaking out of the retirement home for long walks in the woods to feed the aged mouse Mr Jingles. In addition, he misses meals, steals provisions from the kitchen instead, and 'doesn't watch TV during the day' (p. 164). Instead, he goes to the deserted television room in the middle of the night to watch American Movie Channel 'where most of the films are in black and white and none of the women take their clothes off' (p. 165). Watching films he used to watch 'when [he] was a man still walking on the skin of the world, instead of a moth-eaten relic mouldering away in an old folks' home' (p. 164) is his way of keeping his personal integrity.

Edgecombe resists control by disrupting 'Georgia Pines Time' with his own schedule and activities that are not stipulated by the institutional framework. But moreover, because he has been infused by John Coffey with a kind of semi-divine power, his physical temporality defies natural and, with it, institutional boundaries, and this is mirrored by Mr Jingles: Edgecombe is 104 years old, but at least as fit as a man in his late 70s or 80s, and the mouse is about sixty-four years old. While Edgecombe's age may be read as part of the way in which he succeeds in resisting the heteronomous control of his time, it more importantly serves as another way in which the pain of death row is figured and made affectively accessible to the reader. Edgecombe's unnaturally prolonged life span and his uncertainty as to how much longer — ten years? Or fifty? — he may have to live, offer an inverted version of what it means to know the exact hour of one's death when waiting for one's execution, often for years, if not decades.

It should be noted that John Coffey's and Edgecombe's waiting — for an all too certain and an entirely uncertain moment of death — are not painful in the double, paradoxical sense that I have characterized above: unlike most condemned men and most serial readers, Coffey and Edgecombe are not consumed simultaneously by the desire for time to pass and the fear that time/the text may actually come to an end. Instead, because of their beyond-human powers, Coffey and Edgecombe cannot bear life anymore and see in death purely a liberation from pain. When Edgecombe speaks with Coffey about his impending execution, Coffey asserts, 'I *want* to go, boss' (p. 491), and explains:

> I'm rightly tired of the pain I hear and feel, boss. I'm tired of bein on the road, lonely as a robin in the rain. Not never havin no buddy to go on with or tell me where's we comin from or goin to or why. I'm tired of people bein ugly to each other. It feels like pieces of glass in my head. I'm tired of all the times I've wanted to help but couldn't. I'm tired of bein in the dark. Mostly it's the pain. There's too much. If I could end it, I would. But can't. (p. 492)

Similarly, Edgecombe, after the death of Mr Jingles and his friend Elaine Connelly, which he reports on towards the end of the last instalment, wishes for death since everyone he ever loved has now died. Coffey's wish for death, as many critics of the film version have observed, 'translates state slaughter into mercy killing' and undoes any critical stance the film may potentially take towards the death penalty.[23] Edgecombe's similar wish for death at the end of his narrative only heightens the problematic sense of a desire for — rather than a fear of — closure that the reader may share with him towards the end of the novel's last instalment. 'Salvation and damnation' (p. 533), to use Edgecombe's own words, become one and the same thing.

However, while Coffey's and Edgecombe's wish for 'salvation' through death must thus be seen as ideologically highly problematic, the image through which King has Edgecombe express this wish in the very last line of the novel focuses the reader's attention back onto co-experiencing the pain of waiting. Edgecombe conjures up the many nights that he now spends in his bed with insomnia: 'I lie here and wait. I think about Janice [...] and I wait. We each owe a death, there are no exceptions, I know that'; and he concludes: 'but sometimes, oh God, the Green Mile is so long' (p. 536). Through the spatial metaphor of the 'green mile', which Edgecombe here uses to refer to the span of his life, but which simultaneously stands for death row and the novel itself, three levels of painful waiting — Coffey's, Edgecombe's, and the reader's — are related to one another. In referencing and conflating the institutional spaces of death row, the retirement home, and the serial novel and their control over condemned men's, residents', and readers' time through this image, the last line of the novel encapsulates, once again, how each institution fundamentally operates 'in the form of an abuse of power, the arbitrary power of administration', or, in the case of the novel, can at least potentially operate in this way.[24]

The writer-narrator Edgecombe in his frame narrative and the author King in his paratextual comments reinforce the idea that the novel itself functions as an institution that can control its readers. As previously discussed, in the letter that introduces instalment 1, King notes that there is 'one other thing that [he] liked about the idea' of serial publication: 'in a story which is published in instalments, the writer *gains ascendency* over the reader which he or she cannot otherwise enjoy' (p. xv, my emphasis). What King 'likes' about serial writing is clearly described in the language of power relations; that it is essentially a way to control and discipline the reader's behaviour becomes even more obvious when, in the following paragraph, King describes how he once found his mother skipping ahead to the end of an Agatha Christie mystery while she was 'actually' on p. 50, parallels it to eating the filling of Oreo cookies and throwing away the cookies themselves, and states, if facetiously so, that both actions constitute an unforgivable failure to withstand temptation. Edgecombe, even more drastically, finds that 'writing is a special and rather terrifying form of remembrance, I've discovered — there is a totality to it that seems almost like rape' (p. 336). Leaving aside the problematic gender assignations to writer and text/reader for the moment, the image of a 'totality' that can inflict personal injury quite explicitly references the language of the total institution's systemic abuse of power and infliction of pain onto its residents, inmates, or readers.

Creating a constant deferral of gratification through its serial structure and interrupted arcs of suspense, and grounding this structure in thematic reflections on the power that death row, retirement homes, and serial novels can have to control time and inflict pain, *The Green Mile* offers the reader structures to vicariously experience and reflect upon the pain that death row and knowing the time of one's unnatural death creates. The narrator Edgecombe's use of the word 'remembrance' hints towards how this function of the novel is supported, in addition, by its intertextual work.

Intertextuality and Stephen King's Poetic Justice

At the end of the first instalment, King invokes the power of *mémoire involontaire* triggered by smell in an episode based on Proust's *À la recherche du temps perdu*.[25] Brutus Howell, Edgecombe's colleague and friend on E Block, is cleaning out the storage room the winter after John Coffey's execution. He stumbles upon something, and calls on Edgecombe to witness it too: 'The smell of peppermint' (p. 72) as Edgecombe recalls, repeating this line in an incantatory manner.[26] Like Proust's narrator Marcel in the madeleine episode, Brutus and Edgecombe are overcome by involuntary memory upon smelling traces of the peppermint candy that the prisoner Delacroix used to feed Mr Jingles and by the realization that the all-too-human mouse must have hidden pieces of the candy in order to remember Delacroix after his execution.[27] The trigger of the smell gives both men instinctive access to the meaning of the events of the summer and autumn of 1932 that now pass before their eyes: they realize, in fact *feel*, the inhumanity of capital punishment that they have been complicit with, and both apply for a transfer the next day. The peppermint episode measures out the time that the narrative will presumably cover — from Mr Jingles' appearance on the green mile to Edgecombe's and Brutus's decision to quit E Block. The narrative set in 1996, and with it, a clear differentiation between Edgecombe as a remembering self in 1996 versus an experiencing self in 1932, as well as the meta-reflections on time and memory which are interspersed with the 1932 plot, are only introduced at the beginning of instalment 2. The older, Shakespearean English title of Proust's (serial) novel, hinted at in Edgecombe's thoughts on writing, *Remembrance of Things Past*, thus encapsulates King's project of recalling the events of the summer and autumn of 1932 as it is developed in instalment 1, while the newer title, *In Search of Lost Time*, can be read as referencing the larger project of understanding time and its passage that begins with instalment 2 and that Edgecombe, the narrating self, is working through in the remainder of his narrative.

It could be argued that King's rewriting of the madeleine episode does not contribute much to the novel, except that it emphasizes, once more, that its central themes are time and memory. Indeed, readers who miss this reference will still be able to follow the story as well as the reflexive sections fully. King, then, citing one of the most well-known episodes from *À la recherche du temps perdu*, could be seen as (ab)using Proust simply in order to lend high cultural prestige to his own popular text. Indeed, with regard to *Light in August*, King himself casts his intertextual play as rather inconsequential, at best, when he mentions that he renamed 'Luke Coffey [...] John Coffey (with a tip to the *chapeau* to William Faulkner, whose Christ-figure is Joe Christmas)' (p. viii). In downplaying his intertextual work, King understates, however, the degree to which *The Green Mile* is indebted to *Light in August* and other pre-texts beyond *À la Recherche*, which might just be the most obvious one. As I would like to argue briefly in conclusion of this essay, King's intertextual work with *Light in August*, *Of Mice and Men*, and Dickens's forms of serial narrative and sentimental address adds significantly to *The Green Mile*'s complexity and to the cultural work it aspires to perform.

Given that *The Green Mile* essentially tells a conversion narrative about the protagonist's position on capital punishment, and thus loudly speaks to the cultural moment of 1996 when numbers of executions rocketed, setting the main action in 1932 is somewhat unexpected, unless one takes Faulkner's and Steinbeck's pre-texts into account. 1932 marks the publication of *Light in August*, and, like Faulkner's novel, *The Green Mile* begins in the oppressive heat of summer, when John Coffey and Bill Wharton, who committed the rapes and murders that John Coffey is wrongly accused of, arrive on E Block. John Coffey is modelled on both Faulkner's Joe Christmas and Steinbeck's Lennie Small. Like Christmas and Small, Coffey has drifted aimlessly through the Depression South before arriving on death row; like Christmas, he is obsessed with his name as the only thing that truly seems to belong to him; like Small, he is physically big, potentially mentally disabled (or certainly childlike) and does not know his strength — which in Small is purely physical and in Coffey, supernatural. Scars cover Coffey's back, and they can both be read as signifying the scars of slavery that black men still carry in 1932, but also as the scars on Christmas's back, which are a result of his adopted father's frequent beatings. Excessive violence, macabre scenes, desperation, and fear characterize both Faulkner's and King's Depression landscapes in the manner of the Southern Gothic.

In *The Green Mile*, of course, much of the Gothic darkness and senseless evil is eventually countered by Dickensian characters like Edgecombe and Brutal who, despite poverty, crime, and the bureaucratic violence of the prison as an institution, have not lost their capacity for human kindness. In this sense, Coffey can also be read as a counter character to Christmas and Small.[28] Whereas Small accidentally kills a mouse, a dog, and finally 'Curley's wife', Coffey brings Mr Jingles back to life, cures Edgecombe's urinary infection, and saves the life of the warden's wife; whereas Christmas presumably kills his foster father McEachern and Joanna Burden out of personal outrage, Coffey kills Bill Wharton and leaves Percy Wetmore an imbecile. By contrast, Faulkner's Percy Grimm, the white vigilante who castrates and kills Christmas, and who shows the same childish cruelty that Percy Wetmore and Brad Dolan exhibit, goes unpunished. Coffey, in other words, brings about the justice that the legal system in *The Green Mile* does not deliver and that is as unimaginable in the haunted Southern world of Faulkner's Yoknapatawpha County as it is in Steinbeck's similarly hopeless Depression California. One way of reading this 'optimistic' re-writing of Faulkner's and Steinbeck's Gothic/modernist texts would, as a matter of course, be that popular writer King, while tackling serious existential and socio-political questions, comes up with all too facile and individualist, if not outright magical, solutions to more complex and systemic issues.

This reading, while not entirely wrong, misses the ways in which *Light in August* as an intertext may be seen to simultaneously trouble some of *The Green Mile*'s problematic racial dynamics, which function to buttress the legitimacy of the execution that Coffey sees, and that the novel invites the reader to see, as his liberation from Christ-like martyrdom on earth. Daniel LaChance and Linda Williams have thus read the film version as a story of the 'expiation of white sin' and, more specifically, as 'rescu[ing] white Americans from the guilt of putting innocent black men to death', legally as well as extra-legally, historically as well as in 1996.[29] Williams describes Coffey as a figure in the melodramatic 'negro-philic Tom tradition' that inverts, but at the same time also reproduces, 'exaggerated, delusional, and paranoid racial fantasies' of the black, violent rapist. Borrowing from Leslie Fiedler, she sees *The Green Mile* as part of the American dialectic between melodramatic scenarios of 'pro-Tom' sympathy and 'anti-Tom' antipathy.[30] This applies to the novel, too, but here, the melodramatic 'pro-Tom' representation of Coffey is always implicitly paralleled by the ambivalent, modernist 'anti-Tom' representation of Faulkner's Christmas. Whereas Christmas's *desire* to kill McEachern and Joanna Burden is clearly established, the question of whether McEachern in fact died from Christmas's attack as well as Christmas's actual guilt in the murder of Joanna Burden are more uncertain. And much more radically uncertain, of course, is Christmas's racial identity. The fact that he is neither black in terms of skin colour nor considers himself black from the beginning of his life, but slowly 'becomes' black in the eyes of the community and the vigilante who eventually lynches him highlights the constructed nature of race, or race as a lens through which to perceive someone who might otherwise simply be perceived as a fellow human being. Christmas as the parallel or counter character to Coffey, then, challenges readers to view 'race' as less stable than it might seem and guilt, innocence, and larger social responsibility much more complicated to assign than they are when one reads *The Green Mile* as a popular, melodramatic tale cut off from the conversation with a broader literary tradition that it is emphatically engaging in.

Whereas King's intertextual work with *Light in August* and, to a lesser degree,

Of Mice and Men, opens up avenues for more complex readings of the racial dimensions of capital punishment, his positioning of *The Green Mile* as a kind of neo-Dickensian novel, by way of form as well as authorial gesture in his 'Letter', can be read as nothing less than an argument for literature as an institution of equity — and for *popular* literature at that. This argument was timely: the decade before the publication of *The Green Mile* in 1996 had seen the broad institutionalization of literature classes for law students, and in 1995, Martha Nussbaum had published her highly influential *Poetic Justice*. Nussbaum used Dickens's *Hard Times* (1854), alongside Richard Wright's *Native Son* (1940) and E. M. Forster's *Maurice* (1971), to argue that 'literary works typically invite their readers to put themselves in the place of people of many different kinds and to take on their experiences'.[31] Literary reading for legal practitioners can then function as an 'education in empathy', and literature serves as 'an antidote to the fundamental harshness of American law'.[32]

Stephen King's John Coffey is the agent who brings about poetic justice in the traditional sense, that is justice in the world of the novel. Due to his supernatural powers, which include mind-reading and looking into people's past upon touching them, Coffey is able to assign guilt and innocence and, in the novel's Manichean world, to recognize good and evil beyond a reasonable doubt, to draw on legal terminology here. He uses this ability to mete out proportional punishments to the 'evil' characters Bill Wharton and Percy Wetmore for the cruelty they would otherwise get away with. He passes the poison that he sucked out of the warden's wife's brain tumour on to Percy Wetmore and directs him, like a puppet, to shoot Wharton in his sleep — much like Wharton took the twin girls out of their beds to rape and kill them. Wetmore, who was about to be transferred to the psychiatric institution Briar Ridge for an office job, is instead being sent there as a patient who will never regain full consciousness.

King's choice of form and his allegiance to Dickens's sentimental novels, then, works to achieve poetic justice in the real world, or justice through literature, in Nussbaum's sense. This is evident by King's timely choice of Dickens as a predecessor alone, but in his 'Letter' he also emphasizes literature's function of instilling human kindness and togetherness into its readers and, by extension, a love for one's Other. He champions togetherness when he recalls how nineteenth-century readers, as well as his own family in the late 1940s and 50s, used to read out instalments of popular novels aloud so that everyone could partake in the story together and at the same time. He suggests to his contemporary readers: 'Enjoy ... and why not read this aloud, with a friend?'. He concludes his 'Letter' with the following request on how to spend the time between the publication of instalments: 'In the meantime, take care, and be good to one another' (p. xviii). While this is not, in fact, a quote from Dickens, by assuming this well-meaning patriarchal (and also somewhat patronizing) voice, King employs a Dickensian gesture through which he casts himself, the author, as a commanding figure of benevolence and equity. Justice in the real world, then, can be fostered through the poetic practices of writing and reading.

★   ★   ★   ★   ★

The Green Mile, as I hope to have shown, is a 'large loose baggy monster' of a novel with regard to its ideological work. The popular form of the modified horror genre is mired in a melodramatic, Manichean perspective on the world and its ideological implications; it legitimates the death penalty in an implicit embrace of individualist explanations of crime and the justice of talionic punishments. By contrast, the narrator's anti-death penalty sentiments in the frame narrative and, most importantly, his reflections on the pain of time coupled with the novel's painfully serial, or timed, form pull strongly against that conservative, retentionist stance. Intertextual references, in addition, function as thorns in the flesh of a black-and-white world, figuratively and literally. Champions of Jamesian 'deep-breathing economy and organic form' and the integrity and unity of the art work will find reason enough to deride *The Green Mile*. Champions of Dickensian 'queer elements of the accidental and the arbitrary', of an embrace of contemporary messy reality and contradictory sentiments — governed by a desire for a more just and more merciful world — will find much in it to applaud.[33]

Notes to Chapter 10

1. For a comprehensive history of the death penalty in the US, see Stuart Banner, *The Death Penalty: An American History* (Cambridge, MA: Harvard University Press, 2002); for an historically-informed account of the death penalty in the post-*Furman* period, see David Garland, *Peculiar Institution: America's Death Penalty in an Age of Abolition* (Cambridge, MA: Belknap Press of Harvard University Press, 2010).

2. On the Hollywood death penalty cycle of the 1990s, see, for instance, Sean O'Sullivan, 'Representing the "Killing State": The Death Penalty in Nineties Hollywood Cinema', *Howard Law Journal*, 42.5 (December 2003), 485–503.

3. I could identify only five other novels that engage capital punishment in the 1990s. Two novels narrate spectacular death penalty cases of earlier decades. Tema Nason's *Ethel* (1990) treats the execution of the Rosenbergs in 1953, and Ernest J. Gaines's *A Lesson Before Dying* (1993) treats the unsuccessful execution of Willie Francis in 1946 and the successful one in 1947. Apart from *The Green Mile*, two other pieces of genre fiction revolve around a death sentence, John Grisham's *The Chamber* (1994) and Andrew Klavan's *True Crime* (1997), as does Stewart O'Nan's complex homage to Stephen King, *The Speed Queen* (1997).

4. For studies on earlier American literature on capital punishment see, for instance: Barton, *Literary Executions*; DeLombard, *In the Shadow of the Gallows*; Jones, *Against the Gallows*; Guest, *Sentenced to Death*; Algeo, *The Courtroom as Forum*; and Brian Jarvis, *Cruel and Unusual: Punishment and US Culture* (London: Pluto Press, 2004).

5. Harold Bloom, 'For the World of Letters, It's a Horror', *Los Angeles Times*, 19 September 2003, B13; see also Dorothee Birke, 'Challenging the Divide? Stephen King and the Problem of "Popular Culture"', *Journal of Popular Culture* (2014), 520–36 (p. 520); Birke also notes that, ironically, Bloom would edit a critical collection on King's work only four years later, in 2007 (p. 522).

6. For sales numbers see: Doreen Carvajal, 'King's Serial Thriller Rules Best-Seller Lists', *New York Times*, 5 August 1996, <https://www.nytimes.com/1996/08/05/business/king-s-serial-thriller-rules-best-seller-lists.html> [accessed 15 August 2018]; and Blake Morrison, 'Another Year, Another Book: As John Grisham Keeps Up his Phenomenal Workrate, What is the Secret to Avoiding Writer's Block?', *Independent*, 24 January 1999, Features, p. 22; on John Grisham as one of the five US 'megabestsellers' alongside Stephen King, Danielle Steele, Michael Crichton, and Tom Clancy, see Christine Evain, 'John Grisham's Megabestsellers', *Sillages critiques*, 6 (2004), 109–24.

7. As an activist, Grisham has campaigned for the abolition of capital punishment, specifically as a member of the board of directors of the Innocence Project; see Innocence Project, 'Board of Directors', <https://www.innocenceproject.org/disciplines/directors/#JohnGrisham> [accessed 9 August 2018]. In 2006, he published a non-fiction account of the conviction of baseball player Ronald 'Ron' Keith Williamson for rape and murder and his eventual exoneration on DNA evidence (*The Innocent Man: Murder and Injustice in a Small Town*), and his 2010 novel *The Confession*, a fictionalized treatment of the same case, imagines what happens when activist groups, such as the Innocence Project, do not (successfully) intervene and ends with the execution of Donté Drumm, a falsely convicted African American football player.

8. Stephen King's *œuvre* has received increased critical attention after he was honoured by the National Book Foundation, but *The Green Mile* has not been discussed by many King critics. Two reasons for this neglect from within the camp of King scholars may be that, one, their interest in the long-term development of King's *œuvre* takes precedence over a reconstruction of each text's potential timely engagement with socio-political issues, and two, that most studies of King focus on his first fifteen years of writing and thus on novels that can comparatively easily be categorized in the horror genre. In the 1990s, King began to treat the genre more flexibly and pushed its boundaries, including in *The Green Mile*. Scholars in Law and Literature interested in the cultural discourse on the death penalty, on the other hand, have focused on the film version of *The Green Mile* (1999, dir. by Frank Darabont) rather than the novel. This interest in the film may have been due to the fact that it could be discussed as part of Hollywood's larger conversation of capital punishment in the death penalty cycle of films of the 1990s. In the few cases where scholars have discussed the novel, it has been read with a focus on issues such as genetic determinism, race, melodrama, or questions of memory rather than with an interest in its participation in the contemporary debate about the death penalty. See, for example, Heidi Strengell, *Stephen King: Monsters Live in Ordinary People* (Madison: University of Wisconsin Press, 2005), pp. 211–14. Detailed (however, less argumentative than descriptive) treatments can be found in Sharon Russell, *Revisiting Stephen King: A Critical Companion* (Westport, CT: Greenwood Press, 2002), pp. 59–74, and James Arthur Anderson, *The Linguistics of Stephen King: Layered Language and Meaning in the Fiction* (Jefferson, NC: McFarland, 2017), pp. 136–46. On King's treatment of genre, see 'Introduction: A More Subtle Macabre', in *Stephen King's Modern Macabre: Essays on the Later Works*, ed. by Patrick McAleer and Michael A. Perry (Jefferson, NC: McFarland, 2014), pp. 1–8 (pp. 2–3), and Tony Magistrale, *Stephen King: America's Storyteller* (Santa Barbara, CA: Praeger, 2010), p. 17. As Sean O'Sullivan notes, 'The Green Mile was by far the biggest film of the death penalty cycle (of the 1990s) in terms of box office gross', 'Representing the "Killing State"', p. 493.

9. Stephen King, *The Green Mile: The Complete Serial Novel* (New York: Pocket Books, 1999), p. 534; this edition includes the original illustrations. Further page references to this edition are in the main text.

10. Sarat, *When the State Kills*. The third part of Sarat's book is entitled 'The Cultural Life of Capital Punishment', and Sarat has been using and popularizing this phrase with modifications since then, for instance as a title for an edited collection with Boulanger, *The Cultural Lives of Capital Punishment*; see also LaChance, *Executing Freedom*.

11. Sarat, *When the State Kills*, pp. 209–45; Jarvis, *Cruel and Unusual*, p. 190.

12. The most striking example of this change of intertexts is that while the novel *The Green Mile* is set in 1932 to create a parallel to Faulkner's *Light in August*, the film's events are post-dated to 1935 in order to allow for the inclusion of the film *Top Hat* (1935) as a film within the film that, moreover, takes over a memory-triggering function much like the smell of peppermint candy in the novel, modelled on the madeleine episode in *À la recherche du temps perdu*. This is not to say, however, that the novel does not also explicitly employ a number of filmic intertexts from the 1920s and 1930s.

13. The titles of the six instalments are *The Two Dead Girls*, *The Mouse on the Mile*, *Coffey's Hands*, *The Bad Death of Eduard Delacroix*, *Night Journey*, and *Coffey on the Mile*. In subsequent book editions, these titles are sometimes replaced by Part I through VI which correspond to the original instalments. The author's paratexts, 'Introduction' and 'Author's Afterword' (first

included in the book edition) and 'Foreword: A Letter' (preceding the first instalment in the serial publication), are quoted from Stephen King, *The Green Mile: A Novel in Six Parts* (London: Orion Books, 1998): 'Introduction', pp. vii–xi, 'Foreword: A Letter', pp. xiii–xviii; 'Author's Afterword', pp. 451–53.

14. King, 'Foreword: A Letter', p. xviii, and 'Introduction', pp. ix–x. A descriptive account of King's method and the structure of instalments can be found in Russell, *Revisiting Stephen King*, pp. 60–61, 73–74; see also Anderson, *The Linguistics of Stephen King*, p. 137.

15. The most influential studies include Mark Jancovich, *Quality Popular Television: Cult TV, the Industry and Fans* (London: bfi Publishing, 2004); *Quality TV: Contemporary American Television and Beyond*, ed. by Janet McCabe and Kim Akass (London: I. B. Tauris, 2007); *Serielle Formen: von den frühen Film-Serials zu aktuellen Quality-TV- und Online-Serien*, ed. by Robert Blanchet (Marburg: Schüren, 2011); Frank Kelleter, *Serial Agencies: The Wire and Its Readers* (Alresford: John Hunt Publishing, 2014); Jason Mittell, *Complex TV: The Poetics of Contemporary Television Storytelling* (New York: New York University Press, 2015). *The Green Mile*, then, is hardly the only contemporary cultural death-penalty-themed text that takes a serial form. Legal television series such as *Law & Order* (1990–2010), *The Practice* (1997–2004), *Boston Legal* (2004–08), or *The Good Wife* (2009–16), prison dramas such as *Oz* (1997–2003) and *Prison Break* (2005–09, 2017–present), as well as family sagas such as the recent *Rectify* (2013–16) have focused on capital punishment. Beyond television, serial engagements with the death penalty can also be found in the fine arts, for instance in Julie Green's ongoing installation *The Last Supper* (2000–), Robert Priseman's paintings entitled *No Human Way to Kill* (one of which Priseman kindly allowed us to use for this volume's cover), or Lucinda Devlin's photography project entitled *The Omega Suites*. At least two recent poetic series have dealt with capital punishment, George Elliott Clarke's *Execution Poems* and Jill McDonough's *Habeas Corpus* (see Birte Christ, 'State Killing and the Poetic Series: George Elliott Clarke's *Executions Poems* and Jill McDonough's *Habeas Corpus*', *American Studies*, 62.2 (2017), 279–300).

16. Jennifer Hayward, *Consuming Pleasures: Active Audiences and Serial Fiction from Dickens to Soap Opera* (Lexington: University Press of Kentucky, 1997).

17. Sabine Sielke, ' "Joy in Repetition": or, The Significance of Seriality in Processes of Memory and (Re)Mediation', in *The Memory Effect: The Remediation of Memory in Literature and Film*, ed. by Russell J. A. Kilbourn and Eleanor Ty (Waterloo, ON: Wilfrid Laurier University Press, 2013), pp. 37–50.

18. As Jason Mittell has argued, television narratives of the past two decades often take such complexity a step or two further, due to changes in viewing practices and technology (for example, DVDs and streaming) as well as the organization of the industry. They increasingly employ, for instance, unreliable narration, counter-fictional scenarios, and anachrony (see Mittell, *Complex TV*); see also on complexity and the future of television research, Michael Butter, 'Think Thrice, It's Alright: Mad Men's "The Wheel" and the Future Study of Television Narratives', *NARRATIVE*, 25.3 (2017), 374–89. While anachronological narration is integral to *The Green Mile*, too, these and other hallmarks of twenty-first-century serial narratives have no bearing on my present argument.

19. Russell, *Revisiting Stephen King*, p. 73.

20. While the reader will notice these parallels from the start, Edgecombe's meta-narrative suggests that he becomes conscious of the parallels only much later. As late as the beginning of instalment 4 he notes: 'It's as if, by writing about these old times, I have unlocked some unspeakable door that connects the past to the present — Percy Wetmore to Brad Dolan, Janice Edgecombe to Elaine Connelly, Cold Mountain Penitentiary to the Georgia Pines old folks' home' (pp. 254–55). While Edgecombe here sees his writing about the past as unlocking the present, this process could also be seen as functioning vice versa: the fact that Edgecombe finds himself surrounded by institutional and, resulting from that structure, individual circumstances much like in 1932, these circumstances may be seen as triggering his recollections of past events in the sense of Proustian 'involuntary memories'. The madeleine episode from *Du côté de chez Swann* is a theme in King's 1932 plot, as I will detail below.

21. Michel Foucault, *Discipline and Punish: The Birth of the Prison*, trans. by Alan Sheridan (London:

Penguin Books, 1991), p. 149. See also Erving Goffman, *Asylums: Essays on the Social Situation of Mental Patients and Other Inmates* (New York: Doubleday, 1961). It should be noted that Edgecombe's narrative's focus on the structure of institutions, rather than (only) on the sadistic nature of certain individuals — such as Brad Dolan and Percy Wetmore — also demonstrates that the novel is much more concerned with a systemic critique of the penal system than its morality-tale-like film version.

22. Foucault, *Discipline and Punish*, p. 160.

23. Jarvis, *Cruel and Unusual*, p. 191.

24. Foucault, *Discipline and Punish*, p. 266

25. Anderson entitles a chapter in which he discusses *Of Mice and Men* as a pre-text for King's novel '*The Green Mile*: Remembrance of Things Past', but curiously does not mention Proust at all, *The Linguistics of Stephen King*, pp. 136–46.

26. 'A smell of peppermint' (King, *The Green Mile*, p. 73).

27. In *Du côté de chez Swann*, Marcel describes the taste, rather than the smell, of the madeleine dunked into lime flower tea as the trigger for his memories. However, in the reception of this pivotal scene, as Barry Smith has observed, the trigger is often described as olfactory, which is not entirely wrong. On the confusion and conflation of taste and smell in the episode and its reception, see Barry C. Smith, 'Proust, the Madeleine and Memory', in *Memory in the Twenty-First Century: New Critical Perspectives from the Arts, Humanities, and Sciences*, ed. by Sebastian Groes (Basingstoke: Palgrave Macmillan, 2016), pp. 38–41.

28. On Coffey as a counter to Small, see also Anderson, *The Linguistics of Stephen King*, p. 139.

29. LaChance, *Executing Freedom*, p. 112. Linda Williams, 'Melodrama in Black and White: Uncle Tom and *The Green Mile*', *Film Quarterly*, 55.2 (Winter 2001), 14–21 (p. 20).

30. Williams, 'Melodrama in Black and White', p. 15.

31. Martha C. Nussbaum, *Poetic Justice: The Literary Imagination and Public Life* (Boston, MA: Beacon Press, 1995), p. 5.

32. Michael Stanford, 'Poetry, Negative Capability, and the Law: James Wright's "A Poem about George Doty in the Death House" and "At the Executed Murderer's Grave"', *Amerikastudien*, 62.2 (2017), 235–55 (p. 235).

33. Henry James, from 'The Preface' to *The Tragic Muse*, quoted in *The Portable Henry James*, ed. by John Auchard (New York: Penguin, 2003), p. 477.

BIBLIOGRAPHY

ADAMSON, JANE, and others (eds), *Renegotiating Ethics in Literature, Philosophy, and Theory* (Cambridge: Cambridge University Press, 1998)

ADDISON, JOSEPH, and others, *The Spectator*, 6 vols (London: H. D. Symonds, 1796)

ADORNO, THEODOR W., *Notes to Literature* (New York: Columbia University Press, 1991)

—— *Prisms*, trans. by Samuel and Shierry Weber (Cambridge, MA: MIT Press, 1997)

AGAMBEN, GIORGIO, *Homo sacer: il potere sovrano e la nuda vita* (Turin: Einaudi, 1995)

AGUDO MARTÍNEZ, JUSTO, 'Métrica de *Poesías líricas y fragmentos épicos* de José de Espronceda', *Rhythmica*, 11 (2013), 13–43

ALBERTS, PAUL, 'Knowing Life Before the Law: Kafka, Kelsen, Derrida', in *Philosophy and Kafka*, ed. by Brendan Moran and Carlo Salzani (Lanham, MD: Lexington Books, 2013), pp. 179–97

ALEXANDER, JOHN T., *Catherine the Great: Life and Legend* (Oxford: Oxford University Press, 1989)

ALGEO, ANN M., *The Courtroom as Forum: Homicide Trials by Dreiser, Wright, Capote, and Mailer* (New York: Peter Lang, 1996)

ALKALAY-GUT, KAREN, 'The Thing He Loves: Murder as Aesthetic Experience in *The Ballad of Reading Gaol*', *Victorian Poetry*, 35.3 (Fall 1997), 349–66

AMNESTY INTERNATIONAL, 'Annex II: Abolitionist and Retentionist Countries as of 31 December 2017', *Global Report on Death Sentences and Executions 2017* (April 2018), pp. 40–41, <https://www.amnesty.org/download/Documents/ACT5079552018ENGLISH.PDF> [accessed 3 August 2018]

—— 'The Use of the Death Penalty in 2016', *Global Report on Death Sentences and Executions, 2016* (April 2017), pp. 3–10, <https://www.amnesty.org/download/Documents/ACT5057402017ENGLISH.PDF> [accessed 24 February 2018]

—— 'The Use of the Death Penalty in 2017', *Global Report on Death Sentences and Executions 2017* (April 2018), pp. 5–11, <https://www.amnesty.org/download/Documents/ACT5079552018ENGLISH.PDF> [accessed 3 August 2018]

—— 'United States of America', *Amnesty International Report 2017/18. The State of the World's Human Rights*, pp. 384–89, <https://www.amnesty.org/download/Documents/POL1067002018ENGLISH.PDF> [accessed 24 February 2018]

ANDERSON, CHRIS, *Style as Argument: Contemporary American Nonfiction* (Carbondale & Edwardsville: Southern Illinois University Press, 1987)

ANDERSON, JAMES ARTHUR, *The Linguistics of Stephen King: Layered Language and Meaning in the Fiction* (Jefferson, NC: McFarland, 2017)

ANDERSON, WILDA, 'Is the General Will Anonymous? (Rousseau, Robespierre, Condorcet)', *MLN*, 126.4 (2011), 838–52

ANNESLEY, JAMES, *Blank Fictions: Consumerism, Culture and the Contemporary American Novel* (London: Pluto, 1998)

[ANON.], 'Angleterre. Dernières sensations d'un homme condamné à mort', *Le Globe*, 3 January 1828

[ANON.], *The Children in the Wood: A Musical Piece* (Dublin: John Rice, 1794)

[ANON.], 'Le Dernier Jour d'un condamné, roman; par M. Victor Hugo', Le Globe, 4 February 1829

[ANON.], La Journée des Dupes (n.p.: n. pub., 1790)

[ANON.], Le Martyre de Marie-Antoinette d'Autriche, Reine de France (Amsterdam: n. pub., 1794)

[ANON.], Obrashchenie i smert' l.f. Richara, kazennogo v Zhjeneve 11-go iunia 1850 goda, per. s frantsuzskogo (St. Petersburg: Tip. A. Iakobsona, 1877)

APOSTOLIDÈS, JEAN-MARIE, 'La Guillotine littéraire', French Review, 62.6 (May 1989), 985–96

ARASSE, DANIEL, La Guillotine et l'imaginaire de la Terreur (Paris: Flammarion, 1987)

ATWELL, MARY WELEK, Evolving Standards of Decency: Popular Culture and Capital Punishment (New York: Peter Lang, 2004)

—— Wretched Sisters: Examining Gender and Capital Punishment (New York: Peter Lang 2007)

AUSTIN, J. L., How to Do Things with Words (Cambridge, MA: Harvard University Press, 1962)

BACON, LEONARD, 'Shall Punishment Be Abolished?', New Englander and Yale Review, 4.16 (October 1846), 563–88

BADINTER, ROBERT, 'Je vote l'abolition de la peine de mort', L'Histoire, 261 (2002), 56–57

—— 'Préface', in Choses vues à travers Hugo: hommage à Guy Rosa, ed. by Claude Millet and others (Valenciennes: Presses universitaires de Valenciennes, 2007), pp. 7–10

BAECQUE, ANTOINE DE, 'Pamphlets: Libel and Political Mythology', in Revolution in Print: The Press in France 1775–1800, ed. by Robert Darnton and Daniel Roche (Berkeley: University of California Press, 1989), pp. 165–76

BAKHTIN, MIKHAIL, The Dialogic Imagination, trans. by Caryl Emerson and Michael Holquist (Austin: University of Texas Press, 1981)

BANNER, STUART, The Death Penalty: An American History (Cambridge, MA: Harvard University Press, 2002)

BARTH, JOHN, 'A Few Words About Minimalism', New York Times, 28 December 1986, section 7, p. 1

BARTON, JOHN CYRIL, 'Cooper, Livingston, and Death-Penalty Reform', in James Fenimore Cooper Society: Miscellaneous Papers, 27, ed. by Steven Harthorn and Shalicia Wilson (Cooperstown: The Society, 2010), pp. 1–5

—— Literary Executions: Capital Punishment and American Culture, 1820–1925 (Baltimore, MD: Johns Hopkins University Press, 2014)

BAUDELAIRE, CHARLES, Le Spleen de Paris (Petits poèmes en prose), in Œuvres complètes, ed. by Claude Pichois, 2 vols (Paris: Gallimard, 1975–76), I

BECCARIA, CESARE, Dei delitti e delle pene, ed. by Franco Venturi (Turin: Einaudi, 1965; 1994)

—— On Crimes and Punishments, and Other Writings, ed. by Richard Bellamy, trans. by Richard Davies with Virginia Cox and Richard Bellamy (Cambridge & New York: Cambridge University Press, 1995)

BELL, DAVID, The Cult of the Nation in France: Inventing Nationalism, 1680–1800 (Cambridge, MA: Harvard University Press, 2001)

BENNINGTON, GEOFFREY, 'Ex Lex', Oxford Literary Review, 35.2 (2013), 143–63

BERGENGRUEN, MAXIMILIAN, 'Im "gesetzesleeren Raum": Zur inquisitorischen Logik von Rechtssätzen und Rechtssprichworten in Kafkas "Proceß"', Zeitschrift für Deutsche Philologie, 134.2 (2015), 217–49

BIARD, MICHEL, La Révolution hantée (Paris: Vendémiaire, 2012)

BIRÉ, EDMOND, Victor Hugo avant 1830 (Paris: Jules Gervais, 1883)

BIRKE, DOROTHEE, 'Challenging the Divide? Stephen King and the Problem of "Popular Culture"', *Journal of Popular Culture* (2014), 520–36

BJÖRNSSON, BRYNJAR, 'Oscar Wilde and Edgar Allan Poe: Comparison of *The Picture of Dorian Gray* and "William Wilson"' (unpublished essay, University of Iceland, 1987), <https://skemman.is/handle/1946/10612> [accessed 18 August 2017]

BLACKSTONE, WILLIAM, *Commentaries on the Laws of England*, 4 vols (Chicago, IL: University of Chicago Press, 1979)

BLANCHET, ROBERT (ed.), *Serielle Formen: von den frühen Film-Serials zu aktuellen Quality-TV- und Online-Serien* (Marburg: Schüren, 2011)

BLOOM, HAROLD, 'For the World of Letters, It's a Horror', *Los Angeles Times*, 19 September 2003, B13

BOA, ELIZABETH, *Kafka: Gender, Class, and Race in the Letters and Fictions* (Oxford: Clarendon Press, 1996)

BOUDREAU, KRISTIN, *The Spectacle Death: Populist Literary Responses to American Capital Cases* (Amherst, MA: Prometheus Books, 2006)

BOULARD, STÉPHANIE, *Rouge Hugo* (Villeneuve d'Ascq: Presses universitaires du Septentrion, 2014)

BOURDIN, PHILIPPE, 'Les Factions sur les tréteaux patriotiques (1789–1799): combats pour une représentation', in *Représentation et pouvoir: la politique symbolique en France (1789–1830)*, ed. by Natalie Scholz and Christina Schröer (Rennes: Presses universitaires de Rennes, 2007), pp. 23–37

BOURDIN, PHILIPPE, and OTHERS, 'Le programme THEREPSICORE: personnels dramatiques, répertoires et salles de spectacle en province (1791–1813)', *Révolution française*, 367 (2012), 17–48

BOWMAN, FRANK PAUL, 'The Intertextuality of Victor Hugo's *Le Dernier Jour d'un condamné*', in *Alteratives*, ed. by Warren Motte and Gerald Prince (Lexington, KY: French Forum Publishers, 1993), pp. 25–45

BOZON, ÉMILIE, *L'Expression du moi dans 'Le Dernier Jour d'un condamné' de Victor Hugo* (Paris: Le Manuscrit, 2002)

BRECHT, BERTOLT, *Die Maßnahme: Kritische Ausgabe mit einer Spielanleitung von Reiner Steinweg* (Frankfurt am Main: Suhrkamp Verlag, 1972)

BROMBERT, VICTOR, *Victor Hugo and the Visionary Novel* (Cambridge, MA: Harvard University Press, 1984)

BROOKE-ROSE, CHRISTINE, *A Rhetoric of the Unreal: Studies in Narrative and Structure, Especially of the Fantastic* (Cambridge: Cambridge University Press, 1981)

BROWN, MICHELLE, *The Culture of Punishment: Prison, Society, and Spectacle* (New York: New York University Press, 2009)

BRYSON, SCOTT S., *The Chastised Stage: Bourgeois Drama and the Exercise of Power* (Saratoga, CA: ANMA Libri, 1991)

BUDANOVA, N. F., 'Istoriia "Obrashcheniia I smerti" Richara, rasskazannaia Ivanom Karamazovym', *Dostoevskii: Materialy I issledovaniia*, 13 (1996), 106–19

BUGG, JOHN, *Five Long Winters: The Trials of British Romanticism* (Stanford, CA: Stanford University Press, 2014)

BÜRGER, GOTTFRIED AUGUST, 'The Lass of Fair Wone', trans. by William Taylor, *Monthly Magazine*, 1 (1796), 223–24

BURK, TARA, '"A Battleground around the Crime": The Visuality of Execution Ephemera and Its Cultural Significances in Late Seventeenth-Century England', in *Studies in Ephemera: Text and Image in Eighteenth-Century Print*, ed. by Kevin D. Murphy and Sally O'Driscoll (Lewisburg, PA: Bucknell University Press, 2013), pp. 195–218

BURMAN, RUSSELL, *Literature Sets You Free: Literature, Liberty and Western Culture* (Iowa City: University of Iowa Press, 2007)

BUTTER, MICHAEL, 'Think Thrice, It's Alright: Mad Men's "The Wheel" and the Future Study of Television Narratives', *NARRATIVE*, 25.3 (2017), 374–89

C., M. J., *Le Cri de l'innocence, ou le tribunal coupable* (Avignon: Bonnet fils, n.d.)

CABANIS, PIERRE JEAN, *Œuvres complètes de Cabanis*, 5 vols (Paris: Dossange, 1823–25)

CAMUS, ALBERT, 'Réflexions sur la guillotine', in *Œuvres complètes*, ed. by Raymond Gay-Crosier and others, 4 vols (Paris: Gallimard, 2006–08), IV, 125–67

CANUEL, MARK, *The Shadow of Death: Literature, Romanticism, and the Subject of Punishment* (Princeton, NJ: Princeton University Press, 2007)

CARVAJAL, DOREEN, 'King's Serial Thriller Rules Best-Seller Lists', *New York Times*, 5 August 1996, <https://www.nytimes.com/1996/08/05/business/king-s-serial-thriller-rules-best-seller-lists.html> [accessed 15 August 2018]

CHABERT, BENOÎT, 'Sur la peine de mort en France', in *Victor Hugo contre la peine de mort*, ed. by Jérôme Picon and Isabel Violante (Paris: Textuel, 2001), pp. 169–73

CHARBONNEAU, FRANÇOIS, 'Institutionnaliser le droit à l'insurrection: l'article 35 de la constitution montagnarde de 1793', *Tangence*, 106 (2014), 93–112

CHARLIER, GUSTAVE, 'Comment fut écrit *Le Dernier Jour d'un condamné* ?', *Revue d'histoire littéraire de la France*, 22 (1915), 321–60

CHÉNIER, MARIE-JOSEPH DE, *Jean Calas, ou L'École des juges* (Paris: Moutard, 1793)

CHILD, FRANCIS JAMES (ed.), *The English and Scottish Popular Ballads*, 5 vols (New York: Houghton Mifflin, 1898)

CHRIST, BIRTE, 'Rallying Reformers in Anti-Gallows Poetry of the 1840s and 1850s' (forthcoming book chapter)

—— 'State Killing and the Poetic Series: George Elliott Clarke's *Executions Poems* and Jill McDonough's *Habeas Corpus*', *American Studies*, 62.2 (2017), 279–300

COHEN, DANIEL A., 'Blood Will Out: Sensationalism, Horror, and the Roots of American Crime Literature', in *Mortal Remains: Death in Early America*, ed. by Andrew Burstein and Nancy Isenberg (Philadelphia: University of Pennsylvania Press, 2003), pp. 31–55

—— *Pillars of Salt, Monuments of Grace: New England Crime Literature and the Origins of American Popular Culture, 1647–1860* (Liverpool: Liverpool University Press, 1993)

COLERIDGE, SAMUEL, *Biographia Literaria*, ed. by James Engell and Walter Jackson Bate, 2 vols (Princeton, NJ: Princeton University Press, 1983)

COOPER, JAMES FENIMORE, *Correspondence of James Fenimore Cooper*, 2 vols (New Haven, CT: Yale University Press, 1922)

CORRE, ARMAND, 'À propos de la peine de mort et du livre du Professeur Lacassagne, *Peine de mort et criminalité*', in *Archives d'anthropologie criminelle de médecine légale et de psychologie normale et pathologique*, 23 (Lyon: A. Rey et Cie, 1908)

COUNCIL OF EUROPE, 'Protocol No. 6 to the Convention for the Protection of Human Rights and Fundamental Freedoms Concerning the Abolition of the Death Penalty', <https://www.echr.coe.int/Documents/Library_Collection_P6_ETS114E_ENG.pdf> [accessed 24 February 2018]

—— 'Protocol No. 13 to the Convention for the Protection of Human Rights and Fundamental Freedoms, Concerning the Abolition of the Death Penalty in All Circumstances', <https://www.echr.coe.int/Documents/Library_Collection_P13_ETS187E_ENG.pdf> [accessed 24 February 2018]

CULLER, JONATHAN, *Theory of the Lyric* (Cambridge, MA: Harvard University Press, 2015)

CUSACK, ANNE-MARIE, *Cruel and Unusual: The Culture of Punishment in America* (New Haven, CT: Yale University Press, 2009)

DÄLLENBACH, LUCIEN, 'Le Vide plein ou les révélations de l'homme sans tête', in *Hugo dans les marges*, ed. by Lucien Dällenbach and Laurent Jenny (Geneva: Éditions Zoë, 1985), pp. 51–90

DARLOW, MARK, 'Staging the Revolution: the *Fait historique*', *Nottingham French Studies*, 45 (Spring 2006), 77–88

DAVIS, ANGELA Y., *Are Prisons Obsolete?* (New York: Seven Stories Press, 2003)

Déclaration (La) des droits de l'homme et du citoyen, article 6, <http://www.elysee.fr/la-presidence/la-declaration-des-droits-de-l-homme-et-du-citoyen/> [accessed 7 December 2016]

DELEUZE, GILLES, and FÉLIX GUATTARI, *Kafka: Toward a Minor Literature*, trans. by Dana Polan (Minneapolis: University of Minnesota Press, 1986)

DELOMBARD, JEANNINE MARIE, *In the Shadow of the Gallows: Race, Crime, and American Civic Identity* (Philadelphia: University of Pennsylvania Press, 2012)

DE MAN, PAUL, *Allegories of Reading: Figural Language in Rousseau, Nietzsche, Rilke and Proust* (New Haven, CT: Yale University Press, 1979)

DERRIDA, JACQUES, *The Death Penalty*, trans. by Peggy Kamuf (vol. 1) and Elizabeth Rottenberg (vol. 2), 2 vols (Chicago, IL: University of Chicago Press, 2013–17)

—— 'Force of Law: The Mystical Foundation of Authority', *Cardozo Law Review*, 11.5–6 (1990), 920–1045

—— 'The Law of Genre', *Critical Inquiry*, 7.1 (Autumn 1980), 55–81

—— *Margins*, trans. by Alan Bass (Chicago, IL: University of Chicago Press, 1982)

—— '"A Self-Unsealing Poetic Text": Poetics and Politics of Witnessing', in *Revenge of the Aesthetic: The Place of Literature in Theory Today*, ed. by Michael Clark (Berkeley: University of California Press, 2000), pp. 180–207

DICKENS, CHARLES, 'Letter', *Daily News*, 16 March 1846

DIMOCK, WAI CHEE, *Residues of Justice: Literature, Law, and Philosophy* (Berkeley: University of California Press, 1997)

DOSTOEVSKY, FEDOR, *The Best Short Stories of Fyodor Dostoyevsky*, trans. by David Magarshack (New York: The Modern Library, 2001)

—— *The Brothers Karamazov*, ed. and trans. by Susan McReynolds Oddo (New York: W. W. Norton & Company, 2011)

—— *The House of the Dead*, trans. by David McDuff (London: Penguin, 1985)

—— *The Idiot*, trans. by David McDuff (London: Penguin, 2004)

—— *Polnoe sobranie sochinenii v tridtsati tomakh*, 30 vols (Leningrad: Nauka, 1972–90)

DU CAMP, MAXIME, *Paris, ses organes, ses fonctions et sa vie dans la seconde moitié du dix-neuvième siècle*, 6 vols (Paris: Hachette, 1972)

DU CANE, SIR EDMUND, *The Punishment and Prevention of Crime* (London: Macmillan, 1885)

DYZENHAUS, DAVID, 'Positivism and the Pesky Sovereign', *European Journal of International Law*, 22.2 (2011), 363–72

ESPRONCEDA, JOSÉ, *Obras completas*, ed. by Diego Martínez Torrón (Madrid: Cátedra, 2006)

EUROPEAN COMMISSION, INTERNATIONAL COOPERATION and DEVELOPMENT, 'Fight Against the Death Penalty', <https://ec.europa.eu/europeaid/sectors/human-rights-and-governance/democracy-and-human-rights/fight-against-death-penalty_en> [accessed 24 February 2018]

EVAIN, CHRISTINE, 'John Grisham's Megabestsellers', *Sillages critiques*, 6 (2004), 109–24

FAIRER, DAVID, 'Southey's Literary History', in *Robert Southey and the Contexts of English Romanticism*, ed. by Lynda Pratt, Vincent Newey, and Joanne Shattock (London: Ashgate, 2013), pp. 1–18

FALLOWES, GRAHAM, 'Power and Performativity: "Doing Things With Words" in Kafka's *Proceß*', *Oxford German Studies*, 44.2 (2015), 199–225

FARCY, JEAN-CLAUDE, 'La Peine de mort: pratique judiciaire et débats', in *Criminocorpus. Revue hypermédia, histoire de la justice, des crimes et des peines* (13 April 2010), <http://journals.openedition.org/criminocorpus/129> [accessed 5 January 2018]

FAWCETT, F. BURLINGTON (ed.), *Broadside Ballads of the Restoration Period from the Jersey Collection Known as the Osterly Park Ballads* (London: John Lane, 1930)

FEILLA, CECILIA, *The Sentimental Theater of the French Revolution* (Farnham: Ashgate, 2013)

FLAUBERT, GUSTAVE, *Correspondance*, ed. by Jean Bruneau (Paris: Gallimard, 1980)

FOLDY, MICHAEL, *The Trials of Oscar Wilde: Deviance, Morality and Late-Victorian Society* (New Haven, CT: Yale University Press, 1997)

FORTESCUE, G. K., *French Revolutionary Collections in the British Library* (London: The British Library, 1979)

FOUCAULT, MICHEL, *Histoire de la sexualité 1. La Volonté de savoir* (Paris: Gallimard, 1976)

—— '*Il faut défendre la société*': *Cours au Collège de France 1975–1976* (Paris: Gallimard-Seuil, 1997)

—— *Surveiller et punir: naissance de la prison* (Paris: Gallimard, 1975)

—— *Discipline and Punish: The Birth of the Prison*, trans. by Alan Sheridan (New York: Random House, 1977; 1991)

FRANK, JOSEPH, *Dostoevsky: The Seeds of Revolt, 1821–1849* (Princeton, NJ: Princeton University Press, 1976)

—— *Dostoevsky: The Years of Ordeal, 1850–1859* (Princeton, NJ: Princeton University Press, 1983)

—— *Dostoevsky: The Miraculous Years, 1865–1871* (Princeton, NJ: Princeton University Press, 1995)

—— *Dostoevsky: The Mantle of the Prophet, 1871–1881* (Princeton, NJ: Princeton University Press, 2002)

FRANTZ, PIERRE, 'Les Genres dramatiques pendant la Révolution', in *Convegno di studi sul teatro e la Rivoluzione francese*, ed. by Mario Richter (Venice : Accademia Olimpica, 1991), pp. 49–63

—— 'Violence in the Theatre of the Revolution', in *Representing Violence in France, 1760–1820*, ed. by Thomas Wynn (Oxford: SVEC, 2013), pp. 121–35

FRIEDLAND, PAUL, *Seeing Justice Done: The Age of Spectacular Capital Punishment in France* (Oxford: Oxford University Press, 2012)

—— *Political Actors: Representative Bodies & Theatricality in the Age of the French Revolution* (Ithaca, NY: Cornell University Press, 2002)

FRUS, PHYLLIS, *The Politics and Poetics of Journalistic Narrative: The Timely and the Timeless* (Cambridge: Cambridge University Press, 1994)

FULLER, LON L., *The Morality of Law* (New Haven, CT: Yale University Press, 1969)

GARLAND, DAVID, *Peculiar Institution: America's Death Penalty in an Age of Abolition* (Cambridge, MA: Belknap Press of Harvard University Press, 2010)

GENETTE, GÉRARD, *Narrative Discourse: An Essay in Method* (New York: Cornell University Press, 1983)

GEORGEL, J. F., *Mémoires pour servir à l'histoire des événements de la fin du XVIIIe siècle depuis 1760 jusqu'en 1806–1810*, 6 vols (Paris: Eymery, 1820)

GOFFMAN, ERVING, *Asylums: Essays on the Social Situation of Mental Patients and Other Inmates* (New York: Doubleday, 1961)

GOHIN, YVES, 'Les Réalités du crime et de la justice pour Victor Hugo avant 1829', in *Œuvres complètes. Édition chronologique*, ed. by Jean Massin, 18 vols (Paris: Le Club français du livre, 1967–70), III, i–xxv

GONCOURT, EDMOND and JULES, *Histoire de Marie-Antoinette* (Paris: Didot Frères, 1858)

GOODEN, ANGELICA, *Actio and Persuasio* (Oxford: Clarendon, 1986)

GRANT, CLAIRE, *Crime and Punishment in Contemporary Culture* (London: Routledge, 2004)

GREGORY, JAMES, *Victorians Against the Gallows: Capital Punishment and the Abolitionist Movement in Nineteenth-Century Britain* (London: I. B. Taurus, 2012)

GRIMM, FRIEDRICH-MELCHIOR, and OTHERS, *Correspondance littéraire, philosophique et critique* [1747–1793], 16 vols (Paris: Garnier Frères, 1877–82)

GROSSMAN, KATHRYN, *The Early Novels of Victor Hugo: Towards a Poetics of Harmony* (Geneva: Droz, 1986)

GUEST, DAVID, *Sentenced to Death: The American Novel and Capital Punishment* (Jackson: University Press of Mississippi, 1997)

GUYON, LOÏC, *Les Martyrs de la veuve: romantisme et peine de mort* (Oxford: Peter Lang, 2010)

HALSALL, ALBERT, *Victor Hugo et l'art de convaincre: le récit hugolien, rhétorique, argumentation, persuasion* (Montreal: Éditions Balzac, 1995)

HALSTED, CAROLINE A., *Richard III as Duke of Gloucester and King of England* (Philadelphia: Carey and Hart, 1844)

HAWCROFT, MICHAEL, *Reasoning With Fools* (Oxford: Oxford University Press, 2007)

HAYWARD, JENNIFER, *Consuming Pleasures: Active Audiences and Serial Fiction from Dickens to Soap Opera* (Lexington: University Press of Kentucky, 1997)

HEIDSIECK, ARNOLD, *The Intellectual Contexts of Kafka's Fictions: Philosophy, Law, Religion* (Columbia, SC: Camden House, 1994)

HESSE, CARLA, *The Other Enlightenment: How French Women Became Modern* (Princeton, NJ: Princeton University Press, 2002)

—— *Publishing and Cultural Politics in Revolutionary Paris, 1789–1810* (Berkeley: University of California Press, 1991)

HOMESTEAD, MELISSA J., and PAMELA T. WASHINGTON (eds), *E. D. E. N. Southworth: Recovering a Nineteenth Century Popular Novelist* (Knoxville: University of Tennessee Press, 2012)

HOOD, ROGER, and CAROLYN HOYLE, *The Death Penalty: A Worldwide Perspective*, 5th edn (Oxford: Oxford University Press, 2015)

HOSTETTLER, JOHN, *A History of Criminal Justice in England and Wales* (Hook: Waterside Press, 2009)

HUET, MARIE-HÉLÈNE, *Rehearsing the Revolution: The Staging of Marat's Death, 1793–1797* (Berkeley: University of California Press, 1982)

HUGO, VICTOR, *Le Dernier Jour d'un condamné*, ed. by Henri Guillemin (Paris: Seuil, 1963)

—— *Le Dernier jour d'un condamné suivi de Claude Gueux et de l'affaire Tapner*, ed. by Guy Rosa (Paris: Librairie générale française, 1989)

—— *Le Dernier Jour d'un condamné* (Paris: Gallimard, 2000)

—— *Les Misérables*, ed. by Marius-François Guyard, 2 vols (Paris: Garnier Frères, 1957)

—— *Œuvres complètes*, 45 vols (Paris: Ollendorff, 1904–52)

—— *Œuvres complètes. Édition chronologique*, ed. by Jean Massin, 18 vols (Paris: Le Club français du livre, 1967–70)

HUMMER, LAWRENCE, 'I Witnessed the Execution of Dennis McGuire. What I Saw was Inhumane', *Guardian*, 22 January 2014, <https://www.theguardian.com/commentisfree/2014/jan/22/ohio-mcguire-execution-untested-lethal-injection-inhumane> [accessed 15 August 2018]

HUNT, LYNN, 'The Many Bodies of Marie-Antoinette: Political Pornography and the Problem of the Feminine in the French Revolution', in *Marie-Antoinette: Writing on the Body of a Queen*, ed. by Dena Goodman (New York: Routledge, 2003), pp. 117–38

IAROCCI, MICHAEL, *Properties of Modernity: Romantic Spain, Modern Europe, and the Legacies of Empire* (Nashville, TN: Vanderbilt University Press, 2006)

INTERNATIONAL CRIMINAL COURT, ROME STATUTE, 'Part 7: Penalties', <http://legal.un.org/icc/statute/romefra.htm> [accessed 24 February 2018]

IRELAND, RICHARD W., *'A Want of Order and Good Discipline': Rules, Discretion, and the Victorian Prison* (Cardiff: University of Wales Press, 2007)

JACKSON, ROBERT LOUIS, 'The Ethics of Vision I: Turgenev's "Execution of Tropmann" and Dostoevsky's View of the Matter', in *Dialogues with Dostoevsky: The Overwhelming Questions* (Stanford, CA: Stanford University Press, 1993), pp. 29–54

—— 'The Narrator in Dostoevsky's *Notes from the House of the Dead*', in *Studies in Russian and Polish Literature in Honor of Waclaw Lednicki*, ed. by Zbigniew Folejewski and others (The Hague: Mouton, 1962), pp. 192–216

JAMES, HENRY, *The Art of the Novel: Critical Prefaces* (Chicago, IL: University of Chicago Press: 2011)

—— *Partial Portraits* (London: Macmillan, 1888)

—— *The Portable Henry James*, ed. by John Auchard (New York: Penguin, 2003)

JAMESON, FREDRIC, *Postmodernism: Or, the Cultural Logic of Late Capitalism* (London: Verso, 1992)

JANCOVICH, MARK, *Quality Popular Television: Cult TV, the Industry and Fans* (London: bfi Publishing, 2004)

JANES, REGINA, *Losing Our Heads: Beheadings in Literature and Culture* (New York: New York University Press, 2005)

JARVIS, BRIAN, *Cruel and Unusual: Punishment and US Culture* (London: Pluto Press, 2004)

JEAN, RAYMOND, *Écrits de Victor Hugo sur la peine de mort* (Maussane les Alpilles: Actes Sud, 1979)

JOHNSON, JAMES, 'Revolutionary Audiences and the Impossible Imperatives of Fraternity', in *Re-Creating Authority in Revolutionary France*, ed. by Bryant T. Ragan and Elizabeth Ann Williams (New Brunswick, NJ: Rutgers University Press, 1992), pp. 57–68

JOMARON, JACQUELINE DE (ed.), *Le Théâtre en France*, 2 vols (Paris: Armand Colin, 1988)

JONES, PAUL CHRISTIAN, *Against the Gallows: Antebellum American Writers and the Movement to Abolish Capital Punishment* (Iowa City: University of Iowa Press, 2011)

—— 'Revising Uncle Tom's Cabin: Sympathy, the State, and the Role of Women in E. D. E. N. Southworth's *The Lost Heiress*', in *E. D. E. N. Southworth*, ed. by Melissa J. Homestead & Pamela T. Washington (Knoxville: University of Tennessee Press, 2012), pp. 183–204

JOURDA, PIERRE, *Le Théâtre à Montpellier, 1755–1851* (Oxford: Voltaire Foundation, 2001)

JOURDAIN, ELEANOR F., *Dramatic Theory and Practice in France, 1690–1808* (Oxford: Clarendon Press, 1912)

Jugement du Tribunal criminel du Département de l'Hérault, du 19 germinal de l'an deuxième de la fondation de la République française [...] (Affaire dite des Galettes) (Montpellier: Bonnariq and Avignon, an II)

KAFKA, FRANZ, *Drucke zu Lebzeiten: Textband*, ed. by Wolf Kittler (Frankfurt am Main: Fischer, 1994)

—— *Der Proceß: Textband*, ed. by Malcolm Pasley (Frankfurt am Main: Fischer, 1990)

—— *The Trial*, trans. by Willa and Edwin Muir (New York: Schocken, 1984)

KAUFMAN, ROBERT, 'Adorno's Social Lyric, and Literary Criticism Today: Poetics, Aesthetics, Modernity', in *The Cambridge Companion to Adorno*, ed. by Thomas Huhn (Cambridge: Cambridge University Press, 2004), pp. 354–75

KELLETER, FRANK, *Serial Agencies: The Wire and Its Readers* (Alresford: John Hunt Publishing, 2014)

KELLEY, MARY, *Private Woman, Public Stage: Literary Domesticity in Nineteenth-Century America* (New York: Oxford University Press, 1984)

KELSEN, HANS, *Reine Rechtslehre: Einleitung in die rechtswissenschaftliche Problematik* (Leipzig: Franz Deuticke, 1934)

—— *Reine Rechtslehre, mit einem Anhang: das Problem der Gerechtigkeit*, 2nd edn (Vienna: Deuticke, 1960)

——*Pure Theory of Law*, trans. by Max Knight (Berkeley: University of California Press, 1967)

KING, STEPHEN, *The Green Mile: A Novel in Six Parts* (London: Orion Books, 1998)

——*The Green Mile: The Complete Serial Novel* (New York: Pocket Books, 1999)

KIRKPATRICK, SUSAN, *Las románticas: Women Writers and Subjectivity in Spain* (Berkeley: University of California Press, 1989)

KNAPP, LIZA (ed.), *Dostoevsky as Reformer: The Petrashevsky Case*, trans. by Liza Knapp (Ann Arbor, MI: Ardis, 1987)

KRABIEL, KLAUS-DIETER, 'Die Maßnahme', in *Brecht Handbuch in fünf Bänden*, ed. by Jan Knopf, 5 vols (Stuttgart: Metzler, 2001), I, 253–66

KURDZEL, KERSTIN-SUSANNE, *The Machinery of Death on Screen: Die Darstellung der Todesstrafe im US-amerikanischen Spielfilm* (Saarbrücken: Dr. Müller, 2008)

LACHANCE, DANIEL, *Executing Freedom: The Cultural Life of Capital Punishment in the United States* (Chicago, IL: University of Chicago Press, 2016)

LASCOUMES, PIERRE, 'Révolution ou réforme juridique? Les codes pénaux français de 1791 à 1810', in *Révolution et justice pénale en Europe: modèles français et traditions nationales (1780–1830)*, ed. by Xavier Rousseaux, Marie-Sylvie Dupont-Bouchat and Claude Vael (Paris & Montreal: L'Harmattan, 1999), pp. 61–69

LA TOUR DU PIN GOUVERNET, HENRIETTE LUCIE DILLON, MARQUISE DE, *Journal d'une femme de cinquante ans (1778–1815)* (Paris: Chapelot, 1913)

LESSER, WENDY, *Pictures at an Execution: An Inquiry into the Subject of Murder* (Cambridge, MA: Harvard University Press, 1993; 1998)

LOOBY, CHRISTOPHER, 'George Thompson's "Romance of the Real": Transgression and Taboo in American Sensation Fiction', *American Literature, 65* (December 1993), 651–72

LOTMAN, IURII M., 'The Decembrist in Daily Life (Everyday Behavior as a Historical-Psychological Category)', in *The Semiotics of Russian Cultural History*, ed. by Alexander D. Nakhimovsky and Alice Stone Nakhimovsky (Ithaca, NY: Cornell University Press, 1985), pp. 95–149

LOWE-DUPAS, HÉLÈNE, 'Innommable guillotine: la peine de mort dans *Le Dernier Jour d'un condamné* et *Histoire d'Hélène Gillet*', *Nineteenth-Century French Studies, 23* (1995), 341–48

MCALEER, PATRICK, and MICHAEL A. PERRY (eds), *Stephen King's Modern Macabre: Essays on the Later Works* (Jefferson, NC: McFarland, 2014)

MCCABE, JANET, and KIM AKASS (eds), *Quality TV: Contemporary American Television and Beyond* (London: I. B. Tauris, 2007)

MCDONAGH, JOSEPHINE, *Child Murder and British Culture, 1720–1900* (Cambridge: Cambridge University Press, 2003)

MACHÉ, BRITTA, 'The Bürstner Affair and Its Significance for the Courtroom Scenes and the End of Kafka's *Prozeß*', *German Quarterly, 65.1* (1992), 18–34

MACKEY, PHILIP ENGLISH, 'Introduction: An Historical Perspective', in *Voices Against Death: American Opposition to Capital Punishment, 1787–1977* (New York: Burt Franklin, 1977), pp. xi–liii

MCLANE, MAUREEN, *Balladeering, Minstrelsy, and the Making of British Romantic Poetry* (Cambridge: Cambridge University Press, 2008)

MADARIAGA, ISABEL DE, *Russia in the Age of Catherine the Great* (New Haven, CT: Yale University Press, 1981)

MADIVAL, J., and OTHERS (eds), *Archives parlementaires de 1789 à 1860: recueil complet des débats législatifs & politiques des Chambres françaises,* 101 vols (Paris: Librairie administrative de P. Dupont, 1862–)

MAGISTRALE, TONY, *Stephen King: America's Storyteller* (Santa Barbara, CA: Praeger, 2010)

MAILER, NORMAN, *Advertisements for Myself* (Cambridge, MA: Harvard University Press, 1992)

———*Armies of the Night* (New York: Plume, 1968)

——— *The Executioner's Song* (London: Vintage, 1991)

——— 'Introduction', in Jack Henry Abbott, *In the Belly of the Beast* (New York: Vintage, 1991)

MAKDISI, SAREE, *Making England Western: Occidentalism, Race, and Imperial Culture* (Chicago, IL: University of Chicago Press, 2014)

MALLARMÉ, STÉPHANE, *Divagations*, trans. by Barbara Johnson (Cambridge, MA: Harvard University Press, 2009)

——— *Œuvres complètes,* ed. by Bertrand Marchal, 2 vols (Paris: Gallimard, 1998–2003)

MARCANDIER-COLARD, CHRISTINE, *Crimes de sang et scènes capitales: essai sur l'esthétique romantique de la violence* (Paris: Presses universitaires de France, 1998)

MARCOVITCH, HEATHER, *The Art of the Pose: Oscar Wilde's Performance Theory* (Bern: Peter Lang, 2010)

MARÉCHAL, SYLVAIN, *Le Jugement dernier des rois*, in *Théâtre de la Révolution; ou, choix de pièces de théâtre qui ont fait sensation pendant la période révolutionnaire*, ed. by Louis Moland (Paris: Garnier, 1877), pp. 299–325

MARRAST, ROBERT, *Espronceda et son temps: littérature, société, politique au temps du romantisme* (Paris: Klincksieck, 1974)

MASLAN, SUSAN, *Revolutionary Acts: Theater, Democracy and the French Revolution* (Baltimore, MD: Johns Hopkins University Press, 2005)

MASON, LAURA, 'The "Bosom of Proof": Criminal Justice and the Renewal of Oral Culture during the French Revolution', *Journal of Modern History*, 76 (March 2004), 29–61

MAYHEW, HENRY, *The Criminal Prisons of London and Scenes of Prison Life* (London: Griffin, Bohn, 1862)

MAYO, ROBERT, 'The Contemporaneity of the *Lyrical Ballads*', *PMLA* (1954), 486–522

MAZOUR, ANATOLE G., *The First Russian Revolution, 1825*, 2nd printing (Stanford, CA: Stanford University Press, 1961)

MESCHONNIC, HENRI, 'Vers le roman-poème: les romans de Hugo avant *Les Misérables*', in *Œuvres complètes de Victor Hugo*, ed. by Jean Massin. (Paris: Le Club français du Livre, 1967), III, i-xx

MILL, JOHN STUART, *Public and Parliamentary Speeches, November 1850–November 1868*, ed. by John Robson and Bruce Kinzer (Toronto: University of Toronto Press, 1988)

MITTELL, JASON, *Complex TV: The Poetics of Contemporary Television Storytelling* (New York: New York University Press, 2015)

MONESTIER, MARTIN, *Peines de mort: histoire et techniques des exécutions capitales des origines à nos jours* (Paris: Cherche Midi, 1994)

MONNIER, RAYMONDE, 'La Question de la peine de mort sous la Révolution française', in *Révolution et justice pénale en Europe: modèles français et traditions nationales (1780–1830)*, ed. by Xavier Rousseaux, Marie-Sylvie Dupont-Bouchat, and Claude Vael (Paris: L'Harmattan, 1999), pp. 225–42

MONTESQUIEU, *De l'esprit des lois*, in *Œuvres complètes*, ed. by Roger Caillois, 2 vols (Paris: Gallimard, 1951), II, 227–995

MORISI, ÈVE, *Albert Camus contre la peine de mort* (Paris: Gallimard, 2011)

MORRISON, BLAKE, 'Another Year, Another Book: As John Grisham Keeps up his Phenomenal Workrate, What is the Secret to Avoiding Writer's Block?', *Independent*, 24 January 1999Mott, Frank Luther, *Golden Multitudes: The Story of Best Sellers in the United States* (New York: Macmillan, 1947)

MURDOCH, IRIS, 'Vision and Choice in Morality', *Proceedings of the Aristotelian Society*, supplementary vol. 30, (1956), 32–58

NARANJO-HUEBLE, LINDA, ' "The Road to Perdition": EDEN Southworth and the Critics', *American Periodicals*, 16.2 (2006), 123–50

NAVAS RUIZ, RICARDO, *El romanticismo español* (Madrid: Anaya, 1990)

NÉGREL ÉRIC, 'Le Théâtre au service de la Révolution: une rhétorique de l'éloge', in *Une expérience rhétorique: l'éloquence de la Révolution*, ed. by Éric Négrel and Jean-Paul Sermain (Oxford: Voltaire Foundation, 2002), pp. 147–60

NEWMAN, STEVE, *Ballad Collection, Lyric, and the Canon: The Call of the Popular from the Restoration to the New Criticism* (Philadelphia: University of Pennsylvania Press, 2004)

NIETZSCHE, FRIEDRICH, *Zur Genealogie der Moral*, in *Sämtliche Werke: Kritische Studienausgabe*, ed. by Giorgio Colli and Mazzino Montinarie, 15 vols (Berlin: de Gruyter, 1967–77)

NISARD, CHARLES, [REVIEW OF *Le Dernier Jour d'un condamné*] *Le Journal des Débats*, 26 February 1829

NOEL, MARY, *Villains Galore: The Heyday of the Popular Story Weekly* (New York: Macmillan Company, 1954)

NUSSBAUM, MARTHA, *The Fragility of Goodness: Luck and Ethics in Greek Tragedy and Philosophy* (Cambridge: Cambridge University Press, 1986)

—— *Love's Knowledge: Essays on Philosophy and Literature* (Cambridge: Cambridge University Press, 1992)

—— *Poetic Justice: The Literary Imagination and Public Life* (Boston, MA: Beacon Press, 1995)

O'BRIEN, TIM, 'The Ballad of Gary G.', *New York Times*, 15 October 1979, p. 67

OGLETREE, CHARLES J., and AUSTIN SARAT (eds), *Punishment and Popular Culture* (New York: New York University Press, 2015)

OLIVER OLMO, PEDRO, *La pena de muerte en España* (Madrid: Los Libros de la Catarata, 1995)

ORWELL, GEORGE, 'A Hanging' [1931], *Why I Write* (London: Penguin, 2004), pp. 95–101

O'SULLIVAN, SEAN, 'Representing the "Killing State": The Death Penalty in Nineties Hollywood Cinema', *Howard Law Journal*, 42.5 (December 2003), 485–503

OZOUF, MONA, *Festivals and the French Revolution*, trans. by Alain Sheridan (Cambridge, MA: Harvard University Press, 1988)

PAN, DAVID, 'Kafka as a Populist: Re-reading "In the Penal Colony"', *Telos*, 101 (Fall 1994), 3–40

—— 'The Persistence of Patriarchy in Franz Kafka's "Judgment"', *Orbis Litterarum*, 55 (2000), 135–60

—— 'Sacrifice as Political Representation in Bertolt Brecht's *Lehrstücke*', *Germanic Review*, 84.3 (2009), 222–49

—— *Sacrifice in the Modern World: On the Particularity and Generality of Nazi Myth* (Evanston, IL: Northwestern University Press, 2012)

PARENT, YVETTE, 'L'emploi de l'argot dans *Le Dernier Jour d'un condamné*', published by the Groupe Hugo of Université Paris 7 on 8 February 2003, <http://groupugo.div.jussieu.fr/Groupugo/03–02–08Parent.htm> [accessed 5 January 2018]

PARKER, A. A., and E. ALLISON PEERS, 'The Influence of Victor Hugo on Spanish Poetry and Prose Fiction', *Modern Language Review*, 28.1 (January 1933), 50–61

—— 'The Vogue of Victor Hugo in Spain', *Modern Language Review*, 27.1 (January 1932), 36–57

PARKS, ALEXANDER, *The Genre Poissard and the French Stage of the Eighteenth Century* (New York: Columbia, 1935)

PARRISH, STEPHEN MAXFIELD, '"The Thorn": Wordsworth's Dramatic Monologue', *ELH*, 24 (1957), 153–63

PATTEE, FRED LEWIS, *The Feminist Fifties* (New York: D. Appleton-Century, 1940)

PEARSON, HESKETH, *The Life of Oscar Wilde* (London: Methuen, 1954)

PEGENAUTE, PEDRO, *Represión política en el reinado de Fernando VII* (Pamplona: Universidad de Navarra, 1974)

PERCHELLET, JEAN-PIERRE, 'Les Spectacles parisiens et leur public', in *L'Empire des muses: Napoléon, les arts et les lettres*, ed. by Jean-Claude Bonnet (Paris: Belin, 2004), pp. 153–73

PERCY, THOMAS, *Reliques of Ancient English Poetry*, 3 vols (London: Cassell, Petter, and Galpin, 1866)

PEROVIC, SANJA, 'Death by Volcano: Revolutionary Theatre and Marie-Antoinette', *French Studies*, 67.1 (2012), 15–29

PICON, JÉRÔME, and ISABEL VIOLANTE (eds), *Victor Hugo contre la peine de mort* (Paris: Textuel, 2001)

POSNER, RICHARD, *Law and Literature* (Cambridge, MA: Harvard University Press, 1998)

POTTER, HARRY, *Hanging in Judgment: Religion and the Death Penalty in England from the Bloody Code to Abolition* (London: SCM Press, 1993)

POULOSKY, LAURA JEAN, *Severed Heads and Martyred Souls: Crime and Capital Punishment in French Romantic Literature* (New York: Peter Lang, 2003)

PREMINGER, ALEX, and T. V. F. BROGAN (eds), *The New Princeton Encyclopedia of Poetry and Poetics* (Princeton, NJ: Princeton University Press, 1993)

PRITCHARD, JOHN LAURENCE, *A History of Capital Punishment* (New York: The Citadel Press, 1960)

PROUST, MARCEL, *À la recherche du temps perdu*, ed. by Jean-Yves Tadié, 4 vols (Paris: Gallimard, 1987–89)

PUJALS, ESTEBAN, *Espronceda y Lord Byron* (Madrid: Centro Superior de Investigación Científica, 1951)

QUERALT, MARÍA PILAR, *Fernando VII* (Barcelona: Planeta, 1997)

QUINBY, GEORGE WASHINGTON, *The Gallows, the Prison, and the Poor-house: A Plea for Humanity, Showing the Demands of Christianity in Behalf of the Criminal and Perishing Classes* (Cincinnati, OH: G. W. Quinby, 1856)

RADFORD, JEAN, 'Norman Mailer: The True Story of an American Writer', in *American Fiction: New Readings*, ed. by Richard Gray (London: Vision Press, 1983), pp. 222–37

RAEFF, MARC (ed.), *The Decembrist Movement* (Englewood Cliffs, NJ: Prentice-Hall, 1966)

RANCIÈRE, JACQUES, *Mute Speech: Literature, Critical Theory and Politics*, trans. by James Swenson (New York: Columbia University, 2011)

REYNOLDS, DAVID S., 'Radical Sensationalism: George Lippard in his Transatlantic Contexts', in *Transatlantic Sensations*, ed. by Jennifer Phegley, John Barton, and Kristin Huston (Farnham: Ashgate, 2012), pp. 77–96

RICE, JAMES L., 'Dostoevsky's Endgame: The Projected Sequel to *The Brothers Karamazov*', *Russian History*, 33.1 (2006), 45–62

ROBERT, YANN, 'The Everlasting Trials of Jean Calas: Justice, Theatre and Trauma in the Early Years of the Revolution', in *Representing Violence in France, 1760–1820*, ed. by Thomas Wynn (Oxford: SVEC, 2013), pp. 103–19

——*Dramatic Justice: Trial by Theater in the Age of the French Revolution* (Philadelphia: University of Pennsylvania Press, 2019)

ROBESPIERRE, MAXIMILIEN, *Œuvres complètes*, ed. by Eugène Déprez, 10 vols (Paris: E. Leroux, 1910–67)

ROSA, GUY, 'Commentaires du *Dernier Jour d'un condamné*', in *Le Dernier jour d'un condamné suivi de Claude Gueux et de l'affaire Tapner*, ed. by Guy Rosa (Paris: Librairie générale française, 1989)

ROTH, PHILIP, 'Writing American Fiction', *Commentary* (March 1961), 223–33

ROUSSEAU, JEAN-JACQUES, *Du contrat social ou principes du droit politique*, in *Œuvres complètes*, ed. by Bernard Gagnebin and Marcel Raymond, 4 vols (Paris: Gallimard, 1959–69), III

ROUSSET, JEAN, '*Le Dernier Jour d'un condamné* ou l'invention d'un genre littéraire', in *Hugo dans les marges*, ed. by Lucien Dällenbach and Laurent Jenny (Geneva: Éditions Zoë, 1985), pp. 35–50

RUSH, BENJAMIN, *Considerations on the Injustice and Impolicy of Punishing Murder by Death* (Philadelphia: Carey, 1792)

RUSSELL, SHARON, *Revisiting Stephen King: A Critical Companion* (Westport, CT: Greenwood Press, 2002)

RUTTENBURG, NANCY, *Dostoevsky's Democracy* (Princeton, NJ: Princeton University Press, 2008)

SÁNCHEZ MANTERO, RAFAEL, *Fernando VII: un reinado polémico* (Madrid: Temas de Hoy, 1996)

SARAT, AUSTIN, *Gruesome Spectacles: Botched Executions and America's Death Penalty* (Stanford, CA: Stanford University Press, 2014)

—— *The Killing State: Capital Punishment in Law, Politics, and Culture* (New York: Oxford University Press, 1999)

—— *When the State Kills: Capital Punishment and the American Condition* (Princeton, NJ: Princeton University Press, 2001)

SARAT, AUSTIN, and CHRISTIAN BOULANGER (eds), *The Cultural Lives of Capital Punishment; Comparative Perspectives* (Stanford, CA: Stanford University Press, 2005)

SAUREL, FERDINAND, *Un sanglant épisode sous la Terreur à Montpellier, l'affaire dite des Galettes* (Montpellier: Firmin & Montane, 1895)

SAVEY-CASARD, PAUL, *Le Crime et la peine dans l'œuvre de Victor Hugo* (Paris: Presses universitaires de France, 1956)

SCARLETT, ELIZABETH, 'The Metaphysics of Espronceda's Romanticism in *El Estudiante de Salamanca*', *Bulletin of Hispanic Studies*, 93.1 (2016), 29–44

SCHAUS, MARGARET (ed.), *Women and Gender in Medieval Europe: An Encyclopedia* (London: Routledge, 2006)

SCHMID, ULRICH, 'Dostoevsky and Regicide: The Hidden Topographical Meaning of *Crime and Punishment*', *Dostoevsky Studies*, n.s., 19 (2015), 51–62

SCHRADER, ABBY M., *Languages of the Lash: Corporal Punishment and Identity in Imperial Russia* (DeKalb: Northern Illinois University Press, 2002)

SCHUR, ANNA, 'Punishment and Crime', in *Dostoevsky in Context*, ed. by Deborah A. Martinsen and Olga Maiorova (Cambridge: Cambridge University Press, 2015), pp. 30–38

—— *Wages of Evil: Dostoevsky and Punishment* (Evanston, IL: Northwestern University Press, 2012)

SEBOLD, RUSSELL, *Trayectoria del romanticismo español* (Barcelona: Crítica, 1983)

SIELKE, SABINE, ' "Joy in Repetition": or, The Significance of Seriality in Processes of Memory and (Re)Mediation', in *The Memory Effect: The Remediation of Memory in Literature and Film*, ed. by Russell J. A. Kilbourn and Eleanor Ty (Waterloo, ON: Wilfrid Laurier University Press, 2013), pp. 37–50

SLOTKIN, RICHARD, *Regeneration Through Violence: The Mythology of the American Frontier, 1600–1860* (Norman: University of Oklahoma Press, 1973)

SMETS, PAUL F., *Le Combat pour l'abolition de la peine de mort: Hugo, Koestler, Camus, d'autres: textes, prétextes et paratextes* (Brussels: Académie royale de Belgique, 2003)

SMITH, BARRY C., 'Proust, the Madeleine and Memory', in *Memory in the Twenty-First Century: New Critical Perspectives from the Arts, Humanities, and Sciences*, ed. by Sebastian Groes (Basingstoke: Palgrave Macmillan, 2016), pp. 38–41

SMITH, HERBERT F., *The Popular American Novel, 1865–1920* (Boston, MA: Twayne, 1980)

SMITH, PHILIP, *Punishment and Culture* (Chicago, IL: University of Chicago Press, 2008)

SOKEL, WALTER, *Franz Kafka: Tragik und Ironie: Zur Struktur seiner Kunst* (Munich & Vienna: Albert Langen Georg Müller Verlag, 1964)

SOLEINNE, MARTINEAU DE, *Bibliothèque dramatique de Monsieur de Soleinne*, 6 vols (Paris: Administration de l'Alliance des Arts, 1843–1845)

SOLLIER, JOSEPH, 'Love (Theological Virtue)', in *The Catholic Encyclopedia*, <http://www. newadvent.org/cathen /09397a.htm> [accessed 9 August 2018]

SONTAG, SUSAN, *Against Interpretation and Other Essays* (London: Penguin, 2009)

—— *Regarding the Pain of Others* (New York: Picador/Farrar, Straus & Giroux, 2003)

SOUTHEY, ROBERT, *Joan of Arc and Minor Poems* (London: Routledge, 1853)

SOUTHWORTH, E. D. E. N., *The Gipsy's Prophecy* (Philadelphia: T. B. Peterson, 1861)

—— *The Lost Heiress* (Philadelphia: Deacon & Peterson, 1854)

STAINES, JOHN D., *The Tragic Histories of Mary Queen of Scots, 1560–1900: Rhetoric, Passions, and Political Literature* (Farnham & Burlington, VT: Ashgate, 2009)

STANFORD, MICHAEL, 'Poetry, Negative Capability, and the Law: James Wright's "A Poem about George Doty in the Death House" and "At the Executed Murderer's Grave"', *Amerikastudien*, 62.2 (2017), 235–55

STERN, J. P., 'The Law of The Trial', in *On Kafka: Semi-Centenary Perspectives*, ed. by Franz Kuna (London: Elek Books, 1976), pp. 22–46

STEWART, SUSAN, 'Scandals of the Ballad', *Representations*, 32 (1990), 134–56

STRAND, GINGER, 'The Many Deaths of Montgomery: Audiences and Pamphlet Plays of the Revolution', *American Literary History*, 9.1 (1997), 1–20

STRENGELL, HEIDI, *Stephen King: Monsters Live in Ordinary People* (Madison: University of Wisconsin Press, 2005)

SUSSMAN, HENRY, 'The Court as Text: Inversion, Supplanting, and Derangement in Kafka's *Der Prozeß*', *PMLA*, 92.1 (1977), 41–55

SWANN, KAREN, 'Martha's Name, or The Scandal of 'The Thorn', in *Dwelling in Possibility: Women Poets and Critics on Poetry*, ed. by Yopie Prins and Maeera Schreiber (Ithaca, NY: Cornell University Press, 1997), pp. 60–79

THACKERAY, WILLIAM MAKEPEACE, 'Going to See a Man Hanged', *Fraser's Magazine*, 22 (July–December 1840), 150–58

THELWALL, JOHN, *Poems Written in Close Confinement* (London: John Thelwall, 1795)

VALLOIS, MARIE-CLAIRE, 'Écrire ou décrire: l'impossible histoire du "sujet" dans *Le Dernier Jour d'un condamné* de Victor Hugo', *Romantisme*, 48 (1985), 91–104

VANPEE, JANIE, 'Performing Justice: The Trials of Olympe de Gouges', *Theatre Journal*, 51.1 (1999), 47–65

VENIS, LINDA, 'The Problem of Broadside Balladry's Influence on the *Lyrical Ballads*', *Studies in English Literature*, 24 (1984), 617–32

VERHOEVEN, CLAUDIA, *The Odd Man Karakozov: Imperial Russia, Modernity, and the Birth of Terrorism* (Ithaca, NY: Cornell University Press, 2009)

VERNIER, FRANCE, 'Cela "fait mal et ne touche pas"', *La Pensée*, 245 (mai-juin 1985), 41–58

VITORIA, FRANCISCO DE, *Political Writings*, ed. by Anthony Pagden and Jeremy Lawrance (Cambridge: Cambridge University Press, 1991)

VOLGIN, IGOR, *Poslednii god Dostoevskogo: Istoricheskie zapiski* (Moscow: Sovetskii pisatel, 1986)

—— *Propavshii zagovor: Dostoevsky i politicheskii protsess 1849 g.* (Moscow: Izdatel'stvo Libereia, 2000)

WALD LASOWSKI, PATRICK, *Les Échafauds du romanesque* (Lille: Presses universitaires de Lille, 1991)

—— *Guillotinez-moi! Précis de décapitation* (Paris: Le Promeneur, 2007)

WARMINSKI, ANDRZEJ, 'As the Poets Do It...', in *Material Events: Paul de Man and the Afterlife of Theory* (Minneapolis: University of Minnesota Press, 2001), pp. 3–31

WASIOLEK, EDWARD, *Dostoevsky: The Major Fiction* (Cambridge, MA: M.I.T. Press, 1964)

WELLEK, RENÉ, *Immanuel Kant in England, 1793–1838* (Princeton, NJ: Princeton University Press, 1931)

WELSH, ALEXANDER, *Strong Representations: Narrative and Circumstantial Evidence in England* (Baltimore, MD: Johns Hopkins University Press, 1992)

WHITE, HAYDEN, *The Practical Past* (Evanston, IL: Northwestern University Press, 2014)

——*Tropics of Discourse: Essays in Cultural Criticism* (Baltimore, MD: Johns Hopkins University Press, 1985)

WILDE, OSCAR, *The Complete Letters of Oscar Wilde,* ed. by Holland & Hart-Davies (New York: Henry Holt, 2000)

——*The Complete Works of Oscar Wilde*, ed. by Russell Jackson and Ian Small, 6 vols (Oxford: Oxford University Press, 2000–07)

——*The Decay of Lying and Other Essays* (London: Penguin, 2010)

——*The Importance of Being Earnest* (Oxford: Heinemann, 1994)

WILLIAMS, LINDA, 'Melodrama in Black and White: Uncle Tom and *The Green Mile*', *Film Quarterly*, 55.2 (Winter 2001), 14–21

WOLFSON, SUSAN, '*Lyrical Ballads* and the Language of (Men) Feeling: Wordsworth Writing Women's Voices', in *Men Writing the Feminine* (Albany: SUNY Press, 1994), pp. 29–57

WORDSWORTH, WILLIAM, *The Poems. Volume 2*, ed. by John O. Hayden (Harmondsworth: Penguin, 1977)

WORDSWORTH, WILLIAM, and SAMUEL TAYLOR COLERIDGE, *Lyrical Ballads*, ed. by W. J. B. Owen, 2nd edn (Oxford: Oxford University Press, 1979)

WYNN, THOMAS (ed.), *Representing Violence in France, 1760–1820* (Oxford: SVEC, 2013)

——*Sade's Theatre: Pleasure, Violence, Masochism* (Oxford: SVEC, 2007)

YEATS, W. B., *The Oxford Book of Modern Verse, 1892–1935* (Oxford: Clarendon Press, 1936)

YNDURÁIN, DOMINGO, *Análisis formal de la poesía de Espronceda* (Madrid: Taurus, 1971)

ZIMMERMANN, HANS DIETER, 'Die endlose Suche nach dem Sinn: Kafka und die jiddische Moderne', in *Nach erneuter Lektüre: Franz Kafkas Der Proceß*, ed. by Hans Dieter Zimmermann (Würzburg: Königshausen und Neumann, 1992), pp. 211–22

ZIOLKOWSKI, THEODORE, *The Mirror of Justice: Literary Reflections of Legal Crises* (Princeton, NJ: Princeton University Press, 1997)

INDEX

CPSIA information can be obtained
at www.ICGtesting.com
Printed in the USA
LVHW021740230623
750622LV00008B/253

9 781781 885574